Charting

THE NEW TESTAMENT

Charting

THE NEW TESTAMENT

John W. Welch and John F. Hall

Foundation for Ancient Research and Mormon Studies
Provo, Utah

Cover and book design: J. Gregory Welch

The Foundation for Ancient Research
and Mormon Studies (FARMS)
Institute for the Study and Preservation
of Ancient Religious Texts
Brigham Young University
P.O. Box 7113
University Station
Provo, Utah 84602

Library of Congress Cataloging-in-Publication Data

Welch, John W. (John Woodland)
    Charting the New Testament / John W. Welch and John F. Hall
        p.   cm.
    Includes bibliographical references and index.
    ISBN 0-934893-64-0 (alk. paper)
      1. Bible. N.T.—Handbooks, manuals, etc. I. Hall, John Franklin. II. Title.

BS2310 .W45 2002
225'.02'02—dc21

                                                         2002072591

Table of Charts

Preface

This book aims to make the New Testament simple without simplifying this vastly complex text. The New Testament reports with candor and conviction the astonishing events that stunned the world through the ministry of Jesus of Nazareth. Imagine sitting in a wayside inn and listening for the first time as Matthew or John recounted with fervent testimony what they knew.

Unfortunately, such live, original performances are no longer available to us. What remains for us to know about the early decades of Christianity is a collection of books and letters written at different times, by different people, to different audiences, and for different purposes.

This compilation includes many types of information about hundreds of people, scores of events, a multitude of places, and a host of details. Charting this material has not been easy, but in the process many features of the New Testament have become clearer and more meaningful.

This project began several years ago. Modeled largely after the charts in the successful *Charting the Book of Mormon* (Provo, Utah: FARMS, 1999), the charts in this book have been developed, tested, and used in a number of settings. We appreciate what we have learned by using these charts in our university classes, during public lectures, at conferences and workshops, and on travel-study tours in many parts of the Mediterranean world.

We hope that these charts will be useful to readers in many contexts: in classrooms, in family settings, and for personal scripture study. These charts are packed with more information than automatically meets the eye. They usually follow the King James Version but sometimes are based on the ancient Greek text.

Conceptualizing and distilling into charts the extensive and complex world of New Testament scholarship is a daunting task, as anyone who has tried to produce a few charts will quickly realize. For this reason, all these charts invite further research and reflection. Various sources are listed to encourage continued study. We hope that the broad range of subjects covered by these charts and references, including items on doctrinal and textual topics, in addition to geographical or chronological materials, will inspire study in many directions.

This collection of favorites, like any other sampling of graphic aids, is by no means complete. Many more charts could easily be added to this volume, on a wide variety of subjects and displayed in many different layouts. We encourage readers to create charts of their own, as well as to add further details or nuances to the charts included in this volume. As the rising generation of students is increasingly visually oriented, scholars and teachers may find chart presentations more and more useful.

We express our deep appreciation to all who have helped bring this book to completion. In particular, we thank James Gregory Welch for his organizational effectiveness and graphic expertise. Important research and valuable editorial contributions were also made by Amy Osmond Bingham, Katie Worlton Pulham, Victoria Franklin Johnson, other research assistants, and members of the Institute editorial staff.

We dedicate this book to our students who have traveled with us down the paths and through the pages of the world of the New Testament.

John W. Welch
John F. Hall

Abbreviations

Gen	Neh	Obad	Mt	1Tm
Ex	Esth	Jonah	Mk	2Tm
Lev	Job	Micah	Lk	Titus
Num	Ps	Hahum	Jn	Phlmn
Deut	Prov	Hab	Acts	Heb
Josh	Eccl	Zeph	Rom	Jms
Judg	Isa	Hag	1Cor	1Pt
1Sam	Jer	Zech	2Cor	2Pt
2Sam	Lam	Mal	Gal	1Jn
1Kgs	Ezek		Eph	2Jn
2Kgs	Dan		Phlp	3Jn
1Chr	Hos		Col	Jude
2Chr	Joel		1Th	Rev
Ezra	Amos		2Th	

ABD—*Anchor Bible Dictionary* (New York: Doubleday, 1992)

EM—*Encyclopedia of Mormonism* (New York: Macmillan, 1992)

MWNT—*Masada and the World of the New Testament* (Provo, Utah: BYU Studies, 1997)

WRC—*We Rejoice in Christ* (Provo, Utah: BYU Studies, 1995)

SECTION 1

Chronology

New Testament Era Timeline
63 B.C.–A.D. 80

Explanation

Three main cultures intersected in the world into which Jesus was born: Jewish, Greek, and Roman. Each played differing roles in the religious, cultural, and political environment for the initial proclamation of the gospel and the establishment of the kingdom of God.

As these charts show, Jesus was born at a unique moment in history. The Jewish nation had reached the height of its power, flourishing under the political and economic skills of King Herod the Great, who had brought unprecedented unity and unsurpassed prosperity to the Jewish people. At the same time, Augustus Caesar had established an empire-wide era of peace, which allowed the spread of Roman government and law as well as the further extension of the Greek language and its cultural attractions. It was a time of great expectations and new possibilities, but also of challenges to old ways and disruptions in old social orders.

The design of these charts puts events in Judea on center stage, yielding many insights into New Testament history. For example, Julius Caesar, who completed his ascendancy to power over Rome around 45 B.C., granted special privileges to Jews, allowing them to establish synagogues throughout the Roman Empire. This allowed Judaism to enter areas that would become fertile grounds for Christian missionaries one hundred years later, and it created a political climate in which a new religion could be born and thrive.

References

M. Cary and H. H. Scullard, *A History of Rome* (New York: St. Martin's, 1975).
Karl P. Donfried, "Chronology," *ABD*, 1:1002–22.

New Testament Era Timeline
63–1 B.C.

Date	Rome	Judea	Greece and the East
63	Cicero becomes consul; Catilinarian conspiracy occurs.	Hyrcanus is appointed ethnarch of Judea, which comes under Roman control as dependency to Province of Syria.	Pompey annexes remains of Seleucid empire as province of Syria.
53	Pompey, Caesar, and Crassus rule Rome.		Crassus is defeated in Syria by the Parthians.
49	Roman civil war begins.		
48	Caesar consul for the second time.	Julius Caesar gives citizenship to Antipater and his son Herod.	Julius Caesar defeats Pompey at Pharsalus in Greece.
47	Caesar becomes military dictator.		
46	Caesar's legislation grants special rights and privileges to Jews in entire Roman Empire.		
44	Julius Caesar is assassinated.		
43	Marc Antony, Octavian Caesar, and Lepidus form second triumvirate.		
40		Parthians capture Jerusalem and appoint Antigonus ruler of Judea.	Parthia invades Syria.
37		Marc Antony appointed Herod king of Judea; he retakes Jerusalem, deposing Antigonus.	
31	Battle of Actium: Octavian Caesar defeats Antony and Cleopatra.	Herod's kingdom is greatly expanded by Octavian Caesar.	Octavian Caesar conquers Egypt.
27	Principate is established; Octavian Caesar is named Augustus.		
22–18		Herod's Temple is constructed.	
19	Vergil's *Aeneid* is published.		Rome conquers Armenia from Parthia.
16		Marcus Agrippa (Augustus's son-in-law) visits Jerusalem. Herod names his grandson Herod Agrippa.	
10		Herod constructs Caesarea.	
4		Herod dies; his kingdom is divided among his three sons.	

Chart 1-1

New Testament Era Timeline
A.D. 1–50

Date	Rome	Judea	Galilee and Syria
4	Augustus's grandson Gaius Caesar dies. His stepson Tiberius is adopted as heir.		
6		Archelaus is removed as ethnarch. Judea becomes Roman prefecture at the request of Sanhedrin and Jewish leaders.	Herod Antipas becomes tetrarch of Galilee; Quirinius, governor of Syria, conducts regional census.
14	Augustus dies. Tiberius becomes emperor.		
18		Joseph Caiaphas, a Sadducee, becomes High Priest.	
19	Jews are banished from Rome.		
26	Tiberius appoints Pilate prefect of Judea.		
28		John the Baptist begins his ministry.	
31		Christ is crucified (?)	
33		Stephen is martyred (?)	
34		Paul is converted (?)	Tetrarchy of Philip is annexed to Syria.
36		Pilate massacres Samaritans; L. Vitellius, governor of Syria, orders Pilate to return to Rome.	
37	Tiberius dies. Gaius (Caligula) becomes emperor.		
39			Herod Agrippa becomes tetrarch of Galilee; Philo leads embassy of Alexandrian Jews to Rome.
41	Gaius is assassinated; Claudius becomes emperor.	Herod Agrippa is king of Judea.	
43	Britain is conquered.		
44		James is martyred (?) Cuspius procurator.	
48		Cumanas procurator.	
49	Jews are expelled from Rome.	Apostolic Council of Jerusalem is held.	
50			Paul arrives in Corinth.

Chart 1-2

New Testament Era Timeline
A.D. 51–80

Date	Rome	Judea	Other
51			Gallio becomes proconsul of Achaia.
53			Parthians conquer the Roman province of Achaia.
54	Death of Claudius; Accession of Nero.		
58	Corbulo is placed in charge of all Roman holdings and armies in eastern part of empire.		
60	Paul's imprisonment at Rome.		Corbulo defeats Parthians.
61	Paul is acquitted of charges brought by Jews at Jerusalem; release and final travels.		
62		James the Just, brother of the Lord, is executed by Jewish leaders.	
64	Great Fire of Rome. Christians are executed; Death of Peter.		
65	Death of Paul (?)		
66		Jewish zealots seize Jerusalem and kill Jewish leaders, Greeks, and Romans.	
67	Vespasian is given command for Jewish War.		
68	Nero is deposed and commits suicide; Galba becomes emperor.	Vespasian besieges Jerusalem.	
69	"Year of the Four Emperors"; Vespasian emerges from civil wars as sole emperor.		
70		Titus captures Jerusalem.	
73		Flavius Silva captures Masada.	
79	Vespasian dies; Titus becomes emperor; Vesuvius erupts.		
80	The Flavian Amphitheater (Colosseum) is dedicated.		

Chart 1-3

Chart 1-4

The Lunar Jewish Calendar

Explanation

Keeping track of time was extremely important in the life of most Jews during the life-time of Jesus. The weekly Sabbath was meticulously observed by most Jews. In addition, annual festival days were holy celebrations falling on particular days in the month and year. The annual Jewish lunar calendar began in March, as did the Roman calendar ("Beware the Ides of March"). Passover, Pentecost, Day of Atonement (Yom Kippur), Tabernacles (Sukkot), Feast of Dedication (Hanukkah), and other holy days were Sabbath days for purposes of the law.

References

John P. Pratt, "Passover: Was It Symbolic of His Coming?" *Ensign*, January 1994, 38–45.
James C. Vanderkam, "Calendars," *ABD*, 1:814–20.

The Lunar Jewish Calendar

Gregorian	Jewish Month	Observances	Reference
March	**NISAN (abib)** Month 1 – 30 Days	1—New Year's for Reign of Kings 10—Passover Lamb Chosen 14—Passover Lamb Sacrificed 15–21—Seven Days of Passover	Ex 12:2 Ex 12:3 Ex 12:6 Lev 23:6–8
April			
	IYAR (zif) Month 2 – 29 Days		
May			
	SIVAN Month 3 – 30 Days	6—Feast of Firstfruits (Pentecost)	Num 28:26
June			
	TAMMUZ Month 4 – 29 Days	17—Fast	
July			
	AB Month 5 – 30 Days	9—Fast	
August			
	ELUL Month 6 – 29 Days		
September			
	TISHRI (ethanim) Month 7 – 30 Days	1—Feast of Trumpets (Rosh Hashanah) 10—Day of Atonement (Yom Kippur) 15—Feast of Tabernacles (Sukkot) 22—Eighth Day of Feast	Lev 23:24 Lev 23:27 Lev 23:34 Lev 23:36
October			
	HESHVAN (bul) Month 8 – 29/30 Days		
November			
	KISLEV Month 9 – 29/30 Days		
December			
	TEBET Month 10 – 29 Days	25—Feast of Dedication (Hanukkah)	
January			
	SHEBAT Month 11 – 30 Days		
February (Optional 29th Day)	**ADAR (adari I)** Month 12 – 29/30 Days	14—Feast of Esther (Purim)	
March	**VEADAR (adari II)** (Optional Month 13 – 29 Days)		

Chart 1-5

Jewish Celebrations

Explanation

As chart 1-5 shows, many of these Jewish holy days are mentioned in the New Testament. Jesus went to Jerusalem to observe Passover, Tabernacles, and other sacred festivals. Early Christians gathered for the feast of Pentecost, and other days in the life cycle of the people of the day play a role in the texts of the New Testament. The birthday of Herod Antipas is mentioned, probably reflecting Greek or Roman influence, for most Jewish people did not celebrate birthdays. For the pious Jew, life began with circumcision, not birth, and perhaps for this reason, birthday parties do not figure in the New Testament and the birth of Jesus narrative culminates with his presentation at the temple for circumcision (Lk 2:21–39).

References

Abraham P. Bloch, *The Biblical and Historical Background of the Jewish Holy Days* (New York: Ktav, 1978).

James C. Vanderkam, "Weeks, Festival of," *ABD*, 6:895–96.

Jewish Celebrations

Sabbath	Lk 4:16, 6:6, 23:56	Weekly
Passover	Jn 18:39	Spring
Feast of Pentecost	Acts 20:16	50 days after Passover
Feast of Tabernacles	Jn 7:2	Fall
Day of Atonement and fasting	Acts 2:1; 27:9	Fall
Hanukkah or Feast of Dedication	Jn 10:22	Winter
Panegyris	Heb 12:22	Other special occasions
New moon	Col 2:16	Monthly
Birthday	Mt 14:6	Herod's

Chart 1-5

Roman Calendar

Explanation

At the time of Christ, the Roman calendar and dating system were used throughout the Roman Empire. The calendar derived from the old lunar calendar of the Etruscans, which was designed to keep record of times for religious observances and festivals, and which retained as principal days of the month the *kalends* (first), *nones* (fifth or seventh), and *ides* (thirteenth or fifteenth), based originally on the phases of the moon. The months had been restructured by the Romans into a solar calendar of twelve months with several intercalary days at the end of February. March was the first Roman month, making September the seventh, October the eighth, etc. These names derive from the Latin words for seven *(septem)*, eight *(octo)*, and so on. The Roman calendar was reformed by Julius Caesar in 45 B.C., which version operated in New Testament times and still forms the basis of our own modern calendar today.

Roman years were numbered *ab urbe condita*, "from the founding of the city." The year we call 753 B.C. was the Roman year 1, the year that Rome is believed to have been established.

References

John F. Hall, "March Gods and the Etruscan New Year," in *By Study and Also By Faith* (Provo, Utah: FARMS, 1990), 1:643–58.

A. K. Michels, *The Calendar of the Roman Republic* (Princeton: Princeton University Press, 1967).

Roman Calendar

Named for Mars, the god of the New Year	**Martius**
Named for Aprilia, a goddess of spring	**Aprilis**
Named for Maia, an earth goddess	**Maius**
Named for Juno, wife of Jupiter	**Iunius**
Named for Julius Caesar (formerly Quintilis, "Fifth Month")	**Iulius**
Named for Augustus Caesar (formerly Sextilis, "Sixth Month")	**Augustus**
"Seventh Month"	**September**
"Eighth Month"	**October**
"Ninth Month"	**November**
"Tenth Month"	**December**
Named for Janus, a god of gates and doors	**Ianuarius**
"Month of Cleansing"	**Februaris**

Kalendae   First day of the month

Idus   The fifteenth of March, May, July, and October, but the thirteenth of all other months. This was the most important day of the month, used for ritual observances.

Nonae   The seventh of March, May, July, and October, but the fifth of all other months.

All other dates were reckoned backwards from these three dates (e.g., three days before the Kalendae of March).

Chart 1-6

Chart 1-7

Time in the New Testament

Explanation

Chart 1-7 helps modern readers understand references to time in the Gospels. The day began in the morning and ended with sundown. The daytime hours are shown at the top of the chart, with the ancient hours on the outside circle and the modern hours on the inside. For example, the first daytime hour corresponded to our hour between 6:00 A.M. and 7:00 A.M., the seventh hour to our noon hour, and the day ended with the twelfth hour beginning at our 5:00 A.M. The night was divided into four watches. The second watch went until midnight. The third watch ended with the cock crowing.

Scripture references indicate passages in which these times are mentioned.

Reference

Edward J. Brandt, "Everyday Life in Palestine," *Ensign*, September 1974, 22–24.

Time in the New Testament

DAYTIME HOURS

Third Hour
Mt 20:3; Mk 15:25

Sixth Hour
Mt 20:5; 27:45;
Mk 15:33; Lk 23:44;
Jn 4:6, 19:14

Seventh Hour
Jn 4:52

Ninth Hour
Mt 20:5; 27:45–56;
Mk 15:33–34;
Lk 23:44

Tenth Hour
Jn 1:39

Eleventh Hour
Mt 20:6, 9

NIGHTTIME WATCHES

First Watch
Mk 13:35

Second Watch (midnight)
Mt 25:6; Lk 11:5

Third Watch (cock crowing)
Mt 26:74; Mk 14:68, 72;
Lk 22:60–61; Jn 18:27

Fourth Watch
Mt 14:25; Mk 6:48

Chart 1-7

A Jewish menorah on a stone capital excavated at Capernaum on the north shore of the Sea of Galilee (above), and a first-century synagogue inside the fortress of Masada. Photos by John W. Welch

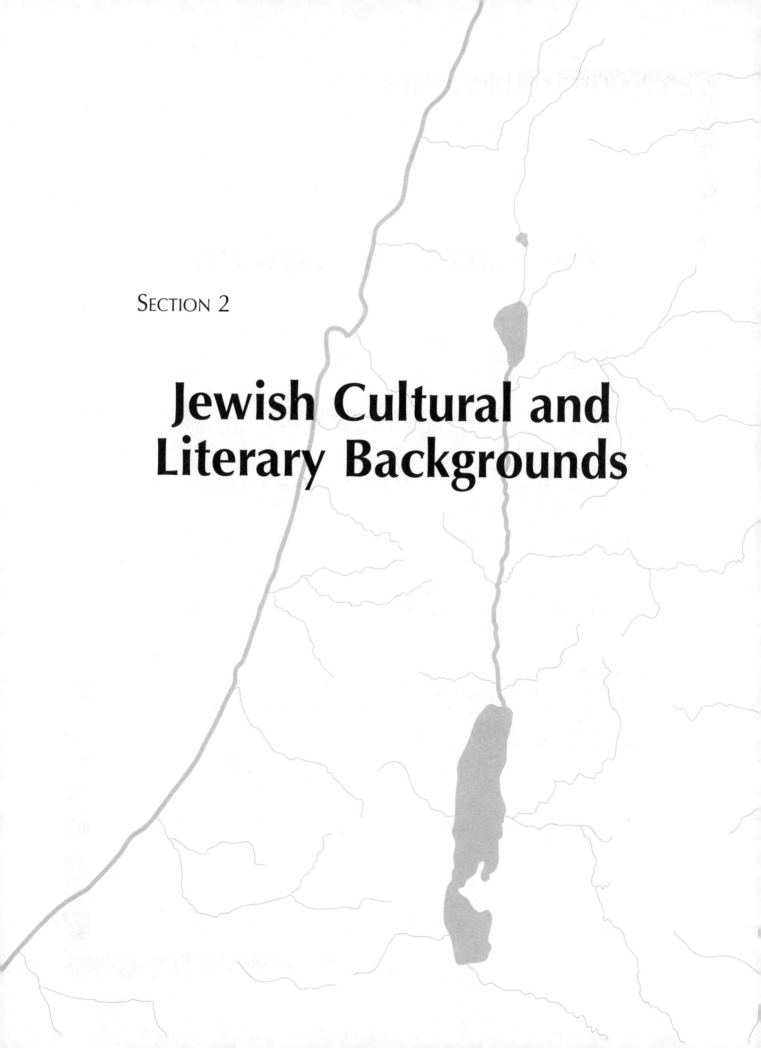

SECTION 2

Jewish Cultural and Literary Backgrounds

Chart 2-1

The Maccabean Dynasty

Explanation

From Mattathias to Mariamme (the first wife of Herod the Great), chart 2-1 traces the genealogy of the Maccabean Dynasty. Mattathias revolted in 167 B.C. against the Greek Seleucid government, which ruled Judea at that time. He killed one of the king's representatives and a Jew who was willing to follow the king's decree requiring Jews to build pagan altars and to sacrifice swine. His sons carried on the fight for Jewish religious purity and independence, and Judas Maccabeus fell in battle. Simon's descendants remained in power for the ensuing century.

From the Maccabeans came the Pharisees of New Testament times, together with strong sentiments encouraging independence, religious extremism, zealousness for the law, protecting the temple, and killing opponents. Precedents regarding the appointment and influence of the High Priest also trace back to Maccabean practices. The Feast of Dedication or Hanukkah, mentioned in John 10:22, celebrates the reclaiming and cleansing of the temple at the time of the Maccabean revolt.

References

Richard Neitzel Holzapfel, "King Herod," *MWNT*, 45.

Gaye Strathearn, "Who Were the Maccabees, and How Did They Influence Jewish History?" *Ensign*, December 1998, 49–53.

Uriel Rappaport, "Maccabean Revolt," *ABD*, 4:433–39.

The Maccabean Dynasty

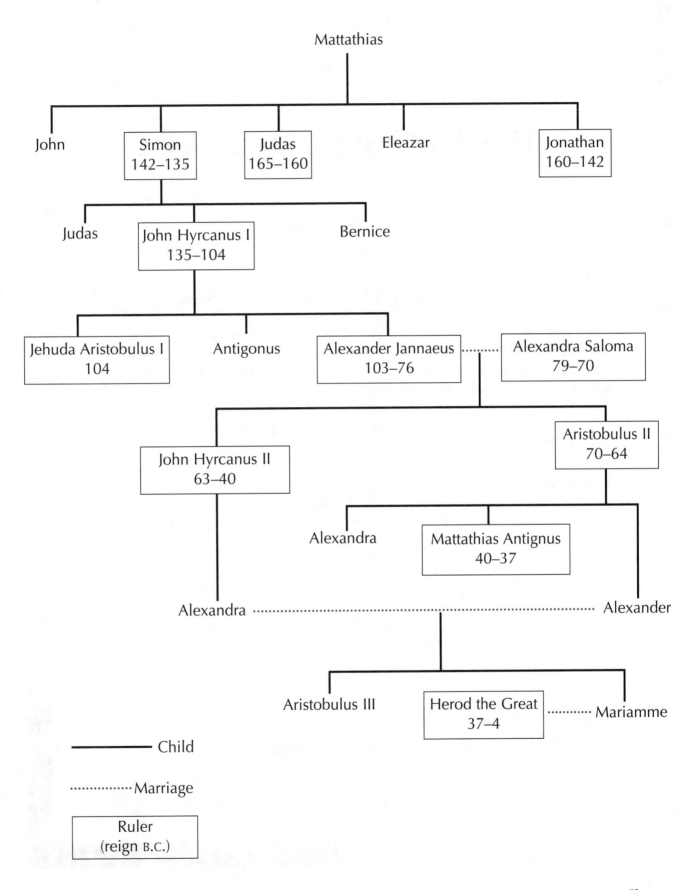

Mattathias

John — Simon 142–135 — Judas 165–160 — Eleazar — Jonathan 160–142

Judas — John Hyrcanus I 135–104 — Bernice

Jehuda Aristobulus I 104 — Antigonus — Alexander Jannaeus 103–76 ········· Alexandra Saloma 79–70

John Hyrcanus II 63–40 — Aristobulus II 70–64

Alexandra — Mattathias Antignus 40–37

Alexandra ····················· Alexander

Aristobulus III — Herod the Great 37–4 ·········· Mariamme

——————— Child

················· Marriage

Ruler
(reign B.C.)

Chart 2-1

Chart 2-2

The Herodian Dynasty

Explanation

The complicated family tree of Herod the Great, beginning with his grandfather and ending with several people mentioned later in the New Testament, is shown on chart 2-2. Eight of his wives are shown. The family was dysfunctional, tumultuous, and sometimes violent. It was said by some that it was better to be a pig than a son of Herod.

Herod Antipas, a son of Herod the Great, beheaded John the Baptist. Antipas had married a "near relative," in violation of the Law of Moses. Their daughter Salome danced and demanded the head of John.

Paul appeared before Felix and Agrippa II, descendants of Herod's brother Phasael and Herod's sister Salome.

References

Richard Neitzel Holzapfel, "King Herod," *MWNT*, 38.
David C. Braund, "Herodian Dynasty," *ABD*, 3:173–74.

The Herodian Dynasty

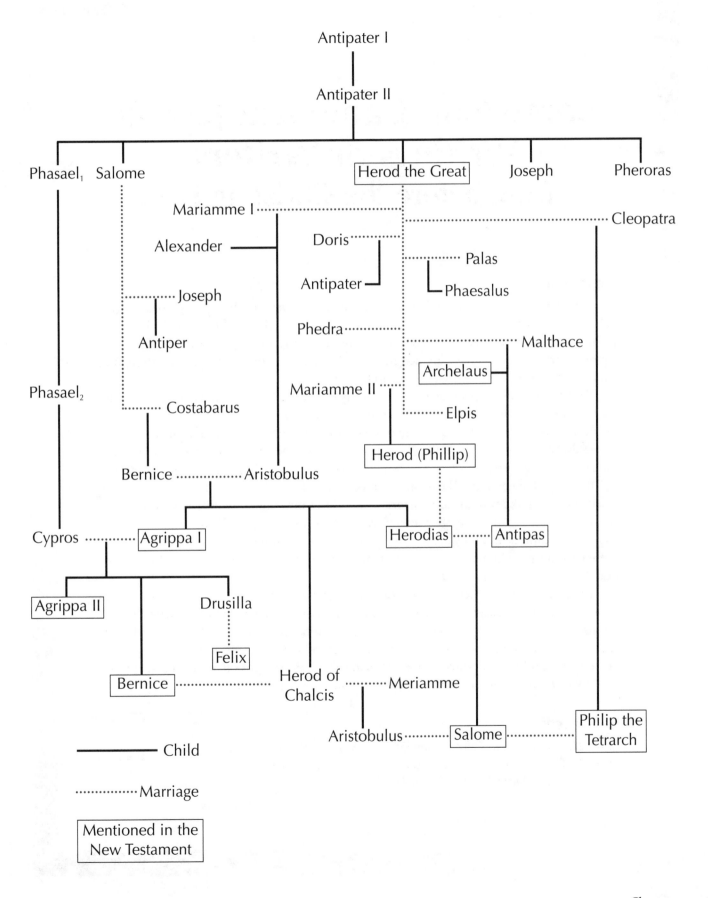

© 2002 Welch, Hall, FARMS

Chart 2-2

Some Non-Canonical Jewish Writings or Writers
from before the Christian Era

Explanation

This chart lists the names and approximate dates of several of the Jewish books known to have existed in the first century B.C. or around the lifetime of Jesus. This was a highly literary world. Scrolls were written and read in Greek and Hebrew, covering a variety of topics and genres. Modern scholars have divided these works into three broad categories although in antiquity they usually existed only as separate scrolls.

The Old Testament Apocrypha, written mostly in Hebrew but preserved in Greek, contains thirteen books that were included in the three main Greek manuscripts of the Bible from the fourth century. They contain a variety of historical, devotional, heroic, and instructional materials. While they were eventually rejected by Luther and early Protestants, during the time of Jesus they were considered by some people to be authoritative or valuable writings.

Books contained in the Old Testament Pseudepigrapha are Jewish (and, later, Christian) works written in the two centuries before or after Jesus but more recently rediscovered and collected. These writings are often attributed to older historic figures and may reflect long-standing traditions, but they are not of equal antiquity with the Old Testament. Some of these writings were influential among Jews and Christians at the time of Jesus. Enoch, for example, is quoted in the Epistle of Jude.

The Dead Sea Scrolls were hidden in caves near Qumran, about ten miles east of Jerusalem, before the fall of Jerusalem to the Romans. This collection of writings contained many biblical scrolls and also a number of interesting sectarian documents, listed in the bottom section of chart 2-3, probably written by Essenes. Although the influence of these writings on the New Testament is probably not direct, these texts show the kinds of books that were being written and used by other Jews during the lifetimes of Jesus, Peter, and Paul.

References

James H. Charlesworth, "Old Testament Apocrypha," *ABD*, 1:292–94.
James H. Charlesworth, "Pseudepigrapha, OT," *ABD*, 5:537–40.
John J. Collins, "Dead Sea Scrolls," *ABD*, 2:85–101.

Some Non-Canonical Jewish Writings or Writers
from before the Christian Era

OLD TESTAMENT APOCRYPHA (180–100 B.C.)

Tobit (c. 180 B.C.)

Ben Sira (c. 180 B.C.)

Judith (c. 150 B.C.)

Additions to Esther (c. 167–14 B.C.)

3 Ezra (1 Esdras) (c. 150–100 B.C.)

Prayer of Azariah

Song of Three Young Men

The History of Susanna

Bel and the Dragon

1 Maccabees

2 Maccabees

Epistle of Jeremiah

1 Baruch

Wisdom of Solomon

OLD TESTAMENT PSEUDEPIGRAPHA (200 B.C.–A.D. 50)

1 Enoch

Treatise of Shem

Apocalypse of Zephaniah

Testaments of the Twelve Patriarchs

Testament of Job

Letter of Aristeas

Jubilees

3 Maccabees

4 Ezra (2 Esdras)

Prayer of Manasseh

Pseudo-Phocylides

Psalms of Solomon

Philo the Epic Poet

Theodotus

Ezekiel the Tragedian

Aristobulus

Aristeas the Exegete

Eupolemus

Cleodemus Malchus

Artapanus

DEAD SEA SCROLLS (BEFORE A.D. 70)

Rule of the Community (1QS)

Damascus Document (CD)

Genesis Apocryphon (1QapGen)

Melchizedek Scroll (11QMelch)

Vision of Amram (4QAmram)

Description of New Jerusalem (1Q32)

Sayings of Moses (4Q159)

Psalms of Joshua (4Q375)

Heavenly Luminaries (4QDibHam)

Commentary on Habakkuk (1QpHab)

Commentaries on Psalms and Prophets

Miqsat Ma'ase ha Torah (4QMMT)

Temple Scroll (11QT)

Thanksgiving Hymns (IQH)

Angelic Liturgy (4QShirShabb)

War Scroll (1QM)

Prayer of Nabonidus (4QPrNab)

Wiles of the Wicked Woman (4Q184)

Chart 2-3

The Old Testament in the New

Explanation

The authors of the New Testament knew their scriptures, but some Old Testament writers were quoted more often than others. As chart 2-4 conveniently shows, Matthew used the Old Testament much more than John. Likewise, the epistles to the Romans and Hebrews (written mainly to Jewish Christians) drew very heavily on the Old Testament, while other letters such as 1 Thessalonians and Colossians (written to Greek audiences) made no direct use of the Old Testament.

Likewise, certain books of the Old Testament are more prevalent than others in the New Testament. The Psalms, Isaiah, and Deuteronomy lead the way, with Genesis and Exodus also being frequently cited. Most of these citations involve only a phrase or two, not the entire verse.

The Hebrew Bible had been translated in Alexandria, Egypt, into Greek around two hundred years before the birth of Jesus. That Greek version of the Old Testament is known as the Septuagint. Because the New Testament was written in Greek, its authors generally used the Greek translation when quoting from the Old Testament. Usually the quotations are quite precise (shown in bold type in chart 2-5), but occasionally the New Testament writers paraphrased or alluded to the Old Testament source. On a few occasions, these renditions may reflect their own translations from the original Hebrew scriptures.

References

Hans Hübner, "New Testament, OT Quotations in the," *ABD,* 4:1096–104.

Barbara Aland, et al., *The Greek New Testament* (Stuttgart: Deutsche Bibelgesellschaft, 1998).

Emanuel Tov, *The Greek and Hebrew Bible: Collected Essays on the Septuagint* (Leiden: Brill, 1999).

Number of Quotations
per Book

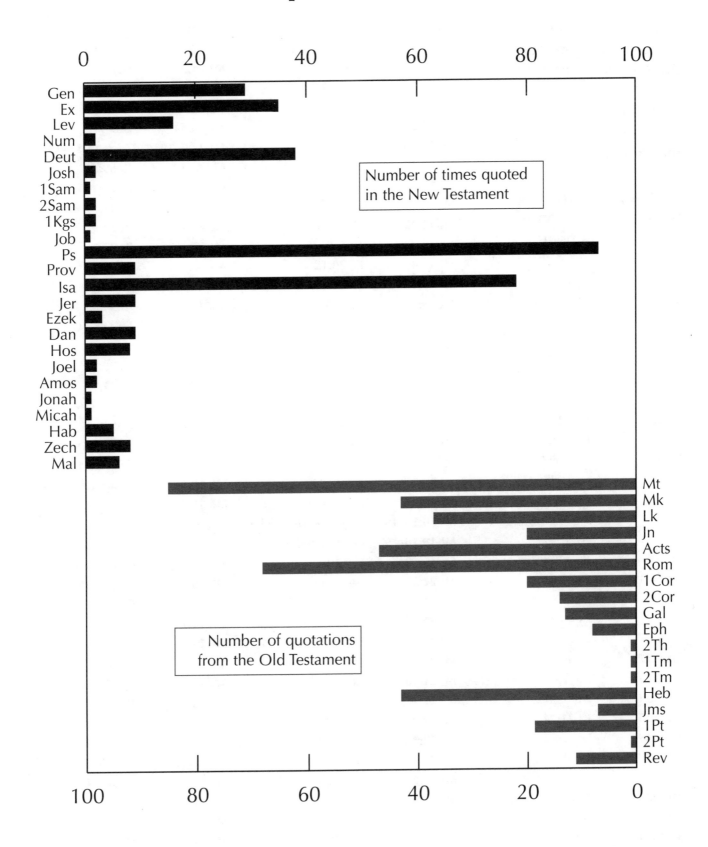

Number of times quoted in the New Testament

Number of quotations from the Old Testament

Chart 2-4

Old Testament Quotations

New Testament	Old Testament		New Testament	Old Testament		New Testament	Old Testament
Text in bold type is a direct quotation from the Greek Septuagint.			Mt 10:35–36	Micah 7:6		Mt 24:15	Dan 9:27
			Mt 11:5	Isa 33:5–6		Mt 24:29	Isa 13:10
			Mt 11:10	Mal 3:1		Mt 24:30	Dan 7:13
Text in italic type is a paraphrase of the text in the Septuagint.			Mt 12:7	Hos 6:6		Mt 26:31	Zech 13:7
			Mt 12:18–20	*Isa 42:1–3*		*Mt 26:64*	*Ps 110:1*
			Mt 12:21	Isa 42:4		Mt 26:64	Dan 7:13
Text in plain type draws on another version of the Old Testament.			Mt 12:40	Jonah 1:17		Mt 27:9–10	Zech 11:12–13
			Mt 12:40	Jonah 2:1		*Mt 27:34, 48*	*Ps 69:22*
			Mt 13:14–15	Isa 6:9–10		Mt 27:35	Ps 22:18
			Mt 13:35	*Ps 78:2*		*Mt 27:39*	*Ps 22:7*
			Mt 13:42	Dan 3:6		Mt 27:43	Ps 22:9
			Mt 13:43	*Dan 12:3*		Mt 27:46	Ps 22:1
Mt 1:23	*Isa 7:14*		Mt 15:4	Ex 20:12		Mt 27:48	Ps 69:22
Mt 1:23	**Isa 8:8, 10**		Mt 15:4	Ex 21:16, 17		Mk 1:2	Mal 3:1
Mt 2:6	**Micah 5:2**		Mt 15:4	Lev 20:9		Mk 1:3	Isa 40:3
Mt 2:15	**Hos 11:1**		Mt 15:4	Deut 5:16		Mk 4:12	Isa 6:9–10
Mt 2:18	*Jer 31:15*		Mt 15:8–9	Isa 29:13		Mk 7:6–7	Isa 29:13
Mt 2:23	Ps 22:6		Mt 16:27	Ps 62:13		Mk 7:10	Ex 20:12
Mt 2:23	Ps 69:9–10		Mt 16:27	Prov 24:12		Mk 7:10	Ex 21:17
Mt 2:23	Isa 52:53		*Mt 16:28*	*Dan 7:13*		Mk 7:10	Deut 5:16
Mt 3:3	**Isa 40:3**		Mt 18:16	Deut 19:15		Mk 7:10	Lev 20:9
Mt 4:4	**Deut 8:3**		Mt 19:4	Gen 1:27		Mk 9:48	Isa 66:24
Mt 4:6	*Ps 91:11–12*		Mt 19:4	Gen 5:2		*Mk 10:4*	*Deut 24:1, 3*
Mt 4:7	**Deut 6:16**		Mt 19:5	Gen 2:24		Mk 10:6	Gen 1:27
Mt 4:10	*Deut 6:13*		*Mt 19:7*	*Deut 24:1*		Mk 10:6	Gen 5:2
Mt 4:15–16	Isa 9:1–2		Mt 19:18–19	Ex 20:12–16		Mk 10:7–8	Gen 2:24
Mt 5:5	*Ps 37:11*		Mt 19:18–19	Deut 5:16–20		Mk 10:19	Ex 20:12
Mt 5:21	**Ex 20:13**		Mt 19:19	Lev 19:18		Mk 10:19	Ex 20:13–16
Mt 5:21	**Deut 5:17**		Mt 21:5	Isa 62:11		Mk 10:19	Deut 5:16–20
Mt 5:27	**Ex 20:14**		Mt 21:5	Zech 9:9		Mk 11:9–10	Ps 118:25–26
Mt 5:27	**Deut 5:18**		Mt 21:9	Ps 118:25–26		Mk 11:17	Isa 56:7
Mt 5:31	*Deut 24:1*		Mt 21:13	Isa 56:7		Mk 11:17	Jer 7:11
Mt 5:33	*Lev 19:12*		Mt 21:13	Jer 7:11		*Mk 12:1*	*Isa 5:2*
Mt 5:33	*Num 30:3*		Mt 21:16	Ps 8:2		Mk 12:10–11	Ps 118:22–23
Mt 5:38	**Ex 21:24**		Mt 21:42	Ps 118:22–23		Mk 12:19	Deut 25:5
Mt 5:38	**Lev 24:20**		Mt 22:24	Deut 25:5		Mk 12:26	Ex 3:6, 15
Mt 5:38	**Deut 19:21**		Mt 22:32	Ex 3:6, 15		Mk 12:29–30	Deut 6:4–5
Mt 5:43	**Lev 19:18**		Mt 22:37	Deut 6:5		Mk 12:31	Lev 19:18
Mt 7:23	**Ps 6:8**		Mt 22:39	Lev 19:18		Mk 12:32	Deut 6:4
Mt 8:17	**Isa 53:4**		Mt 22:44	Ps 110:1		Mk 12:32	Deut 4:35
Mt 9:13	**Hos 6:6**		*Mt 23:38*	*Jer 22:5*		Mk 12:32	Isa 45:21
			Mt 23:39	Ps 118:26		Mk 12:33	Deut 6:5

Chart 2-5 (1)

New Testament	Old Testament	New Testament	Old Testament	New Testament	Old Testament
Mk 12:33	Lev 19:18	Lk 22:37	Isa 53:12	Acts 7:16	Josh 24:32
Mk 12:33	Josh 22:5	*Lk 22:69*	*Ps 110:1*	Acts 7:18	Ex 1:8
Mk 12:36	Ps 110:1	Lk 23:30	Hos 10:8	*Acts 7:26*	*Ex 2:13*
Mk 13:14	Dan 9:27	*Lk 23:35*	*Ps 22:8*	Acts 7:27–28	Ex 2:14
Mk 13:24	Isa 13:10	Lk 23:46	Ps 31:5	*Acts 7:30*	*Ex 3:2*
Mk 13:25	Isa 13:10	Jn 1:23	Isa 40:3	Acts 7:32	Ex 3:6
Mk 13:26	Dan 7:13	Jn 2:17	Ps 69:9	Acts 7:33–34	Ex 3:5, 7–8, 10
Mk 14:27	Zech 13:7	Jn 6:31	Ps 78:24	Acts 7:35	Ex 2:14
Mk 14:62	*Ps 110:1*	Jn 6:45	Isa 54:13	Acts 7:37	Deut 18:15
Mk 14:62	Dan 7:13	Jn 7:38	Isa 12:3	Acts 7:40	Ex 32:1, 23
Mk 15:28	Isa 53:12	*Jn 8:17*	*Deut 19:15*	Acts 7:42–43	Amos 5:25–27
Mk 15:29	*Ps 22:8*	Jn 10:34	Ps 82:6	Acts 7:49–50	Isa 66:1–2
Mk 15:34	Ps 22:1	Jn 12:13	Ps 118:25–26	Acts 8:32–33	Isa 53:7–8
Mk 15:36	*Ps 69:22*	Jn 12:15	Zech 9:9	*Acts 13:22*	*1Sam 13:14*
Mk 27:35	Ps 22:19	Jn 12:38	Isa 53:1	*Acts 13:22*	*Ps 89:21*
Lk 1:15	Num 6:3	Jn 12:40	Isa 6:9–10	Acts 13:33	Ps 2:7
Lk 1:15	Lev 10:9	Jn 13:18	Ps 41:10	Acts 13:34	Isa 55:3
Lk 1:17	*Mal 3:1*	Jn 15:25	Ps 35:19	Acts 13:35	Ps 16:10
Lk 1:17	Mal 4:5–6	Jn 15:25	Ps 69:5	Acts 13:41	Hab 1:5
Lk 2:23	Ex 13:2, 12, 15	Jn 15:25	Ps 109:3	Acts 13:47	Isa 49:6
Lk 2:24	Lev 12:8	Jn 19:24	Ps 22:18	Acts 14:15	Ex 20:11
Lk 3:4–6	Isa 40:3–5	*Jn 19:28–29*	*Ps 69:21*	Acts 14:15	Ps 146:6
Lk 4:4	Deut 8:3	Jn 19:36	Ex 12:10, 46	Acts 15:16–18	Amos 9:11–12
Lk 4:8	Deut 6:13	*Jn 19:36*	*Num 9:12*	Acts 23:5	Ex 22:28
Lk 4:10–11	Ps 91:11–12	Jn 19:37	Zech 12:10	Acts 28:26–27	Isa 6:9–10
Lk 4:12	Deut 6:16	Acts 1:20	Ps 69:26	Rom 1:17	Hab 2:4
Lk 4:18–19	Isa 61:1–2	Acts 1:20	Ps 109:8	Rom 2:24	Isa 52:5
Lk 7:22	Isa 33:5–6	Acts 2:17–21	Joel 2:28–32	Rom 3:4	Ps 51:4
Lk 7:27	Mal 3:1	Acts 2:25–28	Ps 16:8–11	Rom 3:10–12	Ps 14:1–3
Lk 8:10	Isa 6:9–10	*Acts 2:30*	*Ps 132:11*	Rom 3:13	Ps 5:9
Lk 10:27	Lev 19:18	*Acts 2:31*	*Ps 16:10*	Rom 3:13	Ps 140:3
Lk 10:27	Deut 6:5	Acts 2:34–35	Ps 109:1	Rom 3:14	Ps 10:7
Lk 13:27	Ps 6:9	Acts 3:13	Ex 3:6,15	Rom 3:15–17	Isa 59:7–8
Lk 13:35	Ps 118:26	Acts 3:22–23	Deut 18:15–20	Rom 3:18	Ps 36:1
Lk 13:35	*Jer 22:5*	Acts 3:23	Lev 23:29	*Rom 3:20*	*Ps 143:2*
Lk 18:20	Ex 20:12	*Acts 3:25*	*Gen 12:3*	Rom 4:3	Gen 15:6
Lk 18:20	Ex 20:13–16	Acts 3:25	Gen 22:18	Rom 4:7–8	Ps 32:1–2
Lk 18:20	Deut 5:16–20	Acts 3:25	Gen 26:4	*Rom 4:9*	*Gen 15:6*
Lk 19:38	Ps 118:26	Acts 4:11	Ps 118:22–23	Rom 4:17	Gen 17:5
Lk 19:46	Isa 56:7	Acts 4:25–26	Ps 2:1–2	Rom 4:18	Gen 15:5
Lk 19:46	Jer 7:11	Acts 7:3	Gen 12:1	Rom 4:22	Gen 15:6
Lk 20:17	Ps 118:22–23	*Acts 7:5*	*Gen 17:8*	Rom 7:7	Ex 20:17
Lk 20:28	Deut 25:5	Acts 7:5	Gen 48:4	Rom 7:7	Deut 5:21
Lk 20:37	Ex 3:6	Acts 7:6–7	Gen 15:13–14	Rom 8:36	Ps 44:22
Lk 20:42–43	Ps 110:1	Acts 7:7	Ex 3:12	Rom 9:7	Gen 21:12
Lk 21:27	Dan 7:13	Acts 7:14	Gen 46:27	Rom 9:9	Gen 18:10, 14

Chart 2-5 (2)

New Testament	Old Testament	New Testament	Old Testament	New Testament	Old Testament
Rom 9:12	Gen 25:23	1Cor 1:19	Isa 29:14	Eph 1:22	Ps 8:7
Rom 9:13	Mal 1:2–3	*1Cor 1:20*	*Isa 33:18*	*Eph 2:17*	*Isa 57:19*
Rom 9:15	Ex 33:19	*1Cor 1:31*	*Jer 9:23–24*	Eph 4:8	Ps 68:19
Rom 9:17	Ex 9:16	*1Cor 2:9*	*Isa 64:3–4*	Eph 4:25	Zech 8:16
Rom 9:25	Hos 2:25	1Cor 2:16	Isa 40:13	Eph 4:26	Ps 4:4
Rom 9:26	Hos 2:1	1Cor 3:19	Job 5:13	Eph 5:31	Gen 2:24
Rom 9:27–28	Isa 10:22–23	1Cor 3:20	Ps 93:11	Eph 6:2–3	Ex 20:12
Rom 9:29	Isa 1:9	1Cor 5:13	Deut 17:7	Eph 6:2–3	Deut 5:16
Rom 9:33	Isa 8:14	1Cor 6:16	Gen 2:24	*2Th 2:8*	*Isa 11:4*
Rom 9:33	Isa 28:16	1Cor 9:9	Deut 25:4	1Tim 5:18	Deut 25:4
Rom 10:5	Lev 18:5	1Cor 10:7	Ex 32:6	2Tim 2:19	Num 16:5
Rom 10:6	Deut 9:4	1Cor 10:20	Deut 32:17	Heb 1:5	2Sam 7:14
Rom 10:6–8	Deut 30:12–14	1Cor 10:26	Ps 24:1	Heb 1:5	Ps 2:7
Rom 10:11	Isa 28:16	1Cor 14:21	Isa 28:11–12	Heb 1:6	Deut 32:43
Rom 10:13	Joel 2:32	1Cor 15:25	Ps 110:1	Heb 1:6	Ps 96:7
Rom 10:15	Isa 52:7	1Cor 15:27	Ps 8:6	Heb 1:7	Ps 104:4
Rom 10:16	Isa 53:1	1Cor 15:32	Isa 22:13	Heb 1:8–9	Ps 45:6–7
Rom 10:18	Ps 19:4	1Cor 15:45	Gen 2:7	Heb 1:10–12	Ps 102:25–27
Rom 10:19	Deut 32:21	1Cor 15:54	Isa 25:8	Heb 1:13	Ps 109:1
Rom 10:20–21	Isa 65:1–2	1Cor 15:55	Hos 13:14	Heb 2:6–8	Ps 8:4–6
Rom 11:3	1Kgs 19:10, 14	*2Cor 3:3*	*Ezek 11:19*	Heb 2:12	Ps 22:22
Rom 11:4	1Kgs 19:18	*2Cor 3:3*	*Ezek 36:26*	Heb 2:13	Isa 8:17–18
Rom 11:8	Deut 29:3	*2Cor 3:13*	*Ex 34:33*	Heb 3:7–11, 18	Ps 95:7–11
Rom 11:8	*Isa 6:9–10*	2Cor 4:13	Ps 116:10	Heb 3:15	Ps 95:7–8
Rom 11:8	Isa 29:10	2Cor 6:2	Isa 49:8	Heb 4:3, 5	Ps 95:11
Rom 11:9–10	Ps 69:22–23	2Cor 6:16	Lev 26:11–12	Heb 4:4	Gen 2:2–3
Rom 11:26–27	Isa 59:20–21	2Cor 6:16	Ezek 37:27	Heb 4:7	Ps 95:7–11
Rom 11:27	Isa 27:9	2Cor 6:17	Isa 52:11–12	Heb 5:5	Ps 2:7
Rom 11:34	Isa 40:13	2Cor 6:17	Ezek 20:34	Heb 5:6	Ps 110:4
Rom 11:35	Job 41:3	2Cor 6:18	2Sam 7:8, 14	Heb 6:13–14	Gen 22:16–17
Rom 12:16	*Prov 3:7*	2Cor 8:15	Ex 16:18	*Heb 6:20*	*Ps 110:4*
Rom 12:19	Deut 32:35	2Cor 9:9	Ps 112:9	Heb 7:1–2	Gen 14:17–20
Rom 12:20	Prov 25:21–22	2Cor 10:17	Jer 9:22	Heb 7:17, 21	Ps 110:4
Rom 13:9	Ex 20:13–17	2Cor 13:1	Deut 19:15	Heb 8:5	Ex 25:40
Rom 13:9	Lev 19:18	Gal 3:6	Gen 15:6	Heb 8:8–12	Jer 31:31–34
Rom 13:9	Deut 5:17–21	Gal 3:8	Gen 12:3	Heb 9:20	Ex 24:8
Rom 14:11	Isa 45:23	Gal 3:8	Gen 18:18	Heb 10:5–7	Ps 40:6–8
Rom 14:11	Isa 49:18	Gal 3:10	Deut 27:26	Heb 10:16–17	Jer 31:33–34
Rom 14:11	Jer 22:24	Gal 3:11	Hab 2:4	Heb 10:30	Deut 32:35–36
Rom 14:11	Ezek 5:11	Gal 3:12	Lev 18:5	Heb 10:30	Ps 135:14
Rom 15:3	Ps 69:9	Gal 3:13	Deut 21:23	Heb 10:37–38	Hab 2:3–4
Rom 15:9	Ps 18:49	Gal 3:16	Gen 24:7	Heb 11:5	Gen 5:24
Rom 15:10	Deut 32:43	Gal 3:16	Gen 13:15	Heb 11:18	Gen 21:12
Rom 15:11	Ps 117:1	Gal 4:27	Isa 54:1	Heb 11:21	Gen 47:31
Rom 15:12	Isa 11:10	Gal 4:30	Gen 21:10	Heb 12:5–6	Prov 3:11–12
Rom 15:21	Isa 52:15	Gal 5:14	Lev 19:18	*Heb 12:20*	*Ex 19:12–13*

Chart 2-5 (3)

New Testament	Old Testament	Old Testament	New Testament	Old Testament	New Testament
Heb 12:21	**Deut 9:19**	**Gen 1:27**	**Mt 19:4**	**Ex 20:12**	**Lk 18:20**
Heb 12:26	**Hab 2:6**	**Gen 1:27**	**Mk 10:6**	*Ex 20:12*	*Eph 6:2–3*
Heb 12:29	**Deut 4:24**	**Gen 2:3**	**Heb 4:4**	**Ex 20:13–14**	**Jms 2:11**
Heb 13:5	**Deut 31:6, 8**	*Gen 2:7*	*1Cor 15:45*	**Ex 20:12–16**	**Mt 19:18–19**
Heb 13:5	**Josh 1:5**	*Gen 2:24*	*Mt 19:5*	**Ex 20:13–16**	**Lk 18:20**
Heb 13:6	**Ps 118:6**	**Gen 2:24**	**Mk 10:7–8**	**Ex 20:13–16**	**Mk 10:19**
Heb 13:11–12	*Lev 16:27*	**Gen 2:24**	**1Cor 6:16**	**Ex 20:13–17**	**Rom 13:9**
Heb 13:15	**Hos 14:2**	**Gen 2:24**	**Eph 5:31**	**Ex 20:17**	**Rom 7:7**
Jms 2:8	**Lev 19:18**	*Gen 6:3, 5*	*Jms 4:5*	*Ex 21:16*	*Mt 15:4*
Jms 2:11	**Ex 20:13–15**	*Gen 12:1*	*Acts 7:3*	*Ex 21:17*	*Mk 7:10*
Jms 2:11	**Deut 5:17**	*Gen 12:3*	*Acts 3:25*	**Ex 21:24**	**Mt 5:38**
Jms 2:23	**Gen 15:6**	*Gen 12:3*	*Gal 3:8*	**Ex 22:28**	**Acts 23:5**
Jms 4:5	*Gen 6:3, 5*	**Gen 13:15**	**Gal 3:16**	*Ex 24:8*	*Heb 9:20*
Jms 4:6	**Prov 3:34**	**Gen 15:5**	**Rom 4:18**	*Ex 25:40*	*Heb 8:5*
Jms 5:20	**Prov 10:12**	*Gen 15:6*	*Rom 4:3*	**Ex 32:1**	**Acts 7:40**
1Pt 1:16	**Lev 11:44**	**Gen 15:6**	**Gal 3:6**	**Ex 32:6**	**1Cor 10:7**
1Pt 1:16	**Lev 19:2**	**Gen 15:6**	**Jms 2:23**	**Ex 33:19**	**Rom 9:15**
1Pt 1:24–25	**Isa 40:6–8**	Gen 15:13–14	Acts 7:6–7	*Ex 34:33*	*2Cor 3:13*
1Pt 2:6	**Isa 28:16**	**Gen 17:5**	**Rom 4:17**	**Lev 11:44**	**1Pt 1:16**
1Pt 2:7	**Ps 117:22**	Gen 18:10	Rom 9:9	**Lev 12:8**	**Lk 2:24**
1Pt 2:8	**Isa 8:14**	**Gen 18:18**	**Gal 3:8**	*Lev 16:27*	*Heb 13:11–12*
1Pt 2:9	**Ex 19:6**	*Gen 21:10*	*Gal 4:30*	**Lev 18:5**	**Rom 10:5**
1Pt 2:9	**Isa 43:20–21**	**Gen 21:12**	**Rom 9:7**	**Lev 18:5**	**Gal 3:12**
1Pt 2:22	**Isa 53:9**	**Gen 21:12**	**Heb 11:18**	**Lev 19:18**	**Mt 5:43**
1Pt 2:24	**Isa 53:4**	**Gen 22:16–17**	**Heb 6:13–14**	**Lev 19:18**	**Mt 19:19**
1Pt 2:24	**Isa 53:5**	**Gen 22:18**	**Acts 3:25**	**Lev 19:18**	**Mt 22:39**
1Pt 2:24	*Isa 53:11–12*	**Gen 25:23**	**Rom 9:12**	**Lev 19:18**	**Mk 12:31**
1Pt 3:10–12	**Ps 34:13–17**	*Gen 46:27*	*Acts 7:14*	**Lev 19:18**	**Lk 10:27**
1Pt 3:14–15	**Isa 8:12–13**	**Gen 47:31**	**Heb 11:21**	**Lev 19:18**	**Rom 13:9**
1Pt 3:22	Ps 110:1	*Ex 2:13*	*Acts 7:26*	**Lev 19:18**	**Gal 5:14**
1Pt 4:8	**Prov 10:12**	**Ex 2:14**	**Acts 7:27–28**	**Lev 19:18**	**Jms 2:8**
1Pt 4:18	**Prov 11:31**	**Ex 2:14**	**Acts 7:35**	*Lev 20:9*	*Mt 15:4*
1Pt 5:5	**Prov 3:34**	*Ex 3:5, 7–8, 10*	*Acts 7:33–34*	**Lev 24:20**	**Mt 5:38**
1Pt 5:7	*Ps 55:23*	*Ex 3:6*	*Mt 22:32*	*Lev 26:11–12*	*2Cor 6:16*
2Pt 2:22	*Prov 26:11*	*Ex 3:6*	*Mk 12:26*	*Num 9:12*	*Jn 19:36*
Rev 1:17–18	*Isa 44:6*	*Ex 3:6*	*Lk 20:37*	*Num 16:5*	*2Tim 2:19*
Rev 2:8	Isa 44:6–7	**Ex 3:6**	**Acts 7:32**	**Deut 4:24**	**Heb 12:29**
Rev 2:27	**Ps 2:9**	**Ex 9:16**	**Rom 9:17**	**Deut 5:16**	**Eph 6:2–3**
Rev 3:7	*Isa 22:22*	*Ex 12:46*	*Jn 19:36*	**Deut 5:17**	**see Ex 20:13**
Rev 3:19	*Prov 3:11–12*	Ex 13:2	Lk 2:23	**Deut 5:18**	**see Ex 20:15**
Rev 5:6	*Zech 4:10*	**Ex 16:18**	**2Cor 8:15**	**Deut 5:19**	**see Ex 20:14**
Rev 7:16	**Isa 49:10**	*Ex 19:6*	*1Pt 2:9*	**Deut 5:20**	**see Ex 20:16**
Rev 11:4ff.	*Zech 4:2–3, 14*	*Ex 19:12–13*	*Heb 12:20*	**Deut 5:21**	**see Ex 20:17**
Rev 12:14	*Dan 7:25*	*Ex 20:12*	*Mt 15:4*	Deut 6:4–5	Mk 12:29–30
Rev 12:14	*Dan 12:7*	**Ex 20:12**	**Mk 7:10**	Deut 6:5	Mt 22:37
Rev 14:14	*Dan 7:13*	**Ex 20:12**	**Mk 10:19**	Deut 6:5	Lk 10:27

Chart 2-5 (4)

Old Testament	New Testament	Old Testament	New Testament	Old Testament	New Testament
Deut 6:13	*Mt 4:10*	**Ps 8:4–6**	**Heb 2:6–8**	*Ps 91:11–12*	*Mt 4:6*
Deut 6:13	**Lk 4:8**	**Ps 8:6**	**1Cor 15:27**	**Ps 91:11**	**Lk 4:10–11**
Deut 6:16	**Mt 4:7**	*Ps 8:7*	*Eph 1:22*	**Ps 94:11**	**1Cor 3:20**
Deut 6:16	**Lk 4:12**	**Ps 10:7**	**Rom 3:14**	**Ps 95:7–11**	**Heb 3:7–11, 18**
Deut 8:3	**Mt 4:4**	*Ps 14:2–3*	*Rom 3:11–12*	**Ps 95:7–11**	**Heb 4:7**
Deut 8:3	**Lk 4:4**	**Ps 16:8–11**	**Acts 2:25–28**	Ps 97:7	Heb 1:6
Deut 18:15	*Acts 7:37*	**Ps 16:10**	**Acts 13:35**	*Ps 102:25–27*	*Heb 1:10–12*
Deut 18:15–16	Acts 3:22–23	**Ps 18:49**	**Rom 15:9**	**Ps 104:4**	**Heb 1:7**
Deut 18:18–19	*Acts 3:22–23*	*Ps 19:4*	*Rom 10:18*	Ps 109:3	Jn 15:25
Deut 19:15	**Mt 18:16**	**Ps 22:1**	**Mt 27:46**	Ps 109:8	Acts 1:20
Deut 19:15	*Jn 8:17*	**Ps 22:1**	**Mk 15:34**	**Ps 110:1**	**Mt 22:44**
Deut 19:15	**2Cor 13:1**	Ps 22:6	Mt 2:23	**Ps 110:1**	**Mk 12:36**
Deut 21:23	**Gal 3:13**	*Ps 22:7*	*Mt 27:39*	**Ps 110:1**	**Lk 20:42**
Deut 25:4	**1Cor 9:9**	*Ps 22:7*	*Mk 15:29*	**Ps 110:1**	**Acts 2:34**
Deut 25:4	**1Tim 5:18**	*Ps 22:7*	*Lk 23:35*	**Ps 110:1**	**1Cor 15:25**
Deut 25:5	**Mt 22:24**	**Ps 22:8**	**Mt 27:43**	**Ps 110:1**	**Heb 1:13**
Deut 25:5	Mk 12:19	**Ps 22:18**	**Mt 27:35**	Ps 110:1	1Pt 3:22
Deut 25:5	**Lk 20:28**	**Ps 22:18**	**Jn 19:24**	**Ps 110:4**	**Heb 5:6**
Deut 27:26	Gal 3:10	**Ps 22:19**	**Mk 27:35**	*Ps 110:4*	*Heb 6:20*
Deut 29:4	Rom 11:8	**Ps 22:22**	**Heb 2:12**	**Ps 110:4**	**Heb 7:17, 21**
Deut 30:12–14	**Rom 10:6–8**	**Ps 24:1**	**1Cor 10:26**	**Ps 112:9**	**2Cor 9:9**
Deut 31:6, 8	**Heb 13:5**	**Ps 31:5**	**Lk 23:46**	**Ps 116:10**	**2Cor 4:13**
Deut 32:17	**1Cor 10:20**	**Ps 32:1–2**	**Rom 4:7–8**	**Ps 117:1**	**Rom 15:11**
Deut 32:21	Rom 10:19	*Ps 34:12–16*	*1Pt 3:10–12*	*Ps 118:6*	*Heb 13:6*
Deut 32:35	Rom 12:19	**Ps 35:19**	**Jn 15:25**	**Ps 118:22–23**	**Mt 21:42**
Deut 32:35–36	**Heb 10:30**	**Ps 36:1**	**Rom 3:18**	**Ps 118:22–23**	**Mk 12:10**
Deut 32:43	Rom 15:10	*Ps 37:11*	*Mt 5:5*	**Ps 118:22–23**	**Lk 20:17**
Deut 32:43	**Heb 1:6**	**Ps 40:6–8**	**Heb 10:5–7**	**Ps 118:22–23**	**Acts 4:11**
Josh 1:5	**Heb 13:5**	Ps 41:9	Jn 13:18	**Ps 118:22**	**1Pt 2:7**
Josh 24:32	Acts 7:16	**Ps 44:22**	**Rom 8:36**	**Ps 118:26**	**Mt 21:9**
1Sam 13:14	*Acts 13:22*	**Ps 45:6–7**	**Heb 1:8–9**	**Ps 118:26**	**Mt 23:39**
2Sam 7:14	**Heb 1:5**	*Ps 51:4*	*Rom 3:4*	**Ps 118:26**	**Mk 11:9**
2Sam 7:14	**2Cor 6:18**	*Ps 55:22*	*1Pt 5:7*	**Ps 118:26**	**Lk 19:38**
1Kgs 19:14	Rom 11:3	Ps 68:18	Eph 4:8	*Ps 132:11*	*Acts 2:30*
1Kgs 19:18	Rom 11:4	**Ps 69:9**	**Jn 2:17**	**Ps 135:14**	**Heb 10:30**
Job 5:13	**1Cor 3:19**	**Ps 69:9**	**Rom 15:3**	**Ps 140:3**	**Rom 3:13**
Ps 2:1–2	**Acts 4:25–26**	Ps 69:9–10	Mt 2:23	*Ps 143:2*	*Rom 3:20*
Ps 2:7	**Acts 13:33**	*Ps 69:21*	*Mt 27:34, 48*	*Prov 3:7*	*Rom 12:16*
Ps 2:7	**Heb 1:5**	*Ps 69:21*	*Mk 15:36*	**Prov 3:11–12**	**Heb 12:5–6**
Ps 2:7	**Heb 5:5**	*Ps 69:21*	*Jn 19:28–29*	*Prov 3:11–12*	*Rev 3:19*
Ps 2:9	Rev 2:27	*Ps 69:22–23*	*Rom 11:9–10*	**Prov 3:34**	**Jms 4:6**
Ps 4:4	**Eph 4:26**	Ps 69:25	Acts 1:20	**Prov 3:34**	**1Pt 5:5**
Ps 5:9	**Rom 3:13**	Ps 78:2	Mt 13:35	**Prov 10:12**	**Jms 5:20**
Ps 6:8	**Mt 7:23**	*Ps 78:24*	*Jn 6:31*	Prov 10:12	1Pt 4:8
Ps 6:9	*Lk 13:27*	**Ps 82:6**	**Jn 10:34**	*Prov 25:21–22*	*Rom 12:20*
Ps 8:2	*Mt 21:16*	*Ps 89:20*	*Acts 13:22*	*Prov 26:11*	*2Pt 2:22*

Chart 2-5 (5)

Old Testament	New Testament	Old Testament	New Testament	Old Testament	New Testament
Isa 1:9	*Rom 9:29*	*Isa 49:6*	*Acts 13:47*	**Dan 7:13**	**Mk 13:26**
Isa 5:2	*Mk 12:1*	**Isa 49:8**	**2Cor 6:2**	**Dan 7:13**	**Lk 21:27**
Isa 6:9–10	*Mt 13:14–15*	**Isa 49:10**	**Rev 7:16**	*Dan 7:13*	*Rev 14:14*
Isa 6:9–10	*Mk 4:12*	Isa 52:53	Mt 2:23	*Dan 7:25*	*Rev 12:14*
Isa 6:9–10	*Lk 8:10*	Isa 52:5	Rom 2:24	*Dan 12:7*	*Rev 12:14*
Isa 6:9–10	*Jn 12:40*	Isa 52:7	Rom 10:15	**Dan 9:27**	**Mt 24:15**
Isa 6:9–10	*Acts 28:26–27*	Isa 52:11–12	2Cor 6:17	**Dan 9:27**	**Mk 13:14**
Isa 6:9–10	*Rom 11:8*	**Isa 52:15**	**Rom 15:21**	*Dan 12:3*	*Mt 13:43*
Isa 7:14	*Mt 1:23*	**Isa 53:1**	**Jn 12:38**	*Hos 1:10*	*Rom 9:26*
Isa 8:12–13	*1Pt 3:14–15*	**Isa 53:1**	**Rom 10:16**	Hos 2:23	Rom 9:25
Isa 8:14	*Rom 9:33*	**Isa 53:4**	**Mt 8:17**	**Hos 6:6**	**Mt 9:13**
Isa 8:14	**1Pt 2:8**	**Isa 53:4**	**1Pt 2:24**	**Hos 6:6**	**Mt 12:7**
Isa 8:17–18	**Heb 2:13**	*Isa 53:5*	*1Pt 2:24*	**Hos 10:8**	**Lk 23:30**
Isa 9:1–2	Mt 4:15–16	**Isa 53:7–8**	**Acts 8:32–33**	**Hos 11:1**	**Mt 2:15**
Isa 10:22–23	Rom 9:27–28	*Isa 53:9*	*1Pt 2:22*	**Hos 13:14**	**1Cor 15:55**
Isa 11:4	*2Th 2:8*	*Isa 53:11–12*	*1Pt 2:24*	**Hos 14:2**	**Heb 13:15**
Isa 11:10	*Rom 15:12*	**Isa 53:12**	**Mk 15:28**	*Joel 2:28–32*	*Acts 2:17–21*
Isa 12:3	**Jn 7:38**	**Isa 53:12**	**Lk 22:37**	**Joel 2:32**	**Rom 10:13**
Isa 13:10	**Mt 24:29**	**Isa 54:1**	**Gal 4:27**	**Amos 5:25–27**	**Acts 7:42–43**
Isa 13:10	*Mk 13:24*	*Isa 54:13*	*Jn 6:45*	Amos 9:11–12	Acts 15:16–18
Isa 22:13	**1Cor 15:32**	**Isa 55:3**	**Acts 13:34**	**Jonah 2:1**	**Mt 12:40**
Isa 22:22	*Rev 3:7*	**Isa 56:7**	**Mt 21:13**	**Micah 5:2**	**Mt 2:6**
Isa 25:8	**1Cor 15:54**	**Isa 56:7**	**Mk 11:17**	**Hab 1:5**	**Acts 13:41**
Isa 27:9	**Rom 11:27**	**Isa 56:7**	**Lk 19:46**	**Hab 2:3–4**	**Heb 10:37–38**
Isa 28:11–12	1Cor 14:21	*Isa 57:19*	*Eph 2:17*	*Hab 2:4*	*Rom 1:17*
Isa 28:16	**Rom 9:33**	Isa 59:7–8	Rom 3:15–17	**Hab 2:4**	**Gal 3:11**
Isa 28:16	**Rom 10:11**	**Isa 59:20–21**	**Rom 11:26–27**	Hab 2:6	Heb 12:26
Isa 28:16	*1Pt 2:6*	**Isa 61:1–2**	**Lk 4:18–19**	*Zech 4:2–3,14*	*Rev 11:4ff.*
Isa 29:10	Rom 11:8	Isa 62:11	Mt 21:5	*Zech 4:10*	*Rev 5:6*
Isa 29:13	**Mt 15:8–9**	Isa 64:3–4	1Cor 2:9	Zech 9:9	Mt 21:5
Isa 29:13	**Mk 7:6–7**	*Isa 65:1–2*	*Rom 10:20–21*	Zech 9:9	Jn 12:14–15
Isa 29:14	*1Cor 1:19*	Isa 66:1–2	Acts 7:49–50	*Zech 11:13*	*Mt 27:9–10*
Isa 33:5–6	**Mt 11:5**	*Isa 66:24*	*Mk 9:48*	Zech 12:10	Jn 19:37
Isa 33:5–6	**Lk 7:22**	Jer 7:11	Mt 21:13	*Zech 13:7*	*Mt 26:31*
Isa 33:18	*1Cor 1:20*	Jer 7:11	Mk 11:17	*Zech 13:7*	*Mk 14:27*
Isa 40:3	Mt 3:3	Jer 7:11	Lk 19:46	**Mal 1:2–3**	**Rom 9:13**
Isa 40:3	Mk 1:3	*Jer 9:23–24*	*1Cor 1:31*	**Mal 3:1**	**Mt 11:10**
Isa 40:3	**Jn 1:23**	*Jer 22:5*	*Mt 23:38*	**Mal 3:1**	**Mk 1:2**
Isa 40:3–5	Lk 3:4–6	*Jer 22:5*	*Lk 13:35*	*Mal 3:1*	*Lk 1:17*
Isa 40:6–8	*1Pt 1:24–25*	*Jer 31:15*	*Mt 2:18*	**Mal 3:1**	**Lk 7:27**
Isa 40:13	Rom 11:34	Jer 31:31–34	Heb 8:8–12	Mal 4:5–6	Lk 1:17
Isa 40:13	1Cor 2:16	**Jer 31:33–34**	**Heb 10:16–17**		
Isa 42:1–4	Mt 12:18–21	*Ezek 11:19*	*2Cor 3:3*		
Isa 44:6–7	*Rev 1:17–18*	*Ezek 36:26*	*2Cor 3:3*		
Isa 44:6–7	*Rev 2:8*	**Ezek 37:27**	**2Cor 6:16**		
Isa 45:23	Rom 14:11	Dan 7:13	Mt 16:28		

Chart 2-5 (6)

Chart 2-6

Taxes in Judea

Explanation

Taxation was as much a part of the world of the New Testament as it is in our world today. Various kinds of taxes were imposed, by differing authorities, and for an array of purposes. Religious taxes supported the temple and the central Jewish institutions. Imperial taxes went to support the Roman government, and local taxes were levied by Jewish rulers and paid for the infrastructure of Judean commerce. The total tax burden was perhaps as high as 60 percent of all production, but this burden was not primarily imposed by the Romans. As in any age, the combination of these many taxes resulted in popular dissatisfaction.

References

John E. Stambaugh and David L. Balch, *The New Testament in Its Social Environment* (Philadelphia: Westminster, 1986), 74–78.

K. C. Hanson and Douglas E. Oakman, *Palestine in the Time of Jesus: Social Structures and Social Conflicts* (Minneapolis: Fortress, 1998), 113–16.

John A. Tvedtnes, "The Priestly Tithe in the First Century A.D.," *MWNT*, 261–68.

Ronald Z. Domsky, "Taxation in the Bible during the Period of the First and Second Temples," *Detroit College of Law Journal of International Law and Practice* 7 (summer 1998): 225–61.

Taxes in Judea

TYPE OF TAX	APPROXIMATE AMOUNTS	TAX AUTHORITIES
RELIGIOUS		
Annual Temple Tax	Half-shekel per adult male	Chief Priests
Temple Sacrifices	1–2% of goods and animals offered in kind	Chief Priests
Tithing of Herds and Crops	10% of increase to support the priests	Levites
Tithing of Wild Foods	1% of food from hunting and gathering	Chief Priests
Votive Offerings	Dedications connected with vows	Chief Priests
Other Contributions	First dough, first sheering, gleanings, alms	Various
IMPERIAL		
Annual Poll Tax	1 denarius for all adults 14–65 years old	Roman rulers
Property Taxes	1% of value of land, houses, slaves, and ships	Roman rulers
Inheritance Taxes	5% of large bequests from unrelated decedents	Roman rulers
LOCAL		
Sales Taxes	1% of transactions in the market	Local/Roman
Slave Transfer Tax	4% on sales of slaves	Local/Roman
Transit Tolls	2–3% of goods imported	Local/Roman
Conscripted Services	Variable	Local/Roman
Produce Taxes	Could be up to 50% of crop	Local rulers
Resource Use Fees	Variable	Local cities
Total Tax Burden	Governing classes collected a substantial portion of all production	

Chart 2-6

Chart 2-7

Money

Explanation

Greek, Roman, and Jewish coins circulated in Judea and Galilee during New Testament times. Many of these pieces of copper, silver, or gold are mentioned by name in the Gospels. They range from the smallest "widow's mite" to the much larger "denarius" or "stater." Values represented by these coins are important in understanding the meaning of certain passages, such as the coin in the fish's mouth, which was one stater, exactly the amount needed to pay the annual temple tax for two people. A talent was not a coin but a large ingot of metal, weighing from 50 to 92 pounds. Variations occurred from one century to another and from one land to another. One talent of gold was an enormous sum, let alone the 10,000 talent debt owed by the unjust steward to his lord.

References

Christopher Howgego, *Ancient History from Coins* (London: Routledge, 1995).
Nanci DeBloois, "Coins in the New Testament," *MWNT,* 239–51.
John W. Betlyon, "Coinage," *ABD,* 1:1076–89.
T. Edgar Lyon, "Greco-Roman Influences on the Holy Land," *Ensign,* September 1974, 20–21.

Money

Ratios	Greek	Roman	Jewish	Functional Value	Reference
50,000	50,000 silver coins			magical books burned	Acts 19:19
14,616	talent (Tyrian)			42 kilograms	Mt 25:15
6,960	talent (Galilean)			20 kilograms	Mt 25:15
300		300 denarii		value of ointment	Jn 12:5
200		200 denarii		feed multitude	Jn 6:7
				= 50 staters	
120			30 shekels	30 pieces of silver	Mt 26:15
116	mina			= 1/60 talent (Galilean)	Lk 19:16
100		100 denarii		owed to servant	Mt 18:28
25		denarius (gold)			
10	10 drachmai			woman's 10 coins	Lk 15:8
4	stater		shekel	coin in fish's mouth	Mt 17:27
2	didrachm		half shekel	annual temple tax	Mt 17:24
				paid to innkeeper	Lk 10:35
1	drachma	denarius (silver)		render to Caesar	Mt 22:19–21
				a measure of wheat	Rev 6:6
				one day's labor	
				compare one dollar	
.10–.06		assarion		two sparrows	Mt 10:29
				compare one dime or nickel	
.025	kordantes	quadrans		uttermost farthing	Mt 5:26
				widow's mites	Mk 12:42
				compare two cents	
.0125	lepton		prutah	very last mite	Lk 12:59
				smaller in size than a penny	

Bronze lepton

Silver denarius

Silver shekel

Chart 2-7

Chart 2-8

Animals and Plants

Explanation

Local flora and fauna are mentioned expressly in several places in the New Testament. Reading down these lists of animals and plants reminds modern readers of the agrarian and rural setting of the villages and hillsides in which much of the New Testament takes place. Most of the people who heard, wrote, or read the stories of Jesus would have had firsthand awareness of these ordinary features of daily New Testament life.

References

D. Kelly Ogden, *Where Jesus Walked: The Land and Culture of New Testament Times* (Salt Lake City: Deseret Book, 1991).

J. Toynbee, *Animals in Roman Life and Art* (London: Thames & Hudson, 1973).

Edwin Firmage, "Zoology (Fauna)," *ABD*, 6:1109–67.

Animals

Fox	Mt 8:20; Lk 9:58
Wolf	Mt 7:15; Jn 10:12
Bear	Rev 13:2
Leopard	Rev 13:2
Lion	2Tm 4:17; 1Pt 5:8; Rev 4:7
Bull (bous)	Jn 2:14
Ox (bous)	Lk 13:15; 1Cor 9:9; 1Tm 5:18
Bull (tauros)	Mt 22:4; Acts 14:13; Heb 9:13
Calf (moschos)	Lk 15:23; Heb 9:12, 19; Rev 4:7
Heifer (damalis)	Heb 9:13
Kid (eriphos)	Mt 25:32–33
Goat (tragos)	Heb 9:12
Sheep (probaton)	Mt 7:15; 9:36; 10:6; Jn 10:2; 21:16
Lamb (aren)	Lk 10:3
Ram (arnion)	Jn 21:15; Rev 13:11
Horse	Jms 3:3; Rev 6:2
Camel	Mt 3:4; 19:24; 23:24
Donkey (onos)	Mt 21:2; Lk 13:15; Jn 12:15
Colt (polos)	Mt 21:2; Jn 12:14–15
Dog	Lk 16:21
Pig	Mt 7:6; 8:30
Sow	2Pt 2:22
Animal (zoon)	Heb 13:11
Beast (therion)	Acts 28:4
Livestock (thremma)	Jn 4:12
Beast of burden (ktenos)	Lk 10:34
Pack animal (hypozygion)	Mt 21:5
Reptile or Snake (herpeton)	Acts 10:12
Snake (ophis)	Lk 10:19
Poisonous Snake, Asp, Cobra	Rom 3:13
Dragon	Rev 12:3
Frog	Rev 16:13
Scorpion	Rev 9:5
Worm	Mk 9:48
Bird	Mt 6:26; Mk 4:4; 1Cor 15:39
Rooster	Mt 26:34; Jn 13:38
Hen	Mt 23:37; Lk 13:34

Young Bird	Mt 23:37; Lk 13:34
Dove or Pigeon	Mt 10:16; Lk 2:24
Sparrow	Mt 10:29
Eagle or Vulture	Mt 24:28; Rev 12:14
Crow or Raven	Lk 12:24
Locusts or Grasshoppers	Mk 1:6
Gnat or Mosquito	Mt 23:24
Moth	Mt 6:19
Bee	Lk 24:42
Sea Creature (enalion)	Jms 3:7
Fish (ichthus)	Mt 7:10; 14:17; 17:27; Lk 5:6
Small Fish (ichthudion)	Mk 8:7
Sea Monster (ketos)	Mt 12:40

Plants

Lilies of the Field	Mt 6:28
Thorn thistle	Mt 7:16
Reed	Mt 11:7
Tare	Mt 13:25
Mustard	Mt 13:31
Olive Tree	Mt 21:1
Mint	Mt 23:23
Dill, Anise	Mt 23:23
Cummin	Mt 23:23
Fig tree	Mt 24:32
Rue	Lk 11:42
Mulberry tree	Lk 17:6
Sycamore-fig tree	Lk 19:4
Bush	Lk 20:37
Palm tree	Jn 12:13
Wheat	Jn 12:24
Grapevine	Jn 15:1
Hyssop	Jn 19:29
Wormwood	Rev 8:11

Chart 2-8

Chart 2-9

Olive Oil Production

Explanation

The olive crop was a mainstay of Palestinian economy in the days of Jesus. Olive trees were carefully cultivated and took decades to grow. The valuable olive was used for many purposes. The purest oil of the first pressing was especially prized and was used for anointing in the religious ceremonies of Jews, Greeks, and Romans. After separating out the press residue, which was used for fuel, the remaining fluid was re-pressed and separated into oil and *amurca*. The oil served as a basis for medicines and cosmetics, as well as the main source of lamp and cooking oils.

References

John Gee and Daniel C. Peterson, "Graft and Corruption: On Olives and Olive Culture in the Pre-Modern Mediterranean," in *The Allegory of the Olive Tree*, ed. Stephen D. Ricks and John W. Welch (Provo, Utah: FARMS, 1994), 194–95.

Truman G. Madsen, "The Olive Press: A Symbol of Christ," in *The Allegory of the Olive Tree*, ed. Stephen D. Ricks and John W. Welch (Provo, Utah: FARMS, 1994), 1–10.

Wilford M. Hess, "Recent Notes about Olives in Antiquity," *BYU Studies* 39/4 (2000): 115–26.

Olive Oil Production

Olives

First Pressing

1. First Oil

Lighting temple lamps,
Anointings and offerings

2. Press Residue

Presscake, Pomace,
Pulp, Refuse, Oil cake

3. Leftover Mixed Fluid

Second Pressing

4. Olive Oil

Medicine	Lk 10:34
Skin ointment	Mt 6:17
Burning in lamps	Mt 25:1–13
Cooking	1Kgs 17:12

5. *Amurca*

Watery lees, Dregs,
Fertilizer, Herbicide,
Pesticide, New jar cure

Chart 2-9

Chart 2-10

Weights and Measures

Explanation

Chart 2-10 shows the various measures of weight, length, and volume used in New Testament times. In the left-hand column, the basic terms are given (scripture references for those that appear in the New Testament are given in the far right column). Biblical equivalents are given in the second column to facilitate comparisons. In some cases, modern equivalents are known precisely; others are calculated approximations.

Reference

Marvin A. Powell, "Weights and Measures," *ABD,* 6:897–908.

Weights and Measures

BIBLICAL UNITS	ANCIENT EQUIVALENTS	BRITISH, U.S. EQUIVALENTS	METRIC EQUIVALENTS	NEW TESTAMENT OCCURRENCE
WEIGHT				
Tyrian talent		91 pounds	42.5 kilograms	
Galilean talent		45 pounds	20.4 kilograms	Mt 25:15
mina	50 shekels	1.25 pounds	0.6 kilogram	Lk 19:13
litra	Roman pound	12 ounces	327.45 grams	Jn 19:39
shekel	2 bekas	0.4 ounce	11.5 grams	
pim	2/3 shekel	0.27 ounce	7.6 grams	
beka	10 gerahs	0.2 ounce	5.5 grams	
gerah		0.02 ounce	0.6 gram	
LENGTH				
mile *(milion)*		4500 feet	1.380 kilometers	Mt 5:41
furlong *(stadion)*		600 feet	190 meters	Lk 24:13
rod *(kalamos)*		10 feet	3 meters	Rev 11:1
fathom		6 feet	1.8 meters	Acts 27:28
cubit		18 inches	0.5 meter	Mt 6:27
span		9 inches	23 centimeters	
handbreadth		3 inches	8 centimeters	
VOLUME				
kor		11 bushels	393 liters	Lk 16:7
homer	10 ephahs	6 bushels	220 liters	
lethek	5 ephahs	3 bushels	110 liters	
firkin, batos		9 gallons	33 liters	Jn 2:6; Lk 16:6
ephah	10 omers	0.6 bushel, 6 gallons	22 liters	
saton		3 gallons	11 liters	Mt 13:33
modios		0.25 bushel	9 liters	Mt 5:15
seah	0.3 ephah	7 quarts	7.3 liters	
hin	0.17 bath	1 gallon	4 liters	
omer	0.1 ephah	2 quarts	2 liters	
cab	0.06 ephah	1 quart	1 liter	
xestes		0.5 quart	0.5 liter	Mk 7:4
log	0.02 bath	0.33 quart	0.3 liter	

Chart 2-10

Maps of Judea and Galilee

Explanation

Understanding the New Testament requires some understanding of the land where its events transpired. Indeed, the Holy Land has been called by some people another "book" of the Bible. Walking where Mary and Joseph walked, standing where John the Baptist stood, sailing where Peter fished, kneeling where Jesus knelt, and running where John ran adds palpable dimensions of feeling and perspective to the pages of the New Testament.

Chart 2-11 shows the regions around Judea in the first century: Idumea (Herod's homeland) to the south, and moving north through Judea (the Jewish heartland), Samaria (hill country up to the Jezreel Valley), Galilee (an area of Jewish population expansion in the first century B.C.), and on up into Syria. To the east is the Decapolis (ten Hellenistic cities mentioned in the New Testament but apparently not visited by Jesus). This map shows locations of cities, towns, Herodian fortresses, and physical features, many of which are mentioned in the New Testament. From Nazareth to Jerusalem is only 60 miles as the crow flies.

Chart 2-12 focuses on the even smaller region of Galilee. Only 25 miles east of the Mediterranean Sea lies the beautiful Sea of Galilee. Six miles wide and 12 miles long, it feeds the Jordan River, is full of fish, and sits as a jewel amidst the surrounding hills and valleys. One can easily imagine how Jesus and his early Galilean followers loved to be together in this somewhat remote but close-knit and enveloping neighborhood.

References

Andrew Skinner, "A Historical Sketch of Galilee," *MWNT,* 113–25.
Richard A. Horsley, *Galilee: History, Politics, People* (Valley Forge, Penn.: Trinity, 1995).
Charles R. Page II and Carl A. Volz, *The Land and the Book* (Nashville: Abingdon, 1993).

Judea and Surrounding Regions

SYRIA

Mt. Hermon

Mediterranean

Sea

Tyre

Caesarea Philippi (Paneas)

Bathyra

Gischala

GALILEE

Capernaum

Ptolemais

Sea of Galilee

Jotapata

Arbela

Hippos

Sepphoris

Tiberias

Gaba

Jezreel Valley

Jordan River

Gadara

Caesarea

DECAPOLIS

Sebaste

SAMARIA

Samaria

Antipatris

Alexandrium

Mt. Gerizim

Phasaelis

Bethel

Joppa

PEREA

Livias

Emmaus

Cypros

Jericho

Esbus

Jerusalem

Qumran

JUDEA

Hyrcania

Mt. Nebo

Bethlehem

Ascalon

Herodium

Anthedon

Dead

Machaerus

Gaza

Hebron

Sea

En Gedi

Masada

NABATEA

IDUMEA

| 0 | | 25 mi |
| 0 | | 40 km |

Chart 2-11

Galilee at the Time of Jesus

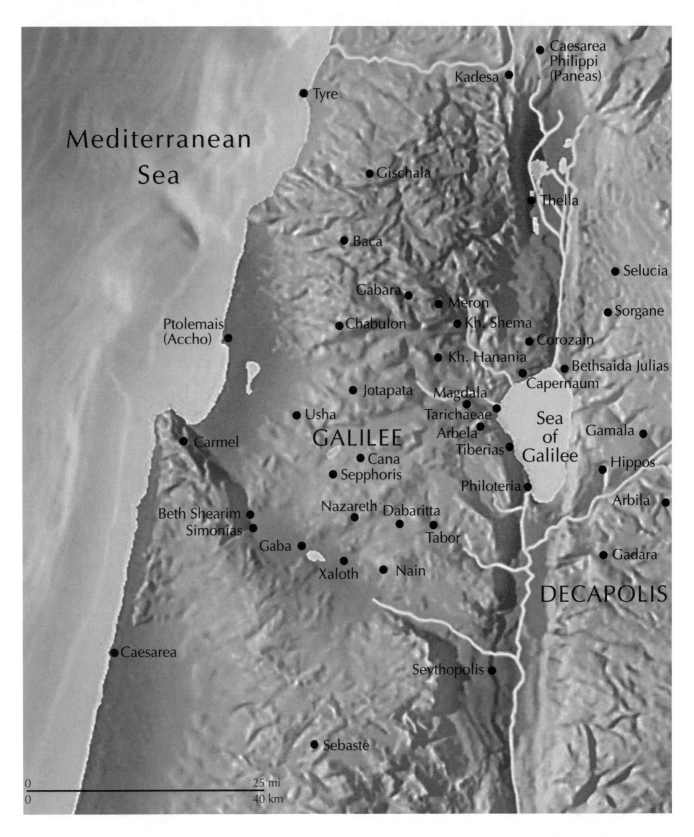

Mediterranean Sea

Caesarea Philippi (Paneas)

Kadesa

Tyre

Gischala

Thella

Baca

Selucia

Gabara

Meron

Sorgane

Chabulon

Kh. Shema

Ptolemais (Accho)

Corozain

Kh. Hanania

Bethsaida Julias

Jotapata

Magdala

Capernaum

Usha

Tarichaeae

Sea of Galilee

GALILEE

Arbela

Gamala

Carmel

Tiberias

Hippos

Cana

Sepphoris

Philoteria

Arbila

Beth Shearim

Nazareth

Dabaritta

Simonias

Tabor

Gadara

Gaba

Xaloth

Nain

DECAPOLIS

Caesarea

Seythopolis

Sebaste

0   25 mi
0   40 km

Chart 2-12

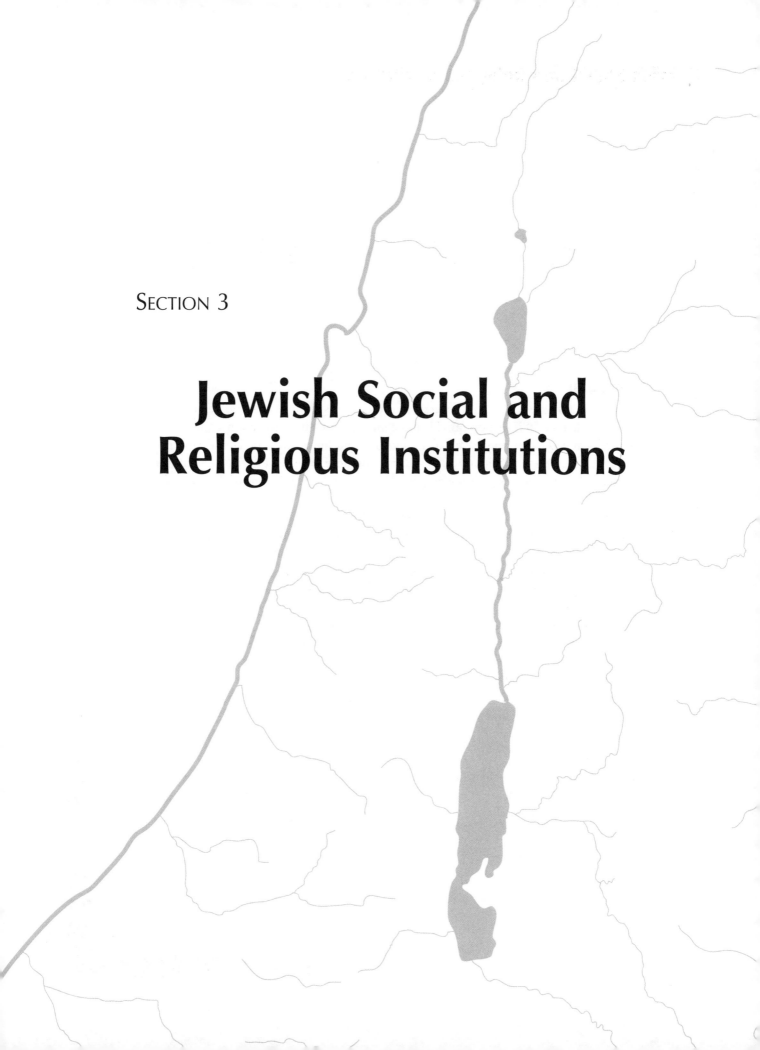

SECTION 3

Jewish Social and Religious Institutions

Chart 3-1

Three Main Jewish Sects

Explanation

The New Testament mentions several Jewish social institutions that can be quite confusing. The charts in this section provide basic information about the main groups with which Jesus interacted or may have had contact. Beyond the aristocratic Herodians, three main Jewish sects were religiously active during the time of Jesus: Pharisees, Sadducees, and Essenes. In addition, many Jews would have been unaffiliated with any of these particular movements.

Pharisaic (separatist) Judaism is known through later rabbinic writings. Jesus clashed with the Pharisees partly because he encountered them often in the outlying villages and also because he shared many of their underlying religious concerns. Friction is often the greatest between groups that are actually the closest to each other.

The Sadducees were largely hellenized Jews who controlled the temple and Sanhedrin in Jerusalem and cooperated with the Romans.

The Essenes, who awaited the impending arrival of the apocalyptic end of the world, occupied one neighborhood in Jerusalem and may have drawn adherents from all around Judea. They were centered at Qumran where they copied biblical scrolls and produced sectarian documents found among the Dead Sea Scrolls. They are never mentioned directly in the New Testament. This chart compares these three main sects on a few of their most salient points of doctrine and practice.

References

Elias J. Bickerman, *The Jews in the Greek Age* (Cambridge: Harvard University Press, 1988).
Victor L. Ludlow, "Major Jewish Groups in the New Testament," *Ensign,* January 1975, 26–29.
Frederick J. Murphy, *The Religious World of Jesus* (Nashville: Abingdon, 1991).

Three Main Jewish Sects

	PHARISEES	SADDUCEES	ESSENES
General	in the world but not of the world	in the world and of the world	neither in the world nor of the world
Law	valued oral law, also accepted old written law	rejected oral law, accepted only old written law	wrote hidden law, accepted and gave interpretations to old law
Interpretation	accurate, precise	pragmatic, accommodating	creative, adaptive
God	participates in events of world	removed from the evil of world	Messiah will destroy the evil of world
Fate	Fate cooperates in human actions	rejected Fate, emphasized agency	accepted Fate
Society	kind to each other, lenient (Mt 5:46; Acts 5:39)	rude to each other, boorish, punitive (compare Acts 5:40)	great attachment to each other
Main Locations	rural villages and cities	urban centers	remote communes, separate quarters
Gentiles	partially accepted	openly accepted	mostly rejected
Property	lived simply	sought wealth	despised wealth, held goods in common
Pleasure			shunned pleasure
Souls	imperishable, good souls alone go on to another body, wicked souls suffer eternal punishment, believed in resurrection	no afterlife, no eternal rewards or punishments	bodies perishable, souls immortal, liberated upon death

Chart 3-1

Sadducees and Pharisees

Explanation

The most influential religious groups in Jesus' world were the Sadducees and Pharisees. As chart 3-2 shows, the Sadducees are rarely mentioned by name in the New Testament. They were influential, however, in the political sphere. They probably controlled a majority of the Sanhedrin and may be identified or closely associated with the Chief Priests (see chart 3-9).

Chart 3-3 shows the most likely legal differences between the Pharisees and Sadducees during biblical times and perhaps later. These issues have been reconstructed out of later Jewish writings, especially the Talmud. One of the main differences between the Pharisees and the Sadducees was what they counted as "law." Jesus was frequently asked questions about how the law should be understood, and from all appearances, this was a controversial topic of the day. The Pharisees included the oral law, or traditional rules that go beyond the legal materials found in the written Torah (the first five books of the Bible). Knowing something about the kinds of legal arguments that were controversial at the time of Jesus helps modern readers understand some of the questions that were asked of him and how his audiences may well have understood the contemporary significance of his answers and teachings.

References

Anthony J. Saldarini, "Pharisees," *ABD,* 5:289–303.

Gary G. Porton, "Sadducees," *ABD,* 5:892–95.

Chart 3-3 is drawn from Gregory R. Knight, "The Pharisees and the Sadducees: Their Respective Outlooks on Jewish Law," *BYU Law Review* (1993): 925–48.

References to the Sadducees

	Mt	Mk	Lk	Acts
Sadducees come with Pharisees to be baptized by John	3:7			
Sadducees and Pharisees ask Jesus for a sign	16:1	[8:11][1]		
Jesus warns of the leaven of the Pharisees and Sadducees	16:6–12	[8:15][2]		
Sadducees question Jesus about the resurrection	22:23	12:18	20:27	
Pharisees learn that Jesus had silenced the Sadducees	22:34			
Sadducees are in the council that tries Peter and John				4:1
Sadducees and the High Priest put apostles in the common prison				5:17
Sadducees are in the divided council that tries Paul				23:6–8

[1]Mentions Pharisees only
[2]Mentions Herod instead of the Sadducees

Chart 3-2

Legal Views
of Pharisees and Sadducees

Issue	Pharisees	Sadducees
POSSIBLE CONTROVERSIES DURING BIBLICAL TIMES		
The use of fire on the Sabbath	Prohibited the *igniting* of fire on the Sabbath but permitted the *use* of fire kindled on Friday before the start of the Sabbath.	Prohibited the use of any fire on the Sabbath.
The *Omer* and the date of *Shavuot*	Interpreted *sabbath* in Lev 23:11 to mean "festival day," the first day of Passover. Thus, the *Omer* was to be performed on the second day of Passover. The festival of *Shavuot* occurred 49 days thereafter.	Interpreted *sabbath* in Lev 23:11 and 16 to mean the weekly Sabbath. Thus, the *Omer* occurs on the Sunday of the Passover week with the *Shavuot* festival taking place 7 weeks later.
Impurity of metals	Believed that metal is subject to impurity and that, just like anything else, it must be purified properly.	Believed that the impurity of metals is limited strictly to the context of Num 31:21–24 (metals captured in war).
Liability for damages caused by a slave	Held that a master is not liable for damages or wrongs committed by his slave as long as the master did not know about or sanction the slave's action.	Believed that a master is liable for the acts of his slave.
Capital punishment	Rejected the idea that a money ransom could be paid in lieu of executing a properly condemned criminal.	Allowed a compensatory payment to substitute for the execution of a criminal.
The water-libations on *Sukkot*	Believed that, although not in the Torah, these ceremonies were part of the oral Torah, which had been given to Moses and handed down by the prophets. All these rituals should be followed.	Rejected these ceremonies and traditions as not having any basis in the written Torah.
The *nizzok*	Believed that the *nizzok* is not unifying. An unbroken stream of liquid will not render the pure pouring vessel impure.	Believed that the *nizzok* is unifying. The impurity of the receiving vessel is transferred to the pure pouring vessel.
Leniency in punishment	Tended toward leniency in enforcing the strict penalties of the Torah.	Tended toward a strict interpretation of the Torah's harsh punishments.

Chart 3-3 (1)

Issue	Pharisees	Sadducees
BASIC BELIEFS		
Resurrection	Believed that souls are immortal. Good souls will be resurrected while evil souls are eternally punished.	Believed that the soul perishes with the body.
Angels	Believed in personal angels.	Rejected the existence of angels or spirits.
Fate	Believed that men are bound by fate in all that they do—both good and evil.	Believed that men have free will and can choose either good or evil. The consequences of our actions are reaped in mortal life.
PROBABLE POST-BIBLICAL CONTROVERSIES		
Hand washing	Pharisaic scholars held that the hands must be washed before worshiping or eating any sacred food or heave offering. Emphasized purity in all situations.	Believed that washing the hands before eating sacred meals was not necessary.
The *'Erub*	Sanctioned the carrying of burdens in or out of the house on the Sabbath based on the legal fiction that a group of houses or even a whole neighborhood could be "merged" into a single household by erecting a symbolic wire around the area.	Rejected the concept of *'Erub*. It is simply inappropriate to carry any burden on the Sabbath.
POSSIBLE LATER CONTROVERSIES		
Lex talionis: "Eye for an Eye"	Allowed monetary compensation to substitute for literal retribution except in capital cases.	Applied the doctrine of *lex talionis* literally. No leniency in retribution.
Impurity of women after childbirth	Believed that during the respective 33- and 66-day cleansing periods, there was no prohibition against marital intercourse.	Forbade marital relations during the cleansing period.
Virgin bride suspected of fornication	Ruled that husband had to produce witnesses to testify that his wife had been unfaithful during the period of the betrothal.	Held that parents had to produce the blood-stained garments as proof of the bride's virginity.
Halizah ceremony	Held that a childless widow must take off her shoe and spit before her brother-in-law in order to release him from the obligation to marry her.	Believed that the childless widow is to spit, literally, in his face.

Chart 3-3 (2)

The Mishnah, Jerusalem, and the Temple

Explanation

Around the time of Jesus, the Mishnah began to take shape. This collection recorded the oral sayings of various Jewish rabbis. Chart 3-4 lists the "six orders" of the Mishnah and the main subjects that are discussed and regulated under each of these headings. Topics included such matters as tithing, Sabbath laws, the temple tax, adultery, divorce, oaths, leprosy, and purity. It is interesting to note that Jesus had something important to say about most of these main subjects.

The heart of Jewish religion and society was Jerusalem and its temple. Chart 3-5 maps some of the main buildings and sites of Jerusalem, where Jesus often went. By modern standards, the city was still relatively small in the days of Jesus. Archaeology allows modern researchers to reconstruct many of the features of the Holy City. This chart shows the walls, gates, pools, buildings, and main areas that Jesus would have frequented. Scripture references locate places mentioned in the New Testament by name.

The floor plan of the temple is given on chart 3-6. This building was spectacular and magnificent, adorned with splendor and wealth. Its design emphasized the sanctity of the inner sanctuary, the Holy of Holies, where the High Priest alone officiated. The New Testament, especially in the Epistle to the Hebrews, recognizes Jesus as the new and eternal High Priest who offered the ultimate atoning sacrifice. The temple proper was contained within the temple complex located on the top of a large platform known as the Temple Mount. In the porticos surrounding that area were money changers, merchants selling sacrificial animals, and meeting places, where Jesus often taught, worked, challenged the established regime and was challenged back. Rendition of the temple courtesy of Michael Lyon.

References

Joachim Jeremias, *Jerusalem in the Time of Jesus* (Philadelphia: Fortress, 1969), 80.
Douglas H. Parker and Ze'ev W. Falk, "Law of Moses," *EM*, 2:810–12.
A. Cohen, *Everyman's Talmud* (New York: Shocken, 1975).

Six Orders of the Mishnah

Hebrew Name	English Name	Main Subjects Regulated
Zera'im	Seeds	Life, plants, benedictions, mixing seeds, sabbatical year, tithes, first-fruits
Mo'ed	Season	Sabbath laws, temple tax, Passover, Day of Atonement, Feast of Tabernacles, sacrifices
Nashim	Women	Levirate marriage, marriage documents, vows, adultery, divorce
Nezikin	Torts	Wrongs, injuries, damages, law courts, punishments, testimonies, oaths, idolatry, inadvertent sin
Kodashim	Sanctities	Temple sacrifices, offerings, firstborns, consecration, excommunication, temple architecture
Tohoroth	Purities	Vessel and tent purity, corpses, defilements, leprosy, menstruation, issues of blood, purification baths

Chart 3-4

Jerusalem

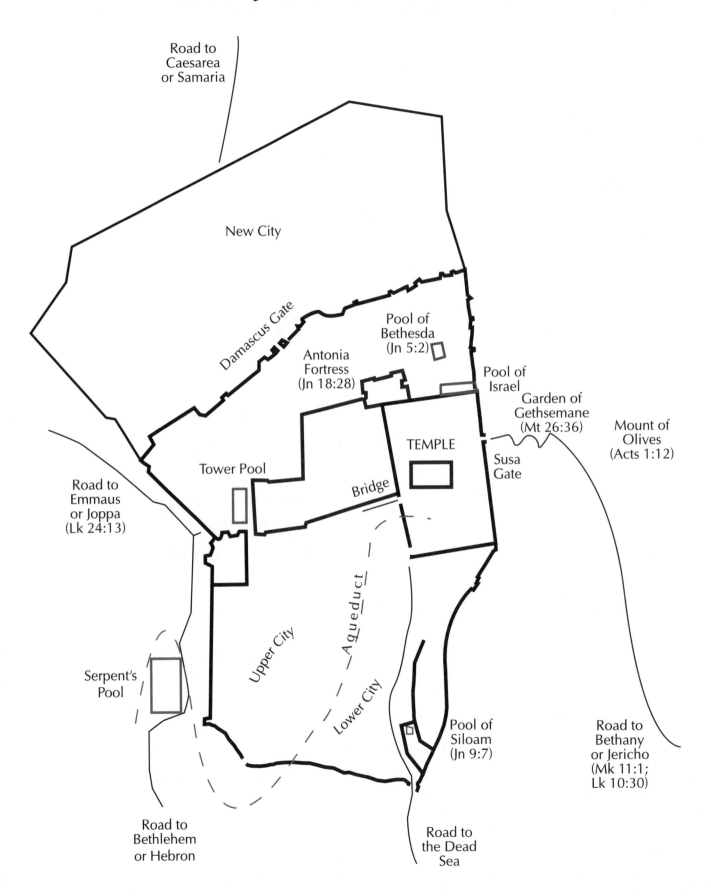

Road to
Caesarea
or Samaria

New City

Damascus Gate

Pool of
Bethesda
(Jn 5:2)

Antonia
Fortress
(Jn 18:28)

Pool of
Israel

Garden of
Gethsemane
(Mt 26:36)

Mount of
Olives
(Acts 1:12)

TEMPLE

Susa
Gate

Tower Pool

Bridge

Road to
Emmaus
or Joppa
(Lk 24:13)

Aqueduct

Upper City

Lower City

Serpent's
Pool

Pool of
Siloam
(Jn 9:7)

Road to
Bethany
or Jericho
(Mk 11:1;
Lk 10:30)

Road to
Bethlehem
or Hebron

Road to
the Dead
Sea

Chart 3-5

The Temple of Herod

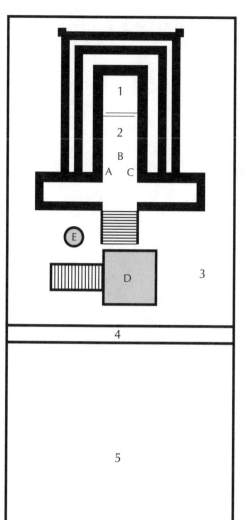

1. Holy of Holies

Former resting place of the ark of the covenant, set apart by two veils. The area was only entered by the High Priest once a year, on Yom Kippur, the Day of Atonement.

2. Holy Place or Sanctuary

Used only by the High Priests of the temple. Contained the altar of incense [A], the table of shewbread [B], and menorah [C].

3. Court of the Priests

Used only by the priests except on special holidays. The area housed the sacrificial altar [D] and the laver (brazen sea for washings) [E].

4. Court of Israel

Any male Jew was generally allowed in this area but no farther.

5. Court of Women

Any Jew was allowed in this area but no farther.

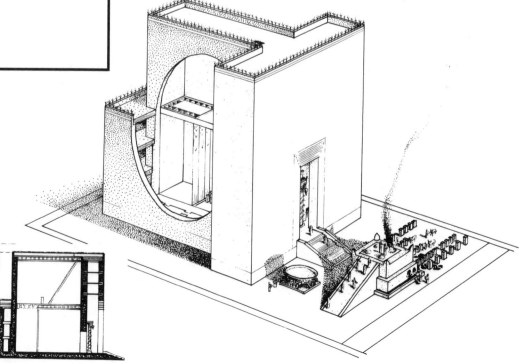

Chart 3-6

Jewish Priests

Explanation

Thousands of people worked in and around the Temple of Jerusalem. Chart 3-7 shows the basic organization of the temple priests, who worked under the direction of the reigning High Priest, a Sadducee. Under him was a council of Chief Priests (see also chart 3-9). They appointed a captain of the temple. His guards or overseers protected the temple and were involved in the arrest of Jesus. Three treasurers maintained the temple treasury, which was opulent. By some estimates, the Temple of Herod housed over 10,000 talents of gold and silver, a staggering amount of wealth (see chart 2-7). The priests were the main officiators in the temple sacrifices and services, while the Levites were distinctly below the priests in status. Both groups are mentioned by Jesus in the parable of the Good Samaritan in Luke 10.

Chart 3-8 lists the High Priests down to the destruction of the temple in A.D. 70. Caiaphas, who was the High Priest at the time of the trial of Jesus, reigned for almost twenty years, an exceptionally long term in office.

Most powerful were the Chief Priests, a small group of extremely influential politicians and managers. As can be seen from chart 3-9, the Chief Priests were the dominant source of sustained opposition to Jesus. Often they worked behind the scenes, frequently alone, but on several occasions they enlisted the involvement of the elders or rulers (venerable or powerful men of the city). Their scribes (who were notaries, lawyers, recorders, readers, or interpreters) were often by their side, yet only rarely did Pharisees have any dealings with them.

References

Drawn from Joachim Jeremias, *Jerusalem in the Time of Jesus* (Philadelphia: Fortress, 1969), 147, 377–78.
Merlin D. Rehm, "Levites and Priests," *ABD*, 4:297–310.

Organization of Jewish Priests

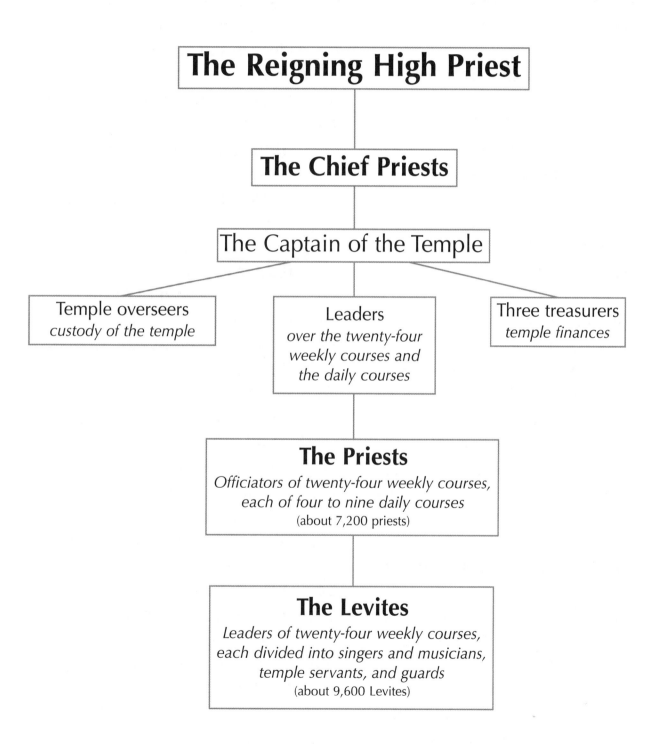

The Reigning High Priest

The Chief Priests

The Captain of the Temple

Temple overseers
custody of the temple

Leaders
over the twenty-four weekly courses and the daily courses

Three treasurers
temple finances

The Priests
Officiators of twenty-four weekly courses, each of four to nine daily courses
(about 7,200 priests)

The Levites
Leaders of twenty-four weekly courses, each divided into singers and musicians, temple servants, and guards
(about 9,600 Levites)

Chart 3-7

High Priests from 200 B.C. to A.D. 70

Pre-Maccabean High Priests (200–159 B.C.)

1. Simon the Righteous (after 200)
2. Onias II (to 175)
3. Jesus (Jason) (175–172)
4. Menelaus (172–162)
5. Jacim (Alcimus) (162–159)

The Maccabean High Priests (152–37)

1. Jonathan (152–143/2)
2. Simon (142/1–132)
3. John Hyrcanus I (134–104)
4. Aristobulus I (104–103)
5. Alexander Jannaeus (103–76)
6. Hyrcanus II (76–67 and 63–40)
7. Aristobulus II (67–63)
8. Antigonus (40–37)

The High Priests (37 B.C. to A.D. 70)

1. Ananel (37–36; again from 34)
2. Aristobulus III, the last Maccabean (35)
3. Jesus, son of Phiabi (to c. 22)
4. Simon, son of Boethus (c. 22–5)
5. Mattaiah, son of Theophilus (5–12 March 4)
6. Joseph, son of Elam (5)
7. Joezer, son of Boethus (4)
8. Eleazar, son of Boethus (from 4 B.C.)
9. Jesus, son of See (until A.D. 6)
10. Annas (6–15)
11. Ishmael b. Phiabi (c. 15–16)
12. Eleazar, son of Annas (c. 16–17)
13. Simon, son of Kamithos (17–18)
14. Joseph Caiaphas (c. 18–37)
15. Jonathan, son of Annas (Easter to Pentecost 37)
16. Theophilus, son of Annas (from 37)
17. Simon Kantheras, son of Boethus (from 41)
18. Matthias, son of Annas
19. Elionaius, son of Kantheras (c. 44)
20. Joseph, son of Kami (c. 45–46)
21. Ananias, son of Nebedaius (47 to at least 55)
22. Ishmael b. Phiabi II (until 61)
23. Joseph Qabi (until 62)
24. Ananus, son of Ananus (62)
25. Jesus, son of Damnaius (c. 62–65)
26. Joshua b. Gamaliel (c. 63–65)
27. Matthias, son of Theophilus (65–67)
28. Pinhas of Habta (67–70)

Chart 3-8

The Chief Priests and Their Associates

CHIEF PRIESTS ACTING ALONE

Mt 2:4	tell Herod where Christ should be born
Jn 12:10	consider putting Lazarus to death
Mt 26:14	meet with Judas to arrange for the betrayal and arrest of Jesus
Mk 14:10	meet with Judas to arrange for the betrayal of Jesus
Mt 27:6–7	refuse to return the thirty pieces of silver to the temple treasury and buy the potter's field
Jn 18:35	deliver Jesus to Pilate (acting in conjunction with entire nation)
Mk 15:3–4	accuse Jesus before Pilate
Mk 15:10	deliver Jesus to Pilate out of envy
Lk 23:4	are told, along with people, of Jesus' innocence by Pilate
Mk 15:11	persuade the crowd to ask for Barabbas to be released
Lk 23:23	prevail in asking for Barabbas to be released
Jn 19:6	cry (with their officers) for the crucifixion of Jesus
Jn 19:21	ask Pilate to change the wording of the title on the cross
Mt 28:11	are told by guards of the resurrection and empty tomb
Acts 9:14	give Saul authority to arrest Christians
Acts 9:21	issue authority to arrest Christians
Acts 26:10	had given Saul authority to arrest Christians
Acts 26:12	had given Saul authority to arrest Christians

Chart 3-9 (1)

CHIEF PRIESTS ACTING WITH ELDERS *(PRESBYTEROI)*, RULERS *(ARCHONTES)*,
CAPTAINS *(STRATEGOI)*, OR THE SANHEDRIN *(SYNHEDRION)*

Mt 21:23	question Jesus in the temple about his authority (elders)
Mt 26:47	arrest Jesus (elders)
Mt 26:59	seek false witnesses against Jesus (Sanhedrin)
Mk 14:56	seek false witnesses against Jesus (Sanhedrin)
Mt 27:1	take council against Jesus (elders)
Lk 22:4	meet with Judas and captains to arrange betrayal
Lk 22:52	arrest Jesus with temple captains and elders
Mt 27:3	refuse the thirty pieces of silver when Judas tries to return them (elders)
Mt 27:12–13	accuse Jesus before Pilate (elders)
Lk 23:13–15	are told, along with the rulers and the people, of Jesus' innocence by Pilate
Mt 27:20	persuade the crowd to ask for Barabbas (elders)
Lk 24:20	with rulers deliver Jesus to be crucified
Mt 28:12–13	bribe guards to say the disciples stole Jesus' body (elders)
Acts 4:18	command Peter and John not to speak of Christ (elders)
Acts 5:24–26	arrest Peter and John and command them again (captains)
Acts 22:30	convene court against Paul (Sanhedrin)
Acts 23:14–15	hear oath of vigilantes against Paul (elders)
Acts 25:15	ask Festus to give judgment against Paul (elders)

CHIEF PRIESTS MENTIONED WITH SCRIBES ONLY

Mt 20:18	Jesus prophesies his betrayal into their hands
Mk 10:33	Jesus prophesies his betrayal into their hands
Lk 20:19	offended by the parable of the rejected cornerstone
Mt 21:15	are displeased at miracles and popularity of Jesus

Chart 3-9 (2)

Mk 11:18	are afraid of his popularity and temple teaching
Lk 22:2	are afraid of his popularity and seek to kill him
Mk 14:1	meet to plot the arrest and death of Jesus
Lk 23:10	accuse Jesus before Pilate
Mk 15:31	mock Jesus on the cross

CHIEF PRIESTS LINKED WITH ELDERS AND SCRIBES

Mt 16:21	Jesus prophesies his suffering and death by them
Mk 8:31	Jesus prophesies his rejection and death by them
Lk 9:22	Jesus prophesies his rejection and death by them
Mk 11:27–28	question Jesus in the temple about his authority
Lk 20:1–2	question Jesus in the temple about his authority
Mt 26:3	meet to plot the arrest and death of Jesus
Lk 19:47	meet to plot the arrest and death of Jesus
Mk 14:43	arrest Jesus
Mk 14:53	assemble against Jesus
Lk 22:66	assemble against Jesus
Mk 15:1	deliver Jesus to Pilate
Mt 27:41	mock Jesus on the cross

CHIEF PRIESTS TOGETHER WITH PHARISEES ONLY

Mt 21:33, 45	hear the parable of the wicked tenants
Jn 7:32	send officers to attempt to arrest Jesus
Jn 7:45–46	listen as officers report that they will not arrest Jesus
Jn 11:47	confer together to discuss arresting Jesus
Jn 11:57	require disclosure of knowledge of Jesus' location
Jn 18:3	send officers to arrest Jesus
Mt 27:62–64	come to Pilate asking for soldiers at the tomb

Chart 3-10

Despised Trades
According to the Mishnah and the Talmud

Explanation

This social picture reminds readers that Jesus was very popular with the Jewish masses, dealing openly with the despised outcasts of his society. Chart 3-10 presents a glimpse into the class structure that pervaded the world of Judea shortly after the New Testament era, especially from the viewpoint of the Pharisees, according to the Mishnah and Talmud. Four Jewish texts list occupations that were despised; they were considered impure, largely because they came in contact with blood or women, or were prone toward fraud or deception. Men in these trades were legally and religiously disadvantaged. Notably on these lists of despised trades, Matthew was a tax collector; Luke was a physician; and Jesus called himself a shepherd, often associated with women, and was accused of being a brigand or robber.

Reference

Developed from a table in Joachim Jeremias, *Jerusalem in the Time of Jesus* (Philadelphia: Fortress, 1969), 304.

Despised Trades
According to the Mishnah and the Talmud

"Wicked Trades," prone to commit fraud

1. Ass driver
2. Camel driver
3. Wagoner
4. Barber
5. Sailor
6. Shepherd
7. Shopkeeper
8. Physician
9. Butcher

"Bogus Trades," ineligible to serve as judges or witnesses

1. Gambler, dice player
2. Usurer, lender
3. Pigeon trainer, racing gambler
4. Seller of produce from the Sabbatical year
5. Herdsman
6. Tax collector, publican
7. Brigands
8. Cheaters in money matters

"Disreputable Trades" that deal with women

1. Jewelry maker
2. Sieve maker
3. Wool-carder, flax comber, weaver
4. Handmill cleaner
5. Peddler
6. Wool dresser, tailor
7. Hairdresser
8. Launderer
9. Bloodletter
10. Bath attendant
11. Leather tanner

"Unsavory Trades," whose wives may divorce them without cause

1. Dung collector
2. Copper smelter
3. Tanner

Chart 3-10

Chart 3-11

Disasters in Jerusalem

Explanation

Times were hard in the ancient world. Weather and other natural disasters disrupted society and dislodged rulers. Although incomplete, historical records provide considerable data about various disasters that befell Jerusalem in the years around the time of Jesus. Catastrophes included war, famine, drought, wind, earthquakes, and epidemics. When Jesus prophesied of impending cataclysms that hung over the city of Jerusalem, and when he warned people to build their house upon a rock and not upon the sand, his audiences would have understood immediately the terrible reality of such disasters.

Reference

Based on data in Joachim Jeremias, *Jerusalem in the Time of Jesus* (Philadelphia: Fortress, 1969), 140–44.

Disasters in Jerusalem

Disaster	Year
Besieged, Famine	163 B.C.
Drought	Before 65 B.C.
Hurricane	64 B.C.
Siege	37 B.C.
Earthquake	31 B.C.
Epidemic	29 B.C.
Famine, drought, sickness, no wool	25–24 B.C.
Famine	A.D. 46–48
Drought	Before A.D. 66
Drought	A.D. 69
Destruction by Roman army	A.D. 70

Chart 3-11

Chart 3-12

Two Profiles of Robbers
in the Ancient World

Explanation

Chart 3-12 gives two profiles of brigands or robbers in the ancient world. Since "robbers" are mentioned seven times in the Greek New Testament (sometimes inaccurately translated as "thieves"), this subgroup on the fringes of the world of the New Testament needs to be understood carefully. From the viewpoint of the dominant government, robbers were vile outlaws; but from the viewpoint of the marginal elements of society, they were heroic Robin Hoods. An understanding of these two profiles explains how Jesus or Barabbas could have been seen as a robber, either favorably or unfavorably, depending on one's social viewpoint. It also discloses important ways in which Jesus and his followers did not conform completely to either of these two profiles.

References

Kent P. Jackson, "Revolutionaries in the First Century," *MWNT*, 129–40.

John W. Welch, "Legal and Social Perspectives on Robbers in First-Century Judea," *MWNT*, 141–53.

Two Profiles of Robbers
in the Ancient World

A. VIEWPOINT OF THE ESTABLISHMENT

1. Robbery was committed blatantly in the open; theft, in secret, a minor offense.

2. Robbers were outsiders and were therefore outside the protection of the law; theft usually occurred within the society.

3. Robbers usually acted with greater force and violence than did thieves.

4. Robbers acted in a group or band (hence, they are called "bandits," highwaymen, brigands); thieves acted alone.

5. Robbers were organized in professional groups. Usually bands of 15 to 40 men, but one had 10,000 men. They often had their own leader, code, priests, and so on, sometimes drawing together dissidents, foreigners, and social outcasts.

6. Robbers bound themselves together with oaths and sacrifices, making them heretics as well as criminals.

7. Robbers kept their hideouts secret, accentuating their sinister reputation.

8. Robbers operated with raids, assassinations, and terrorism.

9. Robbers would harass the highways or disrupt commerce, primarily to weaken local governments.

10. Robbers posed a great military threat to the society.

11. Robbers often demanded ransom or used extortion.

12. Robbers were considered outlaws and could be dealt with under martial law or no law at all.

13. The government bore the duty to clear the highways and keep the bands of robber in check. These bands were usually short-lived.

14. Robbers could be executed; thieves could not.

15. Captured robber leaders were treated especially harshly.

16. Robbers were considered instruments of God's wrath afflicting a wicked nation.

Chart 3-12 (1)

Two Profiles of Robbers
in the Ancient World

B. VIEWPOINT OF THE DISENFRANCHISED

1. Social banditry emerged from circumstances that were perceived by the masses to be unjust and intolerable, including administrative inefficiency, sharp social divisions, economic crises, famines, or prolonged wars.

2. These movements were often rural, giving the poor effective methods of social agitation.

3. These robber groups were often led by marginalized military or political figures.

4. Bandits usually enjoyed the support and protection of their village.

5. Robbers drew strength from people who had been dislocated, displaced, or otherwise alienated from mainstream society.

6. Social brigands were frequently heroes among the poor, defenders and champions of the common people, sharing the basic values and religion of the peasant society.

ROBBERS MENTIONED IN THE GREEK NEW TESTAMENT

1. Casting out the money changers, Jesus used the phrase "den of robbers" [KJV, thieves] (Mt 21:13).

2. In the parable of the good Samaritan, the man fell among robbers [KJV, thieves] (Lk 10:30).

3. The Good Shepherd guards his sheep against thieves and robbers (Jn 10:1, 8).

4. At his arrest, Jesus asked, "Are you come out as against a robber?" [KJV, thieves] (Mt 26:55).

5. Barabbas, a robber, was released instead of Jesus (Jn 18:40).

6. Jesus was crucified in between two robbers [KJV, thieves] (Mt 27:38).

7. On his journeys, Paul was in peril of robbers (2Cor 11:26).

Chart 3-12 (2)

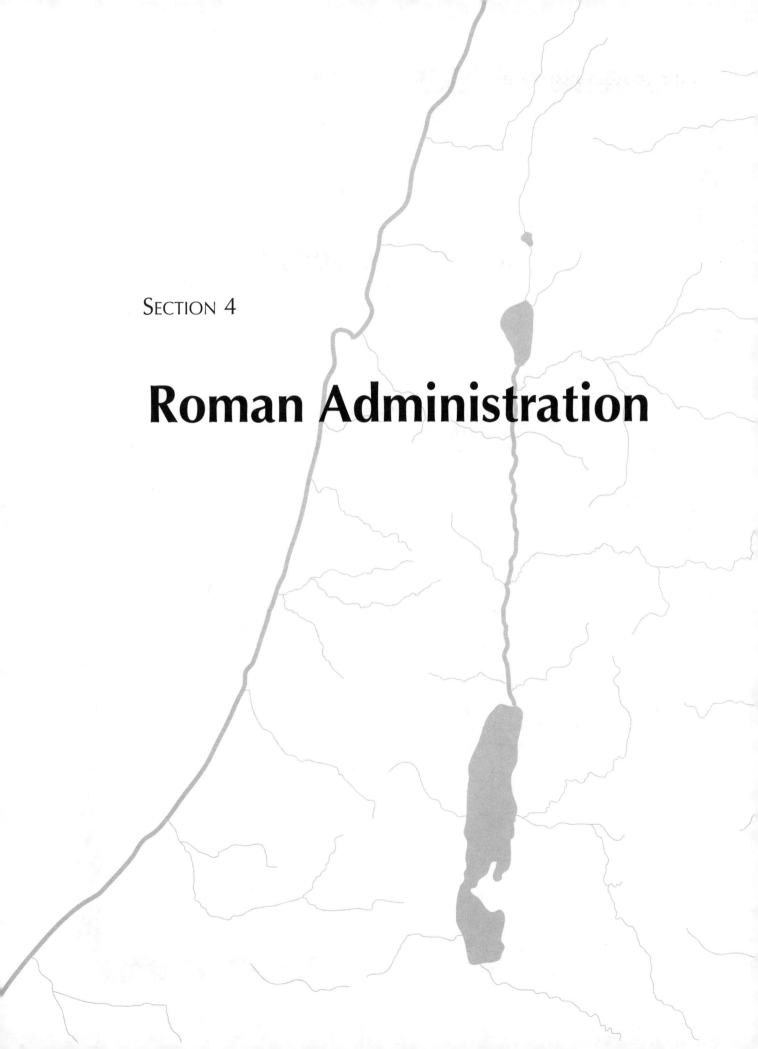

SECTION 4

Roman Administration

Family of Caesar

Explanation

In 48 B.C., Gaius Iulius Caesar, whom we call Julius Caesar, became sole ruler of the Roman world. For the next century Rome and its empire were ruled by Caesar's descendants and heirs. The family had long been known as one of the most prestigious Roman aristocratic clans, claiming descent from Iulus, son of Aeneas, Trojan prince and legendary founder of the Roman race.

The Caesars belonged to the *gens Iulia*, or Julian clan. Their clan or first family name was, therefore, Iulius or Julius, and the branch of the clan they belonged to was the Caesar family whose cognomen was their second family name. The name Caesar later became a title for any supreme ruler of Rome, but originally it referred to only one very distinguished family.

Julius Caesar's grandnephew and adopted son, Augustus, was the first Roman emperor. Other family members were emperors during the era of the New Testament and early Christianity, including Tiberius, Caligula, Claudius, and Nero. The stemma that follows depicts the family tree of the Caesars.

References

John F. Hall, "The Saeculum Novum of Augustus," in *Aufstieg und Niedergang der Römischen Welt* (Berlin: De Gruyter, 1986), 16 no. 2, 2564–89.

Ronald Syme, *The Roman Revolution* (Oxford: Oxford University Press, 1939).

Family of Caesar

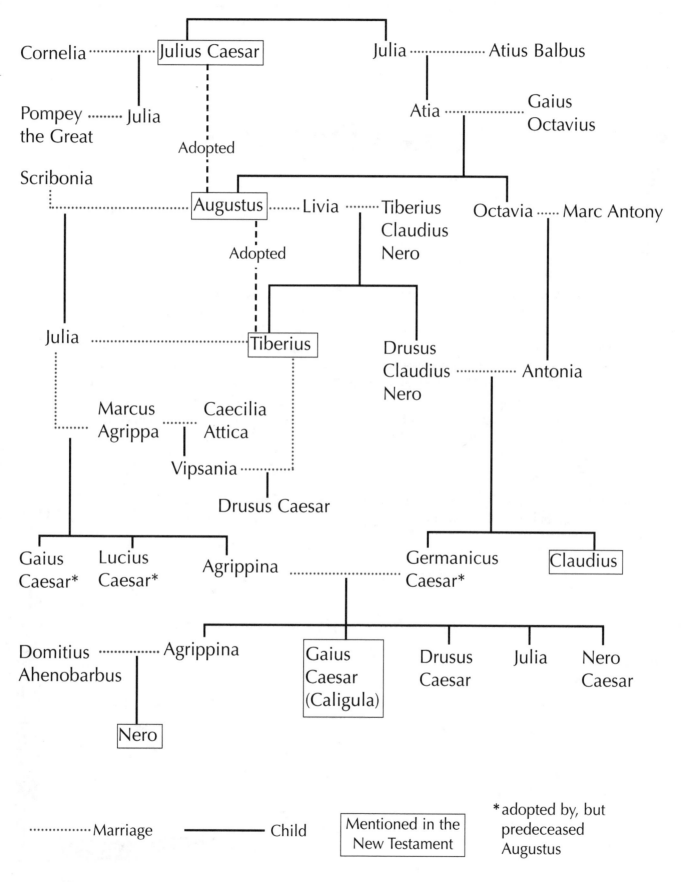

.... Marriage   ———— Child | Mentioned in the New Testament | *adopted by, but predeceased Augustus

© 2002 Welch, Hall, FARMS

Chart 4-1

Chart 4-2

Roman Emperors

Explanation

From the time of Augustus, Rome was ruled by emperors. The manner of their accession to imperial power varied. Some were selected by the Senate, others by the imperial guard, others as a result of revolution, many with the support of one or another faction of the military. Day-to-day governance was accomplished with the assistance of the Senate and an ever-increasing imperial bureaucracy. Usually individual emperors ruled, but on occasion two colleagues governed together, or, as under Diocletian, a college of four emperors. Some reigns were of long duration, others of only a few weeks, as in the calamitous year 69. The chart lists emperors and the dates of their reigns, from Augustus to Constantine, concurrent with the first three centuries of Christian history.

References

Chris Scarre, *Chronicle of the Roman Emperors* (London: Thames & Hudson, 1995).
M. Cary and H. H. Scullard, *A History of Rome* (New York: St. Martin's, 1975).

Roman Emperors

Emperor	Reign (A.D.)	Emperor	Reign (A.D.)
Augustus	27 B.C.–A.D. 14	Maximinus	235–238
Tiberius	14–37	Gordian I	238
		Gordian II	238
Caligula	37–41	Balbinus	238
Claudius	41–54	Pupienus	238
Nero	54–68	Gordian III	238–244
Galba	68–69	Philip	244–249
Otho	69	Decius	249–251
Vitellius	69	Trebonianus	251–253
Vespasian	69–70	Aemilianus	253
Titus	79–81	Valerianus	253–260
Domitian	81–96	Gallienus	253–268
Nerva	96–98	Claudius Gothicus	268–270
Trajan	98–117	Aurelian	270–275
Hadrian	117–138	Tacitus	275–276
Antoninus Pius	138–161	Florianus	276
Marcus Aurelius	161–180	Probus	276–282
Lucius Verus	161–169		
Commodus	180–192	Carus	282–283
Pertinax	193	Carinus	283–285
		Numerianus	283–284
Didius Julianus	193	Diocletian	284–305
Septimius Severus	193–211	Maximian	286–305
Caracalla	211–217	Constantius	292–306
Geta	211–217		
Macrinus	217–218	Galerius	293–311
Elagabulus	218–222	Licinius	311–323
Severus Alexander	222–235	Constantine	306–337

Chart 4-2

Roman Government Officials

Explanation

Out of the old Etruscan monarchy, the Roman Republic was founded in 509 B.C. With the Licinian-Sextian reforms of 346 B.C., the familiar structure of the Republic was put into place and continued basically unchanged past the end of the Republic and through the time of Augustus's principate. The organization of government officials in the Roman Republic is represented in chart 4-3.

Though magistrates were elected by various citizen assemblies, most of these individuals were members of the Senate, a body of elected or hereditarily appointed officials who served for life. In tandem with the Senate, the Republic's magistrates expanded a city-state to an empire that spanned the known world.

As the instruments and machinery of the Republic became archaic and inadequate for the administration of the far-flung empire, changes were effected that ultimately produced the new governmental structures of the empire. The old magisterial offices were preserved but with different functions and modes of selection. Chart 4-4 represents the role of government officials under the empire during New Testament times.

References

Richard J. A. Talbert, *The Senate of Imperial Rome* (Princeton: Princeton University Press, 1984).

Lily Ross Taylor, *Party Politics in the Age of Caesar* (Berkeley: University of California Press, 1949).

[1] Discontinued during Augustus's principate.
[2] Includes the period of the principate of Augustus Caesar (27 B.C.–A.D. 14).
[3] Discontinued in A.D. 222.

Roman Government Officials
of the Republic

Office	Number	Qualifications	Term	Elected by	Duties
Consul	2	Age 42 and 5 years since elected praetor	1 year	Centuriate Assembly	*imperium;* chief officer of state; presided over Senate and Centuriate and Tribal Assemblies; commanded armies; supervised all other officers and governors
Praetor	8	Age 39 and 5 years since elected quaestor	1 year	Centuriate Assembly	*imperium;* judicial official; presided over courts; could command armies
Aedile	4	previously quaestor	1 year	Tribal Assembly	city commissioner; had limited power to regulate business, police, fire, sewer, water, and other public works in Rome
Quaestor	16	Age 30	1 year	Tribal Assembly	financial official in Rome or provinces; oversaw treasury and tax collection
Tribune	6	none	1 year	Tribal Assembly	presided over Tribal Assembly; had veto power in Senate; could protect people from punishment by other officials
Censor[1]	2	previously consul	5 years	Centuriate Assembly	conducted census; placed new citizens in voting tribes; certified senatorial and equestrian ranks

Chart 4-3

and of the Empire

Office	Number	Qualifications	Term	Elected by	Duties
Consul	2	Age 42 and 5 years since elected praetor	1 year	Senate	presided over Senate; supervised other officials and Senate-appointed governors on a limited scale
Praetor	12	Age 39 and 5 years since elected quaestor	1 year	Senate	judicial official; presided over courts
Aedile[2]	4	previously quaestor	1 year	Senate	city commissioner; had limited power to regulate business, police, fire, sewer, water, and other public works in Rome
Quaestor	32	Age 30	1 year	Senate	financial official in Rome or provinces
Tribune[3]	6	none	1 year	Senate	had limited power to judicially protect citizens of Rome

Chart 4-4

Administration
of Roman Provinces

Explanation

Knowing how Rome governed its provinces helps readers understand the situation in Judea during New Testament times. Roman provinces were first formed in the middle of the third century B.C. after the conclusion of the First Punic War. It was standard Roman practice under the republic to dispatch a former magistrate and give him extended authority *(imperium prorogatum)* to act as governor for several years. The Roman governor usually handled judicial or administrative matters involving Roman citizens; but if no Roman citizen was involved, he delegated the matter to local officials who continued to preside over the local populace. The basic premise of Roman provincial government was to have as little direct Roman involvement as possible.

With the advent of imperial government under Augustus, these principles were not abandoned. The most important provinces were governed directly by the emperor, who appointed his own legates, or deputies, with authority to command large complements of troops. Significant provinces were administered directly by the Senate through proconsuls and propraetors. The least important provinces, such as Judea, were assigned to minor officials known as procurators or prefects. Their provinces did not contain Roman armies but only a small contingent of six hundred soldiers to serve as the governor's bodyguard. Pontius Pilate was a low ranking prefect.

References

M. Cary and H. H. Scullard, *A History of Rome* (New York: St. Martin's, 1975).
John F. Hall, "Procurator," *ABD*, 5:473–74.
James S. Jeffers, *The Greco-Roman World of the New Testament Era* (Downers Grove, Ill.: InterVarsity, 1999), 110–79.

Administration
of Roman Provinces

Governor Title	Rank	Province	Appointment	Military Command
Legatus Augusti pro Praetore	consular senator	strategically important large province on frontier	by emperor	3–4 legions with many provincial auxiliaries
Legatus Augusti pro Praetore	praetorian senator	important large province near frontier	by emperor	1–2 legions with provincial auxiliaries
Proconsul	consular senator	important interior province	by Senate	1–2 cohorts with provincial auxiliaries
Propraetor	praetorian senator	interior province	by Senate	1–2 cohorts with a few provincial auxiliaries
Praefectus Aegypti	equestrian	Egypt	by emperor	1 legion with auxiliaries
Procurator	senator	small province	by emperor	1 cohort with a few provincial auxiliaries
Procurator	equestrian	less important small province	by emperor	1 cohort with a few provincial auxiliaries
Praefectus Iudaea	equestrian	Judea (A.D. 6–41)	by emperor	1 cohort with a few provincial auxiliaries

Chart 4-5

Chart 4-6

Rights and Privileges
of Citizenship

Explanation

Paul spoke of his converts as being "no more strangers and foreigners, but fellowcitizens with the Saints" (Eph 2:19). No status was more powerful in Paul's day than that of Roman citizenship. Chart 4-6 lists nine rights and privileges enjoyed by Roman citizens. Within the kingdom of God, parallel rights and privileges were enjoyed by members of the Church. While this arrangement would bolster the esteem and confidence of Christians, it might have been unsettling to people in the Roman Empire who questioned Christian loyalty to Rome.

References

Peter Garnsey, *Social Status and Legal Privilege in the Roman Empire* (Oxford: Clarendon, 1970).
A. N. Sherwin-White, *The Roman Citizenship* (Oxford: Clarendon, 1973).

Rights and Privileges
of Citizenship

ROMAN CITIZENSHIP	KINGDOM OF GOD "CITIZENSHIP"
Right to the triple name	Right to the name of God and a new name written in stone (Eph 3:15; Rev 2:17)
Right to wear the toga	Right to wear the garment (Rev 16:15)
Right to marry a Roman citizen	Right, or duty, to marry within the faith or a fellow citizen of the kingdom (2Cor 6:14; 1Pt 3:7)
Citizen passes to children patrilineally	Right to inherit "all that the Father hath" (Rom 8:17; Gal 4:7; Jms 2:5)
Exemption from tribute	Absolved from payment for sins (Eph 1:7; Jms 5:15)
Right to appointment to government offices	Right, or duty, to serve in the Church (2Tm 1:19; 2Cor 10:8)
Exemption from punishment without trial and appeal	All will be judged by God in perfect justice; none will be punished unjustly; Jesus will act as advocate and mediator for "citizens" of the kingdom (Acts 17:31; Rom 14:10; 1Tm 2:5)
Right to appeal a legal judgment to the emperor	Final judgment rendered by God himself (Jn 5:22; Acts 14:10)
Exempt from authority of non-Roman local officials and protected from accusation by non-Romans	Satan has no power to accuse Christians, nor does he have any authority over them (Lk 9:1; Acts 26:18; Rom 16:20)

Chart 4-6

Chart 4-7

Roman Legal Procedure
Pertaining to the New Testament

Explanation

Roman law gave order to life in the world of the New Testament. Chart 4-7 lists some of the basic aspects of Roman law and suggests some of the ways they would have been pertinent to legal cases involving Jesus and Paul.

The Roman civil and criminal laws would have applied only to Roman citizens, but the *Ius Gentium* would have regulated commercial affairs even in Judea or Galilee. Governors, but not lesser magistrates such as Pilate, would have held the broad legal powers of *imperium*.

Roman officials could hear cases involving non-citizens under their extraordinary jurisdiction, *cognitio extra ordinem*. Cases could either be convened in the town of a person's domicile or in the locale where the infraction occurred. Rights of appeal were limited.

References

John F. Hall, "Appeal to Caesar," *ABD*, 1:317.

A. N. Sherwin-White, *Roman Society and Roman Law in the New Testament* (Oxford: Oxford University Press, 1978).

Wolfgang Kunkel, *An Introduction to Roman Legal and Constitutional History* (Oxford: Clarendon, 1966).

Roman Legal Procedure
Pertaining to the New Testament

PROCEDURE	DEFINITION	APPLICATION
Ius Civile	Civil Law, including rights of *commercium* (contract law), and *connubium* (family law).	Applied only to Roman Citizens.
Ordo	Criminal code and procedure.	Applied only to Roman Citizens.
Ius Gentium	The "right of nations" under which practices of other peoples, similar to Roman practices, are recognized as valid under Roman law.	Allowed non-citizens, both provincials and foreigners, to engage in matters of law, such as *commercium*, with Romans.
Imperium	Religious, judicial, and military authority of Roman magistrates, including the emperor.	Provincial governors derived this authority from the emperor's delegated *imperium*.
Cognitio extra ordinem	Right of judicial inquest over provincials, beyond the scope of Roman *ordo*, thus permitting formal charges and procedure, including scourging as a mode of examination or punishment.	Applied only to non-citizens. The hearing of Jesus before Pilate, or Paul's illegal arraignment at Philippi constitute *cognitio* procedures.
Forum domicilii	The right of a magistrate to transfer venue of a *cognitio* to the magistrate of the defendant's home province.	Pilate exercised this right in referring the compaint about Jesus to Herod Agrippa, tetrarch of Galilee.
Forum delicti	The right of a magistrate to retain venue of a *cognitio* for defendants from another province.	With this authority Pilate finally convened a *cognitio* in the case of Jesus.
Provocatio	The right of a Roman citizen to appeal the jurisdiction of a magistrate.	Paul exercised this citizen right.
Appellatio ad Caesarem	The right of a Roman citizen to a hearing before the emperor at Rome.	Paul exercised this citizen right, and so came to Rome.

Chart 4-7

Roman Administrators

Explanation

In consolidating his power as ruler of Judea, Herod the Great received support from Rome, and in return he became a loyal client of Rome's emperor, Augustus Caesar. Thus, Herod was popular and powerful in certain secular Jewish groups but not in all Jewish circles. After Herod's relatively long reign, his son Archelaus ruled in Judea so poorly in his father's stead that the Sanhedrin and other local Jewish leaders even requested that a Roman administrator be sent to replace Archelaus. Except for a few years when Herod's kingdom was restored under Herod Agrippa (Herod the Great's grandson), Roman governors of minor rank presided over Judea. A single cohort of six hundred men was their only military complement, so Roman domination was not imposed by force. In fact, the Sanhedrin and other Jewish leaders continued to govern the local population. In Galilee, Herod's heirs ruled uninterrupted for a longer period than in Judea but were ultimately supplanted by minor Roman officials. A chronological list of those who ruled over Judea and Galilee is provided in the following two charts.

References

John F. Hall, "The Roman Province of Judea: A Historical Overview," *MWNT,* 319–36.
Richard Neitzel Holzapfel, "King Herod," *MWNT,* 35–73.
Andrew Skinner, "A Historical Sketch of Galilee," *MWNT,* 113–28.

Roman Administrators in Judea

Official	Title	Rank	Date (A.D.)	Emperor
Coponius	Praefectus Iudaeae	equestrian	6–9	Augustus
Ambivulus	Praefectus Iudaeae	equestrian	9–12	Augustus
Rufus	Praefectus Iudaeae	equestrian	12–15	Augustus Tiberius
Valerius	Praefectus Iudaeae	equestrian	15–26	Tiberius
Pontius **Pilate**	Praefectus Iudaeae	equestrian	26–36	Tiberius
Restoration of Herodian kingdom under Herod Agrippa by command of Claudius, A.D. 41–44				
Fadus	Procurator	equestrian	44–46	Claudius
Tiberius Julius Alexander	Procurator	equestrian	46–48	Claudius
Cumanas	Procurator	equestrian	48–52	Claudius
Antonius **Felix**	Procurator	equestrian	52–59/60	Claudius Nero
Porcius **Festus**	Procurator	equestrian	59/60–62	Nero
Albinus	Procurator	equestrian	62–64	Nero
Gessius **Florus**	Procurator	equestrian	66–70	Nero
Titus Flavius Vespasianus (**Vespasian**)	Legatus Augusti pro praetore	senator	67–69	Nero
Titus Flavius Vespasianus (**Titus**)	Legatus Augusti pro praetore	senator	70	Vespasian
Flavius **Silva**	Procurator Legatus Augusti pro praetore	senator	72–75 73–75	Vespasian
Commodus	Procurator	equestrian	75–80	Vespasian Titus
Salvidienus	Procurator	equestrian	80–86	Titus Domitian
Longinus	Procurator	equestrian	86–95	Domitian

Chart 4-8

Rulers and Administrators
of Galilee

Dates	Official	Title	Description of Office	Emperor
Galilee as an affiliated territory under Herodian rule				
37–4 B.C.	Herod the Great	king	client king of Rome	Augustus
4 B.C.– A.D. 39	Herod Antipas	tetrarch	client ruler appointed by Roman emperor	Augustus Tiberius Gaius
39–41	Herod Agrippa I	tetrarch	appointed client ruler	Gaius
Galilee attached to the Roman province of Judea				
41–44	Herod Agrippa I	king	client king of Rome[1]	Claudius
44–46	Fadus	procurator	Roman administrator of equestrian rank	Claudius
46–48	Tiberius Julius Alexander[2]	procurator	Roman administrator of equestrian rank	Claudius
48–52	Cumanas	procurator	Roman administrator of equestrian rank	Claudius
52–59/60	Antonius Felix	procurator	Roman administrator of equestrian rank	Claudius Nero
Galilee attached to kingdom of Herod Agrippa II				
56–95	Herod Agrippa II	king	client king of Rome[3]	Nero Vespasian Titus Domitian

1. Claudius restored the kingdom of Herod the Great with all constituent parts (Judea, Galilee, Perea, etc.) to his friend since boyhood, Herod Agrippa I.

2. A very prominent Jew of Alexandria and brother of the famed Jewish philosopher Philo, he served first as procurator of Judea and later in the high office of prefect of Egypt, giving support to Vespasian in his prosecution of the Jewish War.

3. Herod Agrippa had been previously appointed king of Chalcis and Trachonitis, regions of Phoenicia (modern-day Lebanon) to which Perea and Galilee were added in 56.

Chart 4-9

SECTION 5

Roman Military

Chart 5-1

Roman Army under Augustus

Explanation

At the time of Augustus Caesar, the Roman military was comprised of regular soldiers of Roman or Italian origin organized into legions and stationed through the provinces of the empire as single legions or combined with other legions into an army *(exercitus)*.

Other troops were raised in the provinces and organized utilizing a different structure. They were called "auxiliaries" and served largely to keep order in the provinces by filling police functions or manning guard posts. The legionary units conducted required military operations, although on occasion they were assisted by auxiliary troops, particularly by cavalry units that performed reconnaissance and guarded the flanks of the battle line.

Chart 5-1 shows the organization of both classes of troops, their provenance, function, and command structure around the time when Jesus was born.

Reference

G. Webster, *The Roman Imperial Army of the First and Second Century A.D.* (London: Block, 1979).

Roman Army under Augustus

REGULAR ROMAN UNITS

Unit	Number of Troops	Commander	Unit Type	Origin of Troops
Exercitus (army)	Two or more legions with *auxilia*	Legatus Augusti (Legate of Augustus)	varied	Italy and provinces
Legion	6000 divided into 10 cohorts	Legatus Legionis (Legionary Legate)	infantry	Italy
Cohort	600 divided into 6 centuries	Tribunus Militaris (Military Tribune)	infantry	Italy
Century	up to 100	Centurion	infantry	Italy

PROVINCIAL AUXILIARIES

Auxiliary Cohort	480	Praefectus Militaris (Military Prefect)	light infantry or archers	provinces
Alae	480	Praefectus Militaris	cavalry	provinces
Vexillatio	240	Senior Decurion	cavalry	provinces
Turma	120	Decurion	cavalry	provinces

Chart 5-1

Chart 5-2

Battle Arrangement of a Legion

Explanation

The classical Roman legion depicted on chart 5-2 was invented at the end of the second century B.C. by Rome's military genius Gaius Marius, uncle by marriage of the great Julius Caesar. This amazingly effective arrangement of soldiers in battle supplanted an older legion formation that had been used for the two preceding centuries. The legion was an extremely flexible tactical structure that enabled Roman soldiers to confront vastly superior numbers of enemy forces, absorbing the impact of enemy formations through the use of space and balanced placement of personnel. Due to the power of the legion, Rome conquered the Mediterranean world and large tracts of its hinterland in Europe, Asia, and Africa.

A full legion was comprised of six thousand soldiers, organized into ten cohorts, each of six hundred men. The cohorts were divided into six centuries of one hundred men each (centurions). The legionnaires within each century were also stationed in three lines, the famous Roman triple battle line or *tres acies,* with an interval of approximately a meter between individuals. The second line was staggered by half a meter so as to fill the meter interval of the first line. The triple line arrangement was repeated as the ten cohorts were themselves stationed in three lines, with large intervals between them, as indicated on the chart. The third line, consisting of cohorts VIII, IX, and X, was considered a reserve that could be moved as needed to fill cohort intervals or extend the battle line in a flanking maneuver.

References

H. M. D. Parker, *The Roman Legions* (Oxford: Oxford University Press, 1928).

James S. Jeffers, *The Greco-Roman World of the New Testament Era* (Downers Grove, Ill.: InterVarsity, 1999), 171–78.

Battle Arrangement of a Legion

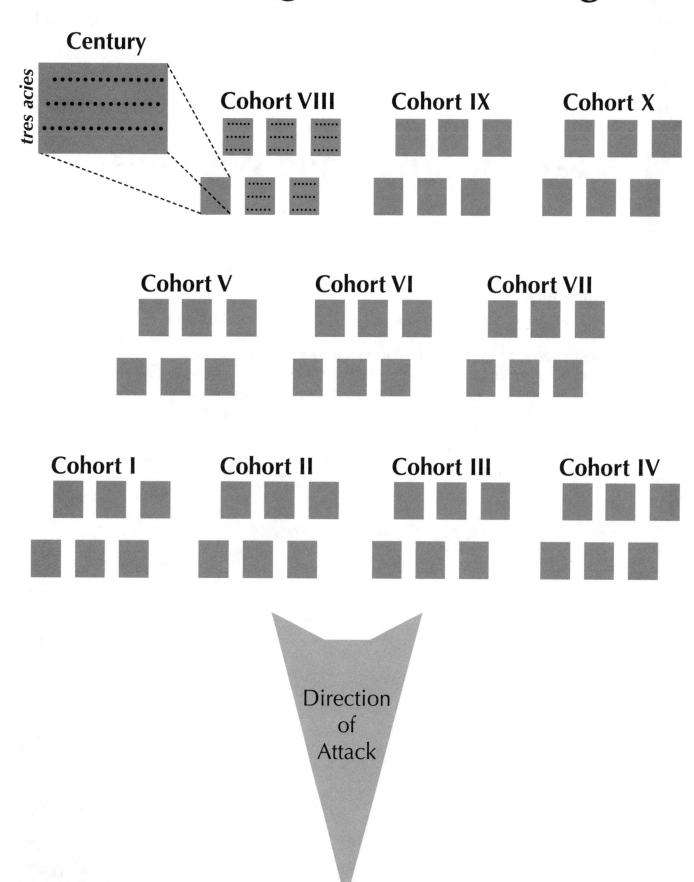

Century

tres acies

Cohort VIII

Cohort IX

Cohort X

Cohort V

Cohort VI

Cohort VII

Cohort I

Cohort II

Cohort III

Cohort IV

Direction of Attack

Chart 5-2

Chart 5-3

Roman Armor and Weapons

Explanation

The common Roman soldier was well equipped with armor of leather manufacture, edged or tipped with iron. His primary defensive weapon was a large rectangular shield, called a *scutum,* which protected much of his body. Major offensive weapons were the *pilum,* a short javelin hurled at the enemy from approximately twenty paces and the much feared *gladius,* a short sword designed for stabbing, used at close range with deadly effect. Compare Ephesians 6:13–17.

Reference

William J. Hamblin, "The Roman Army in the First Century," *MWNT,* 337–49.

Roman Armor and Weapons

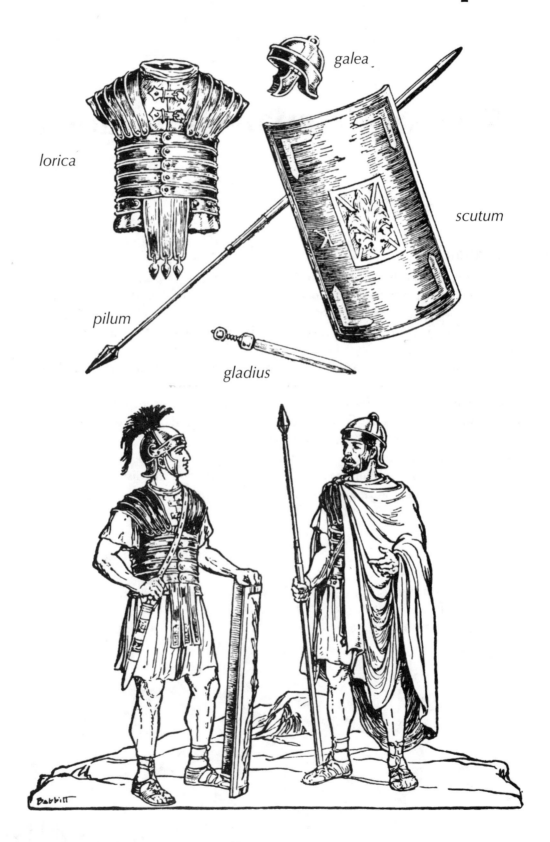

galea

lorica

scutum

pilum

gladius

Chart 5-3

Chart 5-4

Roman Campaigns in Judea

Explanation

Rome became involved in affairs in Judea at the request of Maccabean ambassadors who sought protection from one of Rome's enemies, Seleucid Syria. After Rome became the dominant power in the Near East, Romans were compelled to maintain peace in the region by settling frequent dynastic disputes and civil conflicts in Judea among the Maccabean heirs. After one of these sought to overthrow the legitimate High Priest by introducing Parthian armies into Roman territory, Herod came to power as Rome's loyal client, ruling as king over the Jews.

Although Rome maintained no troops in Judea until A.D. 6, when the first Roman governor was accompanied by a six-hundred-man bodyguard, hatred of the Herods intensified resentment against Rome among fanatical elements of the Jewish populace, Zealots and Sicarii, who for over a century engaged in guerrilla and open warfare against both Roman and Jewish authorities until their final destruction and dispersion.

Chart 5-4 provides information about each of the campaigns Rome was forced to undertake in Judea, either to settle dynastic civil conflict or to repress Zealot insurrection.

References

Fergus Millar, *The Roman Near East* (Cambridge: Harvard University Press, 1993).
F. E. Peters, *The Harvest of Hellenism* (New York: Touchstone, 1970).
John F. Hall, "The Roman Province of Judea," *MWNT,* 319–36.

Roman Campaigns in Judea

Campaign	Date	Circumstances	Commander	Result
Pompey's Disposition of Judea	63 B.C.	Maccabean dynastic dispute, Aristobolus versus his brother Hyrcanus	Pompey the Great, Roman proconsul with extraordinary *imperium* over the Roman East	Judea brought into Roman sphere as a protectorate under Hyrcanus, withdrawal of Roman troops
Gabinius' Resolution of Civil Conflict	55 B.C.	Revolt by Alexander, son of Aristobolus, against his uncle, Hyrcanus	Aulus Gabinius, governor of Syria	Confirmation of Hyrcanus's reign, withdrawal of Roman troops
Antony's Expulsion of Parthians from Judea	40 B.C.	Antigonus, son of Aristobolus, made ruler of Judea with deposition of his great-uncle, Hyrcanus, by the Parthians	C. Sosius, legate of Marc Antony, with Herod	Herod proclaimed King of Judea by the Roman Senate
Jewish Revolt	A.D. 66	Zealots seize Jerusalem and overthrow the Sanhedrin, murdering Jews, Greeks, and Romans	Cestius Gallus	Zealots defeat Gallus, and legion XII (Fulminata) sent from Syria to restore order
Jewish War	A.D. 66–68	The revolt of 66 had developed into a full-scale war	Flavius Vespasianus	The Roman campaign is postponed as Vespasian becomes involved in the A.D. 68 contest for succeeding Nero and emerges from the civil war as emperor
Siege of Jerusalem	A.D. 70	Rome resumes the postponed war in Judea	Titus, son of the emperor Vespasian	Jerusalem invested and order restored in Judea
Masada	A.D. 73	Zealot raids on Jewish towns from mountain strongholds occasion their final destruction	Flavius Silva	Destruction of Masada and other bases of Zealot guerrilla bands
Bar Kochba Rebellion	A.D. 132	Final rebellion of Zealot factions of Jews	Sextus Minucius Iulius Severus	Destruction of Zealots, dispersion of large numbers of Jews, reconstitution of Judea as the Roman province of Palestine

Chart 5-4

Roman Lands

Explanation

The empire of the Romans encompassed the Mediterranean and the surrounding areas in Europe, western Asia, and North Africa. The empire was divided for administrative purposes into provinces. In New Testament times during the reign of Augustus, the empire had achieved boundaries consistent with the natural geography of the lands surrounding the Mediterranean. Britain and Thrace were added as provinces under Claudius and the territory of the empire reached its fullest extent with Trajan's additions of Dacia and the eastern provinces of Armenia, Assyria, and Mesopotamia.

The boundaries of the empire were protected by the Roman legions. Augustus stationed them in more or less permanent quarters in the provinces bordering the frontier. The individual legions and the provinces where they were quartered are listed on the opposite page.

References

M. Cary and H. H. Scullard, *A History of Rome* (New York: St. Martin's, 1975), 436–37.

G. Webster, *The Roman Imperial Army of the First and Second Centuries A.D.* (London: Block, 1979).

Distribution of Legions
in the Early Empire

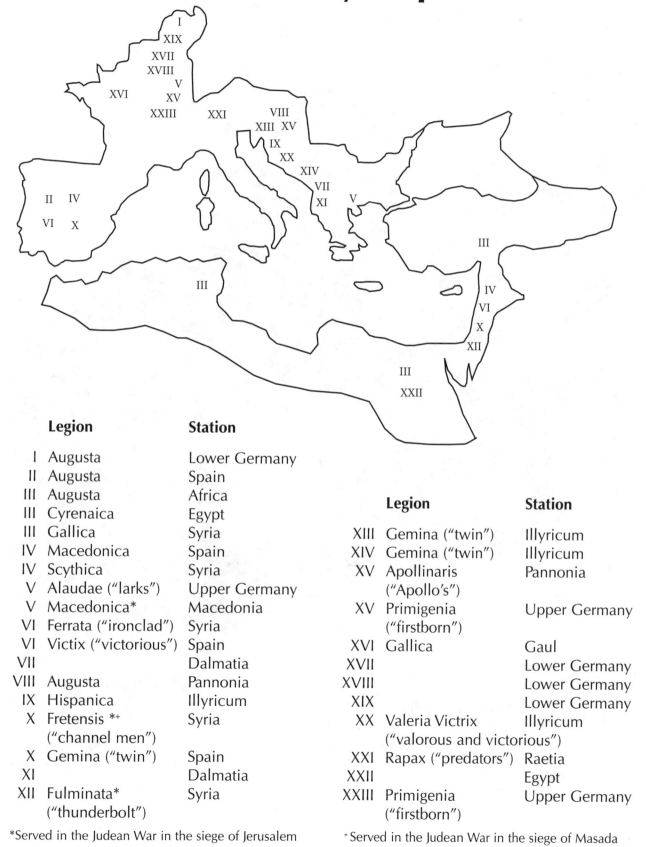

Legion		Station
I	Augusta	Lower Germany
II	Augusta	Spain
III	Augusta	Africa
III	Cyrenaica	Egypt
III	Gallica	Syria
IV	Macedonica	Spain
IV	Scythica	Syria
V	Alaudae ("larks")	Upper Germany
V	Macedonica*	Macedonia
VI	Ferrata ("ironclad")	Syria
VI	Victix ("victorious")	Spain
VII		Dalmatia
VIII	Augusta	Pannonia
IX	Hispanica	Illyricum
X	Fretensis *+ ("channel men")	Syria
X	Gemina ("twin")	Spain
XI		Dalmatia
XII	Fulminata* ("thunderbolt")	Syria

Legion		Station
XIII	Gemina ("twin")	Illyricum
XIV	Gemina ("twin")	Illyricum
XV	Apollinaris ("Apollo's")	Pannonia
XV	Primigenia ("firstborn")	Upper Germany
XVI	Gallica	Gaul
XVII		Lower Germany
XVIII		Lower Germany
XIX		Lower Germany
XX	Valeria Victrix ("valorous and victorious")	Illyricum
XXI	Rapax ("predators")	Raetia
XXII		Egypt
XXIII	Primigenia ("firstborn")	Upper Germany

*Served in the Judean War in the siege of Jerusalem

+Served in the Judean War in the siege of Masada

Chart 5-5

The Roman Empire from

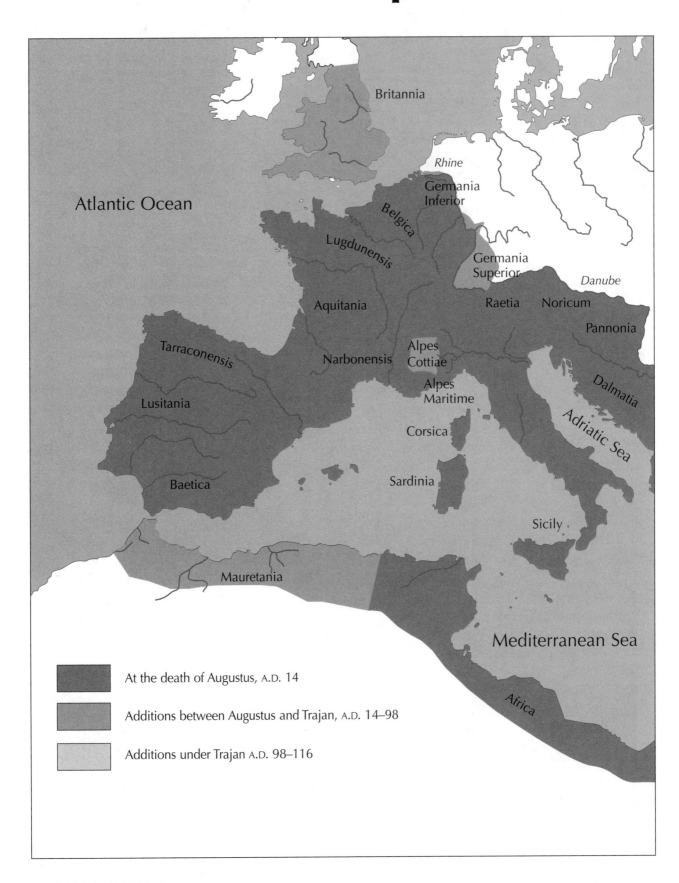

Britannia

Atlantic Ocean

Rhine

Germania Inferior

Belgica

Lugdunensis

Germania Superior

Danube

Aquitania

Raetia

Noricum

Pannonia

Tarraconensis

Narbonensis

Alpes Cottiae

Dalmatia

Lusitania

Alpes Maritime

Adriatic Sea

Corsica

Baetica

Sardinia

Sicily

Mauretania

Mediterranean Sea

Africa

At the death of Augustus, A.D. 14

Additions between Augustus and Trajan, A.D. 14–98

Additions under Trajan A.D. 98–116

Augustus to Trajan

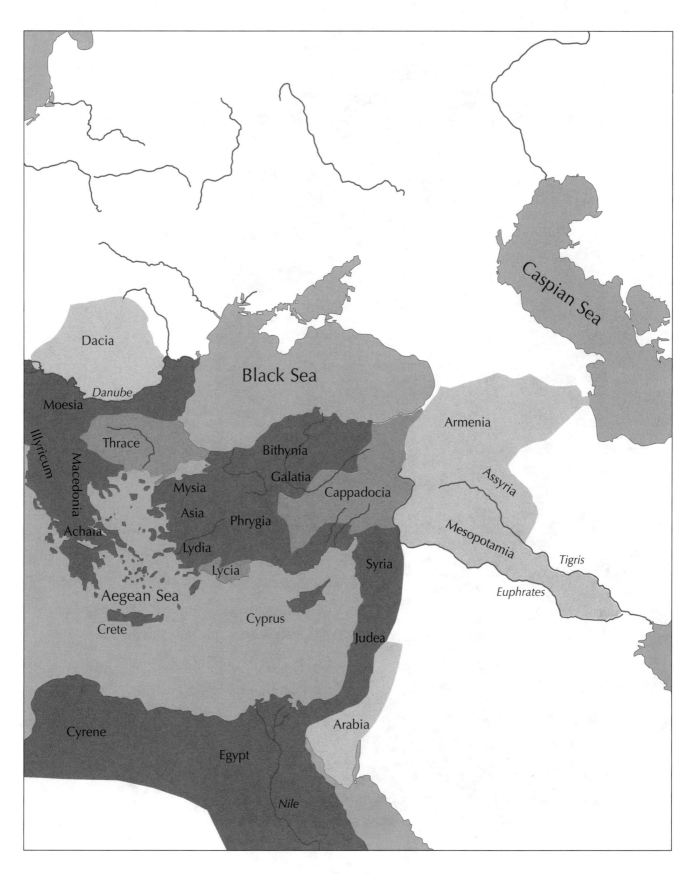

Dacia

Danube

Black Sea

Caspian Sea

Moesia

Illyricum

Thrace

Macedonia

Bithynia

Armenia

Galatia

Assyria

Mysia

Cappadocia

Asia

Phrygia

Mesopotamia

Achaia

Lydia

Tigris

Lycia

Syria

Euphrates

Aegean Sea

Cyprus

Crete

Judea

Cyrene

Arabia

Egypt

Nile

Chart 5-6

Temple of Apollo at Didyma, south of Ephesus, in western Turkey. Photo by John W. Welch

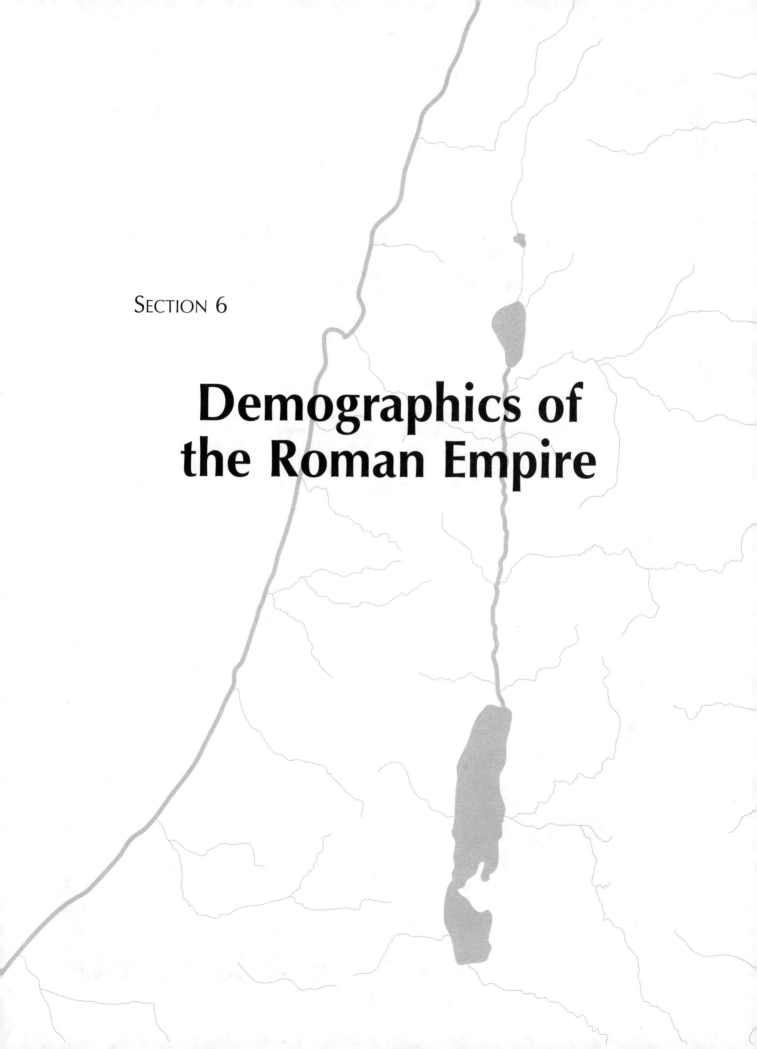

Demographics of the Roman Empire

Chart 6-1

Major Cities of the Eastern Provinces

Explanation

The strength of the Roman Empire was found not only in the municipalities of Italy but also in the major cities of its provinces. Indeed, the most populous cities were located in the provinces of the region the Romans called "the East." Founded by Alexander the Great, the Greek settlement of Alexandria in Egypt was the largest city in the world and, after Rome, the richest during the time of Christ. The second largest was Syria's Antioch, one-time capital of the Seleucid Empire.

Reference

A. H. M. Jones, *The Cities of the Eastern Provinces,* 2nd ed. (Oxford: Oxford University Press, 1971).

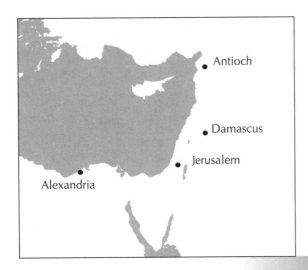

Major Cities of the Eastern Provinces
in order of importance

CITY, PROVINCE	ALEXANDRIA, EGYPT	ANTIOCH, SYRIA	DAMASCUS, SYRIA	JERUSALEM, JUDEA
LOCATION	Mediterranean coast at mouth of Nile	On the Orontes River, ten miles from the Mediterranean	On the Barada River in the center of the Syrian Basin	Central Palestinian hill country
STATUS	Largest city in the world, once capital of Ptolemaic Empire, capital of Roman Egypt	Second largest city in the Roman Empire, once capital of the Seleucid Empire, capital of the Roman province of Syria	Leading city of Syria until the foundation of Antioch	Traditional chief city of Jews from c. 1100 B.C.
POPULATION	1,000,000	400,000–500,000	100,000	30,000
ETHNICITY	Greek, Jewish, Egyptian	Greek, Syrian, Jewish	Syrian, Greek, Jewish	Jewish
FOUNDATION	311 B.C. by Alexander the Great	300 B.C. by Seleucus I	3000 B.C.	c. 2800 B.C.
GOVERNMENT	Roman *Praefectus Aegypti*	Roman *legatus Augusti pro Praetore*	Local dynasts appointed by Rome	High Priest and Sanhedrin
ECONOMIC	Greatest trade center of the Mediterranean	Trade, industry, agriculture	Agriculture	Agriculture
CHRISTIAN PRESENCE	Tradition associates the foundation of Alexandria's very large Christian community with the Evangelist Mark, one-time missionary companion of Peter	Barnabas and Saul/Paul labor to establish the Antiochene Church. After A.D. 49 Antioch seems to have become the headquarters of the Christian church and residence of Peter and other leading brethren (Acts 10–11, 13, and 15)	Christian community well established at the time of Paul's conversion (Acts 9, 22, 26)	From time of Christ until A.D. 66 when most Christians depart

Chart 6-1

Major Cities of Asia Minor

Explanation

The most prosperous of Rome's provinces was Asia, encompassing what is now the western half of modern-day Turkey. Populated by Greeks and the original people of the eastern Aegean region, Asia boasted rich and powerful cities like Pergamum and Smyrna. Most important was Ephesus, the fourth largest city of the empire. Jewish synagogues and many ethnic groups were found amidst these diverse cosmopolitan urban centers.

In all these cities there were soon to be found significant Christian populations. The important role of Antioch is made clear in Acts, but Ephesus and the cities of Asia Minor possessed the largest numbers of Christian inhabitants. Indeed, after the first decades of Christianity and for centuries to follow, Asia Minor was the most important Christian area.

References

David Magie, *Roman Rule in Asia Minor to the End of the Third Century after Christ* (Princeton: Princeton University Press, 1950).

James S. Jeffers, *The Greco-Roman World of the New Testament* (Downers Grove, Ill.: InterVarsity Press, 1999), 259–91.

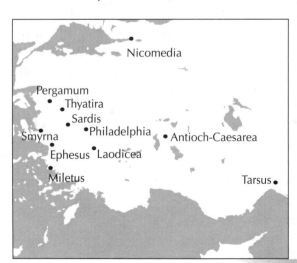

Major Cities of Asia Minor
in order of importance

CITY, PROVINCE	EPHESUS, ASIA	PERGAMUM, ASIA	SMYRNA, ASIA
LOCATION	Coast, where River Cayster enters the Aegean Sea	Valley of the Caicus River, 15 miles inland from the Aegean Sea	At the mouth of the Hermus River, on a large sheltered harbor of the Aegean
STATUS	Provincial capital of Asia	First capital of the Roman province of Asia, by the first century relegated to co-capital of Asia behind Ephesus	Second most important commercial city of Asia
POPULATION	400,000 (4th largest of Roman Empire)	100,000	200,000–250,000
ETHNICITY	Primarily Greek, also Lydian, some Jews, some Romans	Greek and Phrygian	Greek
FOUNDATION	c. 1000 B.C. by Ionian Greeks	c. 700 B.C.	c. 900 B.C. by Aeolian Greeks
GOVERNMENT	Residence of Roman proconsul of Asia; local town council *(boule)*	Roman quaestorian deputy of proconsul of Asia; town council administration *(prytanis and boule)*	Town council *(boule)* and council of elders *(gerousia)*
ECONOMIC	Primary commercial and trade center of Asia Minor	One of three great intellectual centers of the Roman empire with the world's second largest library and most prestigious medical school	Greatest port of Asia and most important trade center
CHRISTIAN PRESENCE	Asia's primary Christian center. Residence of Paul for three years, residence of Apostle John for several decades. Traditional residence of Mary, Mother of Jesus, at the end of her life. Large Christian population, first of the seven churches of Asia in *Revelation* (Acts 15, 18–19; Rev 2)	Mentioned as one of seven churches of Asia, Christian community since time of Paul, but it remained small due to the heavy local influence of cults of Zeus and Asclepius (Rev 2)	One of the seven churches of Asia, large Christian community, perhaps founded by John; Apostolic father Polycarp was bishop of Smyrna (Rev 2)

Chart 6-2 (1)

Major Cities of Asia Minor

CITY, PROVINCE	MILETUS, ASIA	NICOMEDIA, BITHYNIA-PONTUS	TARSUS, PRE-A.D. 60 SYRIA, POST-A.D. 60 CILICIAN CAPITAL
LOCATION	On the coast where the Meander River joins the Latmian Gulf of the Aegean Sea	West coast of the Propontis (Sea of Marmara), 50 miles east of Byzantium	12 miles north of the Mediterranean and 25 miles southeast of the famed Cilician gates
STATUS	For centuries the most prosperous city of Asia, chief city of the Ionian League, destroyed by Persia in 494 B.C.; though rebuilt, it never attained its former greatness	Capital of small Hellenistic kingdom of Bithynia in late 3rd and early 2nd century B.C.; provincial capital of the Roman province of Bithynia-Pontus	Capital of Cilicia
POPULATION	150,000	50,000–75,000	100,000–150,000
ETHNICITY	Greek	Greek	Cilician, Greek, Syrian, large Jewish center
FOUNDATION	c. 2400 B.C. by Minoans, conquered by Mycenaean Greeks c. 1400	264 B.C. by Nicomedes I	c. 2400 B.C.
GOVERNMENT	Town council administration (*prytanis* and *boule*)	Roman proconsular governor, town council	Roman proconsular governor resident but is self-governing under local elected officials
ECONOMIC	Endowed with four fine harbors, Miletus was one of the great trade centers of the Mediterranean	Trade and agriculture	Major center of higher education, agriculture, and trade; the great Asia Minor road from the west and eastern caravan routes terminated at port
CHRISTIAN PRESENCE	Paul visits and meets with elders of Asia there to bid farewell (Acts 19)	A large Christian population is attested by A.D. 115 in the correspondence of Pliny to Trajan requesting information about how to try persons accused of being Christian	Paul's native city and site of his early missionary efforts (Acts 9)

Chart 6-2 (2)

Major Cities of Asia Minor

CITY, PROVINCE	SARDIS, ASIA	ANTIOCH-CAESAREA, PISIDIA	LAODICEA, ASIA
LOCATION	On the River Hermus in the great plain of Sardis, 50 miles east of Ephesus and Smyrna	In central Anatolia on the major road from Phrygia to Galatia	On the upper reaches of the Lycus River, 90 miles east of Ephesus
STATUS	One-time capital of the Lydian Empire	Roman citizen colony	Important regional center
POPULATION	50,000	40,000	50,000
ETHNICITY	Overwhelmingly Lydian, some Greek, large Jewish center	Greek, some Italian, large Jewish center	Greek
FOUNDATION	c. 1200 B.C.	c. 400 B.C.	c. 250 B.C. by Seleucid ruler Antiochus II
GOVERNMENT	Town council	Roman propraetorian governor, town *aediles* and *decuria*	Town council administration (*prytanis* and *boule*)
ECONOMIC	Wealthy and prosperous center of fertile agricultural region and productive gold mining area	Agriculture	Important wool production and banking center
CHRISTIAN PRESENCE	One of the seven churches of Asia (Rev 3)	Paul visits on first, second, and possibly third missionary journeys through Asia Minor (Acts 13)	One of the seven churches of Asia, recipient of Paul's non-extant Epistle to the Laodiceans (Rev 3)

Chart 6-2 (3)

Major Cities of Greece

Explanation

Paul's ministry took him to Asia Minor and then to Greece. By that time, this ancient land of city-states had been ruled by Rome for two centuries. The Romans had organized Greece into two provinces: Macedonia in the north, with Philippi as its provincial capital; and Achaea in the south, with its capital of Corinth. Paul spent significant time in both of these important cities, especially Corinth, which had been largely rebuilt and colonized by Romans and Italians. Consequently, Latin was used as much as Greek by the populations of these cities in the first century. The other cities listed were entirely Greek in their population and language. As a Greek-speaking Roman citizen, Paul was comfortable in either setting. Sizeable numbers of Christians were converted in the Greek cities on the chart, with the possible exception of Athens, which had been the great city of Greece five hundred years earlier.

References

James S. Jeffers, *The Greco-Roman World of the New Testament* (Downers Grove, Ill.: InterVarsity, 1999), 259–91.

J. B. Ward-Perkins, *Cities of Ancient Greece and Italy* (London: Sidgwick & Jackson, 1974).

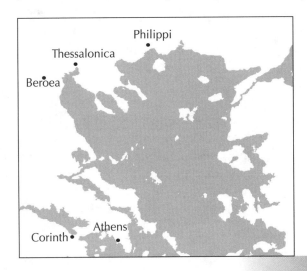

Major Cities of Greece
in order of importance

CITY, PROVINCE	CORINTH, ACHAEA	PHILIPPI, MACEDONIA	ATHENS, ACHAEA	THESSALONICA, MACEDONIA	BEROEA, MACEDONIA
LOCATION	On Isthmus of Corinth bridging Greece and the Peloponnesian Peninsula	10 miles inland from the north coast of the Aegean, on the Via Egnatia	5 miles inland from Saronic Gulf of Aegean Sea	On the Thermaic Gulf of the northwest Aegean Sea	On Mt. Bermion at south end of Macedonian plain, on the Via Egnatia
STATUS	Leading Greek city, Roman citizen colony, capital of Achaea	Capital of province of Macedonia	Most famous city of Greece	Major city of northern Aegean	Populous city of central Macedonia
POPULATION	100,000	50,000	50,000	75,000	50,000
ETHNICITY	Roman, Greek, small groups from many provinces	Roman with some remnant of earlier Greek inhabitants	Greek	Greek	Greek
FOUNDATION	Became Greek c. 2200 B.C. until destruction in 146 B.C., refounded as a Roman city by Julius Caesar in 44 B.C.	c. 550 B.C. by Thasian Greeks, renamed by Philip II in 356 B.C.	1800 B.C. by Mycenaean Greeks	316 B.C.	c. 400 B.C.
GOVERNMENT	Roman proconsular governor of Achaea, town *duoviri, aediles,* and *decuria*	Roman proconsular governor of Macedonia, town *duoviri, aediles,* and *decuria*	Town Council Administration (*boule* and *archontes*)	"Free city" with elected politarches and assembly	Elected politarches and assembly
ECONOMIC	With harbors on both sides of the isthmus, a major trade center, light industry, and agriculture	Gold mining, agriculture	Cultural and educational center	Major port for Macedonia, trade and agriculture	Agriculture
CHRISTIAN PRESENCE	Paul's residence for almost two years, recipient of two extant and two non-extant epistles from Paul, large Christian congregation (Acts 18)	The first European Christian community, established by Paul, and visited on each journey to Greece, large and faithful Christian congregation, home of Lydia, recipient of Epistle to Philippians (Acts 16)	Paul preaches on Mars Hill, no later Christian presence of significance (Acts 17)	Paul establishes church at Thessalonica, recipient of two Pauline epistles (Acts 17)	Paul, Timothy, and Silas found church, which later prospers to become an important Christian center (Acts 17)

Chart 6-3

Chart 6-4

Estimated Distribution of Citizenship
in the Roman Empire

Explanation

Chart 6-4 shows the ratios of Roman citizens to noncitizens and slaves in different parts of the Roman Empire around the middle of the first century.

Because all persons born of Roman parentage in Rome or Italy automatically received full citizen rights, most of the people in that part of the empire were citizens. Rome, and to some degree Italy, was also home to many immigrants from other parts of the empire, who did not possess citizen rights.

Western provinces had a significantly greater number of citizens than eastern provinces. A long process of Romanization in the West had resulted in a ruling class in the towns and municipalities of Gaul and Spain, whose Roman ways and allegiance to the empire acquired Roman citizen rights by virtue of local political office. Of course, all descendants of Roman citizens inherited the prized right of Roman citizenship no matter where they were born.

In the East, very few possessed the privilege of citizenship since it could only be acquired in those provinces by *viritane* grant—as a reward for great services rendered by single individual. The practice of purchasing citizenship was new in this century, and the universal grant of citizenship did not come until later. Most of Paul's work occurred in areas where Roman citizenship was quite uncommon (1–3 percent), perhaps contributing to his practice of not advertising his status.

A substantial population of slaves, generally around 20–30 percent, could be found throughout the empire. The slave population was highest in Rome. People of all races or ethnic origins might find themselves working as slaves in the household of another. Generally, slaves could purchase their freedom if they acquired enough money; others were granted freedom upon the death of their master. Paul's counsel to his converts did not ignore this large segment of the human family; he considered himself a servant (or slave) in the household of God—a vivid image in his day.

Reference

Simon Goldhill, *Being Greek under Rome: Cultural Identity, the Second Sophistic, and the Development of Empire* (New York: Cambridge University Press, 2001).

Estimated Distribution of Citizenship
in the Roman Empire

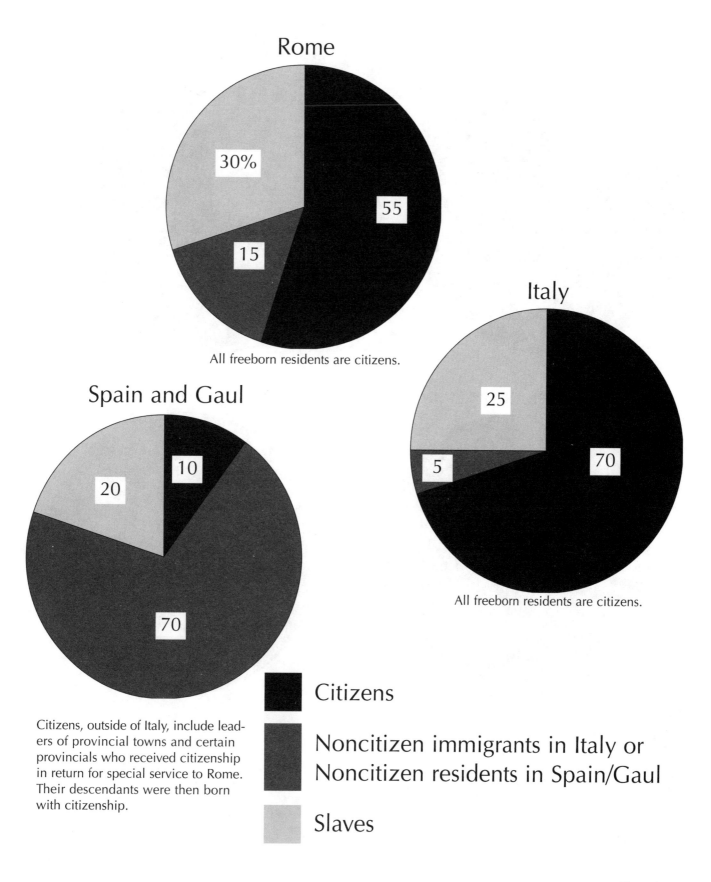

Rome

30%

55

15

All freeborn residents are citizens.

Italy

25

5

70

All freeborn residents are citizens.

Spain and Gaul

10

20

70

Citizens, outside of Italy, include leaders of provincial towns and certain provincials who received citizenship in return for special service to Rome. Their descendants were then born with citizenship.

Citizens

Noncitizen immigrants in Italy or Noncitizen residents in Spain/Gaul

Slaves

Chart 6-4 (1)

Estimated Distribution of Citizenship in the Roman Empire

Other Western Provinces

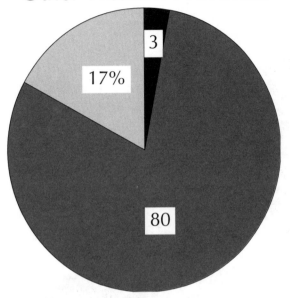

Greece and Asia Minor

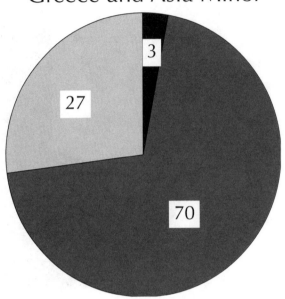

North African Provinces

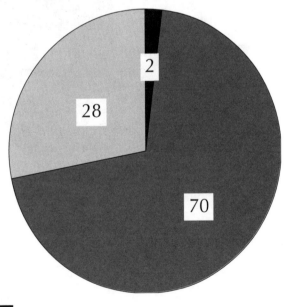

Other Eastern Provinces

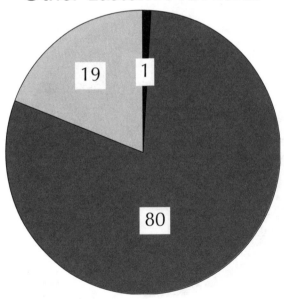

 Citizens

Noncitizen residents

Slaves

A few provincials who performed extraordinary service for Rome received citizenship for themselves and their descendants.

Chart 6-4 (2)

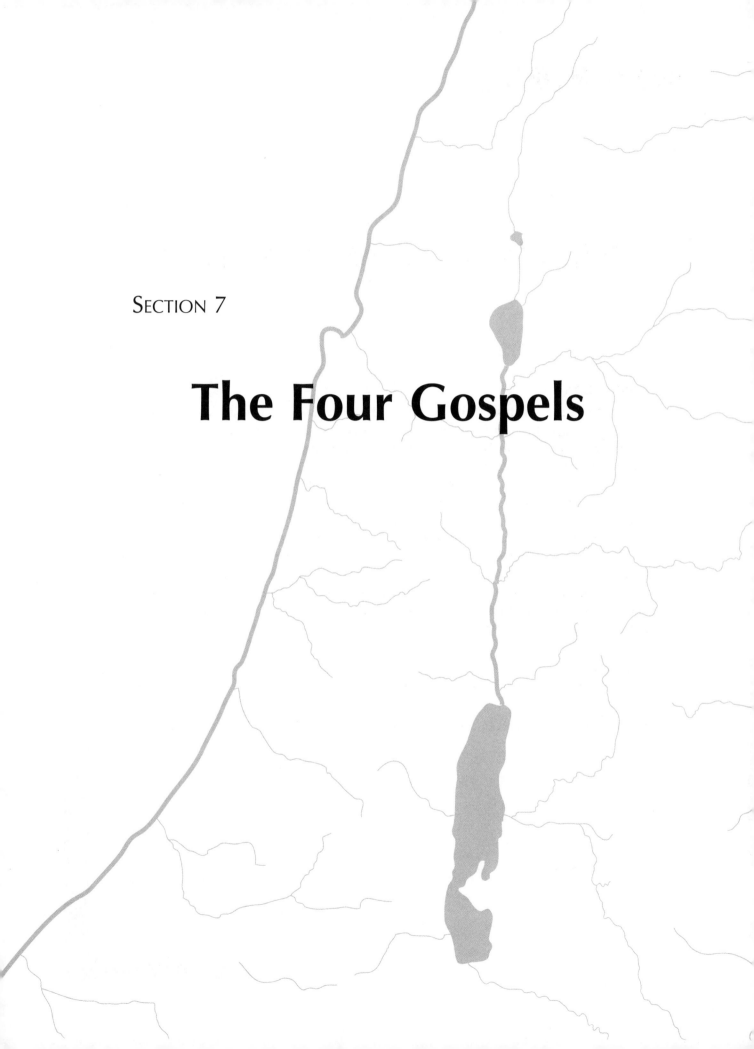

SECTION 7

The Four Gospels

Who Were the Evangelists?

Explanation

The New Testament begins with its four incomparable Gospels. These books comprise the four corners of the sacred written record of the mortal ministry of Jesus Christ. Each Gospel presents an amazingly beautiful and spiritually compelling account of the life and death, words and deeds, suffering and triumph of the Savior.

The charts in this section are designed to help readers understand the contents and purposes of these Gospels: how they differ from each other, and how they are the same; where they overlap, and where they are unique.

A first key of understanding often comes by recognizing the personality of the writer. Chart 7-1 gives information about the four Gospel writers. Among the interesting details about their educational, social, and economic backgrounds, it appears that before their conversions, Matthew and John were Jewish, Luke was Greek, and Mark (the Latin name Marcus) may have been Roman. Thus, these writers personally represent the three main cultures in the world of the New Testament.

References

Neal E. Lambert and Richard H. Cracroft, "The Powerful Voices of the Gospels," *New Era*, January 1973, 36–43.

Kent P. Jackson and Robert L. Millet, eds., *The Gospels* (Salt Lake City: Deseret Book, 1986).

Who Were the Evangelists?

The writers of the four Gospels are called *evangelists,* a term derived from the Greek and Latin words for gospel, *euangelion* and *evangelium.*

MATTHEW

One of the twelve apostles, Matthew is sometimes called Levi (Mk 2:14; Lk 5:27). Mark describes him as a son of Alphaeus, making him perhaps the brother of the lesser James. He was employed as a local tax official of Capernaum. He may have been a man of means since he is said to have given up all that he possessed to follow the Savior. Tradition holds that Matthew spent time in Antioch from where he may have written his gospel during the 70s A.D.

LUKE

Paul's "fellow laborer" in his missionary efforts, Luke is not only the author of the final synoptic gospel but the historian of the early missionary efforts of the apostles as recorded in Acts. Luke's adeptness in using formal Greek historiographical style, as well as his name, suggest Luke's Greek origins. His profession as a physician (Col 4:14) accords with the tradition that Luke was a highly educated Greek convert. Much of Luke's information in both Acts and the Gospel of Luke no doubt derives from his companion Paul. The composition of these works is generally dated to the 70s A.D.

MARK

Mark, or John Mark, was converted to Christianity at Jerusalem where early Christians gathered at the home of Mark's mother, Mary (Acts:12:12). He served as a missionary companion of Paul and Barnabas during Paul's first missionary journey (Acts 12 and 13). His most noted missionary service, however, was as a companion of Peter (see IPt). According to Papias, while associated with Peter, Mark recorded the apostles' words and teachings as a foundation for his written gospel. Probably composed at Rome in the late 60s A.D., the gospel of Mark is considered reflective of Peter's views. Tradition holds that after Peter's death, Mark journeyed to Alexandria where he was instrumental in establishing the Christian community in Egypt.

JOHN

John is known by four names: John the Beloved Disciple, the Apostle John, John the Evangelist, and John the Revelator. John's title as evangelist derives from his composition of the fourth Gospel, in which he refers to himself as the beloved disciple. The Gospel was probably the last of John's writings, following Revelation and the earlier epistles. Its composition may be as late as the first decade of the second century A.D. Clearly it was written to remind an increasingly confused Christian world of the true identity and character of Jesus Christ. The first disciple called by Jesus, John remained one of the leading apostles and, after the death of Peter, presided from Ephesus over the Church of Christ until his translation (D&C 7).

Chart 7-1

Chart 7-2

Four Gospels: Four Beginnings

Explanation

Each Gospel delivers the message of Jesus Christ through its own distinctive style and approach. Significantly, each Gospel traces the origins of Jesus back to a different point. Read from the bottom up, chart 7-2 shows that Matthew takes the genealogy of Jesus only back to David and Abraham, reflecting Matthew's Jewish interests. Luke takes the genealogy back to Adam, reflecting his broader gentile interest in all humankind. Mark gives Jesus no mortal genealogy, for his declared purpose at the outset of his gospel is to emphasize Jesus as the Son of God, not of man. John begins even farther back, where "in the beginning" Jesus was with God and was a God. These points of reference reflect and influence in many ways the different purposes, styles, vocabularies, contents, and characteristics of each of the four Gospels.

References

Philip A. Cunningham, *Jesus and the Evangelists: The Ministry of Jesus and its Portrayal in the Synoptic Gospels* (London: University Press of America, 1993).

Gerd Theissen, *The Gospels in Context: Social and Political History in the Synoptic Tradition* (Minneapolis: Fortress, 1991).

Four Gospels: Four Beginnings

John

Begins with Christ as premortal God

No genealogy mentioned

"in the beginning was the Word,
and the Word was with God, and
the Word was [a] God" (Jn 1:1)

Mark

Begins with Christ as Son of God

No genealogy mentioned

"the beginning of the gospel of Jesus
Christ, the son of God" (Mk 1:1)

Luke

Presents Christ as descendant of Adam

"which was [the son] of Seth, which was [the son]
of Adam, which was [the son] of God" (Lk 3:38)

Matthew

Begins with Christ as descendant of David and Abraham

"the generation of Jesus Christ, the son of David,
the son of Abraham" (Mt 1:1)

Chart 7-2

Purposes and Approaches
of the Four Gospels

Explanation

Because the testimonies of these four witnesses are extremely important in shaping our understanding of the Savior, detailed examination is often necessary. The results are enlightening and rewarding, even though challenges and difficulties often persist. Differences and even inconsistencies between the four Gospels beckon the best of minds to ponder and to reflect on their meaning. Can these differences be constructively understood and explained?

As seen in chart 7-2, where one begins, in any literary work, often determines where the work will also end, for it fundamentally influences the author's outlook, perspective, selection of episodes for inclusion, wording, and the resultant overall character of the work. With respect to the four Gospels, these consequences are demonstrated in chart 7-3, which illustrates how the overall purpose of each Gospel writer is manifested and carried out through several salient particulars in each Gospel.

Reference

Robert C. Patch, "The Gospel in the Gospels," *Ensign*, September 1974, 38–41.

Purposes and Approaches
of the Four Gospels

MATTHEW

Purpose

To show that Jesus is the promised Messiah, the King of Israel, who will restore Israel, the children of Abraham, and royal tribe of Judah

Manifestations of this approach

1. Jesus is born King of the Jews
    2. Baby Jesus is visited by Magi from the East
        3. Jesus is presented as a new Moses, a new lawgiver
            4. Jesus sends twelve disciples to the lost of Israel
                5. Jesus fulfills many Old Testament prophecies

LUKE

Purpose

To show that Jesus is the Savior of all mankind, bringing salvation on earth to the sons and daughters of Adam through his redemption

Manifestations of this approach

1. Jesus is born in humble circumstances
    2. Baby Jesus is visited by shepherds from the hills
        3. Jesus is presented as wise child prodigy
            4. Jesus sends seventy disciples to the nations
                5. Jesus gives many universal, conciliatory parables

MARK

Purpose

To show that Jesus is God here and now on earth, coming in a prophetic mode with divine powers over spirits and forgiveness of sin

Manifestations of this approach

1. No account of the birth is given
    2. Jesus is visited by the Spirit of God descending like a dove
        3. Jesus is told, "Thou art my beloved Son" (1:11)
            4. Jesus' disciples are very slow to understand
                5. Jesus performs many powerful miracles

JOHN

Purpose

To show that Jesus is God forever on earth and in heaven, the great I Am, the image of the Father and his eternal love

Manifestations of this approach

1. Jesus is the Creator of the world
    2. John the Baptist knew the Lamb before his baptism
        3. Jesus is presented as the light and life eternal
            4. Many disciples walk no more with Jesus
                5. Jesus is in control of all from beginning to end

Chart 7-3

Chart 7-4

Author Focus
on the Life of Jesus

Explanation

It is interesting to note that each Gospel tends to place a different degree of emphasis on the words, deeds, death, or resurrection of Jesus. As chart 7-4 shows, Mark, for example, is primarily interested in what Jesus did; his is a gospel of divine power. Matthew and Luke, however, are more interested in telling what Jesus said. John's interest in testifying about the eternal nature of Jesus and his mission is reflected in the fact that his Gospel devotes a very large portion of its attention to the eternally important events of the last supper, the words of Jesus to Pilate, and the resurrection of Jesus.

References

Blake T. Ostler, *The Gospel of Grace in the Writings of John* (Salt Lake City: Deseret Book, 1998).

Adapted from Eta Linnemann, *Is there a Synoptic Problem? Rethinking the Literary Dependence of the First Three Gospels,* trans. Robert W. Yarbrough (Grand Rapids: Baker, 1992).

Author Focus
on the Life of Jesus

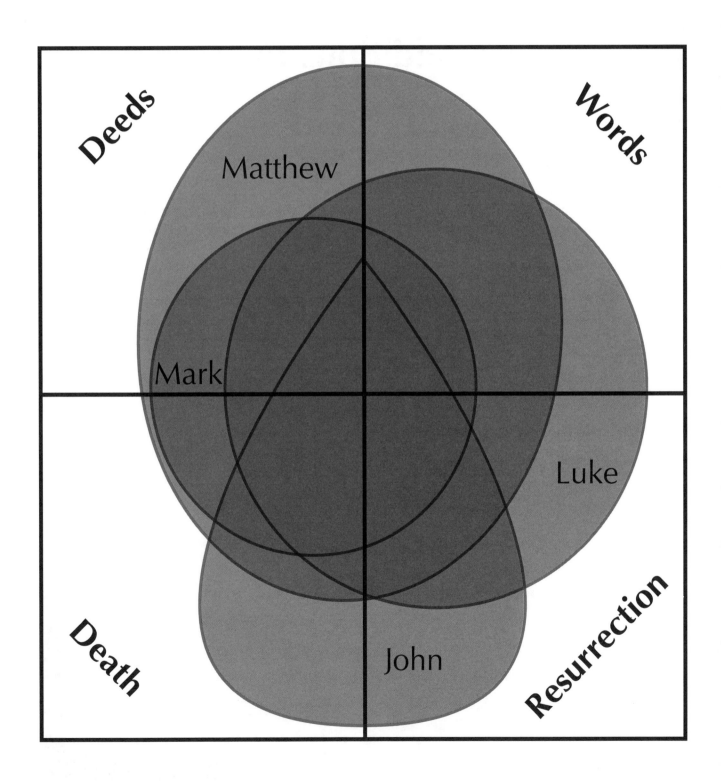

Deeds

Words

Matthew

Mark

Luke

Death

John

Resurrection

Chart 7-4

Chart 7-5

Luke's Additions to Mark

Explanation

It is important to consider the interdependence of the four Gospels. These writers probably knew each other personally. Matthew and John were with Jesus from the early days of his ministry; Luke and Mark were with Paul in the area where John came to live in Ephesus. Thus, it is unlikely that borrowings and similarities between the four Gospels occurred in some kind of compositional isolation on a purely abstract, literary level. They undoubtedly shared several common personal experiences, treasured source materials, and maybe even working conversations. One thing, for example, is quite clear, namely that Luke began with the Gospel of Mark, added seven major blocks of text to it, and omitted a few sections, as chart 7-5 shows.

References

Joachim Jeremias, *New Testament Theology, Part One: The Proclamation of Jesus* (New York: Scribner, 1971), 40–41.

Joseph A. Fitzmyer, *The Gospel According to Luke: A New Translation with Introduction and Commentary* (Garden City, N.Y.: Doubleday, 1981), 67–69.

Luke's Additions to Mark

Material added by Luke

Material ═══════ similar to Mark

[Material omitted by Luke]

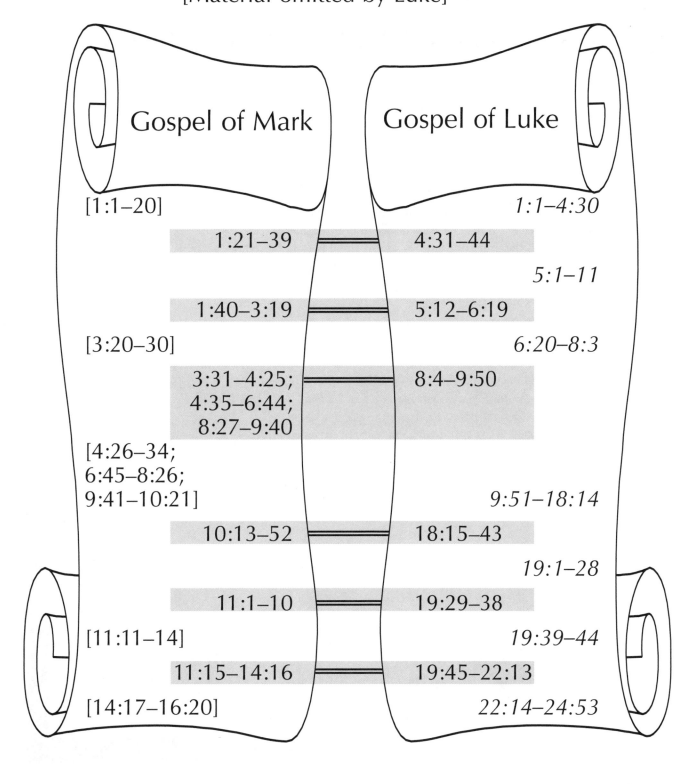

Gospel of Mark   Gospel of Luke

[1:1–20]   *1:1–4:30*

1:21–39 ═══════ 4:31–44

                                            5:1–11

1:40–3:19 ═══════ 5:12–6:19

[3:20–30]   *6:20–8:3*

3:31–4:25;
4:35–6:44;
8:27–9:40 ═══════ 8:4–9:50

[4:26–34;
6:45–8:26;
9:41–10:21]   *9:51–18:14*

10:13–52 ═══════ 18:15–43

                                            19:1–28

11:1–10 ═══════ 19:29–38

[11:11–14]   *19:39–44*

11:15–14:16 ═══════ 19:45–22:13

[14:17–16:20]   *22:14–24:53*

Chart 7-5

Chart 7-6

Synopsis of the Four Gospels

Explanation

Altogether, the four Gospels report 290 episodes, vignettes, or pericopes connected with the life of Jesus. By knowing these 290 segments, modern readers have in broad view all that the Gospels reveal. Chart 7-6 lists all these segments. For convenience, this chart largely follows the order of Matthew. Highlighted in italics are those sections that are found in all three of the so-called synoptic Gospels, Matthew, Mark, and Luke. Although John contains by far the most unique information, Matthew and Luke each present information that no other Gospel preserves.

References

Steven J. Hite, *The Joseph Smith Translation of the Four Gospels: A Harmony: Includes All Textual Changes Made by the Prophet Joseph Smith* (Orem, Utah: S & J, 1989).

Thomas M. Mumford, *Horizontal Harmony of the Four Gospels in Parallel Columns* (Salt Lake City: Deseret Book, 1976).

Bernard Orchard, *A Synopsis of the Four Gospels, in a New Translation* (Macon, Ga.: Mercer University Press, 1982).

"Harmony of the Gospels," Bible Dictionary appendix to the Latter-day Saint edition of the Bible (Salt Lake City: Church of Jesus Christ of Latter-day Saints, 1979), 684–96.

Synopsis of the Four Gospels

GOSPEL AND SYNOPTIC ENTRIES	MATTHEW	MARK	LUKE	JOHN
1. The Word Becomes Flesh				1:1–14
2. Luke's Sources and Purpose			1:1–4	
3. Birth of John the Baptist Foretold			1:5–25	
4. Enunciation to Mary			1:26–38	
5. Mary Visits Elizabeth			1:39–45	
6. Mary's Song of Praise			1:46–56	
7. Birth of John the Baptist			1:57–63	
8. Prophecy of Zacharias			1:64–80	
9. Genealogy of Jesus	1:1–17		3:23–38	
10. Birth of Jesus	1:18–25		2:1–7	
11. Angels Visit the Shepherds			2:8–14	
12. Shepherds Visit Jesus			2:15–20	
13. Presentation of Jesus in the Temple			2:21–39	
14. Wise Men Visit Jesus	2:1–12			
15. Flight to Egypt	2:13–15			
16. Slaying of the Infants by Herod	2:16–18			
17. Return to Nazareth	2:19–23		2:39	
18. Jesus' Childhood			2:40, 52	
19. Jesus as a Boy in the Temple			2:41–52	
20. Preaching of John the Baptist	3:1–12	1:1–8	3:2–18	1:6–8, 15–28

Chart 7-6 (1)

21. John Teaches Generosity and Moderation			3:10–14	
22. John's Messianic Preaching	3:11–12		3:15–18	1:19–28
23. *John's Imprisonment*	*14:3–5*	*6:17–19*	*3:19–20*	
24. John Recognizes Jesus as the Lamb of God				1:29–34
25. *Baptism of Jesus*	*3:13–17*	*1:9–11*	*3:21–22*	
26. *Temptation of Christ*	*4:1–11*	*1:12–13*	*4:1–13*	
27. *First Preaching in Galilee*	*4:12–17*	*1:14–15*	*4:14–15*	
28. *Jesus Calls His First Disciples*	*4:18–22*	*1:16–20*	*5:1–11*	*1:35–51*
29. Wedding of Cana				2:1–11
30. Teaching with Authority and Casting Out a Devil in Capernaum		1:21–28	4:31–37	
31. *Healing Peter's Mother-in-law*	*8:14–15*	*1:29–31*	*4:38–39*	
32. *Evening of Healing*	*8:16–17*	*1:32–34*	*4:40–41*	
33. Departure from Capernaum		1:35–38	4:42–43	
34. *Preaching and Healing in Galilee*	*4:23–25*	*1:39–44*	*4:42–44; 6:17–19*	
35. Miraculous Catch of Fish			5:1–11	
36. Jesus Instructs Nicodemus to Be Born of the Spirit				3:1–21
37. Sermon on the Mount Introduction	5:1–2			
38. The Beatitudes	5:3–12		6:20–23	
39. *Salt of the Earth, Light of the World*	*5:13–16; 6:22–23*	*9:50*	*14:34–35*	
40. Jesus Came to Fulfil the Law	5:17–20			
41. Be Not Angry, Agree with Adversary	5:21–26		12:57–59	
42. The Higher Law on Adultery	5:27–30			

Chart 7-6 (2)

43. *The Higher Law on Divorce*	*5:31–32; 19:9*	*10:11–12*	*16:18*	
44. Swear Not at All	5:33–37			
45. The Higher Law on Retaliation	5:38–42		6:29–30	
46. Love Your Enemies, Bless Them that Curse You	5:43–48; 7:12		6:27–36	
47. Give Alms in Secret	6:1–4			
48. On Prayer	6:5–15; 7:7–11		11:1–13	
49. The Lord's Prayer	6:9–15		11:2–4	
50. On Fasting	6:16–18			
51. Lay Up Treasures in Heaven	6:19–21		12:33–34	
52. The Eye is the Light of the Body	6:22–23		11:34–36	
53. No Man Can Serve Both God and Mammon	6:24		16:13	
54. Take No Thought for the Morrow	6:25–34; 19–21		12:22–34	
55. Ye Shall Be Judged with What Judgment Ye Judge	7:1–5		6:37–42	
56. Cast Not Your Pearls before Swine	7:6			
57. Ask, Seek, Knock	7:7–12		11:9–13	
58. The Golden Rule	7:12		6:31	
59. Strait is the Gate, Narrow the Way	7:13–14, 21–23		13:22–30	
60. A Tree Bears Only One Kind of Fruit	7:15–20; 12:34–35		6:43–45	
61. I Never Knew You	7:21–23		13:25–27	
62. Wise Man Builds House on Rock	7:24–28		6:46–49	
63. Jesus Taught as One with Authority	7:28–29			
64. Samaritan Woman at the Well				4:1–42

Chart 7-6 (3)

65. *Jesus Heals Faithful Leper*	*8:1–4*	*1:40–45*	*5:12–16*	
66. Jesus Heals Centurion's Servant	8:5–13		7:1–10	4:43–54
67. Jesus Raises Widow's Son at Nain			7:11–17	
68. *Jesus Heals the Sick, Casts Out Devils*	*8:16–17*	*1:32–34*	*4:40–41*	
69. Would–be Followers	8:18–22		9:57–62	
70. *Stilling the Tempest*	*8:23–27*	*4:36–41*	*8:22–25*	
71. *Gadarene Demoniacs*	*8:28–34*	*5:1–20*	*8:26–39*	
72. *Easier to Heal Sick or Forgive Sins?*	*9:1–8*	*2:1–12*	*5:17–26*	
73. *Matthew and Tax Collecting*	*9:9–13*	*2:13–17*	*5:27–32*	
74. *Question about Fasting*	*9:14–17*	*2:18–22*	*5:33–39*	
75. *Jairus' Daughter*	*9:18–19, 23–26*	*5:21–24, 35–43*	*8:41–42, 49–56*	
76. *Woman Who Touched Jesus*	*9:20–22*	*5:25–34*	*8:43–48*	
77. Two Blind Men Healed	9:27–31			
78. Dumb Man Healed	9:32–34			
79. Compassion of Jesus	9:35–38			
80. *Calling the Twelve*	*10:1–4*	*3:13–19*	*6:12–16*	
81. *Mission of the Twelve*	*10:1–15*	*6:7–13*	*9:1–6*	
82. *Coming Persecutions*	*10:16–25*	*13:9–13*	*21:12–17*	
83. Confessing Christ before Men	10:32–33; 12:32		12:8–12	
84. Whom to Fear	10:26–33		12:4–7	
85. Not Peace But a Sword	10:34–39		12:49–53; 14:26–27	
86. Conditions of Discipleship	10:37–38		14:26–33	

Chart 7-6 (4)

87. Rewards of Discipleship	10:40–11:1	9:41		
88. Messengers from John the Baptist	11:2–19		7:18–23	
89. Christ's Testimony of John			7:24–35	3:22–30
90. Law and the Kingdom of God	11:12–13		16:14–18	
91. On Testimony				3:31–36
92. Woes to Unrepentant Cities	11:20–24		10:13–15	
93. Christ's Thanksgiving Prayer	11:25–27			
94. Healing at the Pool of Bethesda				5:2–18
95. Authority of the Son				5:19–29
96. Come to Me and Rest	11:25–30			
97. Witnesses to Jesus				5:30–47
98. *Corn on the Sabbath*	*12:1–8*	*2:23–28*	*6:1–5*	
99. *Healing a Withered Hand*	*12:9–14*	*3:1–6*	*6:6–11*	
100. The Chosen Healer-Servant	12:15–21			
101. The Seaside Multitude		3:7–12		
102. The Servant from Capernaum			7:1–10	
103. A Sinful Woman Forgiven			7:36–50	
104. Women Ministering to Jesus			8:2–3	
105. The Accusation of Devilishness	12:22–23		11:14–15	
106. *The Beelzebub Controversy*	*12:22–32*	*3:22–30*	*11:14–23*	
107. A Tree and Its Fruits	12:33–37			
108. *The Demand for a Sign*	*12:38–42*	*8:11–12*	*11:29–32*	
109. Return of the Unclean Spirit	12:43–45		11:24–26	

Chart 7-6 (5)

110. The Brothers of Jesus	12:46–50	3:31–35	8:19–21	2:12
111. Parable of the Sower	13:1–9	4:3–9	8:4–8	
112. Purpose of Parables	13:10–17	4:10–12	8:9–10	
113. Blessedness of Discipleship	13:16–17		10:23–24	
114. The Sower Interpreted	13:18–23	4:13–20	8:11–15	
115. Light under a Bushel		4:21–25	8:16–18; 11:33	
116. Weeds among the Wheat	13:24–30			
117. The Growing Seed		4:26–29		
118. The Wheat and the Tares	13:24–30			
119. The Mustard Seed	13:31–32	4:30–32	13:18–19	
120. The Leaven	13:33		13:20–21	
121. The Use of Parables	13:34–35	4:33–34		
122. Interpretation of the Tares	13:36–43			
123. Pearl of Great Price	13:44–46			
124. Parable of the Great Net	13:47–50			
125. End of the Parable Sermon	13:51–52			
126. Rejection at Nazareth	13:53–58	6:1–6	4:16–30	7:1–9
127. Herod's Opinion of Christ	14:1–2	6:14–16		
128. Death of John the Baptist	14:1–12	6:14–29	9:7–9	
129. Feeding the Five Thousand	14:13–21	6:30–44	9:10–17	6:1–14
130. Walking on the Water	14:22–33	6:45–51		6:15–21
131. Healings at Gennesaret	14:34–36	6:53–56		

Chart 7-6 (6)

132. Traditions of the Jews	15:1–20	7:1–23		
133. The Gentile Woman	15:21–28	7:24–30		
134. Healing of a Deaf Mute		7:32–37		
135. Healing of Many Persons	15:29–31			
136. Feeding the Four Thousand	15:32–39	8:1–9		
137. *Demand for Signs of the Times*	*16:1–4*	*8:11–12*	*12:54–56*	
138. A Discourse on Leaven	16:5–12	8:14–21		
139. The True Bread of Life				6:22–58
140. Words of Eternal Life				6:60–71
141. Feast of the Tabernacles				7:10–24
142. Is This the Christ?				7:25–31
143. Officers Sent to Arrest Jesus				7:32–36
144. Rivers of Living Waters				7:37–39
145. Division among the People				7:40–44
146. Unbelief of the Popular Leaders				7:45–52
147. The Woman Taken in Adultery				8:3–11
148. Light of the World				8:12–20; 9:1–12
149. Healing a Man Born Blind				9:1–12
150. The Blind Man at Bethsaida		8:22–26		
151. Pharisees Investigate				9:13–34
152. *Thou Art the Christ*	*16:13–20*	*8:27–30*	*9:18–21*	
153. *First Prediction of the Passion*	*16:21–28*	*8:31–9:1*	*9:22–27*	

Chart 7-6 (7)

154. Where I Am Going You Cannot Come				8:21–30
155. Conditions of Discipleship	16:24–28	8:34–9:1		8:31–38
156. The Truth Shall Make You Free				8:32
157. Sons of the Devil				8:39–47
158. Before Abraham Was, I Am				8:48–59
159. *The Son of God Transfigured*	*17:1–13*	*9:2–13*	*9:28–36*	
160. The Coming of Elijah	17:10–13	9:11–13		
161. *Healing of an Epileptic Child*	*17:14–21*	*9:14–29*	*9:38–42*	
162. *Second Prophecy of the Passion*	*17:22–23*	*9:30–32*	*9:43–45*	
163. The Temple Tax	17:24–27			
164. *Dispute about Greatness*	*18:1–4*	*9:33–35*	*9:46–48; 22:24–30*	
165. The Strange Exorcist		9:38–41	9:49–50	
166. *About Taking Offense*	*18:6–10*	*9:42–48*	*17:1–2*	
167. Salt of the Earth, Purity		9:49–50		
168. The Lost Sheep	18:11–14		15:1–7	
169. Parable of the Sheepfold				10:1–6
170. Spiritual Blindness				9:35–41
171. The Good Shepherd				10:7–21
172. Christ Rejected by the Jews				10:22–42
173. On Reproving a Brother	18:15–20		17:3–4	
174. Parable of the Unmerciful Servant	18:21–35			
175. The Samaritan Villages			9:51–56	4:1–42
176. Mission of the Seventy			10:1–20	

Chart 7-6 (8)

177. Rejoicing of Jesus			10:21–24	
178. The Good Samaritan			10:25–37	
179. Visiting Mary and Martha			10:38–42	
180. Blessedness of Christ's Mother			11:27–28	
181. Warning against Hypocrisy			12:1–3	
182. Parable of the Rich Fool			12:13–21	
183. Repent or Perish			13:1–5	
184. Parable of the Barren Fig Tree			13:6–9	
185. Healing a Crippled Woman on the Sabbath			13:10–17	
186. Healing a Man with Dropsy			14:1–4	
187. A Lesson to Guests and Hosts			14:7–14	
188. Parable of the Lost Coin			15:8–10	
189. Parable of the Prodigal Son			15:11–32	
190. Parable of the Dishonest Steward			16:1–12	
191. Lazarus and the Rich Man			16:19–31	
192. Unprofitable Servants			17:5–10	
193. Cleansing of Ten Lepers			17:11–19	
194. Parable of the Widow and Judge			18:1–8	
195. Parable of the Pharisee and the Publican			18:9–14	
196. Marriage and Divorce	19:1–10	10:2–12		
197. *Suffer the Little Children*	*19:13–15*	*10:13–16*	*18:15–17*	
198. *The Rich Young Ruler*	*19:16–30*	*10:17–31*	*18:18–30*	
199. Parable of Laborers	20:1–16			

Chart 7-6 (9)

200. *The Third Prophecy of the Passion*	*20:17–19*	*10:32–34*	*18:31–34*	
201. Death of Lazarus				11:1–17
202. Resurrection and the Life				11:18–27
203. Jesus Weeps				11:28–37
204. Lazarus Raised				11:38–46
205. James and John	20:20–28	10:35–45		
206. *Healing Bartimaeus*	*20:29–34*	*10:46–52*	*18:35–43*	
207. Zacchaeus			19:2–10	
208. Parable of the Talents	25:14–30		19:11–27	
209. Plot against Lazarus				12:9–11
210. *The Triumphal Entry*	*21:1–11*	*11:1–11*	*19:28–38*	*12:12–19*
211. The Hour Is Come				12:20–26
212. Voice from Heaven				12:27–30
213. Christ to Be Lifted Up				12:27–36
214. The Unbelief of the Jews				12:36–43
215. Judgment by Jesus' Word				12:44–50
216. Prediction of Jerusalem's Fall			19:39–44	
217. Cursing the Fig Tree	21:18–22	11:12–14, 20–24		
218. *Cleansing the Temple*	*21:12–17*	*11:15–19*	*19:45–48*	*2:13–22*
219. *Lesson of the Fig Tree*	*21:20–22; 24:32–35*	*11:20–26; 13:28–31*	*21:29–33*	
220. *The Question about Authority*	*21:23–27*	*11:27–33*	*20:1–8*	
221. Parable of the Two Sons	21:28–32			
222. *Parable of the Wicked Husbandman*	*21:33–46*	*12:1–12*	*20:9–19*	

Chart 7-6 (10)

223. Parable of the Marriage Feast	22:1–14		14:16–24	
224. *Tribute to Caesar*	*22:15–22*	*12:13–17*	*20:20–26*	
225. *Question on Resurrection*	*22:23–33*	*12:18–27*	*20:27–40*	
226. *The Great Commandment*	*22:34–40*	*12:28–34*	*10:25–28*	
227. Washing the Disciples' Feet				13:1–20
228. *Jesus Foretells His Betrayal*	*26:20–25*	*14:17–21*	*22:21–23*	*13:21–30*
229. The New Commandment				13:31–35
230. *About David's Son*	*22:41–46*	*12:35–37*	*20:41–44*	
231. The Way to the Father				14:1–14
232. Promise of the Spirit				14:14–31
233. The True Vine				15:1–17
234. The World's Hatred				15:18–16:4
235. *Woes against the Scribes and Pharisees*	*23:1–36*	*12:38–40*	*11:39–52; 20:45–47*	
236. The Lament over Jerusalem	23:37–39		13:34–35	
237. The Widow's Mite		12:41–44	21:1–4	
238. Work of the Spirit				16:7–15
239. *Prophecy of the Temple's Destruction*	*24:1–2*	*13:1–2*	*21:5–6, 20–24*	
240. Sorrow Will Turn to Joy				16:16–24
241. I Have Overcome the World				16:25–33
242. *The Last Days*	*24:3–14*	*13:3–31*	*21:7–19*	
243. *The Need for Watchfulness*	*24:15–42*	*13:32–37*	*21:34–38*	
244. The Watchful Householder	24:43–44		12:35–40	
245. Coming of the Kingdom	24:23–28, 37–41		17:20–37	

Chart 7-6 (11)

246. *The Coming of the Son of Man*	24:29–31	13:24–27	21:25–28	
247. The Faithful Servant	24:45–51		12:41–48	
248. The Ten Virgins	25:1–13			
249. The Last Judgment	25:31–46			
250. *Plot to Kill Jesus*	26:1–5, 14–16	14:1–2, 10–11	22:1–2	11:46–57
251. Anointing at Bethany	26:1–13	14:3–9		12:1–8
252. *Betrayal by Judas*	26:14–16	14:10–11	22:3–6	18:1–3
253. *Preparations for Passover*	26:17–25	14:12–21	22:7–13	13:21–30
254. *The Last Supper*	26:17–30	14:12–26	22:7–23	13:21–30
255. The Great Prayer				17:1–26
256. *Peter's Denial Foretold*	26:31–35	14:27–31	22:31–34	13:36–38
257. Purse, Scrip, and Sword			22:35–38	
258. *To Gethsemane*	26:30	14:26	22:39	18:1
259. In Gethsemane	26:36–46	14:32–42	22:39–46	
260. *Jesus Arrested*	26:47–56	14:43–50	22:47–53	18:3–12
261. The Naked Young Man		14:51–52		
262. *Jesus before the Sanhedrin*	26:57–68	14:53–65	22:54–55, 63–71	18:13–14, 19–24
263. *Peter's Denial of Christ*	26:69–75	14:66–72	22:56–62	18:15–18, 25–27
264. Jesus before the High Priest				18:19–24
265. Peter's Second and Third Denial				18:25–27
266. *Mockery and Beating of Jesus*	26:67–68	14:65	22:63–65	
267. *Christ Delivered to Pilate*	27:1–2	15:1	23:1–2	18:28–32
268. Death of Judas	27:3–10			

Chart 7-6 (12)

269. *Trial before Pilate*	*27:11–14*	*15:2–5*	*23:3–5*	18:33–38
270. Christ before Herod			23:6–12	
271. *Jesus Sentenced to Die*	*27:15–26*	*15:6–15*	*23:13–25*	18:39–19:16
272. Mocking by Soldiers	27:27–31	15:16–20		19:2–3
273. *Road to Calvary*	*27:32*	*15:21*	*23:26–32*	
274. *The Crucifixion*	*27:32–44*	*15:21–32*	*23:26–43*	19:16–27
275. *Death on the Cross*	*27:45–56*	*15:33–41*	*23:44–49*	19:28–30
276. Piercing Jesus' Side				19:31–37
277. *Burial of Jesus*	*27:57–61*	*15:42–47*	*23:50–56*	19:38–42
278. Guard at the Tomb	27:62–66			
279. *The Resurrection*	*28:1–10*	*16:1–8*	*24:1–12*	20:1–10
280. Jesus Appears to Mary	28:9–10	16:9–11		20:11–18
281. The Bribed Guard's Report	28:11–15			
282. Appearance on the Road to Emmaus		16:12–13	24:13–35	
283. *Appearance to Ten Disciples*	*28:16–20*	*16:14–18*	*24:36–49*	20:19–23
284. Jesus and Thomas				20:24–29
285. Appearance to Eleven Disciples				20:24–26
286. Appearance to Seven Disciples				21:1–14
287. Jesus and Peter				21:15–19
288. Jesus and John				21:20–25
289. The Ascension of Jesus		16:19–20	24:50–53	
290. Purpose of this Book				20:30–31

Chart 7-6 (13)

Parables, Miracles, John the Baptist, and Disciples

Explanation

Special groupings of segments from the four Gospels are broken out for convenience in the next few charts. Was Jesus a sage who focused mainly on teaching, or was he primarily a man of action? The first two charts in this section show that he equally did both. The forty-nine main parables or metaphors spoken by Jesus are arrayed in chart 7-7, with the forty-two most impressive miracles that he performed, presented on chart 7-8. Jesus was Savior both in word and deed, and thus he praised any person who both "heareth these sayings of mine and doeth them" (Mt 7:24).

Passages on John the Baptist and his followers, most heavily reported in Luke, are shown on chart 7-9. Texts regarding the disciples or apostles of Jesus are listed on chart 7-10. As these charts demonstrate, John and Jesus attracted and instructed a strong group of devoted followers. Jesus organized his disciples into groups of twelve or seventy, and he sent them forth to do the works that he had shown them and to teach the words that he had given them.

References

John R. Donahue, *The Gospel in Parable: Metaphor, Narrative, and Theology in the Synoptic Gospels* (Philadelphia: Fortress, 1988).

Herman Hendrickx, *The Parables of Jesus* (London: Chapman, 1986).

Susan Howe, "Parables," *EM*, 3:1060–62.

Paul C. Hedengren, "Miracles," *EM*, 2:909–10.

Parables and Metaphors of Jesus

	MATTHEW	MARK	LUKE	JOHN
1. The Salt and Light	5:13–16; 6:22–23	9:50	14:34–35	
2. The Light of the Body	6:22–23		11:34–36	
3. Pearls before Swine	7:6			
4. The Narrow Gate	7:13–14, 21–23		13:22–30	
5. By Their Fruits	7:15–20; 12:34–35		6:43–45	
6. A House upon the Sand	7:24–28		6:46–49	
7. The Sheep without a Shepherd	9:36–38			
8. A Tree and Its Fruits	12:33–37			
9. Parable of the Sower	13:1–9	4:3–9	8:4–8	
10. The Sower Interpreted	13:18–23	4:13–20	8:11–15	
11. Light under a Bushel		4:21–25	8:16–18; 11:33	
12. The Growing Seed		4:26–29		
13. The Wheat and the Tares	13:24–30			
14. The Mustard Seed	13:31–32	4:30–32	13:18–19	
15. The Leaven	13:33		13:20–21	

Chart 7-7 (1)

16. Interpretation of the Tares	13:36–43			
17. The Pearl of Great Price	13:44–46			
18. Parable of the Great Net	13:47–50			
19. A Discourse on Leaven	16:5–12	8:14–21		6:26–58
20. The True Bread of Life				6:26–58
21. Rivers of Living Waters				7:37–39
22. The Light of the World				8:12–20; 9:1–12
23. Salt of the Earth — Purity		9:49–50		
24. The Lost Sheep	18:11–14		15:1–7	
25. Parable of the Sheepfold				10:1–6
26. The Good Shepherd				10:7–21
27. Parable of the Unmerciful Servant	18:21–35			
28. The Good Samaritan			10:25–37	
29. Parable of the Rich Fool			12:13–21	
30. Parable of the Barren Fig Tree			13:6–9	
31. Parable of the Lost Coin			15:8–10	
32. Parable of the Prodigal Son			15:11–32	
33. Parable of the Dishonest Steward			16:1–12	

Chart 7-7 (2)

34. Lazarus and the Rich Man			16:19–31	
35. Unprofitable Servants			17:5–10	
36. Parable of the Widow and the Judge			18:1–8	
37. Parable of the Pharisee and Publican			18:9–14	
38. Parable of Laborers	20:1–16			
39. Parable of the Talents	25:14–30		19:11–27	
40. The Grain of Wheat				12:24
41. The Light in Darkness				12:46–47
42. Lesson of the Fig Tree	21:20–22; 24:32–35	11:20–26; 13:28–31	21:29–33	
43. Parable of the Two Sons	21:28–32			
44. Parable of the Wicked Husbandman	21:33–46	12:1–12	20:9–19	
45. Parable of the Marriage Feast	22:1–14		14:16–24	
46. The True Vine				15:1–17
47. The Watchful Householder	24:43–44		12:35–40	
48. The Faithful Servant	24:45–51		12:41–48	
49. The Ten Virgins	25:1–13			

Chart 7-7 (3)

Miracles of Jesus

	MATTHEW	MARK	LUKE	JOHN
1. The Wedding of Cana				2:1–11
2. In the Synagogue at Capernaum		1:21–28	4:31–37	
3. Healing of Peter's Mother-in-law	8:14–15	1:29–31	4:38–39	
4. The Evening of Healing	8:16–17	1:32–34	4:40–41	
5. The Miraculous Catch of Fish			5:1–11	
6. Healing of a Leper	8:1–4	1:40–45	5:12–16	
7. Healing a Centurian's Servant	8:5–13		7:1–10	4:43–54
8. Raising the Widow's Son at Nain			7:11–17	
9. The Healing of Many People	8:14–17	1:29–34	4:38–41	
10. Stilling the Tempest	8:23–27	4:36–41	8:22–25	
11. The Gadarene Demoniacs	8:28–34	5:1–20	8:26–39	
12. Healing a Paralytic	9:1–8	2:1–12	5:17–26	
13. Jairus's Daughter	9:18–19, 23–26	5:21–24, 35–43	8:41–42, 49–56	
14. The Woman Who Touched Jesus	9:20–23	5:25–34	8:43–48	
15. Two Blind Men Healed	9:27–31			
16. A Dumb Man Healed	9:32–34			
17. The Compassion of Jesus	9:35–38			
18. Healing at the Pool of Bethesda				5:2–18
19. Healing a Withered Hand	12:9–14	3:1–6	6:6–11	

Chart 7-8 (1)

#	Event	Matthew	Mark	Luke	John
20.	The Chosen Healer–Servant	12:15–21			
21.	The Seaside Multitude		3:7–12		
22.	The Servant from Capernaum			7:1–10	
23.	A Sinful Woman Forgiven			7:36–50	
24.	Feeding the Five Thousand	14:13–21	6:30–44	9:10–17	6:1–13
25.	Walking on the Water	14:22–33	6:45–51		6:15–21
26.	Healings at Gennesaret	14:34–36	6:53–56		
27.	The Syrophoenician Woman	15:21–28	7:24–30		
28.	Healing of a Deaf Mute		7:32–37		
29.	The Healing of Many Persons	15:29–31			
30.	Feeding the Four Thousand	15:32–39	8:1–9		
31.	Healing a Man Born Blind				9:1–12
32.	The Blind Man at Bethsaida		8:22–26		
33.	Healing of an Epileptic Child	17:14–18	9:14–27	9:38–42	
34.	Healing a Crippled Woman on the Sabbath			13:10–17	
35.	Healing a Man with Dropsy			14:1–4	
36.	Cleansing of Ten Lepers			17:11–19	
37.	Lazarus Raised				11:38–46
38.	Healing Bartimaeus	20:29–34	10:46–52	18:35–43	
39.	The Voice from Heaven				12:27–30
40.	Jesus Arrested, Servant's Ear Healed	26:47–56	14:43–50	22:47–53	18:3–12
41.	The Resurrection	28:1–10	16:1–8	24:1–12	20:1–10
42.	The Ascension of Jesus		16:19–20	24:50–53	

Chart 7-8 (2)

Passages on John the Baptist

	MATTHEW	MARK	LUKE	JOHN
1. The Birth of John Foretold			1:5–25	
2. The Birth of John			1:57–63	
3. Prophecy about John's ministry			1:76–79	
4. The Preaching of John	3:1–12	1:1–8	3:2–18	1:6–8, 15–28
5. John's Sociological Teaching			3:10–14	
6. John's Messianic Preaching	3:11–12		3:15–18	1:19–28
7. John's Imprisonment	14:3–5	6:17–19	3:19–20	
8. The Lamb of God				1:29–34
9. Messengers from John the Baptist	11:2–19		7:19–23	
10. Christ's Testimony of John			7:24–35	3:22–30
11. The Death of John the Baptist	14:1–12	6:14–29	9:7–9	

Chart 7-9

Passages on the Apostles, Disciples, and Followers of Christ

	MATTHEW	MARK	LUKE	JOHN
1. The Call of the First Disciples	4:18–22	1:16–20	5:1–11	1:35–51
2. Would-be Followers	8:18–22		9:57–62	
3. Matthew and Tax Collecting	9:9–13	2:13–17	5:27–32	
4. Calling the Twelve	10:1–4	3:13–19	6:12–16	
5. The Mission of the Twelve	10:1–16	6:7–13	9:1–6	
6. Conditions of Discipleship	10:37–38		14:26–33	
7. Rewards of Discipleship	10:40–11:1	9:41		
8. Women Ministering to Jesus			8:2–3	
9. The Brothers of Jesus	12:46–50	3:31–35	8:19–21	2:12
10. Blessedness of Discipleship	13:16–17		10:23–24	
11. Thou Art the Christ	16:13–20	8:27–30	9:18–21	
12. The Conditions of Discipleship	16:24–28	8:34–9:1		8:31–38
13. The Mission of the Seventy			10:1–20	
14. Visiting Mary and Martha			10:38–42	
15. The Rich Young Ruler	19:16–30	10:17–31	18:18–30	
16. The Death of Lazarus				11:1–17
17. James and John	20:20–28	10:35–45		
18. Zacchaeus			19:2–9	
19. Peter's Denial Foretold	26:31–35	14:27–31	22:31–34	13:36–38
20. The Naked Young Man		14:51–52		
21. Peter's Denial of Christ	26:69–75	14:66–72	22:56–62	18:15–18, 25–27
22. Peter's Second and Third Denial				18:25–27
23. Jesus Appears to Mary	28:9–10	16:9–11		20:11–18
24. Appearance to Ten Disciples	28:16–20	16:14–18	24:36–49	20:19–23
25. Jesus and Thomas				20:24–29
26. Appearance to Eleven Disciples				20:24–26
27. Appearance to Seven Disciples				21:1–14
28. Jesus and Peter				21:15–19
29. Jesus and John				21:20–25

Chart 7-10

The Garden Tomb near Golgatha outside the old city walls of Jerusalem. Photo by John W. Welch

SECTION 8

The Divine Redeemer

Jesus Affirms His Divinity
with the Greek Words ἐγώ εἰμί (I AM)

Explanation

An important feature of the Greek Gospels is the use of the Greek words ἐγώ εἰμί, ego eimi, "I am." These words are used predominantly in John, but they also occur at significant moments in Matthew, Mark, and Luke as well.

When Moses asked God on Mount Sinai, "When they shall say to me, What is his name? What shall I say unto them?", the answer was "I am that I am" (Ex 3:13–14). The Greek version of the Old Testament, widely used in Jesus' day, rendered this text "ἐγώ εἰμί ὁ Ὤν." A similar divine usage is found several places in the Hebrew Bible and in Jewish messianic literature. Thus, when Jesus repeatedly identified himself with these words, his audiences could well have understood that he was affirming his divine identity as the Lord God of Israel.

This chart lists the passages in the Greek that contain the words ἐγώ εἰμί, most of which are in the Gospel of John. Interestingly, Matthew, Mark, and John record this phrase in connection with Jesus' miraculous walking on the water and stilling the storm. Mark emphasizes these words in the pointed answer of Jesus to his accusers who had asked, "Are you the Messiah" (Mk 14:61), just as John preserves them in the open declaration of Jesus to the Samaritan woman at the well. Luke reserves it exclusively for Jesus' final announcement when he appeared to his apostles after his resurrection and Paul consistently testifies that Jesus identified himself this way on the road to Damascus.

Reference

Raymond E. Brown, trans., *The Gospel According to John* (Garden City, N.Y.: Doubleday, 1966), 1:533–38.

Jesus Affirms His Divinity
with the Greek Words ἐγώ εἰμί (I AM)

It *is* I (ἐγώ εἰμί); be not afraid.	Mt 14:27; Mk 6:50; Jn 6:20
I am (ἐγώ εἰμί).	Mk 14:62; Mk 15:4 JST
Ye say that *I am*.	Lk 22:70
It *is* I (ἐγώ εἰμί) myself.	Lk 24:39
The woman saith unto him, I know that Messias cometh, which is called Christ: Jesus saith unto her, *I* that speak unto thee *am he* (ἐγώ εἰμί).	Jn 4:25–26
I am the bread of life.	Jn 6:35
I am the light of the world.	Jn 8:12
I am one that bear witness of myself.	Jn 8:18
If ye believe not that *I am* he, ye shall die in your sins.	Jn 8:24
When ye have lifted up the Son of man, then shall ye know that *I am* he.	Jn 8:28
Before Abraham was born, *I am*.	Jn 8:58
I am the door of the sheep.	Jn 10:7
I am the good shepherd.	Jn 10:11
I am the resurrection and the life.	Jn 11:25
I am the way, the truth, and the life.	Jn 14:6
I am the true vine.	Jn 15:1
I am the vine.	Jn 15:5
I am he.	Jn 18:5, 8
And the Lord said, *I am* (ἐγώ εἰμί) Jesus.	Acts 9:5
And he said unto me, *I am* Jesus of Nazareth.	Acts 22:8
And I said, Who art thou, Lord? And he said, *I am* Jesus.	Acts 26:15

Chart 8-1

Chart 8-2

Witnesses of Jesus' Divinity

Explanation

The New Testament contains numerous witnesses of the divine status or divine mission of Jesus Christ. In addition to the many miraculous deeds and fulfillment of prophecies that demonstrate that Jesus is the Christ and Son of God, these sacred records contain many direct verbal declarations of this crucial truth. This chart lists the main instances of open acknowledgment that Jesus is the Holy One, the Lord, the Son of the living God, the Messiah and Savior. These testimonies are borne by God the Father, Jesus himself, the chief apostle Peter, and the other apostles, including Paul.

Reference

"Birth," "Childhood," and "Christology," *WRC*, 3–10.

Witnesses of Jesus' Divinity

BY GOD

"This is my beloved Son, in whom I am well pleased." (Mt 3:17; 17:5; Mk 1:11; 9:7; Lk 3:22; 9:35)

BY JESUS

The Jews sought the more to kill him, because he … said also that God was his Father, making himself equal with God. (Jn 5:18)

"The Father that sent me beareth witness of me." (Jn 8:18)

"Who is [the Son of God], that I might believe on him?" And Jesus said unto him, "Thou hast both seen him, and it is he that talketh with thee." (Jn 9:35–38)

"I and my Father are one." (Jn 10:30)

I said, "I am the Son of God." (Jn 10:36)

"I am in the Father, and the Father in me." (Jn 14:10–11)

"I am in my Father." (Jn 14:20)

He made himself the Son of God. (Jn 19:7)

BY PETER

He saith unto them, "But whom say ye that I am?" And Simon Peter answered and said, "Thou art the Christ, the Son of the living God." (Mt 16:15–17)

"God hath made this same Jesus, whom ye have crucified, both Lord and Christ." (Acts 2:36)

"The God of Abraham, and of Isaac, and of Jacob, the God of our fathers, hath glorified his Son Jesus." (Acts 3:13)

"But ye denied the Holy One and the Just, … and killed the Prince of life." (Acts 3:14–15)

"God raised up his Son Jesus." (Acts 3:26)

"Jesus Christ is Lord of all." (Acts 10:36)

BY PETER AND THE APOSTLES

"Him hath God exalted with his right hand to be a Prince and a Saviour." (Acts 5:31)

BY PAUL

"This Jesus, whom I preach to you, is Christ." (Acts 17:3)

Shewing by the scriptures that Jesus was Christ. (Acts 18:28)

Chart 8-2

Chart 8-3

Statements by Heavenly Beings

Explanation

Modern secular minds discount the existence of angels or other heavenly beings. Yet the New Testament is full of references to them. Chart 8-3 lists the many occasions on which divine beings or celestial messengers delivered to men and women specific words of joy or knowledge emanating from the presence of God. On thirty-six occasions, such statements came from the angel Gabriel, other angels, God the Father, the risen Lord, the Holy Ghost, or a Macedonian man in a vision to Paul.

Reference

Russell M. Nelson, "Life after Life," *Ensign,* May 1987, 8–10.

Statements by Heavenly Beings

THE ANGEL GABRIEL

1. Tells Zacharias that Elisabeth will give birth to John the Baptist. He is to be consecrated to the Lord and will prepare the way for the Messiah. Zacharias is struck dumb because he disbelieves Gabriel. (Lk 1:13–20)

2. Tells Mary she is to conceive by the Holy Ghost and give birth to the Savior. (Lk 1:28, 30–33, 35–37)

ANGEL(S)

3. Angels announce the birth of the Savior to shepherds near Bethlehem. (Lk 2:10–12,14)

4. An angel tells Joseph not to put Mary away, because the child she carries is of the Holy Ghost. He is the Savior and is to be called Jesus. (Mt 1:20–23)

5. An angel warns Joseph to take Mary and Jesus into Egypt to escape from Herod. (Mt 2:13)

6. An angel tells Joseph to return with Mary and Jesus to Israel. (Mt 2:19–20)

7. Angels greet Mary Magdalene at the tomb of Christ. (Jn 20:13)

8. Angels tell the women at the tomb that Jesus is risen. (Mt 28:5–7; Mk 16:15–18; Lk 24:5–7)

9. "Ye men of Galilee, why stand ye gazing up into heaven? this same Jesus, which is taken up from you into heaven, shall so come in like manner as ye have seen him go into heaven." (Acts 1:11)

10. "Go, stand and speak in the temple to the people all the words of this life." (Acts 5:20)

11. "Arise, and go toward the south unto the way that goeth down from Jerusalem unto Gaza, which is desert." (Acts 8:26)

Chart 8-3 (1)

12. Cornelius's prayer is heard and he is instructed to send for Peter to learn the Gospel. (Acts 10:31–32)

13. An angel frees Peter from prison. (Acts 12:7–8)

14. "Fear not, Paul; thou must be brought before Caesar: and, lo, God hath given thee all them that sail with thee." (Acts 27:24)

THE FATHER FROM HEAVEN

15. Voice of God at the baptism and transfiguration of Jesus. (Mt 3:17; 17:5; Mk 1:11; 9:7; Lk 3:22; 9:35)

16. "I have both glorified [my name], and will glorify it again." (Jn 12:28)

THE RISEN LORD

17. Christ greets Mary Magdalene outside his empty tomb. (Jn 20:15–17)

18. Christ shows himself to Thomas and the rest of the apostles. (Jn 20:26–29)

19. Disciples are instructed to tell the brethren that Christ will meet them in Galilee. (Mt 28:9–10)

20. Apostles of Christ must teach and baptize in the name of the Father, Son, and Holy Ghost. (Mt 28:18–20; Mk 16:15–18)

21. Christ teaches his disciples on the road to Emmaus concerning his resurrection. (Lk 24:17, 19, 25–26)

22. Christ shows himself unto the Ten apostles. (Lk 24:36–49; Jn 20:19, 21)

23. Christ instructs his disciples how to cast their nets in order to catch fish. (Jn 21:5–12)

24. "Lovest thou me more than these?… Feed my sheep." (Jn 21:15–17)

Chart 8-3 (2)

25. Christ prophesies the martyrdoms of the apostles. (Jn 21:18–19)

26. "Follow me." (Jn 21:19)

27. "If I will that he tarry till I come, what is that to thee? follow thou me." (Jn 21:22)

28. The apostles shall receive the Holy Ghost and witness of Christ to the ends of the earth. (Acts 1:7–8)

29. "Saul, Saul, why persecutest thou me?... I am Jesus whom thou persecutest: it is hard for thee to kick against the pricks." (Acts 9:4–6; 26:14–18)

30. Ananias is called to heal and baptize Saul. (Acts 9:10–12, 15–16)

31. "Rise, Peter; kill, and eat.... What God hath cleansed, that call not thou common." (Acts 10:13, 15)

32. "Be not afraid, but speak, and hold not thy peace: For I am with thee, and no man shall set on thee to hurt thee: for I have much people in this city." (Acts 18:9–10)

33. "Be of good cheer, Paul: for as thou hast testified of me in Jerusalem, so must thou bear witness also at Rome." (Acts 23:11)

THE HOLY GHOST	34. Paul is to be bound and imprisoned when he goes to Jerusalem. (Acts 21:11)
	35. Barnabas and Saul are called as missionaries. (Acts 13:2)
A MAN IN A VISION	36. "Come over into Macedonia, and help us." (Acts 16:9)

Chart 8-3 (3)

Chart 8-4

Dating the Birth of Christ

Explanation

The year of the Savior's birth was a matter of controversy in ancient times and remains so today. If the date was known to the friends and associates of Jesus, that knowledge appears to have been lost. By the sixth century the question had become sufficiently pressing to prompt Pope John I to commission a leading scholar of the day, the Scythian monk, Dionysius Exiguus, to determine the year of Christ's birth. Dionysus' researches led him to conclude that Jesus was born in the Roman year 753. By papal decree the Roman dating system was abandoned and the year 753 was renumbered as A.D. 1. That present year of 1278 became the year A.D. 525.

Whether Dionysius was correct in his calculation remains a matter of some dispute, particularly as certain events mentioned in connection with Christ's birth can now be accurately dated through Roman epigraphic and historical records known in modern times, for example, the death of Herod in the year 749 (4 B.C.). Chart 8-4 lists the events for which dates are known or can be conjectured.

The Church of Jesus Christ of Latter-day Saints has not taken an official position on the issue of the year of Christ's birth. Bruce R. McConkie, an apostle, offered what for the present appears to be the most definitive word on the question: "We do not believe it is possible with the present state of our knowledge—including that which is known both in and out of the church—to state with finality when the natal day of the Lord Jesus actually occurred" (*Mortal Messiah,* [Salt Lake City: Deseret Book, 1979–81], 1:349 n. 2).

References

John F. Hall, "April Sixth," *EM,* 1:61–62.

S. Kent Brown, et al., "Book Review of Lefgren's April 6," *BYU Studies* 22 (1982): 375–83.

J. Pratt, "Afterwords: Letter to the Editor," *BYU Studies* 23 (1983): 252–54.

W. E. Filmer, "The Chronology of the Reign of Herod the Great," *Journal of Theological Studies* 17 (1966): 283–98.

H. W. Hoehner, *Chronological Aspects of the Life of Christ* (Grand Rapids: Zondervan, 1977).

Spencer W. Kimball, "Remarks and Dedication of the Fayette, New York, Buildings," *Ensign,* May 1980, 54.

Dating the Birth of Christ

In the Roman year 1278 (A.D. 525), Pope John I commissioned the Scythian monk Dionysius Exiguus to discover through research the year Christ was born. Dionysius concluded the birth occurred in the year 753. New names were then assigned to the years so that 753 became A.D. 1. By examining events related to Jesus' early life, it can be determined whether Dionysius was correct in his dating.

HEROD

Matthew (2:1) and Luke (1:5) place the birth of Christ during the reign of Herod, king of Judea. Both contemporary inscriptions and historical writings date the death of Herod to the Roman year 749 (4 B.C.).

THE WISE MEN AND THE STAR

Matthew's account (2:1–12) has the Wise Men come to Judea to find the king whose birth was heralded by the astral portent of a "star." A triple planetary conjunction of Jupiter, Saturn, and Mars in 7/6 B.C., or a supernova in 5 B.C. may account for the astronomical wonder looked for by the Wise Men.

CENSUS OF AUGUSTUS

Luke (2:1–3) reports that Augustus Caesar decreed the world to be "taxed" (census to be taken) when Quirinius was governor of Syria. Quirinius's governorship began in A.D. 6. Augustus initiated censuses in 28 B.C., 8 B.C., and A.D. 14. It is possible that Luke confused Quirinius with Quinctilius, governor of Syria from 7–4 B.C., and that Augustus's 8 B.C. census began or continued in eastern provinces into 7 or 6 B.C.

SLAUGHTER OF THE INNOCENTS

Matthew (2:1–23) reports that Herod slew all the children in Bethlehem under *two* years of age and that Christ was not brought back from Egypt to Judea until after the death of Herod. The account suggests some time, perhaps as much as two years, passed between the birth of Christ and the death of Herod.

Chart 8-4

The Birth of Jesus:
A Noble King or a Lowly Shepherd?

Explanation

At Christmastime, the accounts of the birth of Jesus in Matthew and Luke are joyously celebrated. The universal appeal of this story derives from many spiritual sources. The hopes and fears of all the years are concentrated together in Christ that night.

As shown in charts 7-2 and 7-3, the New Testament Gospels take different approaches in proclaiming the eternal message of the gospel of Jesus Christ. Those differences manifest themselves in the birth narratives of Matthew and Luke.

Matthew's purpose is to show that Jesus is the promised Messiah and King of Israel, and so his account of the birth of Jesus is filled with regal elements; the male and kingly predominate, with attention focused on Joseph, King Herod the Great, impressive wise men, Chief Priests, government, rulership, gold, swords, intrigue, and other such factors.

Luke's purpose, on the other hand, is to show that Jesus was the Savior of all mankind, bringing peace on earth. Accordingly, his account is populated with humble elements; the female and commonplace predominate, with attention placed on Mary, youth, piety, subjection, shepherds, salvation, peace, all mankind, and openness before God and the world.

The dynamic tension between these two accounts invites people from all stations in life into this story. The two are not mutually exclusive but reciprocally enhancing. Did Jesus come as a noble king or lowly shepherd? Like King David, in whose town Jesus was born, he was both. The Alpha and the Omega embraces and harmonizes both ends of the spectrum.

Reference

Raymond E. Brown, *The Birth of the Messiah* (New York: Doubleday, 1977).

The Birth of Jesus:
A Noble King or a Lowly Shepherd?

MATTHEW'S ACCOUNT	LUKE'S ACCOUNT
An account filled with royal elements	An account emphasizing humble beginnings
Emphasis on Joseph's protection	Emphasis on Mary's nurturing
Born in Bethlehem of Judea, then a powerful kingdom	Born in the city of David, where as a youth David had been a shepherd
During the days of "Herod the king," known for his grand style	During the days of Augustus Caesar, known for his pious goodness
Unstated why they were in Bethlehem	In Bethlehem as tax subjects
Important Wise Men visit him	No Wise Men are mentioned
No shepherds are mentioned	Humble shepherds visit him
The magi are from the East, exotic, learned	The shepherds are from the same country, ordinary, simple
They seek the King of the Jews	They seek a Savior, who is Christ the Lord
Chief Priests rely on interpretation of prophecies to tell where he was born	Shepherds rely on the angel to learn where he was to be found
He will be a "Governor" and rule Israel	He will be a Savior of peace and good will
A star told the time and place of birth, standard omen of a portentous royal birth	The star is not mentioned, the glory of God shone all around and made them afraid
The Wise Men worshiped him	The shepherds praised God
They gave him gold, frankincense, myrrh	No gifts or treasures mentioned
They found him in a house	They found him in a manger
The holy family departed in secret	The shepherds made it known abroad
Babies killed by Herod	The baby circumcised openly at the temple
Joseph kept the matter secret	Mary kept all these things in her heart

Chart 8-5

Lineages of Joseph

Explanation

Chart 8-6 offers comparative stemma of the genealogy of Joseph, known as the legal father of Jesus, as differently depicted in the Gospels of Matthew and Luke. These genealogies serve different purposes: Matthew's demonstrates the Abrahamic descent of Jesus as heir of David; Luke emphasizes that Jesus was the son of God through Adam. Accordingly, Matthew's genealogy descends from Abraham, while Luke's ascends from Jesus and Joseph to Adam and God. Since Luke includes the pre–Abrahamic era, his list of ancestors is much longer, seventy-seven names compared to forty-one in Matthew. However, even in the periods where names overlap, Luke lists fifty-six names to Matthew's forty-one. From the time of David on, the genealogies are quite separate and intersect only on several occasions as is readily apparent with perusal of the chart.

This discrepancy has usually been explained by scholars in two ways. Some say that the lineage given by Matthew is that of Joseph, while the lineage found in Luke could be that of Mary. On the other hand, the more prevalent view among scholars today is that Matthew provides an official genealogy of the Davidic heir to which the names of Joseph and Jesus were attached. The parallel periods of fourteen names each, which Matthew is careful to point out, suggests something of the sort. By contrast, Luke's account is held to reveal the actual ancestors of Joseph who, while being descendants of David, were not the actual heirs to the throne.

References

Raymond E. Brown, *The Birth of the Messiah* (New York: Doubleday, 1977), 57–95.
Joachim Jeremias, *Jerusalem in the Time of Jesus* (Philadelphia: Fortress, 1969), 275–97.
James E. Talmage, *Jesus the Christ* (Salt Lake City: Deseret Book, 1984), 85–87.

Lineages of Joseph
according to (Matthew) and ⟨Luke⟩

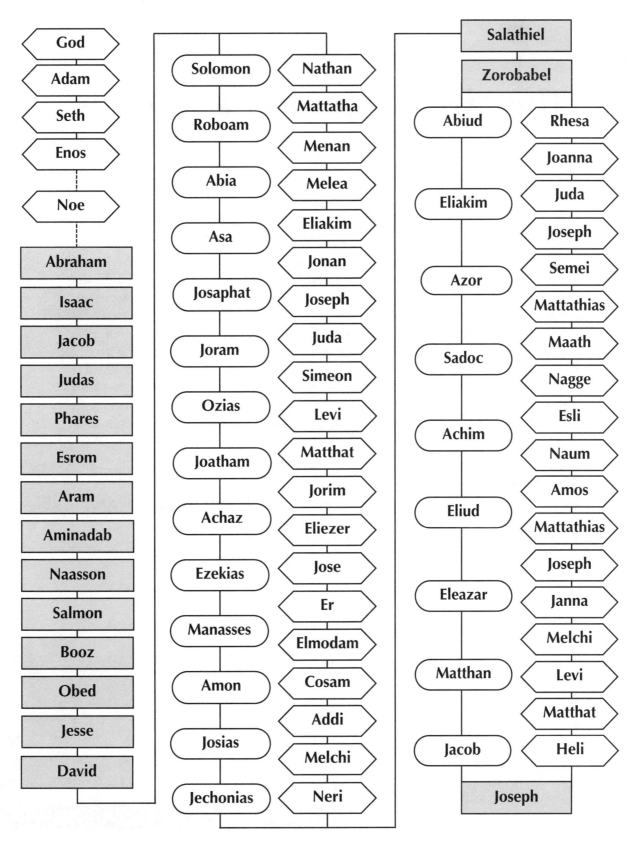

Chart 8-6

Chart 8-7

The Lives of Joseph and Jesus

Explanation

The fact that Jesus was raised under the guardianship of Joseph takes readers back to another Joseph who became an important ruler in Egypt and saved the children of Israel from severe famine. Early Christian writers, especially in the Syriac tradition that grew out of the fledgling congregations at Antioch and Damascus, drew many parallels between the lives of Joseph and Jesus. Both were "shepherds." Both held the birthright. Both were "sold" by brethren. Both were tempted. Both forgave. This chart lists many interesting parallels. Most of them date to sources from early Christian times; others have been newly added or clarified. Some may be fanciful or tenuous, but all contribute to seeing Joseph in Egypt as a type or shadow of Jesus. Because patterns of righteousness are stable and enduring, the exemplary deeds and behavior of all great men and women of God share many common qualities and features.

References

Kristian Heal, "Joseph as a Type of Christ in Syriac Literature," *BYU Studies* 41/1 (2002): 29–49.

Joseph Fielding McConkie, "Joseph of Egypt: Joseph, Son of Jacob," *EM,* 2:760–61.

The Lives of Joseph and Jesus

LIFE OF JOSEPH AS RECOUNTED IN GENESIS	PARALLELS THROUGHOUT THE LIFE OF JESUS
Was a shepherd (Gen 37:2)	The Good Shepherd (Jn 10:11)
Was the son with the birthright (37:3; 43:33)	Was the firstborn Son of God
Was beloved of his father (37:3)	Was the beloved of the Father (Mt 3:17)
His father clothed him in a coat (37:3)	The Father clothed him in a body (Lk 1:35)
Lived with his father in honor before going down to Egypt (37:2–4)	Lived with God before coming to earth (Jn 1:2)
Dreamed dreams but was despised for his prophecies (37:5–11)	Spoke in prophecies but was despised for his prophetic knowledge (Mt 26:68)
Sent by his father to inquire about his brothers (37:13–14)	Sent by his Father to save us all (Jn 3:16)
When his brothers saw him, they said, "Behold, this dreamer cometh.… Come, let us slay him,… and we shall see what shall become of his dreams" (37:18–20)	When the husbandmen saw him they said, "This is the heir to the vineyard. Come, let us kill him, and henceforth the inheritance will be ours" (Mt 21:38; Mk 12:7; Lk 20:14)
Reuben petitioned for the life of Joseph (37:21–22)	Pilate petitioned for the life of Jesus (Mt 27:2–26; Jn 19:4–22)
Was incarcerated twice: the pit and prison	Was enclosed twice: the flesh and the grave
His brothers cast him into a pit (37:24)	His brothers cast him in the grave
His brothers, while eating, intended to slay him (37:25–27)	The Jews, while eating the Passover feast, desired that he be killed
Sold into Egypt at the proposal of Judah (37:26–27)	Sold to the Jews by Judas (Mt 27:3)
Rose up from the pit (37:28)	Rose up from the grave
When his brothers sold him, he said nothing (37:28)	Did not speak a word to judges who judged him
His coat was dipped in the blood of a goat (37:31)	His garment was dipped in blood (Rev 19:13)
His cloak was soaked with blood but his flesh was not harmed at all (37:32)	His flesh was seized but not his divinity

Chart 8-7 (1)

LIFE OF JOSEPH AS RECOUNTED IN GENESIS	PARALLELS THROUGHOUT THE LIFE OF JESUS
Potiphar's wife tempted him unsuccessfully (39:11–12)	Satan tempted him unsuccessfully (Mt 4:8–9)
Potiphar's wife grabbed his clothes, but he escaped (39:13)	His executioners grabbed his garment, but his flesh ascended
Avoided sin yet thrust to prison unjustly (39:16–20)	Conquered sin yet condemned to a tomb unjustly
Thrown into the pit and into prison naked	Hung upon the cross naked (Mt 27:28)
Entered into prison and comforted those who were captive (39:20–23; 40:6–8)	Entered into spirit prison and comforted those there (1 Pt 3:19)
Had the keys to the prison (39:22)	Has the keys to release the dead (Rev 1:18)
Interpreted the dreams of the servants of Pharaoh—the chief butler would return to the courts of Pharaoh, while the chief baker would be hanged (40:1–23)	Told one thief he would join him in paradise, while he left the other thief to be punished (Lk 23:39–43)
Another prisoner (the butler) was released in his stead (40:21–23)	Another prisoner (Barabbas) was released in his stead (Jn 18:40)
In prison for two years (41:1)	In the tomb for two nights
Was brought out from prison on Pharaoh's order, easily interpreted the dreams, and provided the solution to save Pharaoh's people (41:14–37)	Was raised from the dead, proclaiming resurrection and everlasting life, offering to the Father our salvation
Interpreted dreams for the Egyptians and they believed him (41:14–37)	The disciples believed his prophecies, parables, miracles
Interpreted Pharaoh's dreams correctly (41:14–43)	His prophecies were and are fulfilled
Pharaoh clothed him in glorious robes (41:42)	Will be seen clothed in glory at the second coming (Mt 24:30; 25:31)
Took his seat in Pharaoh's chariot and sat upon the throne and was king over all Egypt (41:43)	Ascended into heaven on a cloud of light, took his seat with glory at the Father's right hand (Acts 7:55)
Married the daughter of an Egyptian (41:45)	Took to himself the church from the gentile nations
Was thirty years old when he stood before Pharaoh and became a lord over Egypt (41:46)	Was thirty years old when he was baptized in the Jordan River

Chart 8-7 (2)

LIFE OF JOSEPH AS RECOUNTED IN GENESIS	PARALLELS THROUGHOUT THE LIFE OF JESUS
Went throughout the land to save the people from famine (41:46, 48)	Went out among the people during his ministry to feed and save them
Provided the Egyptians and all countries with bread (41:56–57)	Provided the whole world with the bread of life (Jn 6:48–57)
Purchased the whole of Egypt with bread (41:56)	Purchased the whole of creation with his body
His persecutors bowed and worshiped him (42:6)	Those who persecuted and crucified him will realize who he is and will bow and worship him
After he came up from the pit/prison, he ruled over his brothers	After he rose from the grave, his brothers were subject to him
Judged his judges and cast into prison those who had put him to shame in the pit (42:24)	Will judge those who crucified him (Mt 25:32)
Fed his hungry brothers (43:31–34)	Fed the hungry masses (Jn 6:5–13)
As they ate and drank at his table in his kingdom, he judged the twelve tribes of Israel	"That ye may eat and drink at my table in my kingdom, and sit on thrones judging the twelve tribes of Israel" (Lk 22:30)
As their sovereign, he forgave his brothers	As the Sovereign, he forgave those who crucified him (Lk 23:34)
Revealed himself to his brothers in the chamber (45:1–3)	Revealed himself to his disciples in the upper room (Lk 24:36)
The brothers recognized him on the second occasion	All will recognize and know him at the second coming
When he revealed himself to his brothers they were ashamed and afraid and marveled at his majesty (45:3)	When he is revealed in his majesty at the second coming, his persecutors will be ashamed and afraid
Sent to Egypt by God to preserve the life of his people (45:5–7)	Sent to earth by God to provide everlasting life for all (Mt 27:3–5)
His bones were taken up from Egypt to the promised land (Ex 13:19)	Was resurrected and raised to heaven
Dishonored by men and honored by God	Dishonored by men and honored by God (Jn 5:44)

Chart 8-7 (3)

Moses as a Similitude of Christ

Explanation

Several striking similarities exist between the ministry of Jesus and the life of Moses. Expanding beyond the typology of Joseph (see chart 8-7), parallels between Moses and Jesus have long been noted by Christian scholars and artists. The Gospel of Matthew, in particular, presents Jesus as a new Moses: both came out of Egypt, both spent forty years (or days) in the wilderness, and both delivered commandments and a covenant from a mountain. The basic elements shown in chart 8-8 can be expanded to include other events in the lives of Moses and Jesus, including the working the miracles, the feeding of multitudes, and their experiences of transfiguring theophanies.

Such elements corroborate the understanding that Jesus was a "prophet-like-Moses," as God himself had told Moses he would some day send: "I will raise them up a Prophet from among their brethren, like unto thee" (Deut 18:18; compare 1Ne 21:20; 3Ne 20:23; D&C 133:63). The Sistine Chapel in Rome, most famous for its ceiling, also features a row of six exquisite paintings along the top of one wall depicting scenes from the life of Moses, with six matching paintings on the opposite wall showing parallel scenes in the life of Christ. These elements show that Jesus, the giver of the law, did not come to destroy the law, but to fulfill it (Mt 5:17).

References

Dale C. Allison Jr., *The New Moses: A Matthean Typology* (Edinburgh: T&T Clark, 1993; Minneapolis: Fortress, 1993).

W. D. Davies, *The Sermon on the Mount* (Cambridge: Cambridge University Press, 1966), 10–32.

Frank F. Judd Jr., "Jesus as the New Moses in the Gospel of Matthew" (master's thesis, Brigham Young University, n.d.).

Andrew C. Skinner, "Moses," *EM*, 2:958–59.

Moses as a Similitude of Christ

Escaped being killed as a baby when the decree of a king (Pharaoh) had condemned all male infants to death (Ex 1:8–22)	Escaped being killed as a baby when the decree of a king (Herod) had condemned all male infants to death (Mt 2:1–16)
Was not an Egyptian, but lived among Egyptians (who preserved his life) when an infant (Ex 2:1–10)	Was not an Egyptian, but lived among Egyptians (who preserved his life) when an infant (Mt 2:13–15)
Was raised with the legal right to become a king but belonged to a nation (Israel) oppressed by a pagan and foreign government (Egypt)	Was raised with the legal right to become a king but belonged to a nation (Judah-Israel) ruled by a pagan and foreign government (Rome)
Freed his people from slavery through a "lamb … without blemish, a male of the first year" (Ex 12:5)	Freed his people from sin through his own blood, being the "lamb of God" without blemish (Jn 1:29; 1Pt 1:19)
Came out of Egypt (Ex 13:8–9)	Returned out of Egypt (Mt 2:14–15)
Passed through the Red Sea (Ex 14:21–28)	Passed through the waters of baptism (Mt 3:13–16)
Spent forty years in wilderness (Deut 8:2)	Spent forty days in wilderness (Mt 4:1–2; Mk 1:13; Lk 4:1–2)
Fasted for forty days and forty nights (Ex 24:17–18; Deut 9:9)	Fasted for forty days and forty nights (Mt 4:1–2)
While in the wilderness, was administered to by angels and was tempted (Ex 23:20–23; 17:2, 7)	While in the wilderness, was administered to by angels and was tempted (Mk. 1:12–13; Mt 4:8–11)
Gave the law from a mountain (Ex 19–24)	Gave the new law from a mountain (Mt 5–7)

Chart 8-8

Chart 8-9

Prophecies of Christ's Ministry
in the Meridian of Time

Explanation

The advent of the Savior was indisputably the most important event ever associated with this world. His coming to a particular place and at a particular time when the circumstances were in place to allow the triumph of his atoning mission is not only recognizable in retrospect but served as the subject of numerous, though varied, prophecies. Such prophecies related not only to his birth and mission but also to specific details of his ministry and death. These revelations were given beginning in the earliest epoch and continuing down to the very night before his birth. Prophets in all dispensations, in the Old and New Worlds, declared the coming and the atonement of the Son of God. Chart 8-9 enumerates these prophecies and categorizes them in topical groupings.

References

D. Kelly Ogden and R. Val Johnson, "All the Prophets Prophesied of Christ," *Ensign*, January 1994, 31–37.

Gary Lee Walker, "Jesus Christ: Prophecies about Jesus Christ," *EM*, 2:726–28.

Prophecies of Christ's Ministry
in the Meridian of Time

PROPHECIES	PERSONS SPEAKING/WRITING	REFERENCES
HIS BIRTH		
Jehovah, the Creator of heaven and earth, would take a mortal body in order to redeem mankind	Brother of Jared, Nephi, Jacob, Benjamin, Abinadi, Ammon, Lamoni, John the Baptist	Isa 44:24; 1Ne 19:7–12; 2Ne 9:5; Mosiah 3:5; 7:27; 13:34; 15:1; 19:13; Ether 3:6–16; D&C 93:6–11
He would be the Son of God, the Only Begotten of the Father in the flesh, the God of Israel	Adam, Enoch, Moses, Isaiah, Nephi, Jacob, Abinadi, Alma, John the Baptist	Isa 9:6–7; 1Ne 11:20–21; 22:12; 2Ne 25:12; Jacob 4:5; Mosiah 15:2–5; Alma 5:48; 7:10; 9:26; D&C 93:11–14; Moses 1:6, 33; 2:1, 26; 6–52
His mother would be a virgin, a descendant of Abraham, Isaac, and Jacob through King David; she would live in Nazareth, and her name would be Mary	Moses, Isaiah, Jeremiah, Nephi, Benjamin, Alma	Gen 49:24; Isa 7:14; 11:1; Jer 23:5–6; 33:15–16; 1Ne 11:13–21; Mosiah 3:8; Alma 7:10
Heavenly signs would attend his birth	Samuel the Lamanite	Hel 14:3–7
HIS NAME		
The Messiah would be called "Salvation" (in Hebrew, *Yeshua;* in other languages, *Jesus*)	Moses, Isaiah	Ex 15:2; Isa 12:2–6
His name would be Jesus Christ	Adam, Enoch, Noah, brother of Jared, Nephi, Jacob, Benjamin, Abinadi, Alma	2Ne 10:3; 25:19; 31:10; Jacob 4:11; Mosiah 3:8, 17; 7:27; Alma 5:48; Ether 3:14–16; Moses 6:52, 57; 8:23–24

Chart 8-9 (1)

Time and Place of Birth		
Jesus would be born in the meridian of time, that is, within 600 years after Lehi left Jerusalem or 5 years after Samuel's prophecy	Adam, Enoch, Moses, Lehi, Nephi, Samuel the Lamanite	1Ne 10:4; 19:8; 2Ne 25:19; Hel 14:2; Moses 5:57; 6:57, 62; 7:45–46
Christ would be born among the Jews near Jerusalem at Bethlehem	Micah, Jacob, Alma	Micah 5:2; 2Ne 10:3; Alma 7:10
Details of His Ministry		
A messenger prophet would prepare the way for the Messiah	Isaiah, Lehi	Isa 40:3; 1Ne 10:7–9
He would come up out of Egypt	Hosea	Hos 11:1
He would be a child in Nazareth	Nephi	1Ne 11:13, 20
He would be baptized by the forerunner near Bethabara; the prophet would testify of him, and the Holy Ghost would descend on him as a dove	Lehi, Nephi	1Ne 10:9–10; 11:27; 2Ne 31:4–8
He would suffer temptations, hunger, and thirst	Isaiah, Benjamin, Abinadi, Alma	Isa 53:3; Mosiah 3:7; 15:5; Alma 7:11
He would call twelve apostles in the Old World and twelve disciples in the New World	Nephi	1Ne 11:29, 34; 12:8–10
He would preach glad tidings to the meek and the captives	Isaiah	Isa 61:1
He would care for his followers as a shepherd	Isaiah, Ezekiel	Isa 40:10–11; Ezek 34:11–31

Chart 8-9 (2)

He would be a priest forever after the order of Melchizedek	Moses, David, Alma	Gen 14:25–28 JST; Ps 110:1–4; Alma 13:7–9
He would minister in power and glory, performing miracles, healing the sick, raising the dead	Isaiah, Nephi, Jacob, Benjamin, Abinadi, Alma	Isa 59:16–19; 1Ne 11:28, 31; 2Ne 10:4; Mosiah 3:5–6;15:6; Alma 5:50
He would come to Zion (Jerusalem)	Isaiah	Isa 59:20
He would come as a king riding on a young ass	Zechariah	Zech 9:9
He would be a man of sorrows, without beauty, a stumbling block to his people, who would despise and reject him	David, Isaiah, Nephi, Jacob	Ps 118:21–22; Isa 8:13–14; 53:3; 1Ne 19:13; 2Ne 10:3–5; 25:12; Jacob 4:15
He would be betrayed by his friends for thirty pieces of silver	David, Zechariah	Ps 41:9; Zech 11:12–13; 13:6
HIS ATONING SUFFERING		
Christ would yield himself to suffer	Isaiah, Nephi, Abinadi	Isa 50:6; 53:7; 1Ne 19:9–10; Mosiah 15:5–6
He would be innocent of violence and deceit	Isaiah	Isa 53:9
He would suffer to atone for our sins and help our sicknesses; blood would come from every pore	Isaiah, Jacob, Benjamin, Alma, Amulek, Aaron	Isa 53:3–12; 2Ne 9:21–22; Mosiah 3:7; Alma 7:11–13; 21:9; 34:8–9
He would be judged and placed in prison	Isaiah, Nephi	Isa 53:8; 1Ne 11:32
Foreshadowings of his suffering	Abraham and Isaac, Moses	Gen 22:1–14; Lev 16:7–10

Chart 8-9 (3)

HIS CRUCIFIXION

Christ would die voluntarily	Isaiah, Lehi, Nephi, Abinadi	Isa 53:7, 9, 12; 1Ne 19:9–10; 2Ne 2:6–7; Mosiah 15:5, 7
He would be crucified by and for his people	Enoch, Zenock, Neum, Lehi, Nephi, Jacob	1Ne 10:11; 11:32–33; 19:10; 2Ne 6:9; 10:3–5; 25:13; Moses 7:47, 55
His hands and feet would be pierced	David, Isaiah, Zechariah	Ps 22:16; Isa 22:23–25; Zech 12:10; 13:6
He would be mocked and suffer pain and thirst	David, Isaiah	Ps 22:7–8; Isa 50:6
He would be given vinegar to drink	David	Ps 69:20–21
He would speak specific words from the cross	David	Ps 22:1; 31:5
None of his bones would be broken	David	Ps 34:19–20
Lots would be cast for his garments	David	Ps 22:18
He would be buried in a sepulchre	Zenos, Nephi	1Ne 19:10; 2Ne 25:13
Physical signs would attend his death	Zenos, Nephi, Samuel the Lamanite	1Ne 12:4–6; 19:10–13; Hel 14:20–28
Foreshadowings of his atonement and death	Adam, Eve, Enoch, Abraham, Isaac, Moses, Ezekiel, Nephi, Jacob, Alma, Nephi (son of Helaman)	Gen 22:1–14; Ex 12; 16:12–35; 17:1–7; 29; Lev 1–17; 21–23; Num 19; 21:5–9; Ezek 43:18–27; 45:18–25; 1Ne 17:41; Jacob 4:4–5; Alma 33:18–23; Hel 8:13–15; Moses 5:4–7; 6:63–65

Chart 8-9 (4)

HIS RESURRECTION		
Jesus would rise from death after three days and show himself to witnesses	Lehi, Nephi, Benjamin	1Ne 10:11; 2Ne 26:1; Mosiah 3:10
Foreshadowings of his resurrection	Jonah	Jonah 1:17; 2:1–10
All would be resurrected because he overcame death	Enoch, Samuel, Job, David, Isaiah, Ezekiel, Hosea, Jacob, Abinadi, Alma, Amulek, Samuel the Lamanite	1Sam 2:6; Job 19:25–27; Ps 16:9–10; Isa 25:8; 26:19; Ezek 37:12–13; Hos 13:14; 2Ne 2:8; 9:4–13; Mosiah 13:33–35; 15:20–24; 16:7–11; Alma 11:42–45; 33:22; 40:2–23; Hel 14:25; Moses 7:55–56, 62
HIS ATONEMENT		
Christ's atonement would be infinite	Nephi, Jacob, Amulek	2Ne 9:7; 25:16; Alma 34:8–14
His sacrifice would satisfy the demands of justice and mercy	Jacob, Abinadi, Alma, Amulek	2Ne 9:25–26; 25:16; Mosiah 15:8–9, 26–27; Alma 34:14–18; 42:13–30
His atonement would redeem all mankind from physical death brought about by Adam's fall	Lehi, Jacob, Abinadi, Alma, Amulek	2Ne 2:8–9; 9:4–15; Mosiah 15:7–9, 20–27; Alma 11:39–45; 12:21–25; 40:23; 41:2–15
His atonement would make available the forgiveness of sins for all who have faith in him, repent, are baptized, receive the Holy Ghost, and endure; they thus become his sons and daughters and receive joy and eternal life	Adam, Eve, Noah, brother of Jared, Isaiah, Lehi, Nephi, Jacob, Benjamin, Abinadi, Alma, Amulek, Aaron, John the Baptist	Ether 3:14; Isa 1:16–18; Mt 3:11; 1Ne 10:4–6; 2Ne 2:3–29; 9:10–42; 31:10–21; Mosiah 3:11–19; 4:5–30; 5:6–15; 15:10–19; Alma 5:6–62; 11:36–43; 12:12–37; 22:14; 34:2–41; 42:2–28; Moses 5:8–11; 6:51–68; 8:23–24

Chart 8-9 (5)

Chart 8-10

Baptism of Jesus
in the Four Gospels

Explanation

Each of the four Gospels gives an account of the baptism of Jesus, and further information is added by the Joseph Smith Translation of Matthew. Most of the details are consistent among these accounts concerning where and how Jesus was baptized. Because of minor differences, however, major questions have arisen. Was the Spirit that descended that of God himself (Matthew) or the Holy Ghost (Luke) or just "the Spirit" (Mark, John)? Did the Spirit perhaps descend only once, or perhaps twice: once before the baptism (John) and again right after? Did the voice from heaven come right after the baptism, or apparently afterward as Jesus was praying (Luke)? Did the voice say to John, "*This is* my beloved Son" (Matthew), with the added words "Hear ye him" (Matthew JST), or did the voice say to Jesus, "*Thou art* my beloved Son" (Mark, Luke), or did only the Baptist testify, "This is the Son of God" (John)?

The purpose of this chart is not to create confusion but to display the source of considerable scholarly inquiry. The solution to these problems may rest in the fact that concurrent recipients of a spiritual experience may each receive a version of that divine manifestation suited to their own vantage point. Thus, John the Baptist could have heard "This is my beloved Son," at precisely the same time that Jesus heard "Thou art my beloved Son." Jesus could have been offering up a prayer while John was baptizing him. If God can listen simultaneously to prayers from multiple people, he can also respond to them both simultaneously and individually.

Reference

S. Brent Farley, "The Baptism and Temptations of Jesus," in *Studies in Scripture Vol. 5: The Gospels*, ed. Kent P. Jackson and Robert L. Millet (Salt Lake City: Deseret Book, 1986), 175–87.

Baptism of Jesus
in the Four Gospels

Matthew 3:13–17	Matthew 3:40–46 JST	Mark 1:9–11	Luke 3:21–22	John 1:28–34
From Galilee to the Jordan		From Nazareth in the Jordan		In Bethabara beyond Jordan
				Behold the lamb of God, This is he
	John bearing record			
John forbade him	John forbade him			
Suffer it now	Suffer me to be baptized of thee			
Jesus being immersed		Jesus was immersed	Jesus having been immersed	
Straightway coming up out of the water	Went up straightway out of the water	Straightway coming up from the water		
Heavens opened (to him)	And John saw, and lo, the heavens were opened unto him	Heavens split open	Jesus was praying Heaven was opened	From heaven
He saw the Spirit of God descending like a dove and coming upon him	And he saw the Spirit of God descending like a dove and lighting upon Jesus	He (John) saw the Spirit descending like a dove into (or unto) him	Holy Ghost descended in a bodily shape like a dove upon him	I (John) saw the Spirit descending like a dove and it abode upon him
Voice from the heavens	And lo, he heard a voice from heaven,	Voice came from the heavens	Voice came from heaven	
This is my beloved Son in whom I am well pleased	This is my beloved Son, in whom I am well pleased. Hear ye him	Thou art my beloved Son; in thee I am well pleased	Thou art my beloved Son; in thee I am well pleased	
				God had said to John: Upon whom thou shalt see the Spirit descending, and remaining on him, the same is he which baptizeth with the Holy Ghost
				I saw and bear record: This is the Son of God

Chart 8-10

Jesus and the Temple

Explanation

A strong thread runs through all four Gospels: whenever Jesus was in Jerusalem, he spent time at the temple. Jesus did not reject the idea of the temple. Instead, he desired to replace the temple system in Jerusalem with a new ritual order, a sacred way of holiness and purity. The temple was very important to Jesus.

The bar graph in chart 8-11 displays the total number of verses in the Gospels. The darker section of each bar shows the percent of verses that describe Jesus' sayings and doings in the temple at Jerusalem. While John devotes the highest percentage of writings to these themes, Luke uses thirty-one more verses describing what Jesus said and did there.

Chart 8-12 shows that the earliest Christians remembered vividly many things that Jesus said and did at the temple. All four Gospel writers remember Jesus walking and teaching in the temple. In the Synoptics, directly following his triumphal entry onto the holy mount, Jesus drove out the money changers. The temple was seen in the Jewish world as a source of God's power. From this sacred place flowed streams of living water and divine blessing. Jesus was unwilling to misuse those powers. Recollections of Jesus at the temple are even stronger in the Gospel of John, and not just at the end of Jesus' ministry as in the other Gospels, but on many occasions for Passover and on other holy celebrations.

In this light, it is instructive to connect what Jesus said with where he said it. Some of his most memorable teachings about obedience, chastity, marriage, lordship, authority, priesthood, tithing, consecration, judgment, and the afterlife were given at the temple.

References

D. Kelly Ogden, "Jesus and the Temple," *Ensign*, April 1991, 12–19.

Paul M. Mortensen, "The Temple Mount: The Center for Christ's Teachings and Activities in Jerusalem," *A Symposium on the New Testament* (Salt Lake City: The Church of Jesus Christ of Latter-day Saints, 1980), 142–45.

Verses in the Temple
by Gospel

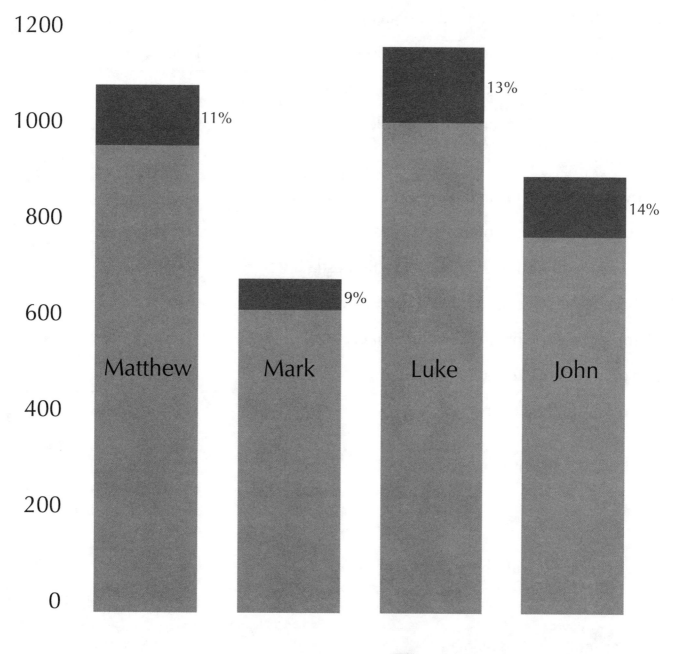

1200

1000 — 11%

800

600 — 9%

400

200

0

Matthew Mark Luke John

13%

14%

Number of
verses in
each Gospel

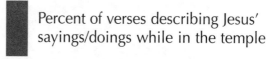

Percent of verses describing Jesus'
sayings/doings while in the temple

Chart 8-11

Jesus at the Temple

Gabriel there foretold the Lord's coming	Lk 1:17–19
Jesus circumcised there on eighth day	Lk 2:21
Simeon held and proclaimed the Savior	Lk 2:27–35
Anna gave thanks for Jesus' redemption	Lk 2:38
Jesus amazed the elders there at age twelve	Lk 2:42, 46
Tempted at the pinnacle of the temple	Mt 4:5–7; Lk 4:9–12
Regularly went there for Passover	Jn 2:13
Drove out merchants and their sacrificial animals	Jn 2:14–17
Encouraged payment of the temple tax	Mt 17:24–27
Cleansed man at the temple pool of Bethesda	Jn 5:14–16
At Tabernacles declared himself God's emissary	Jn 7:14, 28
There forgave a woman taken in adultery	Jn 8:2–11
Spoke in the treasury about light	Jn 8:12–20
Drove out money changers	Mt 21:12–13; Mk 11:15–19; Lk 19:45
Walked and taught there daily	Mt 21:23; 26:55; Mk 11:27; 12:35–40; 14:49; Lk 19:45–48; 20:1; 22:52; Jn 10:23
Reasoned there with the Jewish leaders	Mt 21:23–23:39; Mk 11:27–12:44; Lk 19:45–48; 21:37
Had his authority challenged	Mt 21:23; Mk 11:27–28; Lk 20:2

Chart 8-12 (1)

Gave the parable of the two sons on obedience	Mt 21:28–32
Taught of the wicked tenants' rejection of the son	Mt 21:33–46; Mk 12:1–12; Lk 20:9–19
Gave parable of the marriage feast on chosenness	Mt 22:1–14
Was asked about what belongs to Caesar or God	Mt 22:17; Mk 12:14; Lk 20:22
Sadducees asked about marriage and the afterlife	Mt 22:24; Mk 12:19; Lk 20:28
Pharisees asked about the greatest commandment	Mt 22:36; Mk 12:28
Pharisees asked about Christ and the son of David	Mt 22:42; Mk 12:35; Lk 20:41
Jesus warned about the pride of the Scribes	Mk 12:38; Lk 20:46
Saw the widow offer her two mites	Mk 12:42; Lk 21:2
Approved Pharisaic teaching but not action	Mt 23:3
Taught his priesthood leaders to be servants	Mt 23:11
Gave eight woes upon the scribes and Pharisees regarding their exclusivity, long prayers, misleading converts, improper temple oaths, missing the spirit of tithing, having external purity only, outward appearances, and rejecting the prophets	Mt 23:13–34
Mentioned the murder of Zacharias in the temple	Mt 23:35
Lamented over the temple's coming destruction	Mt 24:1–2; Mk 13:1–2; Lk 21:6
Spoke of the return of "the master of the house"	Mk 13:34–35
Used imagery of "my Father's house"	Jn 14:2
Rending of the veil of the temple	Mt 27:51; Mk 15:38; Lk 23:45
Earliest Christians continue to meet there	Lk 24:53

Chart 8-12 (2)

Chart 8-13

Two Healings on the Sabbath

Explanation

In John 5, at the pool of Bethesda, just north of the temple, Jesus healed a man who had been infirm for thirty-eight years; and in John 9, at the pool of Siloam, south of the temple, he healed a man who had been blind since birth. Chart 8-13 displays the similar conduct of Jesus in both of these cases and at the same time points out the common literary structure of the two accounts.

One may wonder why the two stories are so similar. There may be many reasons. The consistency may well reflect the orderly practice of the Lord, who does not vary unpredictably from one case to the next. These two accounts, typical of other similar doublets in the scriptures, stand as two witnesses of the truth of what they report. In Job 33:14, Elihu says, "For God speaketh once, yea twice," and yet man still does not understand. Twice-told truths serve as double notice to reinforce their importance in hopes of promoting their acceptance.

Reference

Bruce J. Malina and Richard L. Rohrbaugh, *Social-Science Commentary on the Gospel of John* (Minneapolis: Fortress, 1998), 109.

Two Healings on the Sabbath

JOHN 5	JOHN 9
1. In Jerusalem for feast (5:1)	1. In Jerusalem for Feast of Tabernacles
2. Sabbath healing (5:10)	2. Sabbath healing (9:14)
3. Old, proven infirmity (5:5)	3. Old, proven infirmity (9:1)
4. Illness and sin (5:14 "sin no more")	4. Illness and sin (9:2 "who sinned")
5. At pool of Bethesda (5:2)	5. At pool of Siloam (9:7)
6. Command ("rise, take," 5:7) obedience/cure (5:9)	6. Command ("go, wash," 9:7) obedience/cure (9:7)
7. Court of inquiry (5:9–16) healed man charge: Sabbath violation defense (5:31–47)	7. Court of inquiry (9:13–34) healed man charge: Sabbath violation defense (9:30–34)
8. Question: who is he? (5:12–13)	8. Questions: where is he? (9:12) what do you say of him? (9:17)
9. Subsequent meeting Jesus found him (5:14) no Christophany	9. Subsequent meeting Jesus found him (9:35) Christ declares himself (9:35–38)
10. Judgment they judge Jesus (5:9–16) Jesus judges them (5:38–47)	10. Judgment they judge Jesus (9:13–34) Jesus judges them (9:39–41)

Chart 8-13

Christ, His High Priesthood and Eternal Sacrifice

Explanation

The Epistle to the Hebrews drives home the point that Jesus was the greatest High Priest who performed an eternal sacrifice of everlasting covenant with God. Nowhere in the New Testament is the atonement of Jesus Christ more comprehensively taught than in the heart of this important text. Many features of this atonement, which fulfills and transcends the atoning sacrifices previously performed by the Levitical priests under the Law of Moses, are clearly presented here, particularly its compassion, power, sworn certainty, immortal operation, perfection, authority, mediation, sacrificial efficacy, covenantal sealing, and remitting generosity. To the witness of Hebrews, the briefer testimonies of Romans and 1 Peter are also added.

Reference

Craig R. Koester, *Hebrews: A New Translation with Introduction and Commentary* (New York: Doubleday, 2001), 352–62, 393–416.

Christ, His High Priesthood and Eternal Sacrifice

Jesus the compassionate High Priest	Heb 4:14–5:10
Melchizedek Priesthood greater than the Levitical	Heb 7:11–14
Melchizedek Priesthood binds with an eternal oath	Heb 7:15–19
Christ's priesthood operates beyond death	Heb 7:20–26
The perfection of Christ as the heavenly High Priest	Heb 7:27–28
Christ officiates in the divine temple	Heb 8:1–5
Christ is the mediator of a better covenant	Heb 8:6–13
The efficacy of Christ's sacrifice	Heb 9:11–14
Christ seals the new covenant with his blood	Heb 9:15–28
Christ's sacrifice brings remission of sins	Heb 10:11–18
Christ died for the ungodly and sinners	Rom 5:6–11
God has bought you back with Christ's blood	1Pt 1:17–21

Chart 8-14

The Roles of the High Priest

Explanation

The Epistle to the Hebrews draws particular attention to the parallels between the traditional roles of the Jewish High Priest and the ways in which Jesus fulfilled many of those functions. A major teaching of this letter is to prove "that we," as Christians, "have such an High Priest" (Heb 8:1). Jesus serves as the great atoning High Priest, although not by entering "into the holy places made with hands, which are figures of the true; but into heaven itself, now to appear in the presence of God for us" (Heb 9:24).

Chart 8-15 contrasts some of the main ceremonial functions performed by the Jewish High Priest with the corresponding elements in the ministration of Jesus. These range from his status and birth, to his designation, ordination, performance of vicarious sacrifices for the benefit of others, and his standing before God as mediator and judge of his people. To people who understand the commission of the High Priest under the Law of Moses, the counterparts in the mission of Jesus are transparent.

Reference

Craig R. Koester, *Hebrews: A New Translation with Introduction and Commentary* (New York: Doubleday, 2001), 240–42, 298–99, 416–51.

The Roles of the High Priest

JEWISH HIGH PRIEST

JESUS' FULFILLMENT

JEWISH HIGH PRIEST	JESUS' FULFILLMENT
A teacher of the law (Deut 33:10; Lev 10:10–11)	A teacher of the law (Sermon on the Mount, Mt 5–7; the Sabbath law, Mt 12:1–12; the great commandment, Mk 12:28–31)
Communicator of the divine will (Num 27:21)	"I seek not mine own will, but the will of the Father which hath sent me" (Jn 5:31)
Blesses the people in the name of the Lord (Num 6:22–27)	Christ prays for blessing on his disciples and people (Jn 16 and 17)
Does not take the office upon himself but is chosen of God (Num 16:5; Heb 5:4)	"Called of God an High Priest" (Heb 5:10)
A firstborn son (Ex 13:2; Num 3:12)	God's only begotten Son (Jn 3:16) Mary's firstborn son (Lk 2:7)
Was washed (Ex 29:4)	Baptized by John the Baptist (Mt 3:13–17)
Clothed with garments (Ex 29:5–6)	Wears robes of the atonement (Rev 1:13; 19:13)
Anointed with holy oil (Ex 29:7)	"God hath anointed [Christ] with the oil of gladness" (Heb 1:9)
Sin offering to put away sin (Ex 29:36)	Christ frees us from sin (Rom 6:11)
Burnt offering to indicate the full and complete surrender to God (Lev 1:3)	"Not my will, but thine, be done" (Lk 22:42)
Makes peace/consecration offering (Lev 7:11–21)	Prince of Peace (Isa 9:6)
Sabbath sacrifice (Num 28:9–10)	The Son of Man is Lord of the Sabbath (Mt 12:8)
Was a mediator between his people and God	"One mediator between God and men, the man Jesus Christ" (1Tm 2:5)
Wore the breastplate of judgment	"The Father judgeth no man, but hath committed all judgment unto the Son" (Jn 5:22)
Crown of gold engraved with "Holiness to the Lord" (Ex 28:36; 29:6)	"I looked, and behold … the Son of man, having on his head a golden crown" (Rev 14:14)
Performs the service on the Day of Atonement (Lev 16)	Performed the atonement for all mankind (Jn 17–20; Heb 10:10)
Lifetime office (Ex 29:9)	"Thou art a priest forever" (Heb 7:21)
Enters Holy of Holies (Lev 16:17)	The saints enter the Holy of Holies by the blood of Jesus (Heb 10:19–20)

Chart 8-15

Names and Titles of Christ

Explanation

Jesus Christ, God's Son, Savior, is known by many names and titles within the writings of the New Testament. Chart 8-16 lists alphabetically over 150 such proper names or descriptive expressions. Much can be learned and gleaned by pondering each of these terms. They all reveal different facets of Jesus, his love, his roles, his functions, his being. No sweeter sound is known than his blessed name, and no other name given is under heaven through which one may successfully approach God and enter back into his presence. The name of Jesus Christ is itself manifold. It invites his followers into an eternal sphere of abundance and effulgence.

The copiousness of names and titles used for Jesus, from the very earliest days of Christianity, is itself a remarkable testimony of the unsurpassed explosion of spiritual knowledge that burst onto the scene in Galilee and Judea with the advent of the Savior as the Word became flesh and dwelt on this earth. Great religions typically do not evolve slowly, as Darwin might suggest, from single cells to complex organisms. True revelations shatter old, narrow, erroneous perceptions with a sudden blast that sends out refractions glistening off of its clear and brilliant fulness. The many names and titles by which Jesus immediately came to be known is a strong symptom of precisely such an expansive phenomenon.

References

Jeffrey R. Holland, "Whom Say Ye That I Am?" *Ensign*, September 1974, 6–11.
Stephen E. Robinson, "Jesus Christ, Names and Titles of," *EM*, 2:740–42.

Names and Titles of Christ

Able to Save to the Uttermost	Heb 7:25
Advocate with the Father	1Jn 2:1
Almighty	Rev 1:8; 4:8; 16:7
Alpha and Omega, the Beginning and the End	Rev 1:8, 11; 21:6; 22:13
Amen	Rev 3:14
Apostle	Heb 3:1; 4:14; 10:21
Appears in the Presence of God for Us	Heb 9:24
Author and Finisher of Our Faith	Heb 12:2
Author of Eternal Salvation	Heb 5:9
Beginning of the Creation of God	Rev 3:14
Beloved Son of God	Mt 3:17; 17:5; Mk 9:7; Lk 3:22
Better than the Angels	Heb 1:4
Blessed for Evermore	2Cor 11:31
Bread of Life	Jn 6:35, 41, 48
Bright and Morning Star	Rev 22:16
Brightness of God's Glory	Heb 1:3
Captain of Man's Salvation	Heb 2:10
Carpenter	Mk 6:3
Carpenter's Son	Mt 13:55
Chief Cornerstone	Eph 2:20
Chosen of God	Lk 23:35; 1Pt 2:4
Christ of God	Lk 9:20
Consecrated for Evermore	Heb 7:28
Consolation of Israel	Lk 2:25
Crowned with Glory and Honour	Heb 2:9
Deliverer	Rom 11:26
Door of the Sheep	Jn 10:7, 9
End of the Law for Righteousness	Rom 10:4
Express Image of God's Person	Heb 1:3
Faithful	Heb 2:17; Rev 19:11
Faithful Witness	Rev 1:5; 3:14
First and the Last	Rev 1:17; 2:8; 22:13
First Begotten	Heb 1:6
First Begotten of the Dead	Rev 1:5
Firstfruits of Them that Slept	1Cor 15:20, 23
Forerunner	Heb 6:20

Chart 8-16 (1)

Foundation of the Church	1Cor 3:11
God Manifest in the Flesh	1Tm 3:16
God's Anointed	Acts 4:27
God's Holy Child Jesus	Acts 4:27, 30
Good Shepherd	Jn 10:11, 14
Governor that shall Rule Israel	Mt 2:6
Great God	Titus 2:13
Great Shepherd of the Sheep	Heb 13:20; 1Pt 5:4
Harmless	Heb 7:26
He that Came by Water and Blood	1Jn 5:6
He that Cometh in the Name of the Lord	Mt 21:9; Mk 11:9
He that Is Holy, He that Is True, He that Hath the Key of David	Rev 3:7
He that Liveth and Was Dead	Rev 1:18; 2:8
Head of Every Man	1Cor 11:3; cf. Eph 4:15
Head of the Church	Eph 5:23
Heir of All Things	Heb 1:2
High Priest	Heb 2:17
High Priest of Good Things to Come	Heb 9:11
High Priest of our Confession	Heb 3:1; 4:14; 10:21
Holy	Heb 7:26
Holy One and the Just	Acts 3:14
Hope of Glory	Col 1:27
Image of God	2Cor 4:4
In Whom Is Salvation	2Tm 2:10
Jesus of Galilee	Mt 26:69
Jesus of Nazareth	Mt 26:71; Mk 1:24; 10:47; 14:67; 16:6; Lk 4:34; 18:37; 24:19; Jn 1:45; 18:5, 7; 19:19; Acts 2:22; 3:6; 4:10; 6:14; 10:38; 22:8; 26:9
Joseph's Son	Lk 4:22; Jn 1:45; 6:42
Judge of Quick and Dead	Acts 10:42
Just One	Acts 7:52; 22:14
King of Israel	Mt 27:42; Mk 15:32; Jn 1:49; 12:13
King of Kings	Rev 17:14; 19:16
King of Sion	Mt 21:5; Jn 12:15
King of the Jews	Mt 2:2; 27:11, 37 Mk 15:9, 12, 18, 26; Lk 23:3, 38; Jn 18:33, 39; 19:3,14–15, 19, 21

Chart 8-16 (2)

King that Cometh in the Name of the Lord	Lk 19:38; Jn 12:13
Lamb	Rev 5:6, 8, 12–13; 6:16; 7:9, 14, 17; 12:11; 14:1, 4, 10; 15:3; 17:14; 19:7, 9; 21:9, 14, 22, 27; 22:1, 3
Lamb of God	Jn 1:29, 36
Lamb without Blemish and without Spot	1Pt 1:19
Life	Jn 14:6
Light	Jn 1:7–8
Light of the World	Jn 8:12; 9:5; 12:46
Lion of the Tribe of Judah	Rev 5:5
Living Bread	Jn 6:51
Living Stone	1Pt 2:4
Lord	Mt 28:6; Mk 16:19–20; Lk 2:11; 22:61; 24:3, 34; Jn 11:2; 20:2, 18, 20, 25; Acts 2:36; 8:24–25, 39; 9:5–6, 10–11, 15, 17, 31, 35, 42; 10:48; 11:21, 23; 13:12, 48–49; 14:3, 23; 15:35; 16:10, 32; 18:8–9, 25; 20:19; 21:20; 22:10, 16; 23:11
Lord both of Dead and Living	Rom 14:9
Lord from Heaven	1Cor 15:47
Lord Jesus	Lk 24:3; Acts 7:59; 8:16; 9:29; 11:17, 20; 15:11, 26; 16:31; 19:5, 10, 13, 17; 20:21, 24, 35; 21:13; 28:31
Lord of All	Acts 10:36
Lord of Glory	Jms 2:1
Lord of Lords	Rev 17:14; 19:16
Lord of the Sabbath	Mk 2:28
Lord's Christ	Lk 2:26
Made Higher than the Heavens	Heb 7:26
Made of a Woman, Made Under the Law	Gal 4:4
Mediator between God and Men	1Tm 2:5
Mediator of a Better Covenant	Heb 8:6; 12:24
Mediator of the New Testament	Heb 9:15
Meek and Lowly	Mt 21:5; see Zech 9:9; Mt 12:19
Merciful	Heb 2:17
Messias	Jn 1:41; 4:25
Minister of the Circumcision for the Truth of God	Rom 15:8

Chart 8-16 (3)

Minister of the Sanctuary and of the True Tabernacle	Heb 8:2
Nazarene	Mt 2:23
One Body	1Cor 12:12
One with the Father	Jn 10:30
Only Begotten of the Father	Jn 1:14, 18
Only Wise God Our Savior	Jude 1:25
Our Life	Col 3:4
Our Passover	1Cor 5:7
Our Peace	Eph 2:14
Our Savior	1Tm 2:3; 2Tm 1:10; Titus 2:10, 13; 3:6
Power of God and the Wisdom of God	1Cor 1:24
Precious	1Pt 2:4
Prince	Acts 5:31
Prince of Life	Acts 3:15
Prince of the Kings of the Earth	Rev 1:5
Prophet	Jn 4:19; 7:40; 9:17
Prophet of Nazareth	Mt 21:11
Propitiation for Our Sins	1Jn 2:2; 4:10
Propitiation for the Sins of the Whole World	1Jn 2:2; 4:10
Propitiation through Faith	Rom 3:25; 1Jn 2:2
Rabbi	Jn 1:38, 49; 3:2, 26; 6:25
Rabboni	Jn 20:16
Resurrection and the Life	Jn 11:25
Righteous Judge	2Tm 4:8
Righteous Man	Lk 23:47
Root and Offspring of David	Rev 22:16
Root of David	Rev 5:5
Samaritan (by the Jews)	Jn 8:48
Same Yesterday, Today, and Forever	Heb 13:8
Savior	Phlp 3:20; Mt 1:21; Lk 2:11; Acts 5:31; 13:23
Savior of Israel	Acts 13:23
Savior of the Body	Eph 5:23
Savior of the World	Jn 4:42; 1Jn 4:14
Seed of Abraham	Gal 3:16; Heb 2:16
Seed of David	2Tm 2:8
Separate from Sinners	Heb 7:26
Shepherd and Bishop of Souls	1Pt 2:25

Chart 8-16 (4)

Son	Lk 2:48
Son of David	Mt 9:27; 12:23; 15:22; 20:30–31; 21:9, 15; Mk 10:47–48; 12:35; Lk 18:38–39; 20:41
Son of David/Abraham	Mt 1:1
Son of Mary	Mk 6:3
Son of the Blessed	Mk 14:61
Son of the Highest	Lk 1:32
Son of the Living God	Mt 16:16
Son of the Most High God	Mk 5:7
Spiritual Rock	1Cor 10:4
Surety of a Better Testament	Heb 7:22
Tasted Death for Every Man	Heb 2:9
Teacher Come from God	Jn 3:2
True	Rev 19:11
True Vine	Jn 15:1
Truth	Jn 14:6
Undefiled	Heb 7:26
Vine	Jn 15:5
Way	Jn 14:6
Which Delivereth Us from the Wrath to Come	1Th 1:10
Who Bare Our Sins in His Own Body	1Pt 2:24; 3:18; 4:1
Who Came into the World to Save Sinners	1Tm 1:15
Who Did No Sin	1Pt 2:22
Who Died and Rose Again	1Th 4:14
Who Gave Himself for Our Sins	Gal 1:4
Who Gave Himself for Us	Titus 2:14
Who Is Passed into the Heavens	Heb 4:14; 8:1; 9:24; 1Pt 3:22
Who Knew No Sin	2Cor 5:21; Heb 4:15
Who Shall Judge the Quick and Dead	2Tm 4:1
Who Sitteth on the Right Hand of God	Col 3:1; Heb 1:3; 10:12; 12:2
Who Suffered for Us	1Pt 2:21
Who Was Raised from the Dead	2Tm 2:8
Wisdom, Righteousness, Sanctification, and Redemption unto Us	1Cor 1:30
Word	Jn 1:1, 14
Word of God	Rev 19:13
Word of Life	1Jn 1:1
Worthy	Heb 3:3

Chart 8-16 (5)

The Temple Mount from the south of Jerusalem in the early twentieth century. Photo by Karl Gröber

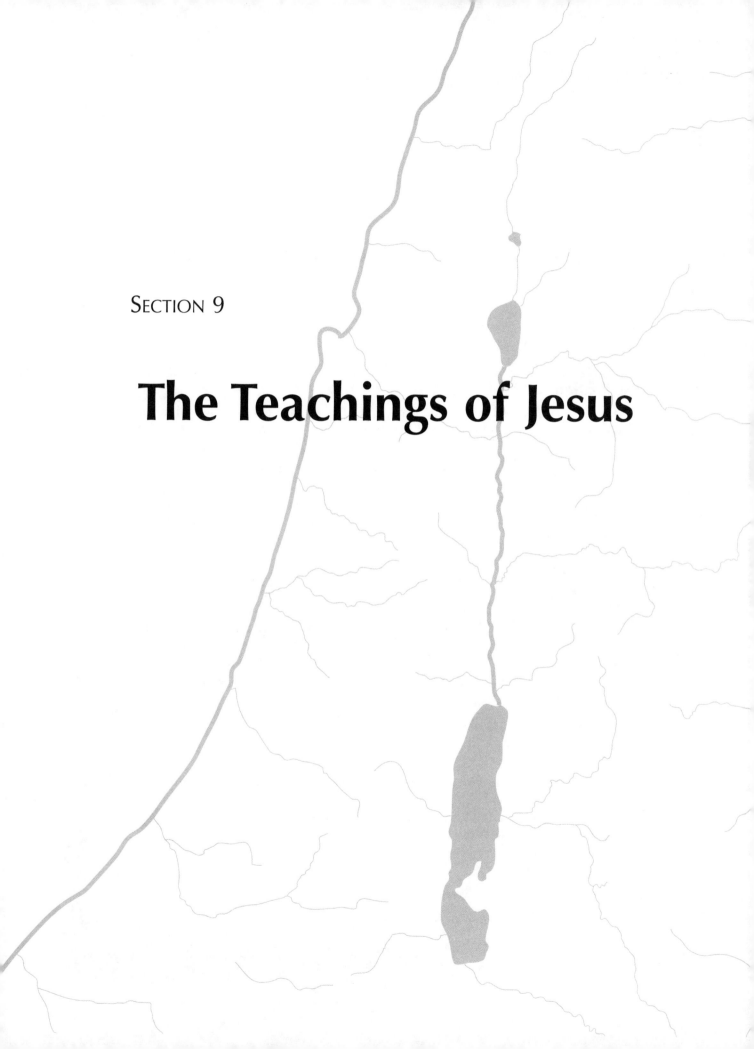

SECTION 9

The Teachings of Jesus

The Sermon on the Mount

Explanation

Chart 9-1 compares five versions of the Lord's Prayer. Each one is slightly different. In addition to the four prayers found in the scriptures, the fifth comes from a very early Christian handbook of instructions known as the Didache. Because the early Christians understood that this prayer was not to be rigidly recited verbatim, the surviving variations are not unexpected.

Similarly, chart 9-2 displays the Beatitudes found at the beginning of the Sermon on the Mount. These statements, beginning with the word "blessed" (in Greek, *makarios;* in Latin, *beatus*), promise ultimate blessedness, happiness, or beatification, especially in the afterlife, to individuals who have acquired the requisite attributes of righteousness. This chart compares the Beatitudes in three versions of the Sermon. Jesus gave basically the same sermon on several occasions, modifying details to suit the particular audience or setting. In Matthew 5–7, Jesus addressed faithful disciples at the outset of his ministry. In Matthew 5–7 JST, he addressed his Twelve Apostles as he sent them forth as missionaries. In 3 Nephi 12–14, he again presented essentially the same speech but now modified it to instruct a group of righteous people gathered at the temple in the city of Bountiful following his resurrection. Some people seek to find "the original version" of the Sermon on the Mount, but that quest may be guided by the faulty assumption that Jesus gave the Sermon only on one occasion. Ministering for over three years, he would have repeated his basic messages on several occasions.

References

John W. Welch, *Illuminating the Sermon at the Temple and Sermon on the Mount* (Provo, Utah: FARMS, 1999), 79–82.

John W. Welch, "Two Notes on the Lord's Prayer," in *Pressing Forward with the Book of Mormon* (Provo, Utah: FARMS 1999), 228–30.

Ernst Lohmeyer, *"Our Father": An Introduction to the Lord's Prayer* (New York: Harper & Row, 1965).

The Lord's Prayer

King James Version of Matthew 6	Joseph Smith Translation Matthew 6	Greek Version in Luke 11	Book of Mormon 3 Nephi 13	Didache 8:2
9. Our Father which art in heaven[s], hallowed be thy name.	10. Our Father who art in heaven, hallowed be thy name.	2. Father hallowed be thy name.	9. Our Father who art in heaven, hallowed be thy name.	Our Father in heaven, hallowed be thy name.
10. Thy kingdom come.	11. Thy kingdom come.	Thy kingdom come.		Thy kingdom come.
Thy will be done in earth, as it is in heaven.	Thy will be done on earth, as it is done in heaven.		10. Thy will be done on earth as it is in heaven.	Thy will be done, on earth as it is in heaven.
11. Give us this day our daily bread.	12. Give us this day, our daily bread.	3. Give us day by day our daily bread.		Give us this day our daily bread
12. And forgive us our debts, as we forg[a]ve also our debtors.	13. And forgive us our trespasses, as we forgive those who trespass against us.	4. And forgive us our sins; for we also forgive every one that is indebted to us.	11. And forgive us our debts, as we forgive our debtors.	and forgive us our debt [singular], as we [now] forgive our debtors.
13. And lead us not into temptation, but deliver us from [the] evil.	14. And suffer us not to be led into temptation, but deliver us from evil.	And lead us not into temptation.	12. And lead us not into temptation, but deliver us from evil.	And lead us not into temptation, but deliver us from [the] evil.
For thine is the kingdom, and the power, and the glory, forever. Amen.	15. For thine is the kingdom, and the power, and the glory, forever and ever, Amen.		13. For thine is the kingdom, and the power, and the glory, forever. Amen.	For thine is the power and the glory forever.

Chart 9-1

The Beatitudes

1. **Blessed are ye if ye shall give heed unto the words of these twelve whom I have chosen from among you to minister unto you, and to be your servants; and unto them I have given power that they may baptize you with water, behold, I will baptize you with fire and with the Holy Ghost; therefore** blessed are **ye if ye** shall believe **in** me **and be baptized, after that ye have seen me and know that I am.**

2. And again, more blessed are they who shall believe **in** your words **because that** ye shall testify that ye have seen me, **and that ye know** that I am.
   Yea, blessed are they who shall believe **in** your words, and come down into the depths of humility and be baptized, for they shall be visited **with** fire and with the Holy Ghost, and shall receive a remission of their sins.

3. Blessed are **they who** shall believe **on** me;

   and again, more blessed are they who shall believe **on** your words, **when** ye shall testify that ye have seen me and that I am.

4. Yea, blessed are they who shall believe **on** your words, and come down into the depth of humility, and be baptized **in my name;** for they shall be visited with fire and the Holy Ghost, and shall receive a remission of their sins.

Chart 9-2 (1)

KING JAMES VERSION MATTHEW 5	BOOK OF MORMON 3 NEPHI 12	JOSEPH SMITH TRANSLATION MATTHEW 5
3. Blessed are the poor in spirit: for theirs is the kingdom of heaven.	3. Yea, blessed are the poor in spirit who come unto me, for theirs is the kingdom of heaven.	5. Yea, blessed are the poor in spirit, who come unto me; for theirs is the kingdom of heaven.
4. Blessed are they that mourn: for they shall be comforted.	4. And again, blessed are **all** they that mourn, for they shall be comforted.	6. And again, blessed are they that mourn; for they shall be comforted.
5. Blessed are the meek: for they shall inherit the earth.	5. And blessed are the meek, for they shall inherit the earth.	7. And blessed are the meek; for they shall inherit the earth.
6. Blessed are they **which** do hunger and thirst after righteousness: for they shall be filled.	6. And blessed are all they **who** do hunger and thirst after righteousness, for they shall be filled with the Holy Ghost.	8. And blessed are all they **that** do hunger and thirst after righteousness; for they shall be filled with the Holy Ghost.
7. Blessed are the merciful: for they shall obtain mercy.	7. And blessed are the merciful, for they shall obtain mercy.	9. And blessed are the merciful; for they shall obtain mercy.
8. Blessed are the pure in heart: for they shall see God.	8. And blessed are all the pure in heart, for they shall see God.	10. And blessed are all the pure in heart; for they shall see God.
9. Blessed are the peacemakers: for they shall be called the children of God.	9. And blessed are all the peacemakers, for they shall be called the children of God.	11. And blessed are all the peacemakers; for they shall be called the children of God.
10. Blessed are they **which** are persecuted for **righteousness'** sake: for theirs is the kingdom of heaven.	10. **And** blessed are all they **who** are persecuted for my name's sake, for theirs is the kingdom of heaven.	12. Blessed are all they **that** are persecuted for my name's sake; for theirs is the kingdom of heaven.
11. Blessed are ye, when men shall revile you, and persecute you, and shall say all manner of evil against you falsely, for my sake.	11. And blessed are ye when men shall revile you and persecute, and shall say all manner of evil against you falsely, for my sake;	13. And blessed are ye when men shall revile you, and persecute you, and shall say all manner of evil against you falsely, for my sake.
12. **Rejoice,** and be exceeding glad: for great **is** your reward in heaven: for so persecuted they the prophets which were before you.	12. For ye shall have great joy and be exceedingly glad, for great shall be your reward in heaven; for so persecuted they the prophets **who** were before you.	14. For ye shall have great joy, and be exceeding glad; for great shall be your reward in heaven; for so persecuted they the prophets which were before you.

Chart 9-2 (2)

Sermon on the Mount Overview

Explanation

No text in the New Testament is more important than the Sermon on the Mount. It has been called the "sermon of sermons," the Lord's most masterful speech, and some consider it the greatest discourse ever given. Understanding the Sermon on the Mount is crucial to understanding the New Testament. These three chapters in the Gospel of Matthew have probably influenced Christian values and lifestyle more than any other section of the New Testament.

Chart 9-3 offers an overview of the Sermon on the Mount. Many people have wondered whether the Sermon is a single coherent text or whether it is, instead, a scrapbook of miscellaneous sayings without any particular structure or organizing principle. Recent scholarship, however, has begun to see the Sermon as a baptismal catechism or an instructional text teaching baptized Christians their advanced duties as members of the kingdom of God. While the Sermon on the Mount certainly contains many ethical and social teachings, it also goes far beyond the regular scope of an ordinary moral discourse.

References

John W. Welch, *Illuminating the Sermon at the Temple and Sermon on the Mount* (Provo, Utah: FARMS, 1999), 102–3.

Hans Dieter Betz, *The Sermon on the Mount* (Minneapolis: Fortress, 1995).

Herman Hendrickx, *The Sermon on the Mount* (London: Chapman, 1984).

"Sermon on the Mount," *WRC*, 49–52.

Sermon on the Mount Overview
Matthew 5–7

Beatitudes, ultimate blessings in the kingdom of heaven	5:2
Rejoice and be glad	5:12
Commission to be the salt of the earth and the light of the world	5:13
Instruction to obey all the commandments in their fullness	5:17
Prohibition against anger, ridicule, or brotherly unkindness	5:21
Requirement to reconcile and settle disputes quickly	5:23
Prohibition against adultery and lust	5:27
Protection of marriage and chastity against divorce and fornication	5:31
Swear your oaths not by heaven or earth, but by honestly saying "Yes"	5:33
Love your neighbor, turn other cheek, go the second mile, love your enemy	5:38
Be ye therefore perfect as is your Father in Heaven	5:48
Requirement to give alms to the poor	6:1
Pray privately in your closet	6:5
Pray together with the faithful, the Lord's Prayer as an example	6:9
Fasting, washing, anointing	6:16
Lay up treasures in heaven, for where your treasure is there is your heart	6:19
Have an eye single, consecrated and pure, that you may be full of light	6:22
Choose this day between loving God or mammon	6:24
God will clothe you in glorious garments	6:30
God will give you sufficient for your daily needs	6:33
God will judge you as you have judged others, the mote and the beam	7:1
Give not your holy thing to the dogs, neither cast your pearls before swine	7:6
Ask, seek, and knock	7:7
Your Father gives good gifts	7:11
Do unto others as you would have them do unto you	7:12
Enter in at the strait gate on the narrow path	7:13
Beware of false prophets	7:15
By their fruits ye shall know them	7:17
Not everyone that saith Lord, Lord, shall enter into his presence	7:21
Some will be told to depart	7:23
Hear and do, build your house on a rock, the wise man and the foolish man	7:24

Chart 9-3

Chart 9-4

Two Sermon Settings

Explanation

Matthew 5–7 reports Jesus' Sermon on the Mount. Luke 6 gives the Sermon on the Plain. The two texts are similar in many respects, the two speeches following essentially the same order. Luke begins with certain beatitudes, followed by a set of woes or curses. Brief instructions are given regarding loving enemies, turning the other cheek, giving to those who ask, lending to sinners, being merciful and doing well unto others (the last point being one of the few major elements taken out of order from the Matthean text). Luke then skips all the material found in Matthew 6 (some of which is found when Jesus speaks in private to his apostles in Luke 11), and then presents most of the items found in Matthew 7. In chart 9-4, the shared elements are in italic type.

Luke's selection of materials can be explained by the different settings in which the two speeches were given. The Lucan speech was delivered to a large, public audience of Jews and gentiles who had come to hear Jesus probably for the first time. Jesus gave them the more public elements of his gospel message. Missing from the speech in Luke are elements that one would expect to be reserved for the closer circle of disciples, such as the commission to be the light of the world, the issuance of commandments, and the explanation of sacred practices found in the Sermon on the Mount.

References

John W. Welch, *Illuminating the Sermon at the Temple and Sermon on the Mount* (Provo, Utah: FARMS, 1999), 221–26.

Hans Dieter Betz, *The Sermon on the Mount* (Minneapolis: Fortress, 1995), 50–70.

Two Sermon Settings

SERMON ON THE MOUNT		SERMON ON THE PLAIN
Mt 5:3–11	*Promises of present and ultimate blessings*	Lk 6:20–26
5:12	Rejoicing	
5:13–16	Commissioning	
5:17–20	Fulfillment of the law	
5:21–22	Prohibition against anger, ill-speaking, ridicule of brethren	
5:23–26	Reconciliation before offering	
5:27–32	The new law of chastity	
5:33–37	Swear by saying only "yes" or "no"	
5:38–47	*The new law of love and kindness*	Lk 6:27–36
5:48	Transition to a higher order	
6:1–4	The new law of almsgiving	
6:5–15	The new order of prayer, the Lord's Prayer	Lk 11:1–4
6:16–18	Fasting, washing, anointing	
6:19–24	The new law of single-minded consecration	
6:25–34	Promises to the disciples	
7:1–5	*Preparing for the final judgment*	Lk 6:37–38, 41–42
7:6	A requirement of confidentiality	
7:7–11	A three-fold petition to the Father	
7:12	*The Golden Rule*	Lk 6:31
7:13–14	Entering through the narrow door	
7:15–20	*Bringing forth good fruit*	Lk 6:43–45
7:21–22	*Entering into the Lord's presence*	Lk 6:46
7:23–27	*The wise man blessed, the foolish man warned*	Lk 6:48–49

Chart 9-4

Lessons for Leaders

Explanation

After the transfiguration, Jesus spent time especially with his disciples, teaching them many important lessons that they would need to learn in order to direct the affairs of the kingdom following the death and departure of the Savior. These lessons were taught in many ways, through object lessons, parables, explanations, aphorisms, and many other challenging and persuasive methods. All leaders in the Church of Jesus Christ today will be strengthened in their callings by knowing and observing the leadership training given by the Lord to the leaders whom he had called. The principles of faith, fasting, prayer, loyalty, humility, not offending the weak, seeking the lost, handling disputes, forgiving, strengthening marriages, giving to the poor, struggling, and keeping perspective apply as much today as they did in the days of Jesus.

Reference

"Teachings in General," and "Teaching Techniques," *WRC*, 54–59, 108–9.

Lessons for Leaders
Teachings to the Apostles following the Transfiguration—Matthew 17–20

Have faith as a grain of mustard seed (17:20)

Use prayer and fasting (17:21)

Do not offend political powers, but remember your true independence (17:26–27)

Be converted and become as humble as little children (18:3–4)

Receive, bless, and care for the little children (18:5; 19:15)

Do not offend or despise even the least of the Saints (18:6, 10)

Seek to find the lost sheep (18:12)

Seek first to resolve disputes in private (18:15)

Involve proper witnesses and disciplinary councils to try to recover lost souls (18:16)

Forgive over and over again (18:22, 35)

Try to keep marriages together, as God has ordained, even if all may not succeed (19:6, 11)

Consecrate your property, sell and give to the poor (19:22)

Remember that with God all things are possible (19:26)

The first shall be last, and the last shall be first (19:30; 20:16)

Know that God will reward all as he sees fit, not as we might think is fair (20:15)

Many are called, but few chosen (20:16)

Be prepared to drink of the difficult cup of struggle and suffering (20:23)

Whoever will be great or chief, let them be ministers and servants (20:26–27)

Chart 9-5

Parables

Explanation

Jesus was a masterful teacher who often used parables to convey different levels of meaning to audiences with different levels of faith or understanding. See chart 7-7 for a full list of the parables. On two occasions reported in the Gospel of Matthew, Jesus took his disciples aside and told them the deeper meaning of his parables, for those who had eyes to see and ears to hear. Chart 9-6 illustrates the explanation he gave of the parable of the sower, and chart 9-7 shows the meaning of the parable of the wheat and the tares, both found in Matthew 13. The Prophet Joseph Smith affirmed that Jesus actually explained the symbolic meaning behind each of his parables: "The parables were all plainly elucidated" by Jesus to his disciples. Chart 9-8 displays the explanations given by Joseph Smith of the meanings behind the other parables in Matthew 13.

References

Joseph Fielding Smith, ed., *The Teachings of the Prophet Joseph Smith* (Salt Lake City: Deseret Book, 1972), 98–102.

V. George Shillington, ed., *Jesus and His Parables: Interpreting the Parables of Jesus Today* (Edinburgh: T&T Clark, 1997).

Parable of the Sower
Recorded in the Book of Matthew

Symbol	Jesus' Interpretation
1 Seeds by the wayside (13:4)	"When any one heareth the word of the kingdom, and understandeth it not" (13:19)
Fowls which come and devour (13:4)	"wicked one … catcheth away that which was sown in his heart" (13:19)
2 Seeds in stony places with no root (13:5)	"he that heareth the word, and anon with joy receiveth it; yet hath he not root in himself" (13:20–21)
Sun which scorches seeds (13:6)	"tribulation or persecution ariseth because of the word, and by and by he is offended" (13:21)
3 Seeds among thorns (13:7)	"he that heareth the word; and the care of this world, and the deceitfulness of riches, choke the word, and he becometh unfruitful" (13:22)
4 Seeds in good ground (13:8)	"he that heareth the word, and understandeth it; which also beareth fruit, and bringeth forth, some an hundredfold, some sixty, some thirty" (13:23)

Chart 9-6

The Wheat and the Tares
Matthew 13:24–43

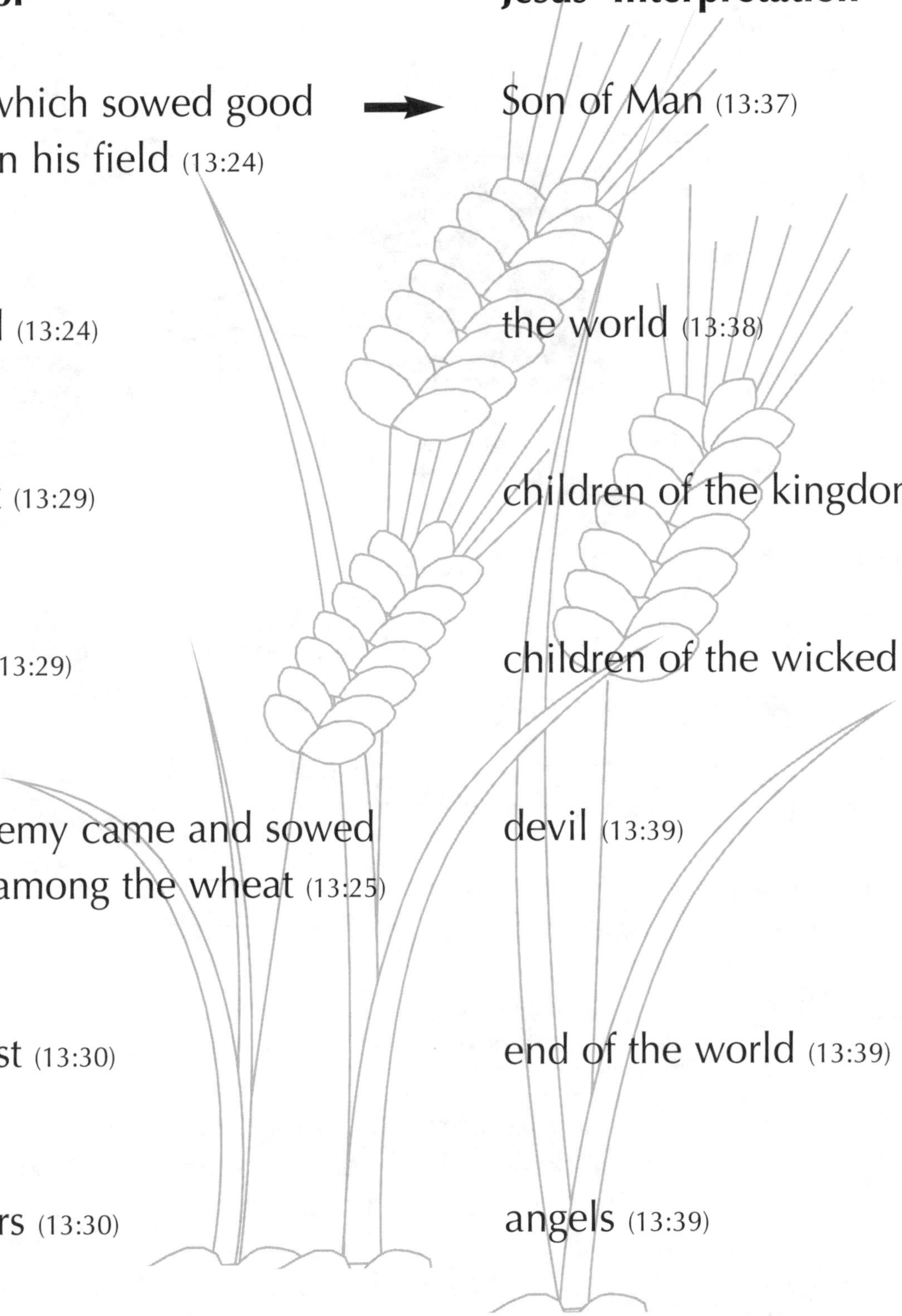

Symbol

Jesus' Interpretation

man which sowed good
seed in his field (13:24) ➞ Son of Man (13:37)

a field (13:24)
the world (13:38)

wheat (13:29)
children of the kingdom (13:38)

tares (13:29)
children of the wicked one (13:38)

an enemy came and sowed
tares among the wheat (13:25)
devil (13:39)

harvest (13:30)
end of the world (13:39)

reapers (13:30)
angels (13:39)

Chart 9-7

Joseph Smith's Explanations
of the Parables in Matthew 13

MUSTARD SEED (vv. 31–32)

The expansive growth of the restored kingdom through the sprouting of the Book of Mormon out of the earth "in the last days"

LEAVEN (v. 33)

The rise of the Church of Jesus Christ out of "a little leaven that was put into three witnesses"

TREASURES HIDDEN IN THE FIELD (v. 44)

The Latter-day Saints, selling all that they have, and gathering themselves together unto a place that they may purchase

MAN SEEKING GOODLY PEARLS (vv. 45–46)

Men traveling to find places for Zion,… who, when they find the place for Zion, or the pearl of great price, straightway sell all that they have, and buy it

NET CAST INTO THE SEA (vv. 47–48)

The seed of Joseph, spreading forth the Gospel net upon the face of the earth

SCRIBE BRINGING FORTH OUT OF HIS TREASURY BOTH OLD AND NEW (v. 52)

The restoration of old truths and covenants through the Book of Mormon coming forth…, also the translation of the Bible—thus bringing forth out of the heart things new and old

Chart 9-8

The Good Samaritan

Explanation

One of the most influential parables is that of the good Samaritan (Lk 10:30–35). People all over the world speak of being a good Samaritan, of helping people who are in need. Jesus told this parable to a lawyer who asked, "Master, what shall I do to inherit eternal life?" As dramatic and crucial as this parable's plain practical content clearly is, a time-honored but now almost forgotten tradition sees this story also as an impressive allegory of the fall and redemption of all mankind. The roots of this interpretation reach deep into early Christian literature. Writing in the late second century A.D., Origen stated that this interpretation came down to him from "one of the elders":

> The man who was going down is Adam. Jerusalem is paradise, and Jericho is the world. The robbers are hostile powers. The priest is the law, the Levite is the prophets, and the Samaritan is Christ. The wounds are disobedience, the beast is the Lord's body, the inn, which accepts all who wish to enter, is the Church. And further, the two coins mean the Father and the Son. The manager of the inn is the head of the Church, to whom its care has been entrusted. And the fact that the Samaritan promises he will return represents the Savior's second coming.

Indeed, to a listener who understands the plan of salvation, each element in this allegory can be seen as corresponding significantly with an important step in the journey of all mankind toward eternal life. Understood in this way, this parable is not only about a man who went down to Jericho but also about every person who comes down to walk upon this earth.

Reference

John W. Welch, "The Good Samaritan: A Type and Shadow of the Plan of Salvation," *BYU Studies* 38/2 (1999): 50–115.

The Good Samaritan

LUKE 10	LDS TYPES AND SHADOWS
a man	all mankind
went down	left premortal existence
from Jerusalem	presence of God
to Jericho	a telestial world
fell	fallen state, sins
among robbers	Satan, expected trials
stripped him	stripping authority, garment
wounded him	blows of mortality
departed	required to depart
left him half dead	two deaths
by chance	not by the original divine plan
priest and Levite	those with partial authority
passed by	lacked higher power to save
Samaritan	Christ, most humble, despised
saw	knowing him and seeing all
had compassion	pure love of Christ
went to him	succoring him in need
bound his wounds	binding, covenant
pouring in	gushing forth and filling up
oil	healing, anointing, Holy Spirit
wine	atoning blood
on his own beast	with helper, triumphal rescue
inn	church, but not a final destination
took care	Jesus personally cares for all
on the morrow	dawning of new day, born again
two denaria	two days, annual temple tax
the innkeeper	any church leader
when I come again	second coming of Christ
repay	cover all costs, reward well

Chart 9-9

Seven Signs
in the Gospel of John

Explanation

Scholars suspect that when the apostle John wrote his Gospel, he had in front of him or knew of a record that scholars have called hypothetically the "Book of Signs." Whether such an independent source existed or not, the Gospel of John features several miracles that validate the teaching of Jesus by showing that he had divine powers. Interestingly, seven miracles are reported in John, a number that occurs prominently in the book of Revelation (see chart 17-1).

Reference

Robert T. Fortna, "Signs/Semeia Source," *ABD*, 6:18–22.

Seven Signs
in the Gospel of John

SIGN	REFERENCE
1. Changing water into wine	Jn 2:1–11
2. Healing an official's son	4:46–54
3. Healing a lame man	5:2–9
4. Feeding the multitude	6:1–13
5. Walking on the water	6:17–21
6. Giving sight to a blind man	9:1–8
7. Raising Lazarus from the dead	11:1–45

Chart 9-10

Repentance
and Obtaining Forgiveness

Explanation

Over and over, Jesus and John the Baptist called people to repentance. When Jesus sent forth his twelve, "they went out, and preached that men should repent" (Mk 6:12). Jesus said, "Except ye repent, ye shall all likewise perish" (Lk 13:5). Some of his most notable parables, including the stories of the prodigal son and the unmerciful servant, deal with the crucial themes of repenting and obtaining forgiveness. Chart 9-11 helps readers to identify some of the key steps of repentance that are reflected in the scriptures that guide people through the process of obtaining forgiveness and reconciliation through the atonement of Jesus Christ.

Reference

Spencer W. Kimball, *The Miracle of Forgiveness* (Salt Lake City: Bookcraft, 1969).

Repentance
and Obtaining Forgiveness

Recognize that an attitude or action is out of harmony with God's will

Remorse, feel genuinely sorry with a broken heart and contrite spirit

Resolve and truly desire to make a permanent change

Report, confess sins to the Lord or bishop and talk with people whom you trust

Rely on the merits and mercy of God and put yourself in his hands

Respond to priesthood guidance

Request forgiveness from the Lord

Receive God's gift of forgiveness

Restitution, repair all possible damage to relationships with God or man

Renew your life through a realization of redemption

Reform your conduct by adopting new patterns of behavior

Reciprocate by forgiving others

Retain a remission by giving generously to those in need

Reinstatement in the household of faith by making new commitments

Repeat the resolve, especially during the sacrament

Rejoice, expressing thanks to God and testimony to others

Chart 9-11

Women and Children

Explanation

During his ministry Jesus interacted often with women and children, and in his teachings he often addressed them. Charts 9-12 and 9-13 show twenty-eight instances and many statements reflecting his concerns for women, widows, mothers, mothers-in-law, and friends who were dear to him. Charts 9-14 and 9-15 demonstrate eight episodes and many expressions of his love for and interest in the children of world who model humility and goodness. Modern readers should not overlook these unusually sensitive manifestations of the Savior's love.

References

John L. Nebeker, "Is There Marrying and Giving in Marriage in Heaven?" *Improvement Era*, March 1912, 391–95.

Michaelene P. Grassli, "Roles of Children," *EM*, 1:266–69.

Teachings and Prophecies of Jesus
Concerning Women

Those who lust after a woman have committed adultery in their hearts	Mt 5:28
Jesus discusses the ramifications of divorce	Mt 5:31–32; Lk 16:18
Jesus explains that he sets the daughter against her mother and the daughter-in-law against her mother-in-law	Mt 10:35; Lk 12:53
Jesus' followers must love him more that they love their mothers, sisters, and daughters	Mt 10:37; Lk 14:26
Jesus prophesies of the queen of the south	Mt 12:42; Lk 11:31
Jesus teaches about marriage and divorce	Mt 19:1–12; Mk 10:2–12
Those who forsake their mothers and wives for him shall inherit eternal life and gain mother and wife in eternity	Mt 19:29; Mk 10:29–30; Lk 18:29–30
Earthly marriages do not last beyond this life	Mt 22:23–33; Mk 12:18–27; Lk 20:27–38
The sorrow of a woman in labor turns to joy at the birth of a child	Jn 16:21
The hardship of women who will be pregnant and nursing preceding the second coming is a measure of their trials	Mt 24:19; Mk 13:17
Two women grinding at the mill prior to the second coming	Mt 24:41; Lk 17:35
Jesus tells the Old Testament story of Elias and a widow	Lk 4:25–26
Until the second coming, as in Noah's day, men and women will continue to marry	Mt 24:38; Lk 17:27
The parable of the ten bridesmaids	Mt 25:1–13
The parable of the woman who puts leaven into bread	Mt 13:33; Lk 13:21
The parable of the woman who finds the lost silver coin	Lk 15:8–10
The parable of the widow and the unjust judge	Lk 18:1–8

Chart 9-12

Jesus' Interactions with Women

After searching for him, Mary finds her young son Jesus teaching in the temple	Lk 2:48
Jesus' mother Mary asks him to turn water to wine at the wedding in Cana	Jn 2:3–5
Jesus goes to Capernaum with his mother	Jn 2:12
Jesus heals Peter's mother-in-law	Mt 8:14–15; Mk 1:29–31; Lk 4:38–39
Jesus talks to the Samaritan woman at the well	Jn 4:6–28
Jesus raises a widow's son at Nain after walking much of the night from Capernaum	Lk 7:11–17
A woman touches Jesus' robe and is healed; he commends her faith	Mt 9:20–22; Mk 5:25–34; Lk 8:43–48
Jesus forgives a sinful woman	Lk 7:36–50
Mary Magdalene, Joanna, Susanna, and many other women minister to Jesus	Lk 8:2–3
Jesus' mother and brothers desire to speak with him	Mt 12:46–50; Mk 3:31–35; Lk 8:19–21
On two occasions, women are among the thousands fed with a few loaves and fishes	Mt 14:21; 15:38
Jesus heals the Syrophenician woman's daughter	Mt 15:21–28; Mk 7:24–30
Jesus does not accuse the woman taken in adultery	Jn 8:3–11
Jesus visits Mary and Martha	Lk 10:38–42
Jesus visits Mary and Martha and raises their brother Lazarus from the dead	Jn 11:1–46

Chart 9-13 (1)

A woman in a crowd blesses Jesus' mother	Lk 11:27–28
Jesus heals a crippled woman on the Sabbath	Lk 13:10–17
Jesus talks to the mother of James and John	Mt 20:20–23
Jesus witnesses a widow give her only mites to the treasury; he praises her generosity	Mk 12:41–44; Lk 21:1–4
A woman anoints Jesus with oil and Jesus defends her actions to the disciples	Mt 26:6–13; Mk 14:3–9
Mary of Bethany anoints Jesus with oil	Jn 12:1–8
Women follow Jesus to his crucifixion and weep; he tells them to weep for themselves and their children	Lk 23:27–30
Women who followed Jesus from Galilee view his crucifixion from afar	Mt 27:55; Mk 15:40; Lk 23:49; Jn 19:25
Jesus entrusts his mother's care to John	Jn 19:26–27
Mary Magdalene and Mary mark where Jesus was laid in the sepulchre so that they can return after the Sabbath to complete burial procedures	Mt 27:61; Mk 15:47; Lk 23:55
Women tend to Jesus' body	Lk 23:56
Mary Magdalene and Mary visit the sepulchre after Jesus' resurrection	Mt 28:1–8; Mk 16:1–8; Lk 24:1–10
The resurrected Jesus first appears to Mary Magdalene	Mt 28:9–10; Mk 16:9–11; Jn 20:11–18

Chart 9-13 (2)

Teachings and Prophecies of Jesus Involving Children

Peacemakers shall be called the children of God	Mt 5:9
This generation is like children in a marketplace	Mt 11:16; Lk 7:32
It is better to be thrown into the sea with a millstone around one's neck than to offend a little child	Mk 9:42; Lk 17:2
Those who love their enemies will be the children of God	Mt 5:44–45
God knows how to give good things to his children	Mt 7:9–11; Lk 11:13
Jesus calls his disciples the children of the bridechamber	Mt 9:15; Mk 2:19; Lk 5:34
Kings do not tax their own children	Mt 17:25–26
Jesus foretells a time when children shall rise up against their parents	Mt 10:21; Mk 13:12
Jesus sets son against father, daughter against mother, and daughter-in-law against mother-in-law	Mt 10:35; Lk 12:53
Those who forsake their children for him shall inherit eternal life and gain their children in eternity	Mt 19:29; Mk 10:29–30; Lk 18:29–30
Jesus' followers must love him more than they love their children	Mt 10:37; Lk 14:26
Children should honor their mother and father	Mt 15:4–6; Mk 7:10–12
Jesus weeps over Jerusalem and prophesies that their children will be destroyed	Lk 19:44
Children are the deeds and works that justify wisdom	Mt 11:19; Lk 7:35
Jesus instructs the people to be children of light	Jn 12:36
Jesus refers to his disciples as "little children"	Jn 13:33
Jesus explains that the children of Abraham would do the works of Abraham	Jn 8:39

The daughters of Jerusalem should weep for their children rather than for Jesus	Lk 23:28
A man who gives a drink of cold water to a child in the name of a disciple will not lose his reward	Mt 10:42
The parable of the prodigal son	Lk 15:11–32
The parable of the two sons	Mt 21:28–32
The parable of the tares: the good seed are the children of the kingdom; the tares are the children of the wicked one	Mt 13:36–43
The parable of the wicked husbandmen who kill the householder's son	Mt 21:33–41; Lk 20:9–18
Children of the resurrection	Lk 20:36

Chart 9-14

Jesus' Interactions
with Children

Raising the widow's son at Nain	Lk 7:11–17
Healing Jairus's twelve-year-old daughter	Mt 9:18–19, 23–26; Mk 5:22–24, 35–43; Lk 8:41–42, 49–56
Using a lad's loaves and fishes to feed the five thousand	Jn 6:9
Children are among the thousands fed by a few loaves and fishes on two occasions	Mt 14:21; Mt 15:38
Healing the Syrophenician woman's daughter	Mt 15:21–28; Mk 7:24–30
Healing an epileptic child	Mt 17:14–21; Mk 9:14–29; Lk 9:37–42
Jesus calls a child out of the crowd to use as an example of humility and righteousness	Mt 18:1–6, 10, 14; Mk 9:36–37; Lk 9:46–48
Jesus suffers the little children to come to him and he blesses them	Mt 19:13–15; Mk 10:13–16; Lk 18:15–17

Chart 9-15

Chart 9-16

Questions Jesus Asked

Explanation

The teaching style of Jesus involved the use of many questions. Chart 9-16 classifies this vast collection of questions used for teaching, demonstration, and reproof. Jesus' questions were pedagogical, forensic, argumentative, and rhetorical. Unlike Socrates and Plato, who constructed long and elaborate dialogues asking question after question, Jesus mostly posed a single question to make an irrefutable point. His questions were penetrating and perceptive. They forced listeners to stop, think, evaluate, and act. This teaching style has much to offer to parents, teachers, and leaders today.

Questions Jesus Asked

MORALIZING, PARABLES, & TEACHING

If the salt have lost his savour, wherewith shall it be salted?
Mt 5:13; Mk 9:50; Lk 14:34

For if ye love them which love you, what reward have ye? do not even the publicans the same? And if ye salute your brethren only, what do ye more than others? do not even the publicans so?
Mt 5:46–47; Lk 6:32–34

Is not the life more than meat, and the body than raiment?
Mt 6:25

Which of you by taking thought can add one cubit unto his stature?
Mt 6:27; Lk 12:25

If God so clothe the grass of the field, shall he not much more clothe you?
Mt 6:30; Lk 12:28

And why beholdest thou the mote that is in thy brother's eye, but considerest not the beam that is in thine own eye? Or wilt thou say to thy brother, Let me pull out the mote out of thine eye; and, behold, a beam is in thine own eye?
Mt 7:3–4; Lk 6:41–42

Or what man is there of you, whom if his son ask bread, will he give him a stone? Or if he ask fish, will he give him a serpent? If ye then, being evil, know how to give good gifts unto your children, how much more shall your Father which is in heaven give good things to them that ask?
Mt 7:9–11; Lk 11:11–13

Do men gather grapes of thorns, or figs of thistles?
Mt 7:16

Wherefore think ye evil in your hearts? For whether is easier, to say, Thy sins be forgiven thee; or to say, Arise, and walk?
Mt 9:5; Mk 2:8–9; Lk 5:22–23

Can the children of the bridechamber mourn, as long as the bridegroom is with them?
Mt 9:15; Mk 2:19; Lk 5:34

If they be called the master of the house Beelzebub, how much more shall they call them of his household?
Mt 10:25

Are not two sparrows sold for a farthing?
Mt 10:29; Lk 12:6

And if Satan cast out Satan, he is divided against himself; how shall then his kingdom stand? And if I by Beelzebub cast out devils, by whom do your children cast them out?
Mt 12:26–27; Mk 3:23; Lk 11:18–19

Or else how can one enter into a strong man's house, and spoil his goods, except he first bind the strong man?
Mt 12:29

Who is my mother? and who are my brethren?
Mt 12:48; Mk 3:33

For what is a man profited, if he shall gain the whole world, and lose his own soul? or what shall a man give in exchange for his soul?
Mt 16:26; Mk 8:36–37; Lk 9:25

What thinkest thou, Simon? of whom do the kings of the earth take custom or tribute? of their own children, or of strangers?
Mt 17:25

Who is the greatest in the kingdom of heaven?
Mt 18:1

Chart 9-16 (1)

How think ye? if a man have an hundred sheep, and one of them be gone astray, doth he not leave the ninety and nine, and goeth into the mountains, and seeketh that which is gone astray?
Mt 18:12; Lk 15:4

Why callest thou me good?
Mt 19:17; Mk 10:18; Lk 18:19

The baptism of John, whence was it? from heaven, or of men?
Mt 21:25; Mk 11:30; Lk 20:4

When the lord therefore of the vineyard cometh, what will he do unto those husbandmen?
Mt 21:40

Did ye never read in the scriptures, The stone which the builders rejected, the same is become the head of the corner: this is the Lord's doing, and it is marvellous in our eyes?
Mt 21:42

Whose is this image and superscription?
Mt 22:20; Mk 12:16; Lk 20:24

But as touching the resurrection of the dead, have ye not read that which was spoken unto you by God, saying, I am the God of Abraham, and the God of Isaac, and the God of Jacob?
Mt 22:31–32; Mk 12:26

How then doth David in spirit call him Lord, saying, The Lord said unto my Lord, sit thou on my right hand, till I make thine enemies thy footstool? If David then call him Lord, how is he his son?
Mt 22:44–45; Mk 12:35–37; Lk 20:41, 43

See ye not all these things?
Mt 24:2

Who then is a faithful and wise servant, whom his lord hath made ruler over his household, to give them meat in due season?
Mt 24:45

Know ye not this parable? and how then will ye know all parables?
Mk 4:13

Is a candlestick brought to be put under a bushel, or under a bed? and not to be set on a candlestick?
Mk 4:21

Whereunto shall we liken the kingdom of God? or with what comparison shall we compare it?
Mk 4:30; Lk 13:18, 20

Seest thou these great buildings?
Mk 13:2

Can the blind lead the blind? shall they not both fall into the ditch?
Lk 6:39

Tell me therefore, which of them will love him most?
Lk 7:42

Seeth thou this woman?
Lk 7:44

Which now of these three, thinkest thou, was neighbor unto him that fell among the thieves?
Lk 10:36

Which of you shall have a friend, and shall go unto him at midnight, and say unto him, Friend, lend me three loaves; For a friend of mine in his journey is come to me, and I have nothing to set before him?
Lk 11:5–6

Ye fools, did not he that made that which is without make that which is within also?
Lk 11:40

Who then is that faithful and wise steward, whom his lord shall make ruler over his household, to give them their portion of meat in due season?
Lk 12:42

I am come to send fire on the earth; and what will I, if it be already kindled?
Lk 12:49

Chart 9-16 (2)

Suppose ye that I am come to give peace on earth?
Lk 12: 51

Suppose ye that these Galilaeans were sinners above all the Galilaeans, because they suffered such things?… Or those eighteen, upon whom the tower in Siloam fell, and slew them, think ye that they were sinners above all men that dwelt in Jerusalem?
Lk 13:2, 4

For which of you, intending to build a tower, sitteth not down first, and counteth the cost, whether he have sufficient to finish it?
Lk 14:28

Or what king, going to make war against another king, sitteth not down first, and consulteth whether he be able with ten thousand to meet him that cometh against him with twenty thousand?
Lk 14:31

Either what woman having ten pieces of silver, if she lose one piece, doth not light a candle, and sweep the house, and seek diligently till she find it?
Lk 15:8

If therefore ye have not been faithful in the unrighteous mammon, who will commit to your trust the true riches? And if ye have not been faithful in that which is another man's, who shall give you that which is your own?
Lk 16:11–12

But which of you, having a servant plowing or feeding cattle, will say unto him by and by, when he is come from the field, Go and sit down to meat? And will not rather say unto him, Make ready wherewith I may sup, and gird thyself, and serve me, till I have eaten and drunken; and afterward thou shalt eat and drink? Doth he thank that servant because he did the things that were commanded him?
Lk 17:7–9

And shall God not avenge his own elect, which cry day and night unto him, though he bear long with them?… Nevertheless when the Son of man cometh, shall he find faith on the earth?
Lk 18:7–8

Wherefore then gavest not thou my money into the bank, that at my coming I might have required mine own with usury?
Lk 19:23

What is this then that is written, The stone which the builders rejected, the same is become the head of the corner?
Lk 20:17

For whether is greater, he that sitteth at meat, or he that serveth? is not he that sitteth at meat?
Lk 22:27

For if they do these things in a green tree, what shall be done in the dry?
Lk 23:31

Have ye here any meat?
Lk 24:41; Jn 21:5

Art thou a master of Israel, and knowest not these things?
Jn 3:10

Are there not twelve hours in the day?
Jn 11:9

Know ye what I have done to you?
Jn 13:12

Do ye enquire among yourselves of that I said, A little while, and ye shall not see me: and again, a little while, and ye shall see me?
Jn 16:19

Put up thy sword into the sheath: the cup which my Father hath given me, shall I not drink it?
Jn 18:11

Sayest thou this thing of thyself, or did others tell it thee of me?
Jn 18:34

Chart 9-16 (3)

Sabbath & Legal

Have ye not read what David did, when he was an hungered, and they that were with him; How he entered into the house of God, and did eat the shewbread, which was not lawful for him to eat, neither for them which were with him, but only for the priests?
Mt 12:34; Mk 2:25–26; Lk 6:3–4

Or have ye not read in the law, how that on the sabbath days the priests in the temple profane the sabbath, and are blameless?
Mt 12:5

What man shall there be among you, that shall have one sheep, and if it fall into a pit on the sabbath day, will he not lay hold on it, and lift it out? How much then is a man better than a sheep?
Mt 12:11–12; Lk 14:3, 5

Are ye also yet without understanding? Do not ye yet understand, that whatsoever entereth in at the mouth goeth into the belly, and is cast out into the draught?
Mt 15:16–17; Mk 7:18–19

Have ye not read, that he which made them at the beginning made them male and female, And said, For this cause shall a man leave father and mother, and shall cleave to his wife: and they shall be one flesh?
Mt 19:4–5

Are ye come out as against a thief with swords and staves for to take me?
Mt 26:53–54; Mk 14:48; Lk 22:52

Is it lawful to do good on the sabbath days, or to do evil? to save life, or to kill?
Mk 3:4

What did Moses command you?
Mk 10:3

What is written in the law? how readest thou?
Lk 10:26

Did not Moses give you the law, and yet none of you keepeth the law? Why go ye about to kill me?
Jn 7:19

Are ye angry at me because I have made a man every whit whole on the sabbath day?
Jn 7:23

Woman, where are those thine accusers? hath no man condemned thee?
Jn 8:10

Is it not written in your law, I said, Ye are gods?
Jn 10:34

Is it not written, My house shall be called of all nations the house of prayer?
Mk 11:17

Is it lawful on the sabbath days to do good, or to do evil? to save life, or to destroy it?
Lk 6:9; 14:3

Thou hypocrite, doth not each of you on the sabbath loose his ox or his ass from the stall, and lead him away to watering? And ought not this woman, being a daughter of Abraham, whom Satan hath bound, lo, these eighteen years, be loosed from this bond on the sabbath day?
Lk 13:15–16

Criticizing & Vipers

What went ye out in the wilderness to see? A reed shaken with the wind?… A man clothed in soft raiment?… A prophet?
Mt 11:7–9; Lk 7:24–26

But whereunto shall I liken this generation?
Mt 11:16; Lk 7:31

O generation of vipers, how can ye, being evil, speak good things?
Mt 12:34

Why do ye also transgress the commandment of God by your tradition?
Mt 14:3

Chart 9-16 (4)

O ye hypocrites, ye can discern the face of the sky; but can ye not discern the signs of the times?
Mt 16:3; Lk 12:56

O faithless and perverse generation, how long shall I be with you? how long shall I suffer you?
Mt 17:17; Mk 9:19; Lk 9:41

Yea; have ye never read, Out of the mouth of babes and sucklings thou hast perfected praise?
Mt 21:16

Why tempt ye me, ye hypocrites?
Mt 22:18; Lk 20:23

Ye fools and blind: for whether is greater, the gold, or the temple that sanctifieth the gold?
Mt 23:17

Ye fools and blind: for whether is greater, the gift, or the altar that sanctifieth the gift?
Mt 23:19

Ye serpents, ye generations of vipers, how can ye escape the damnation of hell?
Mt 23:33

Why doth this generation seek after a sign?
Mk 8:12

How is it that ye have sought me? wist ye not that I must be about my Father's business?
Lk 2:49

And why call ye me, Lord, Lord, and do not the things which I say?
Lk 6:46

If I have told you earthly things, and ye believe not, how shall ye believe, if I tell you of heavenly things?
Jn 3:12

How can ye believe, which receive honour one of another, and seek not the honour that cometh from God only?
Jn 5:44

Doth this offend you? What and if ye shall see the Son of man ascend up where he was before?
Jn 6:61–62

Why do ye not understand my speech?
Jn 8:43

Which of you convinceth me of sin? And if I say the truth, why do ye not believe me?
Jn 8:46

Many good works have I shewed you from my Father; for which of those works do ye stone me?
Jn 10:32

Say ye of him, whom the Father hath sanctified, and sent into the world, Thou blasphemest; because I said, I am the Son of God?
Jn 10:36

If I have spoken evil, bear witness of the evil: but if well, why smitest thou me?
Jn 18:23

Miracles

Believe ye that I am able to do this?
Mt 9:28

How many loaves have ye?
Mt 15:34; Mk 6:38; 8:5

What will ye that I shall do unto you?
Mt 20:32; Mk 10:36; 10:51; Lk 18:41

Why trouble ye this woman?
Mt 26:10; Mk 14:6

What is thy name?
Mk 5:9; Lk 8:30

Who touched my clothes?
Mk 5:30; Lk 8:45

Why make ye this ado, and weep?
Mk 5:39

Chart 9-16 (5)

Why reason ye, because ye have no bread? perceive ye not yet, neither understand? have ye your heart yet hardened? Having eyes, see ye not? and having ears, hear ye not? and do ye not remember? When I brake the five loaves among five thousand, how many baskets full of fragments took ye up?… And when the seven among four thousand, how many baskets full of fragments took ye up?… How is it that ye do not understand?
Mk 8:17–21

What question ye with them?
Mk 9:16

How long is it ago since this came unto him?
Mk 9:21

Were there not ten cleansed? but where are the nine?
Lk 7:17

Woman, what have I do to with thee?
Jn 2:4

Wilt thou be made whole?
Jn 5:6

Whence shall we buy bread, that these may eat?
Jn 6:5

Where have ye laid him?
Jn 11:34

Said I not unto thee, that, if thou wouldest believe, thou shouldest see the glory of God?
Jn 11:40

Woman, why weepest thou? whom seekest thou?
Jn 20:15

If I will that he tarry till I come, what is that to thee?
Jn 21:23

INTERROGATION OF DISCIPLES' FAITH

Why are ye fearful, O ye of little faith?
Mt 8:26

Have ye understood all these things?
Mt 13:51

O thou of little faith, wherefore didst thou doubt?
Mt 14:31; Mk 4:40

O ye of little faith, why reason ye among yourselves, because ye have brought no bread? Do ye not understand, neither remember the five loaves of the five thousand, and how many baskets ye took up? Neither the seven loaves of the four thousand, and how many loaves ye took up? How is it that ye do not understand that I spake it not to you concerning bread, that ye should beware of the leaven of the Pharisees and of the Sadducees?
Mt 16:8–11

Whom do men say that I the Son of man am?
Mt 16:13; Mk 8:27; Lk 9:18

But whom say ye that I am?
Mt 16:15; Mk 8:29; Lk 9:20

Are ye able to drink of the cup that I shall drink of, and to be baptized with the baptism that I am baptized with?
Mt 20:22

What think ye of Christ? whose son is he?
Mt 22:42

What, could ye not watch with me one hour?
Mt 26:40; Mk 14:37

Thinkest thou that I cannot now pray to my Father, and he shall presently give me more than twelve legions of angels? But how then shall the scriptures be fulfilled, that thus it must be?
Mt 26:53–54; Mk 14:48; Lk 22:52

Chart 9-16 (6)

What was it ye disputed among yourselves by the way?
Mk 9:33

Ye know not what ye ask: can ye drink of the cup that I drink of? and be baptized with the baptism that I am baptized?
Mk 10:39

Where is your faith?
Lk 8:25

When I sent you without purse, scrip, and shoes, lacked ye anything?
Lk 22:35

Why sleep ye?
Lk 22:46

Judas, betrayest thou the Son of man with a kiss?
Lk 22:48

What manner of communications are these that ye have one to another, as ye walk, and are sad?
Lk 24:17

What things?
Lk 24:19

Ought not Christ to have suffered these things, and to enter into his glory?
Lk 24:26

Why are ye troubled? and why do thoughts arise in your hearts?
Lk 24:38

What seek ye?
Jn 1:38

Because I said unto thee, I saw thee under the fig tree, believest thou?
Jn 1:50

But if ye believe not his writings, how shall ye believe my words?
Jn 5:47

Will ye also go away?
Jn 6:67

Have not I chosen you twelve, and one of you is a devil?
Jn 6:70

Dost thou believe on the Son of God?
Jn 9:35

Believest thou this?
Jn 11:26

Wilt thou lay down thy life for my sake?
Jn 13:38

Have I been so long time with you, and yet hast thou not known me, Philip? he that hath seen me hath seen the Father; and how sayest thou that, Shew us the Father? Believest thou not that I am in the Father, and the Father in me?
Jn 14:9–10

Do ye now believe?
Jn 16:31

Simon, son of Jonas, lovest thou me more than these?… Simon, son of Jonas, lovest thou me?… Simon, son of Jonas, lovest thou me?
Jn 21:15–17

MISCELLANEOUS

My God, my God, why hast thou forsaken me?
Mt 27:46

Whom seek ye?
Jn 18:7

Why asketh thou me?
Jn 18:21

Chart 9-16 (7)

Chart 9-17

Questions Asked of Jesus

Explanation

Just as Jesus asked many questions of other people, his friends and foes are frequently shown asking questions of him. Chart 9-17 lists the questions and groups them on a spectrum that ranges from faithful and helpful questions to argumentative and hostile questions. As is shown on the last page of this chart, ninety-four questions were asked, spread fairly evenly over the spectrum. The questions asked by the disciples are supportive and constructive; the questions asked by the people in general are fairly neutral; the questions asked by the Jews who opposed Jesus are mainly polemical. Much is revealed by the words that come from a person's own mouth.

Questions Asked of Jesus

Asked by Disciples

Asked by General Disciples

Question	Faithful	Seeking	Marvelling	Worried	Rhetorical	Argumentative	Polemical	Hostile
Why speakest thou unto them in parables? Mt 13:10		X						
Knowest thou that the Pharisees were offended, after they heard this saying? Mt 15:12				X				
Whence should we have so much bread in the wilderness, as to fill so great a multitude? Mt 15:33; Mk 8:4			X					
Why then say the scribes that Elias must first come? Mt 17:10; Mk 9:11		X						
Why could not we cast him out? Mt 17:19; Mk 9:28	X							
Who then can be saved? Mt 19:25; Mk 10:26; Lk 18:26		X						
Tell us, when shall these things be? and what shall be the sign of thy coming, and of the end of the world? Mt 24:3; Mk 13:4		X						
To what purpose is this waste? Mt 26:8; Mk 14:4		X						
Where wilt thou that we prepare for thee to eat the passover? Mt 26:17; Mk 14:12; Lk 22:9	X							
Master, carest thou not that we perish? Mk 4:38				X				
Thou seest the multitude thronging thee, and sayest thou, Who touched my clothes? Mk 5:31; Lk 8:45			X		X			
Shall we go and buy two hundred pennyworth of bread, and give them to eat? Mk 6:37		X						
What might this parable be? Lk 8:9		X						
Master, but when shall these things be? and what sign will there be when these things shall come to pass? Lk 21:7		X						
Lord, shall we smite with the sword? Lk 22:49		X						
Master, who did sin, this man, or his parents, that he was born blind? Jn 9:2		X						
Master, the Jews of late sought to stone thee; and goest thou thither again? Jn 11:8		X						

Chart 9-17 (1)

	Faithful	Seeking	Marvelling	Worried	Rhetorical	Argumentative	Polemical	Hostile
ASKED BY JOHN THE BAPTIST								
I have need to be baptized of thee, and thou comest to me? Mt 3:14	X							
ASKED BY DISCIPLES OF JOHN								
Why do we and the Pharisees fast oft, but thy disciples fast not? Mt 9:14; Mk 2:18; Lk 5:33		X						
Art thou he that should come, or do we look for another? Mt 11:3; Lk 7:19, 20		X						
ASKED BY JAMES AND JOHN								
Lord, wilt thou that we command fire to come down from heaven, and consume them, even as Elias did? Lk 9:54	X							
ASKED BY SIMON PETER								
Lord, how oft shall my brother sin against me, and I forgive him? till seven times? Mt 18:21	X							
Behold, we have forsaken all, and followed thee; what shall we have therefore? Mt 19:27	X							
Lord, speakest thou this parable unto us, or even to all? Lk 12:41		X						
Lord, to whom shall we go? Jn 6:68	X	X						
Lord, dost thou wash my feet? Jn 13:6	X		X					
Lord, who is it? Jn 13:25		X						
Lord, whither goest thou? Jn 13:36		X						
Lord, why cannot I follow thee now? Jn 13:37		X						
Lord, which is he that betrayeth thee? Jn 21:20		X						
Lord, and what shall this man do? Jn 21:21		X						
ASKED BY TWELVE APOSTLES								
Lord, is it I? Mt 26:22; Mk 14:19		X		X				
ASKED BY NATHANAEL								
Whence knowest thou me? Jn 1:48		X	X					

Chart 9-17 (2)

	Faithful	Seeking	Marvelling	Worried	Rhetorical	Argumentative	Polemical	Hostile
ASKED BY ANDREW								
There is a lad here, which hath five barley loaves, and two small fishes: but what are they among so many? Jn 6:9		X						
ASKED BY THOMAS								
Lord, we know not whither thou goest; and how can we know the way? Jn 14:5		X						
ASKED BY JUDAS (NOT ISCARIOT)								
Lord, how is it that thou wilt manifest thyself unto us, and not unto the world? Jn 14:22		X						
ASKED BY NICODEMUS								
How can a man be born when he is old? can he enter the second time into his mother's womb, and be born? Jn 3:4		X						
How can these things be? Jn 3:9		X	X					
ASKED BY MARY, MOTHER OF JESUS								
Son, why hast thou thus dealt with us? Lk 2:48				X				
ASKED BY MARTHA								
Lord, dost thou not care that my sister hath left me to serve alone? Lk 10:40		X		X				
ASKED BY A WOMAN OF SAMARIA								
Sir, thou hast nothing to draw with, and the well is deep: from whence then hast thou that living water? Jn 4:11		X						
Art thou greater than our father Jacob, which gave us the well, and drank thereof himself, and his children, and his cattle? Jn 4:12		X						
ASKED BY A YOUNG MAN								
Good Master, what good thing shall I do, that I may have eternal life? Mt 19:16; Mk 10:17; Lk 10:25; 18:18	X	X						
All these things have I kept from my youth up: what lack I yet? Mt 19:20		X						
ASKED BY MAN CURED OF BLINDNESS								
Who is he, Lord, that I might believe on him? Jn 9:36	X	X						

Chart 9-17 (3)

Asked by the People

ASKED BY UNIDENTIFIED PEOPLE

	Faithful	Seeking	Marvelling	Worried	Rhetorical	Argumentative	Polemical	Hostile
Is not this the son of David? Mt 12:23	X		X	X				
Lord, are there few that be saved? Lk 13:23		X						
Rabbi, when camest thou hither? Jn 6:25			X					
What shall we do, that we might work the works of God? Jn 6:28	X							
What sign shewest thou then, that we may see, and believe thee? what dost thou work? Jn 6:30		X						
We have heard out of the law that Christ abideth for ever: and how sayest thou, The Son of man must be lifted up? who is this Son of man? Jn 12:34		X						

ASKED BY PEOPLE OF JESUS' OWN COUNTRY

	Faithful	Seeking	Marvelling	Worried	Rhetorical	Argumentative	Polemical	Hostile
Whence hath this man this wisdom, and these mighty works? Is not this the carpenter's son? is not his mother called Mary? and his brethren, James, and Joses, and Simon, and Judas? and his sisters, are they not all with us? Whence then hath this man all these things? Mt 13:54–56; Mk 6:2–3; Lk 4:22					X	X		X

ASKED BY ALL IN CITY OF JERUSALEM

	Faithful	Seeking	Marvelling	Worried	Rhetorical	Argumentative	Polemical	Hostile
Who is this? Mt 21:10			X					

ASKED BY SOLDIERS/OFFICERS HOLDING JESUS CAPTIVE

	Faithful	Seeking	Marvelling	Worried	Rhetorical	Argumentative	Polemical	Hostile
Prophesy, who is it that smote thee? Lk 22:64								X
Answerest thou the High Priest so? Jn 18:22					X			X

ASKED BY PONTIUS PILATE

	Faithful	Seeking	Marvelling	Worried	Rhetorical	Argumentative	Polemical	Hostile
Art thou the King of the Jews? Mt 27:11; Mk 15:2; Lk 23:3; Jn 18:33		X						
Hearest thou not how many things they witness against thee? Mt 27:13			X					
Am I a Jew? Thine own nation and the chief priests have delivered thee unto me: what hast thou done? Jn 18:35					X	X		
Art thou a king then? Jn 18:37		X						
Whence art thou? Jn 19:9			X					
Speakest thou not unto me? knowest thou not that I have power to crucify thee, and have power to release thee? Jn 19:10					X		X	

Chart 9-17 (4)

	Faithful	Seeking	Marvelling	Worried	Rhetorical	Argumentative	Polemical	Hostile

ASKED BY DEVILS

	Faithful	Seeking	Marvelling	Worried	Rhetorical	Argumentative	Polemical	Hostile
What have we to do with thee, Jesus, thou Son of God? art thou come hither to torment us before the time? Mt 8:29; Mk 1:24; 5:7; Lk 4:34; 8:28							X	

Asked by the Jews

ASKED BY PHARISEES

	Faithful	Seeking	Marvelling	Worried	Rhetorical	Argumentative	Polemical	Hostile
Is it lawful to heal on the sabbath days? Mt 12:10						X		
Is it lawful for a man to put away his wife for every cause? Mt 19:3; Mk 10:2						X		
Why did Moses then command to give a writing of divorcement, and to put her away? Mt 19:7					X	X		
Tell us therefore, What thinkest thou? Is it lawful to give tribute unto Caesar, or not? Mt 22:17; Mk 12:14–15; Lk 20:22						X		
Master, which is the greatest commandment in the law? Mt 22:36; Mk 12:28						X		
Why do ye that which is not lawful to do on the sabbath days? Lk 6:2						X		
What shall I do to inherit eternal life? Lk 10:25						X	X	
And who is my neighbour? Lk 10:29						X	X	
Where, Lord? Lk 17:37								
Where is thy Father? Jn 8:19					X	X	X	
Are we blind also? Jn 9:40						X	X	

ASKED BY SCRIBES AND PHARISEES

	Faithful	Seeking	Marvelling	Worried	Rhetorical	Argumentative	Polemical	Hostile
Why do thy disciples transgress the tradition of the elders? Mt 15:2						X		
Why walk not thy disciples according to the tradition of the elders, but eat bread with unwashen hands? Mk 7:5					X	X		
Why do ye eat and drink with publicans and sinners? Lk 5:30						X		
Now Moses in the law commanded us, that such should be stoned: but what sayest thou? Jn 8:5					X	X		

ASKED BY SADDUCEES

	Faithful	Seeking	Marvelling	Worried	Rhetorical	Argumentative	Polemical	Hostile
Therefore in the resurrection, whose wife shall she be of the seven? Mt 22:28; Mk 12:23; Lk 20:33						X		

Chart 9-17 (5)

	Faithful	Seeking	Marvelling	Worried	Rhetorical	Argumentative	Polemical	Hostile
ASKED BY THE CHIEF PRIESTS, ELDERS, AND/OR SCRIBES								
Hearest thou what these say? Mt 21:16								X
By what authority doest thou these things? and who gave thee this authority? Mt 21:23; Mk 11:28; Lk 20:2							X	X
Art thou the Christ? Lk 22:67							X	
Art thou then the Son of God? Lk 22:70							X	
ASKED BY THE HIGH PRIESTS								
Answerest thou nothing? what is it which these witness against thee? Mt 26:62; Mk 14:60; 15:4						X		
Art thou the Christ, the Son of the Blessed? Mk 14:61						X		
ASKED BY OTHER JEWS								
What sign shewest thou unto us, seeing that thou doest these things? Jn 2:18		X						
Forty and six years was this temple in building, and wilt thou rear it up in three days? Jn 2:20						X		X
Thou hast a devil: who goeth about to kill thee? Jn 7:20								X
Who art thou? Jn 8:25; 21:12		X				X		
How sayest thou, Ye shall be made free? Jn 8:33						X	X	
Say we not well that thou art a Samaritan, and hast a devil? Jn 8:48								X
Art thou greater than our father Abraham, which is dead? and the prophets are dead: whom makest thou thyself? Jn 8:53						X	X	X
Thou art not yet fifty years old, and hast thou seen Abraham? Jn 8:57					X	X	X	
How long dost thou make us to doubt? Jn 10:24							X	

Chart 9-17 (6)

TOTALS ASKED OF EACH TYPE

	Faithful	Seeking	Marvelling	Worried	Rhetorical	Argumentative	Polemical	Hostile
TOTALS ASKED BY DISCIPLES								
Totals asked by disciples in general	2	10	2	3	1			
Totals asked by John the Baptist	1							
Totals asked by disciples of John		2						
Totals asked by James and John	1							
Totals asked by Simon Peter	4	7	1					
Totals asked by Twelve Apostles		1		1				
Totals asked by Nathanael		1	1					
Totals asked by Andrew		1						
Totals asked by Thomas		1						
Totals asked by Judas (not Iscariot)		1						
Totals asked by Nicodemus		2	1					
Totals asked by Mary, mother of Jesus				1				
Totals asked by Martha		1		1				
Totals asked by woman of Samaria		3	1					
Totals asked by a young man	1	2						
Totals asked by man cured of blindness	1	1						
TOTALS ASKED BY THE PEOPLE								
Totals asked by general people	2	3	2		1			
Totals asked by the people of Jesus' own country					1	1		1
Totals asked by all in city of Jerusalem			1					
Totals asked by soldiers/officers holding Jesus captive					1			2
Totals asked by Pontius Pilate		2	2		2	1	1	
TOTALS ASKED BY JEWS								
Totals asked by Jews in general		2			1	4	5	4
Totals asked by Pharisees						2	10	4
Totals asked by Scribes and Pharisees						2	4	
Totals asked by Sadducees							1	
Totals asked by Chief Priests, Elders, and/or Scribes							3	2
Totals asked by High Priests							2	
Totals asked by devils								1
TOTAL QUESTIONS ASKED OF JESUS								
Totals of each type of question asked	12	40	11	6	7	10	26	14

Chart 9-17 (7)

Chart 9-18

Main Prophetic Predictions
by Jesus

Explanation

Jesus was known as a prophet. When he asked his disciples, "Whom do men say that I the Son of man am?" (Mt 16:13), they said that some people said he was John the Baptist, or Elijah, and others said he was one of the prophets. Deuteronomy 18:18 has prophesied that the Lord would "raise up a Prophet" at a future date, like unto Moses, who would speak in the name of the Lord and to whom the people should hearken. As a prophet, Jesus issued many predictions about future events, including coming persecutions, actions of individual people, his own death, woes and laments, the last days, his second coming, and the final judgment. This dimension of his ministry was more potent than many readers realize.

References

Richard D. Draper, *The Savior's Prophecies* (American Fork, Utah: Covenant Communications, 2001).

Ben Witherington III, *Jesus the Seer: The Progress of Prophecy* (Peabody, Mass.: Hendrickson, 1999).

"Eschatology (Destruction of Jerusalem and the Latter Days)," *WRC*, 13–14.

Main Prophetic Predictions
by Jesus

	MATTHEW	MARK	LUKE	JOHN
Blessings shall be given to the poor in spirit, the mournful, the meek, the righteous, the merciful, the pure in heart, the peacemakers, and the persecuted	5:1–12		6:20–26	
"One jot or one tittle shall not pass"	5:17–18			
COMING PERSECUTIONS				
Cities that do not receive or listen to the apostles will be condemned at the last judgment	10:14–15	6:11	10:11–12	
The apostles are sent to preach as "sheep in the midst of wolves"	10:16			
The apostles will be "deliver[ed] up to the councils" and will be "scourg[ed] in their synagogues; And ye shall be brought before governors and kings for my sake"	10:17–18	13:9	21:12	16:2
"Take no thought beforehand what ye shall speak, neither do ye premeditate," for "I will give you a mouth of wisdom, which all your adversaries shall not be able to gainsay nor resist"	10:19–20	13:11	21:13–15	
The apostles will be betrayed by both family and friends and some will be put to death at their hands	10:21	13:12	21:16	
"Ye shall be hated of all men for my name's sake," but those that endure to the end will be saved and "there shall not an hair of your head perish"	10:22; 24:13	13:13	21:12, 17–19	15:20–21
"All ye shall be offended"	26:31	14:27		
"Ye shall not have gone over the cities of Israel, till the Son of man be come"	10:23			
James and John will suffer	20:20–23	10:35–39		
ACTIONS OF UPPER ROOM OWNER				
In the city you "shall meet a man bearing a pitcher of water"		14:13	22:10	
He will enter into a house. Follow him.		14:13	22:10	
"He will shew you a large upper room furnished and prepared"		14:15	22:12	

Chart 9-18 (1)

	MATTHEW	MARK	LUKE	JOHN
JUDAS'S AND PETER'S ACTIONS				
"One of you shall betray me"	26:21	14:18		13:21
"The hand of him that betrayeth me is with me on the table"			22:21	
"He that dippeth his hand with me in the dish, the same shall betray me"	26:23	14:20		13:26
"Woe to that man by whom the Son of man is betrayed! Good were it for that man if he had never been born"	26:24	14:21	22:22	
Judas asks, "Master, is it I?" and Jesus replies, "Thou hast said"	26:25			
Peter shall deny	26:34	14:30	22:34	13:36–38
DEATH AND RESURRECTION OF JESUS				
"Little children, yet a little while I am with you. Ye shall seek me"				13:33
"I will not drink henceforth"	26:29	14:25		
First prediction of his own death	16:21–28	8:31–9:1	9:22–27	16:16–20
Second prediction of his own death	17:22–23	9:30–32	9:43–45	
Third prediction of his own death	20:17–19	10:32–34	18:31–34	
"The third day I shall be perfected"			13:32	
"Son of man be risen again from the dead" on the third day	12:39–40; 16:4; 17:9; 26:32	9:9–10; 14:28	11:29–30	12:32–33
"I will go before you into Galilee"	26:32	14:28		
WOES AGAINST SCRIBES AND PHARISEES				
Scribes and Pharisees will slay and persecute prophets of the Lord	23:34		11:49	
Blood of the prophets to be required of this generation	23:36		11:50–51	
Scribes and Pharisees "shall receive greater damnation"	23:14, 33	12:40	20:47	
LAMENT OVER JERUSALEM				
If thou hadst known the things that could have been yours, "but now they are hid from thine eyes"	23:37		13:34; 19:42	
This house is left desolate	23:38		13:35	
"Ye shall not see me henceforth, till ye shall say, Blessed is he that cometh in the name of the Lord"	23:39		13:35	

Chart 9-18 (2)

	MATTHEW	MARK	LUKE	JOHN
JERUSALEM'S FALL				
"For the days shall come upon thee, that thine enemies shall cast a trench about thee, and compass thee round, and keep thee in on every side"			19:43	
The city will be leveled and its people buried in the ground			19:44	
When Jerusalem is surrounded with armies, its desolation is nigh			21:20	
Woe to the mothers with infants "in those days! for there shall be great distress in the land, and wrath upon this people"			21:23	
"And they shall fall by the edge of the sword"			21:24	
Israel will be scattered in bondage in all nations			21:24	
"And Jerusalem shall be trodden down of the Gentiles, until the times of the Gentiles be fulfilled"			21:24	
Destruction of the Temple of Herod	24:1–2	13:1–2	21:5–6, 20–24	
THE LAST DAYS				
"The father shall be divided against son, and the son against the father; the mother against the daughter, and the daughter against the mother"			12:53	
When preaching the gospel in the last days, do not premeditate your words; the Holy Ghost will give you utterance	10:19	13:11	21:13–15	
Family members shall betray and kill each other	10:21	13:12	21:16	
"Many shall come in my name, saying, I am Christ; and shall deceive many"	23:5	13:6	21:8	
You shall hear of wars and rumors of wars	24:6	13:7	21:9	
"All these things must come to pass, but the end is not yet"	24:6	13:7	21:9	
"Nation shall rise against nation, and kingdom against kingdom"	24:7	13:8	21:10	
"There shall be famines, and pestilences, and earthquakes, in diverse places"	24:7	13:8	21:11	
Persecution of the disciples	24:9	13:9	21:12	
Many will be offended, betrayed, and hated	24:10			

Chart 9-18 (3)

	Matthew	Mark	Luke	John
"Many false prophets shall rise and shall deceive many"	24:11, 24	13:22		
Iniquity shall abound and the love of many shall wax cold	24:12			
"This gospel of the kingdom shall be preached in all the world for a witness unto all nations; and then shall the end come"	24:14	13:10		
The righteous will need to flee to holy places	24:15–20	13:14–18	21:21	
"Woe unto them that are with child, and to them that give suck in those days!"	24:19	13:17	21:23	
There shall be greater tribulation than has been since the beginning of this world	24:21	13:19		
"Days shall be shortened"	24:22	13:20		
Apostasy and error: "False Christs, and false prophets shall shew great signs and wonders" and will deceive many	24:24	13:21–22	17:23	
Those who sacrifice in selflessness will have their lives preserved			17:33	
"The sea and the waves roaring"			21:25	
"Upon the earth distress of nations"			21:25	
"Men's hearts failing them"			21:26	
"When ye shall see these things come to pass, know that it is nigh, even at the doors"		13:29	21:31	
"This generation shall not pass, till all these things be done"		13:30	21:32	

COMING OF THE KINGDOM

	Matthew	Mark	Luke	John
Will not come to one specific, observable place, but will come within you			17:20	
"For there shall be new heavens, and a new earth, wherein dwelleth righteousness"			17:39 JST	
The earth will be cleansed of all sin			17:40 JST	
The Holy Ghost will come				6:7; 14:16; 15:26

Chart 9-18 (4)

	Matthew	Mark	Luke	John
COMING OF THE SON OF MAN				
His own second coming				14:3; 16:16
Sorrow will turn to joy				16:20
The false Christs will say "He is in the desert. He is in the secret chambers," but do not believe them	24:26			
"As the lightning cometh out of the east, and shineth even unto the west; so shall the coming of the Son of man be"	24:27		17:24	
Sun and moon will be darkened and the stars will fall from heaven, and the powers of heaven will be shaken	24:29	13:24–25	21:25, 26	
"The days will come, when ye shall desire to see one of the days of the Son of man, and ye shall not see it"			17:22	
"Then shall appear the sign of the Son of man in heaven"	24:30			
"Then shall all the tribes of the earth mourn, and they shall see the Son of man coming in the clouds of heaven with power and great glory"	24:30	13:26	21:27	
Angels will sound trumpets with great glory, gathering his elect from all ends of heaven and earth	24:31	13:27		
Only the Father knows the day and hour of the second coming	24:36	13:32		
Coming of the Son of Man likened to the coming of the flood in the day of Noah	24:37–39		17:26–27	
Days before the coming of the Son of Man likened to the days of Lot in Sodom when "it rained fire and brimstone from heaven, and destroyed them all. Even thus shall it be in the day when the Son of man is revealed"			17:29–30	
Coming of the Son of Man likened to "a man taking a far journey, who left his house, and gave authority to his servants, and to every man his work, and commanded the porter to watch"	24:43	13:34		
He comes "in such an hour as ye think not"	24:44			
The Saints will be gathered and angels will descend and gather the remainder of the Saints from all places			17:37–38 JST	

Chart 9-18 (5)

	MATTHEW	MARK	LUKE	JOHN
The Son of Man will come in glory with angels around him and will sit on the throne of glory	25:31			
All nations will appear before him	25:32		13:29	
"He shall separate them one from another"	25:32			
THE LAST JUDGMENT				
Unrepentant cities will not be tolerated in the judgment day	11:24		10:14	
Secrets will be revealed and preached from the housetops			12:2–3	
Many will not be able to enter the strait gate because the Lord will not recognize the sinful and will tell them to depart	7:13, 23		13:24–27	
There will be weeping and gnashing of teeth when the sinful see Abraham, Isaac, Jacob, and all the prophets in the kingdom of God and they themselves are thrust out			13:28	
One of every two will be left behind	24:40		17:34–36	
The last shall be first and the first shall be last			13:30	
"And he shall set the sheep on his right hand, but the goats on the left"	25:33			
The King will invite those on his right hand to inherit the kingdoms prepared for them since the foundation of the world	25:34			
The righteous will question their good works in humility	25:37–39			
The King will curse those on his left hand to depart from him and enter everlasting fire prepared for the devil	25:41			
The unrighteous will defend their works in pride	25:44			
The unrighteous will suffer everlasting punishment, but the righteous will inherit eternal life	25:46			

Chart 9-18 (6)

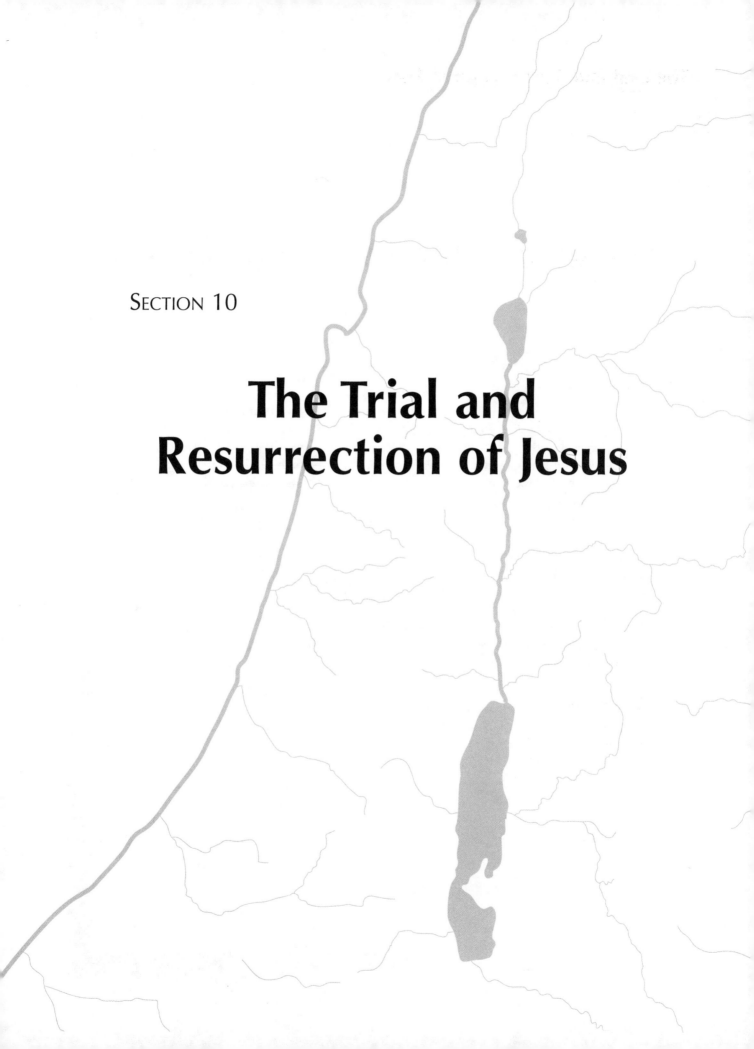

SECTION 10

The Trial and
Resurrection of Jesus

Chart 10-1

Features in the Four Approaches

Explanation

Central to any interpretation of the New Testament is an understanding of the trial and resurrection of Jesus. Everything in the Gospels builds to the concluding hours of his life, and virtually everything in Christianity turns on how one views these critical events.

The death of Jesus, however, is not easy to understand. From the beginning, it was difficult for many of his followers to understand and accept. Most messianic expectations assumed that the Anointed One would come in a glorious fashion, even though Isaiah 53 had prophesied otherwise; and the fact that Jesus was hung on a tree was a scandal to many, who used this shameful execution in denigrating him.

In light of the importance and complexity of these historic moments, it is not surprising that the four Gospels take different approaches to these far-reaching events. Consistent with the varying approaches taken in the Gospels generally (see charts 7-2 and 7-3), each of the four Gospels emphasizes different aspects of the trial and death of Jesus. Luke consistently features humanitarian and public elements; Matthew draws upon Israelite factors; Mark gives a straightforward, powerful account; and John consistently directs attention toward eternal and divine elements.

References

John W. Welch, "Latter-day Saint Reflections on the Trial and Death of Jesus," *Clark Memorandum* (fall 2000): 2–13.
"Passion Week," *WRC*, 41–46.

Features in the Four Approaches

MATTHEW: Israelite Features	MARK: Power Features	LUKE: Populist Features	JOHN: Eternal Features
Twelve legions of angels (compare the twelve tribes of Israel)	When the ear is cut off and healed, no words, just actions	Concern about lowly servant, healing his ear	Foreknowledge of the actions of Judas
Jesus is taken directly to high priest, adjudicator of Jewish law	They arrest Jesus under heavy guard	The arresters blaspheme Jesus (the popular world rejects Jesus)	Concern over impurity in Praetorium
False witnesses testify (compare witnesses against Naboth)	False witnesses are powerless	No actual accusation until before Pilate (making it a public affair)	Concern over who has power to deliver
Jesus shows respect for the Jewish Temple with power over it	Jesus said, "I will destroy this temple"	Allegations involve ordinary public offenses: he stirs up the people	God as king? "We have no king but Caesar"
Focus on blasphemy, violation of Jewish law	Jesus responds powerfully, "I am"	Herod's soldiers play games	"My kingdom is not of this world"
Israelites willing to take responsibility: "His blood be upon us"	Those with power move against Jesus, all condemning Jesus	Women are mentioned; Jesus prophesies to them	"For this cause came I into the world"
When the earth shook, dead Israelites arose	Guards beat Jesus	Jesus asks the Father to forgive those who crucified him	Casting of lots, thirsting, side pierced; all fulfilled prophecy
	Crowd is very demanding, threatening riot	The robber on the cross invited into paradise	Jesus said, "It is finished"
	Roman soldiers mock Jesus' power	The crowd beats their breasts	
	Joseph of Arimathea, a powerful member of the Sanhedrin, mentioned		

Chart 10-1

Unique Information or Features
in Matthew, Mark, Luke, John, and the JST

Explanation

Each of the four Gospels provides unique information about the arrest, interrogations, trials, and execution of Jesus. The following charts spell out the data that is found exclusively in each of these accounts. Charts 10-3 through 10-6 are based on the Greek text of the New Testament, further details of which are conveniently displayed in tabular form in Kurt Aland, *Synopsis of the Four Gospels*, published by the German Bible Society. Careful readers of the New Testament will gain appreciation for each of the four Gospels by seeing how each one uniquely contributes to our understanding of the trial of Jesus. Chart 10-2 points out the details supplied exclusively by the Joseph Smith Translation.

References

Raymond E. Brown, *The Death of the Messiah* (New York: Doubleday, 1994).
John W. Welch and Matthew G. Wells, "Recent Bibliography on the Trials of Jesus," *BYU Studies* 32/4 (1992): 78–86.

Unique Information or Features in the JST

1. Jesus healed the servant's ear by touching it *with his finger* (Compare Mk 14:47; 14:53 JST).

2. The disciples fled *because they heard this saying* (Mk 14:50; 14:56 JST).

3. The young man who fled was *a disciple* (Mk 14:51; 14:57 JST).

4. The young man who fled *saved himself from the arresters* (Mk 14:52; 14:57 JST).

5. Jesus answered Pilate, "Thou sayest *truly; for thus it is written of me*" (Mt 27:11; 27:12 JST).

6. Jesus answered Pilate, "*I am, even as thou sayest*" (Mk 15:2; 15:4 JST).

7. Pilate's wife had a *vision* (Mt 27:19; 27:20 JST).

8. Pilate told the Jews, "See *that ye do nothing unto him*" (Mt 27:24; 27:26 JST).

9. Golgotha means *"place of burial"* (Mt 27:33; 27:35 JST; Mk 15:22; 15:25 JST; Jn 19:17; 19:17 JST).

10. In his words from the cross, Jesus expressly forgave only *the soldiers* who crucified him (Lk 23:34; 23:35 JST).

11. Pilate *himself* wrote the title, "King of the Jews" (Mt 27:37; 27:39 JST; Mk 15:26; 15:29 JST).

Chart 10-2

Unique Information or Features in Matthew

1. The arresting crowd was "great" (26:47).

2. Jesus said he could call down twelve legions of angels (26:53).

3. The crowd took Jesus directly to Caiaphas (mentioned by name; 26:57).

4. The council sought *false* testimony (26:59).

5. Jesus had said, "I *am able* to destroy the Temple of God" (26:61).

6. The High Priest tried to get Jesus to swear under oath that he was the son of God, but Jesus wouldn't answer with an oath (26:63).

7. The High Priest said, "he has uttered blasphemy" (26:65).

8. The death of Judas is recorded (27:3–10; Luke places this in Acts).

9. Pilate's wife requested Jesus' release because of a dream (27:19).

10. Jesus was undressed before the robe was put on him (27:28).

11. Pilate acted because a riot was beginning (27:24).

12. Pilate washed his hands and said, "I am innocent of this man's blood" (27:24).

13. All the people said, "His blood be on us, and on our children" (27:25).

14. Jesus "gave up the spirit" [KJV, yielded up the ghost] (27:50).

15. The earth shook, rocks split, tombs opened, and dead were raised and appeared to many (27:51–53).

16. The centurion and others were filled with great fear (27:54).

17. The Chief Priests and Pharisees asked Pilate to place a guard at the tomb, but he told them to use their own guards; they sealed and guarded the tomb (27:62–66).

Unique Information or Features in Mark

1. Jesus says nothing when the High Priest's slave's ear is cut off (14:48).

2. Judas told the crowd to take Jesus away "under guard" (14:44).

3. Jesus had taught in the temple "right before" the crowd's eyes, not just there or with them (14:49).

4. A young man flees naked (14:51–52).

5. Jesus said, "I *will* destroy this temple," not just "I am able to" (14:58).

6. The false witnesses did not agree with each other (14:56, 59).

7. Jesus said, "I am" (14:62).

8. All present in the Sanhedrin condemned Jesus (14:64).

9. The Jewish guards took and beat Jesus (14:65).

10. Pilate turned Jesus over to the crowd in order to satisfy them (15:15).

11. The Roman soldiers bowed down in mock homage (15:19).

12. Simon of Cyrene was the father of Alexander and Rufus (15:21).

13. Jesus was crucified the third hour of the day (15:25).

14. Jesus "expired" [KJV, gave up the ghost] (15:37).

15. Salome, who had ministered to and followed Jesus in Galilee, was with the other women at the cross (15:40–41).

16. Jesus was crucified on the day of preparation, the day before the Sabbath (15:42).

17. Joseph of Arimathea "took courage" [KJV, went in boldly] to ask for the body of Jesus (15:43).

18. Pilate wondered and asked a centurion whether Jesus was already dead (15:44).

Unique Information or Features in Luke

1. Disciples asked Jesus whether they should "strike with the sword" (22:49).

2. Jesus healed the servant's ear (22:51; also Mk 14:53 JST "put forth his finger").

3. In the arresting crowd were the Chief Priests, officers of the temple, and elders (22:52).

4. Jesus said, "This is your hour" (22:53).

5. The arresting crowd took Jesus to the High Priest's *house* (22:54).

6. Upon Peter's third denial, "the Lord turned, and looked upon Peter," and then Peter remembered what Jesus had said (22:61).

7. The arresters "blasphemed" Jesus (22:65).

8. Jesus told the elders, "If I tell you, you will not believe" (22:67).

9. The Jews accused Jesus first after taking him to Pilate (23:2).

10. Jesus was accused of perverting the nation, forbidding taxation, and saying he was Christ King (23:2).

11. An accusation of blasphemy against Jesus is never mentioned.

12. Once Pilate said he found no fault with Jesus, the Chief Priests and multitudes were "urgent, saying 'He stirs up the people, teaching throughout all Judea, from Galilee even to this place'" (23:5).

13. Jesus was taken to Herod, who was glad to see him and who hoped to see a sign. Herod's men mocked Jesus and dressed him in a gorgeous robe (23:6–11).

Chart 10-5 (1)

14. The Chief Priests and scribes vehemently accused Jesus (23:10).

15. Pilate proposed to flog Jesus and let him go (23:16).

16. Pilate said three times, "What evil has he done?" (23:4, 13–16, 22).

17. The crowd *all* urgently cried for Jesus' crucifixion (23:18, 23).

18. Pilate wanted to release Jesus (23:22).

19. Pilate gave *formal sentence* that the crowd's demand for Jesus to be killed be granted (23:24).

20. Jesus prophesied to the women as he was led to the hill (23:28–31).

21. Along with the women, at a distance, were "all his acquaintance[s]" (23:49).

22. The two criminals executed with Jesus were led out with him (23:32).

23. Jesus said, "Father, forgive them" (23:34).

24. Dialogue between Jesus and the thieves crucified with him; Jesus said, "Today you will be with me in paradise" (23:39–43).

25. The sun's light failed between the sixth and the ninth hours (23:44–45).

26. Jesus said, "Father, into thy hands I entrust my spirit" [KJV, commend my spirit] (23:46).

27. The crowds returned home beating their breasts (23:48).

28. Joseph of Arimethea had not consented to the Sanhedrin's purpose and deed (23:51).

Chart 10-5 (2)

Unique Information or Features in John

1. Judas had *procured* the arresting crowd, not just led or come with it (18:3).

2. The arresting crowd consisted of a "band of soldiers" and officers [KJV, men and offices] from the Chief Priests and Pharisees (18:3).

3. The arresting crowd came with lanterns and torches (18:3).

4. Jesus spoke to his arresters, not just Judas, in the garden (18:4–9).

5. Upon hearing Jesus say "I am," the arresters fell to the ground (18:6).

6. Peter was the disciple who drew his sword (18:10).

7. The High Priest's servant was named Malchus (18:10).

8. The crowd took Jesus to Annas (18:13).

9. Another disciple followed the crowd with Peter (18:15).

10. That other disciple entered the High Priest's hall (18:15).

11. One of the officers struck Jesus and told him not to evade the High Priest's question (18:22).

12. The second person to ask Peter whether he knew Jesus was a kinsman of the man whose ear Peter had cut off (18:26).

13. To avoid impurity, the Jews did not go into the Praetorium (18:28).

14. The Jews claimed they lacked power to execute Jesus (18:31).

15. Jesus spoke extensively to Pilate (18:33–38).

16. Barabbas was a robber (18:40).

17. Jews taunted Pilate, "you are no friend of Caesar" (19:8–15).

18. Pilate scourged Jesus (19:1).

19. Pilate said "behold the man" to the Jews (19:5).

20. Pilate became very afraid (19:8).

Chart 10-6 (1)

21. Pilate, when Jesus did not answer his question, asked if Jesus knew Pilate had the power to release or to crucify him (19:10).

22. Jesus said, "he who delivered me unto [Pilate] hath the greater sin" (19:11).

23. The Jews said, "We have no king but Caesar" (19:15).

24. Pilate himself wrote the words of the title for the cross (19:19; also Mt JST, Mk JST).

25. Many of the Jews read the titlus because the place of crucifixion was near the city and the sign was written in three languages—Hebrew, Latin, and Greek (19:20).

26. Pilate said, "What I have written I have written" (19:22).

27. The coat of Jesus had no seam (19:23).

28. The casting of lots for Jesus' garments fulfilled scripture (19:24).

29. Jesus put his mother into the care of the disciple (19:26–27).

30. Jesus said, to fulfill scripture, "I thirst" (19:28).

31. The reed used to pass the sponge of vinegar up to Jesus was hyssop (19:29).

32. Jesus said, "It is finished" and "gave over his spirit" [KJV, gave up the ghost] (19:30).

33. The soldiers pierced Jesus' side, and this fulfilled scripture (19:34–36).

34. Joseph of Arimathea was a secret disciple of Jesus (19:38).

35. Nicodemus went with Joseph of Arimathea, bringing a mixture of myrrh and aloes (19:39).

36. The tomb was in a garden (19:41).

Chart 10-7

The Arrest of Jesus

Explanation

The arrest of Jesus took place at night on the Mount of Olives. But who arrested him? Did Judas actually kiss Jesus? What happened with Peter's sword and the servant's ear? Where was Jesus taken immediately after the arrest? These and several other similar questions can be asked about the arrest of Jesus. The answers are not always as clear as we would like them to be. Wrestling with limited textual evidence is challenging but essential in sorting out what actually happened, who was involved, and how and why certain events transpired.

Reference

Paula Fredriksen, *Jesus of Nazareth: King of the Jews* (New York: Vintage, 1999).

The Arrest of Jesus

THE MULTITUDE

The multitude who arrested Jesus was "from the chief priests and elders of the people."	Mt 26:47
The multitude was "from the chief priests and the scribes and the elders."	Mk 14:43
In the "multitude" were "the chief priests, and captains of the temple, and the elders."	Lk 22:47, 52
The arresting crowd consisted of "a band of men and officers from the chief priests and Pharisees."	Jn 18:3

THE KISS

Judas said, "Hail, master," and kissed Jesus.	Mt 26:49
Judas said, "Master, master," and kissed Jesus.	Mk 14:45
Judas "drew near unto Jesus to kiss him," but Jesus asked, "Judas, betrayest thou the Son of man with a kiss?"	Lk 22:47–48
There is no mention of Judas kissing Jesus.	Jn 18:5

THE SWORD

Jesus told the disciple who cut off the ear of the High Priest's servant to put his sword away.	Mt 26:52
There is no mention of Jesus saying anything to the disciple who cut off the High Priest's servant's ear.	Mk 14:47
Disciples asked Jesus whether they should "smite with the sword," and Jesus answered "Suffer ye thus far," after one cut off the High Priest's servant's right ear.	Lk 22:49
Jesus told Peter to put away his sword after he cut off the right ear of Malchus, the High Priest's servant.	Jn 18:10–11

THE HEALING

There is no mention of Jesus healing the servant's ear.	Mt 26:51
Jesus healed the servant's ear by touching it with his finger.	Mk 14:47 JST
There is no mention of Jesus healing the servant's ear.	Mk 14:47
Jesus healed the servant's ear.	Lk 22:51
There is no mention of Jesus healing the servant's ear.	Jn 18:11

THE HIGH PRIEST

The crowd took Jesus to Caiaphas, the High Priest.	Mt 26:57–58
The crowd took Jesus to the High Priest.	Mk 14:53
The crowd took Jesus to the house of the High Priest.	Lk 22:54
The crowd took Jesus to Annas, the father-in-law of Caiaphas, the High Priest.	Jn 18:13

Chart 10-7

Chart 10-8

The Hearing before the Council

Explanation

One of the greatest difficulties in reconstructing the events of the trial of Jesus is ascertaining what happened, or most likely happened, when he was interrogated before the Jewish council. Many important legal issues remain very obscure. Who were these people? Was this an official trial, or something akin to a grand jury investigation, only an informal hearing? When did the council meet? How many judges were there? Were witnesses produced? What questions was Jesus asked? How did he answer? Were those questions directly related to alleged crimes, or were they simply probing for further allegations? Was an actual accusation and verdict reached, or did the council just express outrage? What was the purpose and intent behind humiliating and shaming Jesus? On close inspection, different conclusions emerge from the different Gospels.

Reference

Haim Cohn, *The Trial and Death of Jesus* (New York: Ktav, 1977), 94–141.

The Hearing before the Council

THE COUNCIL

The council assembled at night.	Mt 26:57, 59, 74
The council assembled at night.	Mk 14:53, 55, 68
The council assembled "as soon as it was day."	Lk 22:66
The council assembled at night or very early in the morning.	Jn 18:28

THE WITNESSES

Two false witnesses said that Jesus had said, "I am able to destroy the temple of God, and to build it in three days."	Mt 26:61
Certain witnesses said that Jesus had said, "I will destroy this temple that is made with hands, and within three days I will build another made without hands."	Mk 14:58
There is no mention of witnesses being brought against Jesus.	Lk 22:71
There is no mention of witnesses being brought against Jesus.	Jn 18:19, 23

THE QUESTIONS

Caiaphas asked Jesus if he was the Christ, and Jesus answered, "Thou hast said."	Mt 26:63–64
When asked if he was the Christ, Jesus answered, "Thou sayest truly; for thus it is written of me."	Mt 27:11 JST
Caiaphas asked Jesus if he was the Christ; Jesus answered, "I am."	Mk 14:61–62
The council asked Jesus if he was the Christ, and Jesus answered, "If I tell you, ye will not believe: And if I also ask you, ye will not answer me, nor let me go…. Ye say that I am."	Lk 22:67–70
There is no mention of Jesus being asked whether he was the Christ.	Jn 18:19

THE ACCUSATIONS

Caiaphas rent his clothes, saying, "He hath spoken blasphemy; what further need have we of witnesses?" The council said Jesus was "guilty of death."	Mt 26:65–66
Caiaphas rent his clothes and said, "What need we any further witnesses? Ye have heard the blasphemy." All the council found Jesus "to be guilty of death."	Mk 14:63–64
The council said, "What need we any further witness? for we ourselves have heard of his own mouth."	Lk 22:71
There is no mention of witnesses or of Jesus declaring he is the Christ.	Jn 18:28

THE HUMILIATION

The council spit in Jesus' face, buffeted him, and "smote him with the palms of their hands, Saying, Prophesy unto us, thou Christ, Who is he that smote thee?"	Mt 26:67–68
Some of the council "began to spit on him, and to cover his face, and to buffet him, and to say unto him, Prophesy: and the servants did strike him with the palms of their hands."	Mk 14:65
The "men that held Jesus" mocked him, smote him, blindfolded him, and asked him to "prophesy" who it was that smote him.	Lk 22:63–64
One of the officers struck Jesus with the palm of his hand.	Jn 18:22

Chart 10-8

Comparative Details

Explanation

The trial of Jesus is one of the most complicated historical matters in the entire New Testament and perhaps in all of legal history. Commentators have greatest difficulty dealing with varying details in the four accounts, particularly when those variations contradict each other. Chart 10-9 spells out the varying details. In these cases, it is possible to reconcile the accounts by assuming that both are correct, even though this may produce puzzling or awkward results. Chart 10-10 shows twenty ways in which the accounts of the trials of Jesus contradict each other. In these instances, reconciliation is less obvious. Usually a reader must choose to follow one account or another. Chart 10-11 points out well-attested elements in the trial of Jesus that are absent in some of the Gospels but are present in all three of the other accounts. John contains by far the greatest amount of unique information, but Luke also has expanded his account well beyond those of Mark and Matthew.

Reference

Kurt Aland, *Synopsis of the Four Gospels: Greek-English Edition of the Synopsis Quattuor Evangeliorum,* 10th ed. (Stuttgart: German Bible Society, 1993).

Varying Details

1. Did Jesus speak to Judas (Mt 26:50; Lk 22:48), his arresters (Jn 18:4), or both?

2. Did Jesus say to Judas "wherefore art thou come?" (Mt 26:50), or "betrayest thou the Son of man with a kiss" (Lk 22:48)?

3. Was it not just an ear (Mt 26:51; Mk 14:47) but the right ear (Lk 22:50; Jn 18:10) of the servant that was cut off by a disciple in the garden?

4. Did the council seek witnesses who may have been honest (Mk 14:55), or did they perversely seek false witnesses (Mt 26:59)?

5. Regarding being the son of God, did Jesus answer "I am" (Mk 14:62), "Thou hast said" (Mt 26:64; Lk 22:70), or both?

6. Did the High Priest say "You have heard the blasphemy" (Mt 26:65; Mk 14:64), did the assembly say "We ourselves have heard [enough] from his own mouth" (Lk 22:71), or both?

7. Did the High Priest tear his robes (Mt 26:65; Mk 14:63)? Nothing is said of this in Luke or John.

8. Did the Jewish council find Jesus worthy of death (Mt 22:66; Mk 14:64), or did they not reach an explicit verdict (Luke is silent on this point)?

9. Was Jesus bound (Mt 27:2; Mk 15:1), taken (Lk 23:1; Jn 18:28), or both?

10. Was Pilate amazed (Mt 27:14; Mk 15:5), did he simply find no fault in Jesus (Lk 23:4; Jn 18:38), or both?

11. Did the Roman soldiers put a reed in Jesus' right hand (Mt 27:29), did they strike his head with a reed (Mk 15:19), or both?

12. Did the Roman soldiers mock Jesus after Pilate had consented to his death (Mt 27:27–31; Mk 15:15–20), or did the Roman soldiers do this before Pilate had finished talking to Jesus (Jn 19:2–4), or both?

13. Was the drink offered to Jesus at the outset (Mt 27:34; Mk 15:23), at the end (Jn 19:29–30), or both?

14. Was the robe purple (Mk 15:17; Jn 19:2; Mt 27:27 JST) or scarlet (Mt 27:28), or do the Greek words synonymously describe the same color?

15. Was Jesus struck by the men of the assembly after the trial at Caiaphas's palace (Mt 26:67–68; Mk 14:65), by the arresters before the trial (Lk 22:64), by a Jewish officer during the trial (Jn 18:23), or by all of them?

16. Did the soldiers say, "This man was the Son of God" (Mt 27:54; Mk 15:39), "This was a righteous man" (Lk 23:47), or both?

Chart 10-9

Unresolved Differences

1. Did Judas actually kiss Jesus (Mt 26:49; Mk 14:45), or only try to (Lk 22:47)?

2. Did the disciples escape (Mk 14:50), or did Jesus negotiate their release (Jn 18:8)?

3. Did they take Jesus to Caiaphas (Mt 26:57), or to Annas and then Caiaphas (Jn 18:13, 24)?

4. Were men gathered at the house of the High Priest (Mt 26:57; Mk 14:53), or was the High Priest alone (as Jn 18:13–16 and Lk 22:54 imply)?

5. Was the whole Sanhedrin gathered (Mt 27:1; Mk 15:1), or did some simply gather together (Lk 22:66)?

6. Were there two meetings of the council of the Sanhedrin—one at night and one at daybreak (Mt 26:59; 27:1; Mk 14:55; 15:1), just one meeting at daybreak (Lk 22:66), or just one before the arrest of Jesus (Jn 18:3)?

7. Did a council of the Sanhedrin meet at night (Mt 26:59; Mk 14:55), or only when day came (Lk 22:66)?

8. Did Jesus answer nothing about his teaching about the temple (Mt 26:62–63; Mk 14:60–61), or did he converse with the High Priest about his teaching (Jn 18:20–23)?

9. Did the High Priest say "what further need have we of witnesses?" (Mt 26:65; Mk 14:63), or did the assembly say this (Lk 22:71)?

10. Did the assembly all condemn Jesus (Mk 14:64; 15:1), or did some abstain (Lk 23:27)?

11. Did Jesus remain silent before Pilate (Mt 27:14), or did he speak much (Jn 18:34–37)?

12. Did Pilate propose to release Barabbas in place of Jesus (Mt 27:17), or did the crowd ask him to (Mk 15:11; Lk 23:18; Jn 18:40)?

13. Was it Pilate's custom to release a prisoner on Passover (Mt 27:15), or did Pilate think it was the Jews' custom (Jn 18:39), or did the people bring up the idea of releasing Barabbas (Lk 23:18)? Some manuscripts say that Pilate had to release a prisoner (Lk 23:17).

14. Did the soldiers put Jesus' clothes back on him right after they had mocked him (as Mt 27:31 and Mk 15:20 imply), or did he wear the robe and thorns as Pilate took him out and presented him again to the Jews (Jn 19:5)?

15. Did Pilate order his soldiers to scourge Jesus in the Praetorium and then crucify him (Mt 27:26; Mk 15:15), or did he hand Jesus over to the Jews for execution (Lk 23:25; Jn 19:16)?

16. Did Pilate simply hand Jesus over to the Jews (Jn 19:16), or did he give a formal sentence to grant their demand (Lk 23:24)?

17. Did the Jews alone (Mk 15:29–32) or both Jews and soldiers (Mt 27:31; Lk 23:35–39) mock Jesus?

18. Was the wine mixed with gall (Mt 27:34; Mk 15:23 JST), or with myrrh (Mk 15:23)?

19. Did one (Lk 23:39) or both robbers on the cross mock Jesus (Mt 27:44; Mk 15:32)?

20. Did the veil of the temple tear before Jesus died (Lk 23:45), or after (Mt 27:51; Mk 15:38)?

Chart 10-10

Conspicuous Omissions

Details left out though included in all three other Gospels

Matthew

None

Mark

1. Jesus rebukes disciple who struck with a sword
   (Mt 26:52–54; Lk 22:51; Jn 18:11)

2. Jesus gives a hedging answer to whether he is the Christ
   (Mt 26:64; Lk 22:70; Jn 18:21)

Luke

1. Arresters come with weapons
   (Mt 26:47; Mk 14:43; Jn 18:3)

2. Jesus prophesies about destroying temple
   (Mt 26:61; Mk 14:57–58; Jn 2:19)

3. Caiaphas accuses Jesus of blasphemy
   (Mt 26:65; Mk 14:64)

4. Roman soldiers scourge Jesus
   (Mt 27:26; Mk 15:15; Jn 19:1)

5. Jesus wears crown of thorns
   (Mt 27:29; Mk 15:17; Jn 19:2)

6. Roman soldiers mock Jesus
   (Mt 27:27–31; Mk 15:16–20; Jn 19:2–3)

7. Women at cross are named
   (Mt 27:56; Mk 15:40; Jn 19:25)

8. Pilate gives permission for Joseph of Arimathea to take body of Christ
   (Mt 27:58; Mk 15:45; Jn 19:38)

John

1. Disciples fall asleep in the garden
   (Mt 26:36–46; Mk 14:32–42; Lk 22:39–46)

2. Judas betrays Christ with a kiss
   (Mt 26:49; Mk 14:45; Lk 22:47)

3. Jesus prophesies of Peter's denial
   (Mt 26:34; Mk 14:30; Lk 22:34)

4. Peter denies Christ three times
   (Mt 26:69–75; Mk 14:66–72; Lk 22:56–62)

5. Chief priests and elders accuse Jesus
   (Mt 27:12–13; Mk 15:3–5; Lk 23:9–10)

6. Jews mock Jesus at Caiaphas's palace
   (Mt 26:67–68; Mk 14:61–65; Lk 22:63–65)

7. Jewish council meets in the morning
   (Mt 27:1; Mk 15:1; Lk 22:66)

8. Crowd desires Jesus to be crucified
   (Mt 27:22–23; Mk 15:13–14; Lk 23:18–23)

9. Simon of Cyrene carries Jesus' cross
   (Mt 27:32; Mk 15:21; Lk 23:26)

10. Crowd mocks Jesus at Golgotha
    (Mt 27:39–44; Mk 15:29–32; Lk 23:35–38)

11. Thieves speak to Jesus
    (Mt 27:44; Mk 15:32; Lk 23:39–43)

12. Darkness covers the earth from the 6th to 9th hour
    (Mt 27:45; Mk 15:33; Lk 23:44)

13. Temple curtain tears
    (Mt 27:51; Mk 15:38; Lk 23:45)

14. Marys come to sepulchre
    (Mt 27:61; Mk 15:47; Mk 23:55)

Chart 10-11

Chart 10-12

The Prevalent Factor of Fear

Explanation

Although the factor of fear is rarely mentioned by New Testament commentators, fear may well provide the consistent driving undercurrent that best explains all the irregularities and vagaries of the so-called trials of Jesus. Powerful and pervasive, this consistent factor runs through the story as an underlying emotion (even though all people were not afraid of the same thing). Consequently, the legal proceedings before the Jewish council and Pontius Pilate should not be viewed as wholly rational affairs. As chart 10-12 shows, many people arrayed around Jesus were afraid of one thing or another. Most often, they were deeply afraid of the supernatural. Jesus' healings and control of physical elements were open and impressive. They must have been the cause of profound concern to anyone who took these miracles seriously and did not believe that he was the Son of God. The only other option was to reject him as an evil wonder-worker or deceiving magician.

Reference

John W. Welch, "The Factor of Fear in the Trial of Jesus," in *Jesus Christ, Son of God, Savior,* ed. Paul H. Peterson, Gary L. Hatch, Laure D. Card (Provo, Utah: BYU Religious Studies Center, 2002), chap. 13.

The Prevalent Factor of Fear

General reaction to miracles was fear	Mt 9:8; Lk 5:26; 7:16; 8:37; Jn 6:19
Herod Antipas feared John the Baptist	Mk 6:20
Herod Antipas feared the people	Mt 14:5
Joseph of Arimathaea feared the Jews	Jn 19:38
The apostles fled from Gethsemane	Mk 14:50
Peter denied Jesus outside Caiaphas's house	Mt 26:69–70; Jn 18:26–27
Chief Priests feared retribution from the Romans	Jn 11:48
Chief Priests feared the people	Mt 21:46
Chief Priests feared Jesus	Mk 11:18
Pilate feared exceedingly	Jn 19:8
One robber on the cross feared God	Lk 23:40
Soldiers at Golgatha feared greatly	Mt 27:54
All the people left Golgatha fearful	Lk 23:48
The tomb guards feared the angel	Mt 28:4
The women at the tomb were afraid	Mk 16:8
The apostles met in fear on the first day	Jn 20:19
The apostles were terrified seeing the Lord	Lk 24:37
Initial reaction to angels was fear	Lk 1:12; 1:30; 2:10

Chart 10-12

Chart 10-13

Peter's Three Denials of Christ

Explanation

An important detail in the trial of Jesus is the so-called denial of Peter. All four Gospels report this event, but they do so in different ways. To begin with, the exact words of Jesus' prophecy differ. Would the cock crow once or twice? Would Peter deny that he knows Jesus or that he was a disciple of Jesus? Did Peter actually deny in response to all three of the different questioners, or did he simply profess that he did not understand the question? In any event, it is clear that, unlike John who followed Jesus into the council room, Peter did not step forward and defend Jesus (perhaps for very good reason, under the circumstances). Nevertheless, a close reading of these accounts shows that he did not deny that Jesus was the Christ, only that he had not been in the garden, or a disciple, or one who knew Jesus.

Reference

Richard Lloyd Anderson, "Simon Peter," *Ensign*, February 1975, 40–41.

Peter's Three Denials of Christ

	MATTHEW 26:34, 69–75	MARK 14:30, 66–72	LUKE 22:34, 54–62	JOHN 13:38; 18:15–18, 25–27
Jesus' Prophecy				
What did Christ prophesy?	this night, before the cock crows, deny me thrice	this night, before the cock crows twice, deny me thrice	before cock crows thrice you will deny you know me	before cock crows, deny me thrice
First Denial				
Who addressed Peter?	maid	maid of High Priest	maid	maid at the door
What was said?	you were also with Jesus of Galilee	you were also with Jesus of Nazareth	you were also with Jesus	are not you one of the disciples?
Peter's answer	I do not understand	I do not understand	I do not know him	I am not a disciple
Second Denial				
Who addressed Peter?	another maid	maid of High Priest/ another man	another man	a group
What was said?	you were also with Jesus of Nazareth	you are one of the disciples	you are also one of the disciples	are not you one of the disciples?
Peter's answer	I do not know him, with an oath/curse	plain denial, he denied it	I am not a disciple	I am not a disciple
Third Denial				
Who addressed Peter?	group	group	another man	kinsman of the man whose ear Peter cut off
What was said?	are not you one of the disciples? your accent betrays you	are you not one of the disciples? you are a Galilean; your accent betrays you	you were also with Jesus; you are a Galilean	did I not see you in the garden with him?
Peter's answer	I do not know him, with an oath/curse	I do not know him, with an oath/curse	I do not understand	plain denial
Results				
Cock crowed	1 time	2 times	1 time	1 time
Peter's reaction	remembered the word of Jesus; went out; wept bitterly	remembered the word of Jesus; wept	Lord turned and looked at Peter; he remembered the word of Jesus; went out; wept bitterly	no information

Chart 10-13

Seven Words from the Cross

Explanation

As Jesus hung on the cross, he spoke seven times. Interestingly, six of these seven sayings are reported by only one of the four Gospel writers, and the one saying reported by Matthew and Mark does not appear in either Luke or John. John, who was present at the cross, records three of the statements; Luke gives three others, including the famous words of forgiveness to his crucifiers and of assurance to the repentant robber next to him. Moreover, each of the Gospels uses different words to describe the death of Jesus, from simply breathing his last, to giving up his spirit, to placing his spirit into God's hands, to giving over or surrendering his spirit. One wonders if these differences are intentional and significant. They seem to be consistent with the overall messages of the individual Gospel writers.

Reference

James E. Talmage, *Jesus the Christ* (1915; reprint, Salt Lake City: Deseret Book, 1984), 607–14.

Seven Words from the Cross

1. And about the ninth hour Jesus cried with a loud voice, saying, "Eli, Eli, lama sabachthani? that is to say, My God, my God, why hast thou forsaken me?" (Mt 27:46; Mk 15:34).

2. Then said Jesus, "Father, forgive them; for they know not what they do" (Lk 23:34).

3. And Jesus said unto [the robber], "Verily I say unto thee, To day shalt thou be with me in paradise" (Lk 23:43).

4. When Jesus therefore saw his mother, and the disciple standing by, whom he loved, he saith unto his mother, "Woman, behold thy son!" Then saith he to the disciple, "Behold thy mother!" (Jn 19:26–27).

5. After this, Jesus knowing that all things were now accomplished, that the scripture might be fulfilled, saith, "I thirst" (Jn 19:28).

6. When Jesus therefore had received the vinegar, he said, "It is finished" (Jn 19:29–30).

7. And when Jesus had cried with a loud voice, he said, "Father, into thy hands I commend my spirit" (Lk 23:46).

In **Matthew and Mark**, Jesus expresses abandonment, quoting Hebrew scripture in which King David recognized the abandonment of Israel (Ps 22:1). He gives up his spirit.

In **Mark**, Jesus simply breathes his last and expires.

In **Luke**, even on the cross Jesus continues teaching salvation, offering forgiveness and placing his spirit into the hands of the Father.

In **John**, Jesus shows eternal love toward his mother and disciple. He thirsts, completes his work, and surrenders his spirit.

Chart 10-14

Chart 10-15

Isaiah 53 and the Messiah

Explanation

One of the most striking prophecies of the Old Testament is the Suffering Servant song in Isaiah 53. It poignantly affirms that the Lord's servant will suffer pain and grief, according to the will of God. Not only will he suffer, he will die. Indeed, he will die young, without posterity and innocently. Yet he would go voluntarily and be numbered "with the transgressors" (53:12; Lk 22:37). His suffering will benefit all humanity, for the expiation of sin would not come through him. His offering will satisfy the demands of justice and will bring about a reconciliation and atonement between God and mankind. But, according to the prophet, each person will need to accept his offering in order for it to become efficacious. In this way, the Lord shall have spiritual offspring, and he will be able to reward and prosper his people at the day of judgment. These eternal blessings, the spoils of the ultimate war against evil, will be turned over to the servant for division among his followers. Although it remains difficult to determine how many of the earliest Christians fully connected this prophecy with the death of Jesus, Isaiah 53 is quoted several times in the New Testament (see chart 2-5) and recent evidence from the Dead Sea Scrolls makes it more likely that the Suffering Servant was understood messianically even before the time of Christ.

References

Israel Knohl, *The Messiah before Jesus: The Suffering Servant of the Dead Sea Scrolls,* trans. David Maisel (Berkeley: University of California, 2000).

John W. Welch, "Isaiah 53, Mosiah 14, and the Book of Mormon," in *Isaiah in the Book of Mormon,* ed. Donald Parry and John Welch (Provo, Utah: FARMS, 1998), 293–312.

Isaiah 53 and the Messiah

He "shall grow up before him [the Father] as a tender plant" (53:2)

"As a root [the root of Jesse] out of a dry ground [Israel]" (53:2)

He will have "no form nor comeliness" (53:2)

"There is no beauty that we should desire him" (53:2)

"He is despised and rejected ..., we esteemed him not" (53:3)

"We [his friends] hid as it were our faces from him" (53:3)

"We did esteem him stricken, smitten of God, and afflicted" (53:4)

He will be "a man of sorrows, and acquainted with grief" (53:3)

"Surely he hath borne our griefs, and carried our sorrows" (53:4)

"He was wounded for our transgressions, bruised for our iniquities" (53:5)

"He was oppressed, and he was afflicted" (53:7)

"He was taken from prison and from judgment" (53:8)

"Yet it pleased the Lord to bruise him; he hath put him to grief" (53:10)

"He made his grave with the wicked, and with the rich in his death" (53:9)

"He hath poured out his soul unto death" (53:12)

"He was cut off out of the land of the living" (53:8)

They would number him "with the transgressors" (53:12)

"He had done no violence, neither was any deceit in his mouth" (53:9)

"He opened not his mouth: as a lamb to the slaughter" (53:7)

"The chastisement of our peace was upon him" (53:5)

"With his stripes we are healed" (53:5)

"The Lord hath laid on him the iniquity of us all" (53:6)

"For the transgression of my people was he stricken" (53:8)

"For he shall bear their iniquities" (53:11)

"He made intercession for the transgressors" (53:12)

The Father "shall see of the travail of his soul, and shall be satisfied" (53:11)

"His soul [will be] an offering for sin" (53:10)

"By his knowledge shall my righteous servant justify many" (53:11)

"The pleasure of the Lord shall prosper in his hand" (53:10)

"I will divide him a portion with the great" (53:12)

"He shall divide the spoil with the strong" (53:12)

Chart 10-15

Chart 10-16

Parallels between the Trials
of Jeremiah and Jesus

Explanation

Another Old Testament precursor to the trial of Jesus was the trial of Jeremiah. Found in Jeremiah 26, this account reports how Jeremiah was accused of false prophecy, brought before a council of rulers, and accused by the priests and how he defended the genuineness of his mission. In a literary sense, the narratives of the trial of Jesus may echo the trial of Jeremiah. Because Jesus was associated in the minds of some people with Jeremiah (Mt 16:14), and like Jeremiah he had prophesied the destruction of the temple, both may have been exposed to the charge of being a false prophet, which under Deuteronomy 13 and 18 could be viewed as a capital offense.

Reference

Drawn from Bernard S. Jackson, "The Trials of Jesus and Jeremiah," *BYU Studies* 32/4 (1992): 63–77.

Parallels between the Trials
of Jeremiah and Jesus

Occasion	Jeremiah	Jesus
The prophet preaches in the court of the temple.	26:1–2	Mt 21:23–23:36; Mk 11:27–12:40; Lk 19:47–48
He does so following a divine mission but with no guarantee of success.	26:3	Mt 21:33–39; Mk 12:1–8; Lk 20:9–15
He prophesies the destruction of the temple.	26:4–7	Mt 24:1–2; Mk 13:1–2; Lk 21:5–6
There is priestly involvement in arresting and charging the prophet alleged to be prophesying falsely.	26:8–9	Mt 26:47, 59; Mk 14:43, 55–64; Lk 22:52
There is some form of hearing in the temple itself (i.e., within priestly jurisdiction).	26:9	Mt 26:57; Mk 14:53; Lk 22:54
The secular authority then convenes a court.	26:10	Mt 27:11; Mk 15:1–2; Lk 23:1
The priests frame the accusation before the secular authority.	26:11	Mt 27:12; Mk 15:3; Lk 23:2
The accused prophet defends himself, reasserting the genuineness of his mission.	26:12	Mt 26:64; Mk 15:2; Lk 22:67–69; 23:13
The secular rulers tell the priests that they have decided to exonerate the prophet.	26:16	Mt 27:23; Mk 15:14; Lk 23:4, 13–14
Comparison is made with the fate of another accused (Uriah, Barabbas).	26:20–22	Mt 27:15–26; Mk 15:6–15; Lk 23:18–25
Uriah and Jesus suffer execution.	26:23	Mt 27:32–50; Mk 15:21–37; Lk 23:26–46
Jeremiah and Barabbas escape this fate, but stress is placed upon the potential role of the people as being responsible for the life-or-death decision.	26:24	Mt 27:20–23; Mk 15:12–15; Lk 23:18–25

Chart 10-16

Chart 10-17

Passover Prophecy Fulfillment

Explanation

Although it is not completely clear which day of the week or in which year Jesus was crucified, no one doubts that the trial of Jesus occurred near or at the time of the Passover. Chart 10-17 compares the normal sequence of events observed by Jews at the time of Passover with elements in the final days of Jesus. In this way, one may see how the Passover came to be seen by early Christians as a type and shadow of the death of Jesus as an eternal Paschal lamb.

References

Lenet H. Read, "Symbols of the Harvest: Old Testament Holy Days and the Lord's Ministry," *Ensign,* January 1975, 32–36.

John P. Pratt, "Passover: Was It Symbolic of His Coming?" *Ensign,* January 1994, 38–45.

Passover Prophecy Fulfillment

On the eve of Passover Jews begin to remove all leaven from their houses

After the last supper and betrayal, Christ is found worthy to be "cast out"

Sunset

Sunrise

Leaven must be eaten until midday then it is strictly forbidden

Jesus' preparations for the crucifixion

Slaughter of Paschal lambs begins at midday and continues until sundown

Crucifixion begins at noon
Death occurs at the ninth hour (3 P.M.)

Sunset
Christ's body is entombed

Firstfruit sheaf is cut down and the Paschal lamb is consumed

Sunrise

Paschal Sabbath

Sunset

Sunrise

Early morning, the sheaf of firstfruits is "lifted up before the Lord"

Christ is resurrected, the "Firstfruits of the Dead," and the tomb is left empty

Chart 10-17

Witnesses to the Resurrection

Explanation

Each of the four Gospels concludes with an account of Jesus' resurrection. Taken together with the additional witnesses, mentioned especially by Paul and in the Book of Mormon, numerous people bear testimony of the reality of the resurrection of the Lord Jesus Christ. Chart 10-18 lists eighteen recorded appearances of the resurrected Christ. In most cases, the time and place of the appearance are known, and specific details of the event are reported. These true and faithful witnesses are more numerous than people usually recognize. In the mouth of many witnesses, this all-important event has been established for all the world to see and, hopefully, accept.

References

John Gee, "Jesus Christ: Forty-day Ministry and Other Post-Resurrection Appearances of Jesus Christ," *EM*, 2:734–35.
Douglas L. Callister, "Resurrection," *EM*, 3:1222–23.
"Postresurrection Appearances," and "Resurrection," *WRC*, 46–49.

Witnesses to the Resurrection

Persons Visited	Scripture Reference	Date or Time	Place of Appearance	What Transpired	Items of Interest
Mary Magdalene	Jn 20:1–18	Resurrection, early morning	At the tomb of Jesus Christ	Mary talked with Jesus; she did not recognize him at first but was soon convinced it was him.	
Other women	Mt 28:1–10	Resurrection day, early morning	Somewhere between the tomb and Jerusalem	They held Jesus by the feet and worshiped him.	
Two disciples	Mk 16:12–13; Lk 4:13–32	Resurrection day, afternoon	On the road to Emmaus	They walked, talked, and ate with Jesus, not recognizing him until he broke bread. Their hearts burned within them.	The hymn "Abide with Me; 'Tis Eventide" (*Hymns*, no. 165) recalls this event.
Simon Peter	Lk 24:34; 1Cor 15:5	Sometime on the day of the resurrection	Not specified	Not specified	
Ten of the Twelve	Lk 24:36–53; Jn 20:19–24	Resurrection day, evening	A room with shut doors somewhere in Jerusalem	Jesus invited them to handle him so they would know that he had flesh and bone. He ate fish and honey before them.	Although Lk 24:33 refers to "the eleven," it seems certain that neither Judas nor Thomas was present.
Eleven of the Twelve	Jn 20:26–31; Mk 16:14	Eight days after the resurrection	Apparently the same room as above	Jesus showed Thomas his hands and his side; this was convincing evidence for Thomas.	
Seven of the Twelve	Jn 21:1–14	Morning, at a time subsequent to the episode with Thomas	On the shore of the Sea of Tiberias (Galilee)	After the seven had fished all night and caught nothing, Jesus gave them directions from the shore; they caught a multitude of fish. They recognized him and went to shore. He ate with them.	This is similar to the first draught of fishes (see Lk 5) that accompanies Jesus' call of Peter and others to the ministry.
Eleven of the Twelve	Mt 28:16–20	Not specified	A mountain in Galilee, by previous appointment of Jesus Christ	Jesus appeared to them on the mountain. They talked with him and worshiped him.	
More than 500 brethren	1Cor 15:6	Not specified	Not specified	No information	This visitation probably took place in Galilee.
James	1Cor 15:7	Not specified	Not specified	No information	

Chart 10-18 (1)

Persons Visited	Scripture Reference	Date or Time	Place of Appearance	What Transpired	Items of Interest
Eleven apostles at the ascension	Mk 16:14, 19; Lk 24:50–51; Acts 1:3–11	Forty days after the resurrection	Near Bethany	Jesus bade farewell to the apostles and ascended to heaven. They watched him ascend.	
Paul	1Cor 9:1; 15:8		Near Damascus	As Paul traveled toward Damascus to persecute believers, Jesus identified himself and spoke to him. Paul was blinded for three days but was converted to Christ.	Paul saw Jesus but the time of his appearance is not clear (see Acts 9:3–18). Paul's own account of the event near Damascus tells of seeing a light and hearing the Savior's voice (see Acts 22:5–11; 26:12–18). Other participants speak of seeing a light but not hearing a voice (see Acts 9:7 JST).
John	Rev 1:9–18	Between A.D. 81 and 96	Isle of Patmos, in the Aegean Sea	Jesus appeared to John, spoke to him, and touched him with his hand.	The scripture gives one of the few descriptions of the glorified Savior.
2,500 Nephites	3 Nephi 11:1–18:39; 19:2, 15–26:15	About A.D. 34, soon after the ascension	Land of Bountiful in America, by the temple	The multitude saw Jesus, heard him, and went forth one by one. They touched him and knew of a surety that he had risen.	Jesus visited the Nephites several times; not all of the visits are talked about in detail (see 3 Nephi 26:13).
The Nephite Twelve	3 Nephi 27:1–28:12	After previous appearance to the Nephite people	Not specified	They saw Jesus and conversed with him. He touched all but three with his finger.	The three Nephite disciples not touched by Jesus would remain on earth until his second coming.
The lost tribes of Israel	3 Nephi 16:1–5; 17:4	No information, but soon after appearance to Nephites	Not specified	Jesus said he would show himself to them and they would hear his voice.	
Moroni	Ether 12:39	Not specified	Not specified	Moroni saw Jesus who instructed him in "plain humility."	Moroni's father, Mormon, was also "visited of the Lord" (Mormon 1:15).
Joseph Smith	Joseph Smith—History 1:14–20	Spring 1820	Sacred Grove, near Manchester, New York	Joseph Smith saw the Father and the Son and conversed with them. The Father introduced the Son.	In subsequent visits Joseph Smith and Sidney Rigdon saw the Lord and conversed with him (see D&C 76:14–24). Joseph Smith and Oliver Cowdery saw him in the Kirtland Temple; they describe him in D&C 110:1–10.

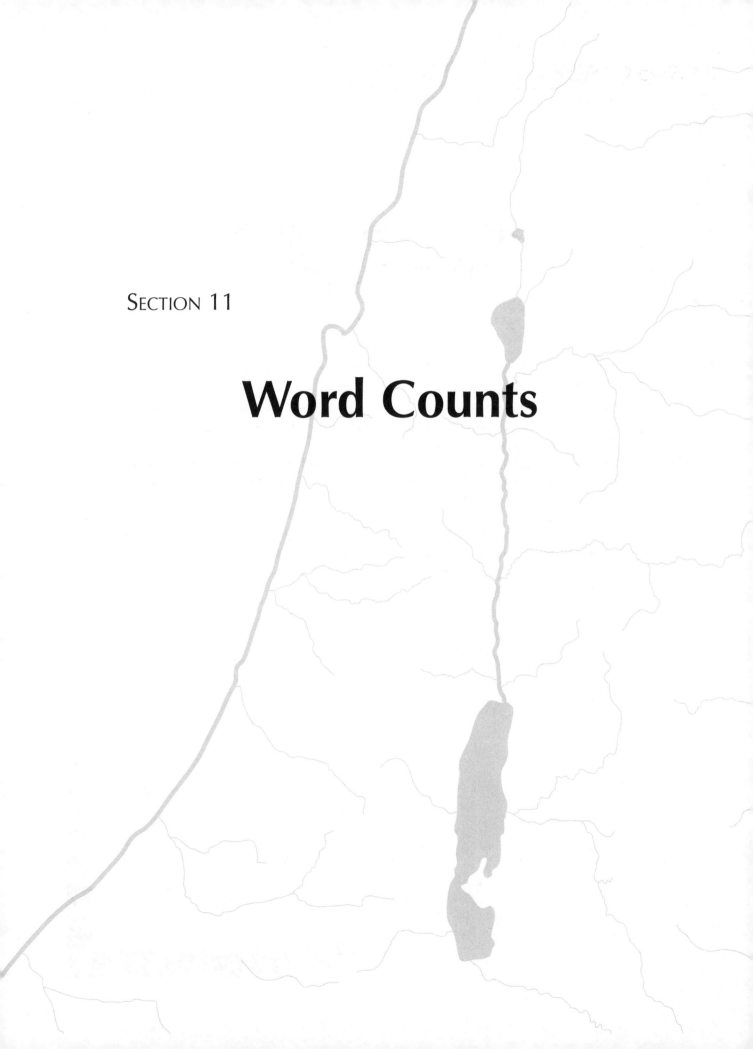

SECTION 11

Word Counts

Greek and English Word Counts

Explanation

This section presents ten charts that count and compare interesting data about the vocabulary of the New Testament. Living in a world that extracts meaning from unsuspected details, readers may find these charts to be more than mere curiosities.

Charts 11-1 through 11-4 compare the total word counts in the ancient Greek and more recent English versions of the New Testament. Not only does this allow a quick visual comparison of the lengths of the books of the New Testament, but one readily sees that Greek is a more efficient language than English. Greek uses fewer words to express the same thoughts. This means that translators must often turn to longer idiomatic English expressions to attempt to capture and express the original intent of the New Testament writers. Chart 11-5 shows that Peter is harder to render into English in a word-for-word manner, whereas John can be translated much more directly.

Total Word Counts

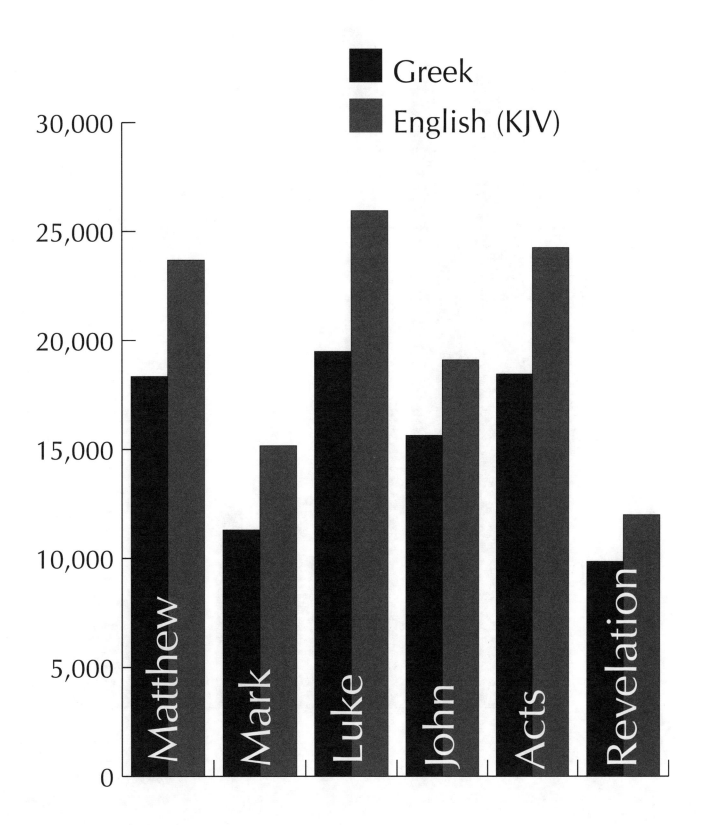

Total Word Counts

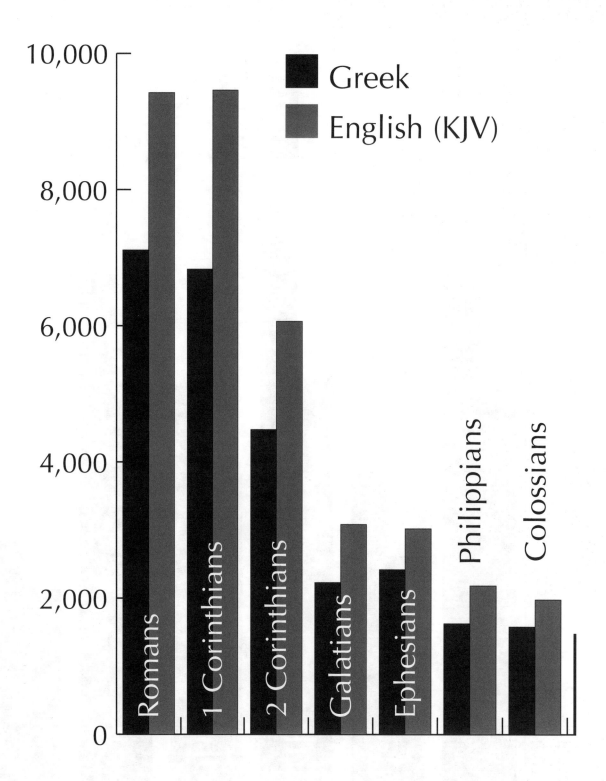

Total Word Counts

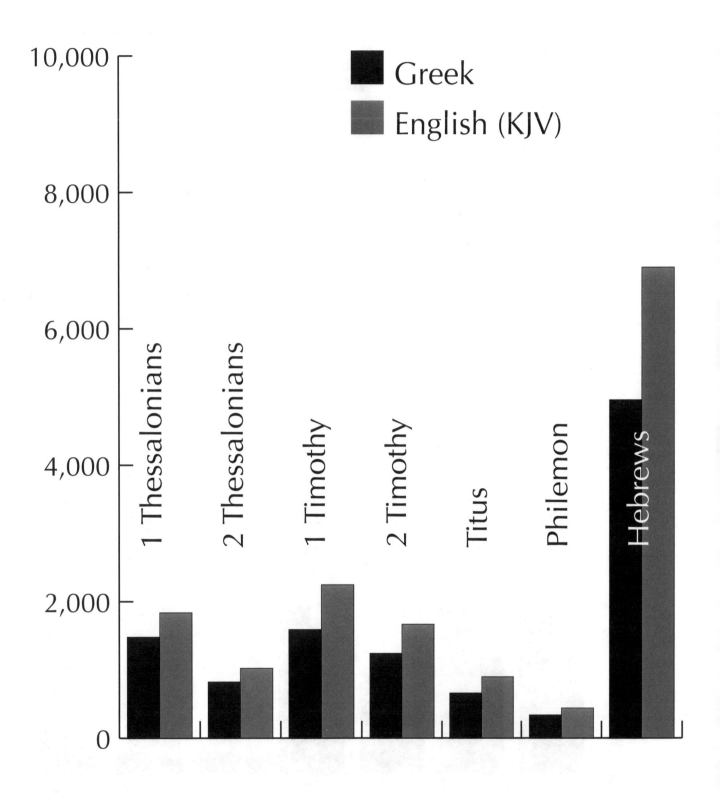

Total Word Counts

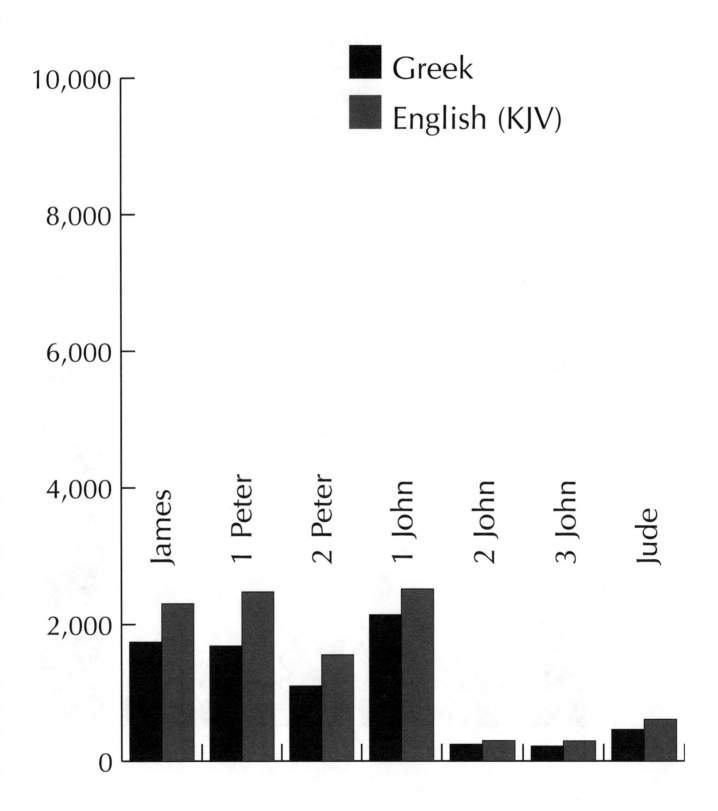

Chart 11-4

Translation Size Comparison
English/Greek by author

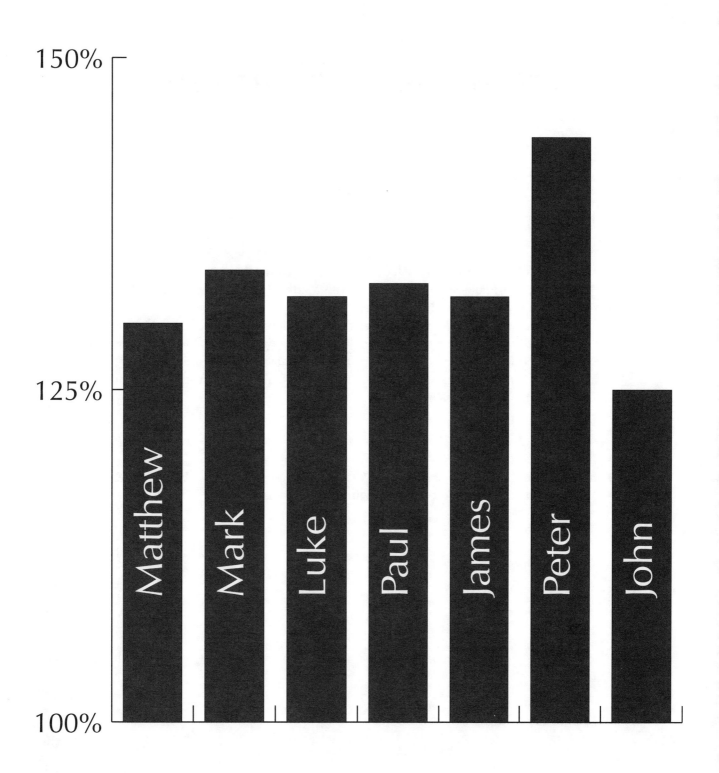

Chart 11-5

Synoptic Comparisons

Explanation

Charts 11-6 through 11-8 reveal some interesting features of the vocabularies of Matthew, Mark, and Luke. This information may be relevant in assessing the degree of dependence or independence of these writers on each other. Chart 11-6 shows that some of Mark's words are unique to that work; others he shares only with Matthew and Luke; and over half are fairly common throughout the New Testament.

Chart 11-7 examines the degree of overlap that exists between the material of Matthew with that of the other two synoptic writers and, similarly, between the material of Luke and the other two. Interestingly, all three Gospels contain a fair amount of unique material, although Luke contains the most information (almost 40 percent) not mentioned in the others. In addition, all three share a significant amount of common ground, as chart 11-8 confirms.

Reference

Eta Linnemann, *Is there a Synoptic Problem? Rethinking the Literary Dependence of the First Three Gospels,* trans. Robert W. Yarbrough (Grand Rapids: Baker, 1992).

Greek Vocabulary of Mark

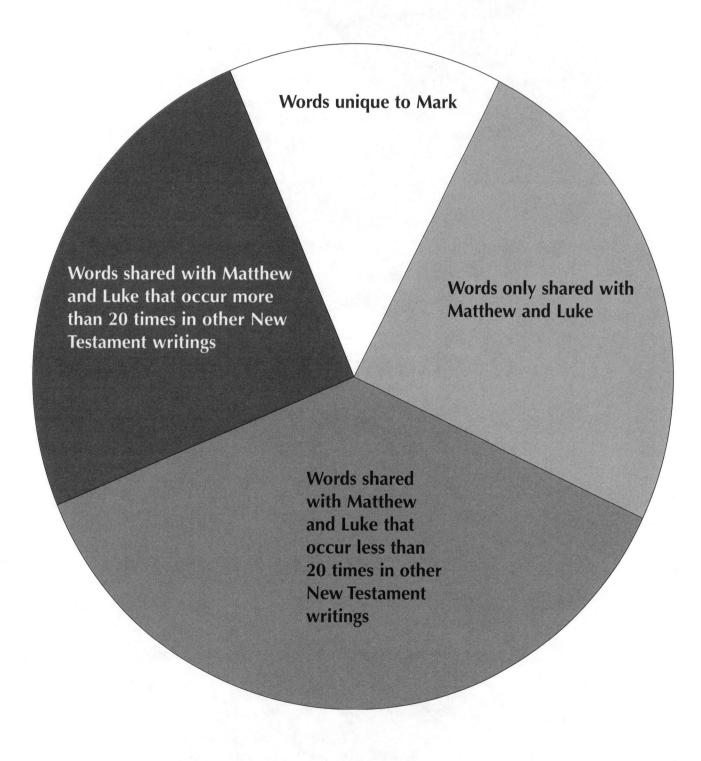

Words unique to Mark

Words only shared with Matthew and Luke

Words shared with Matthew and Luke that occur more than 20 times in other New Testament writings

Words shared with Matthew and Luke that occur less than 20 times in other New Testament writings

Chart 11-6

Matthew's Overlap with Mark and Luke

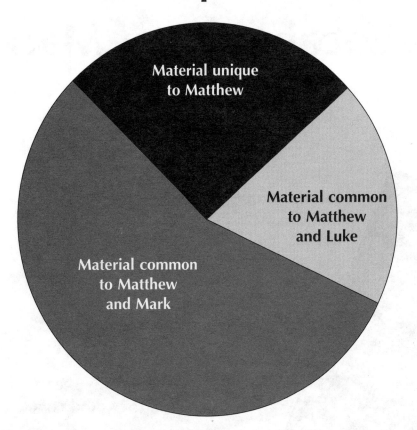

Material unique to Matthew

Material common to Matthew and Luke

Material common to Matthew and Mark

Luke's Overlap with Mark and Matthew

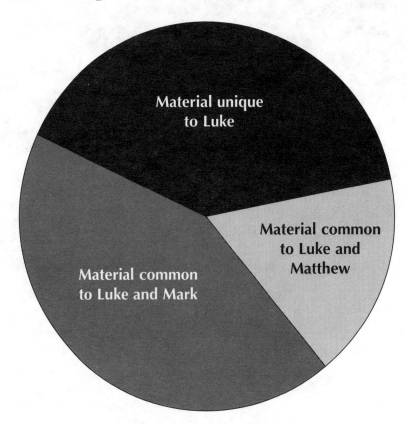

Material unique to Luke

Material common to Luke and Matthew

Material common to Luke and Mark

Chart 11-7

Comparison of Parallel Synoptic Passages' Vocabulary

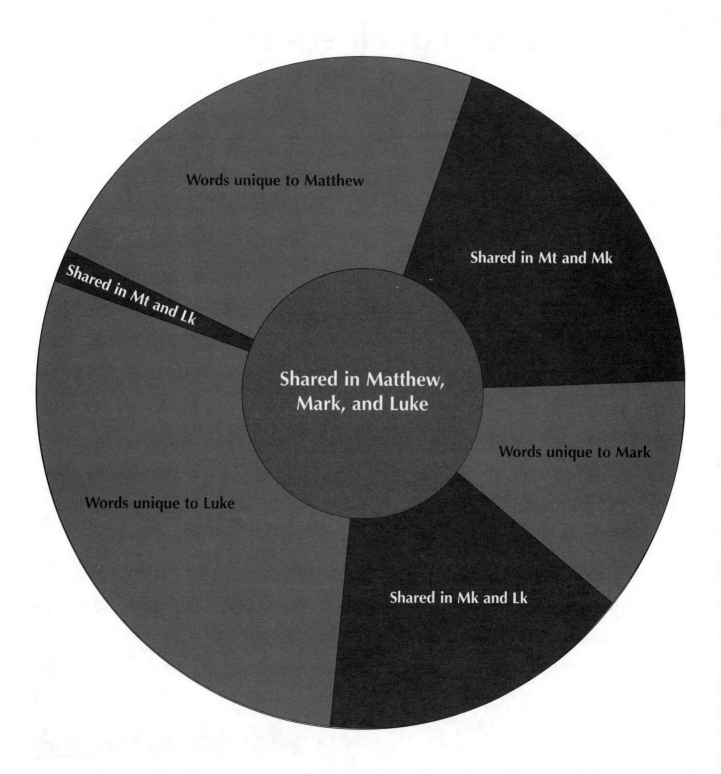

Words unique to Matthew

Shared in Mt and Mk

Shared in Mt and Lk

Shared in Matthew, Mark, and Luke

Words unique to Mark

Words unique to Luke

Shared in Mk and Lk

Chart 11-8

Paul's Greek Vocabulary

Explanation

Chart 11-9 displays the vocabulary of Paul, measured according to the Greek. People are often interested in determining which letters may be safely attributed to the apostle Paul. Unusual vocabulary can sometimes offer a clue that a letter was not written by the same person who wrote other letters, but according to the data contained on this chart such words may not prove conclusive in this regard. Each letter of Paul contains unique vocabulary not found in any other of his letters. While the percentage of unique vocabulary ranges from a low of 7 percent to a high of 33 percent even undisputed letters of Paul such as Romans and 1 Corinthians score among the highest in terms of unique vocabulary. Ephesians and Colossians register only 13 percent of their words as unique. For the most part, all that can be concluded from this is that the longer a letter, the more unique its vocabulary tends to become. Moreover, the letter to the Hebrews, while containing a large percentage of Pauline words, has an above average number of unique words because it is the only letter in the New Testament addressed to that particular audience.

Paul had and used an enormous vocabulary. Counting all fourteen Pauline epistles, over a fourth of his words appear in one and only one of his letters. Chart 11-10 tabulates this versatility. Over half are used by him alone of all the New Testament writers. Only 45 percent of his words appear again anywhere else within the New Testament.

Paul's Unique Greek Vocabulary
by Individual Epistle

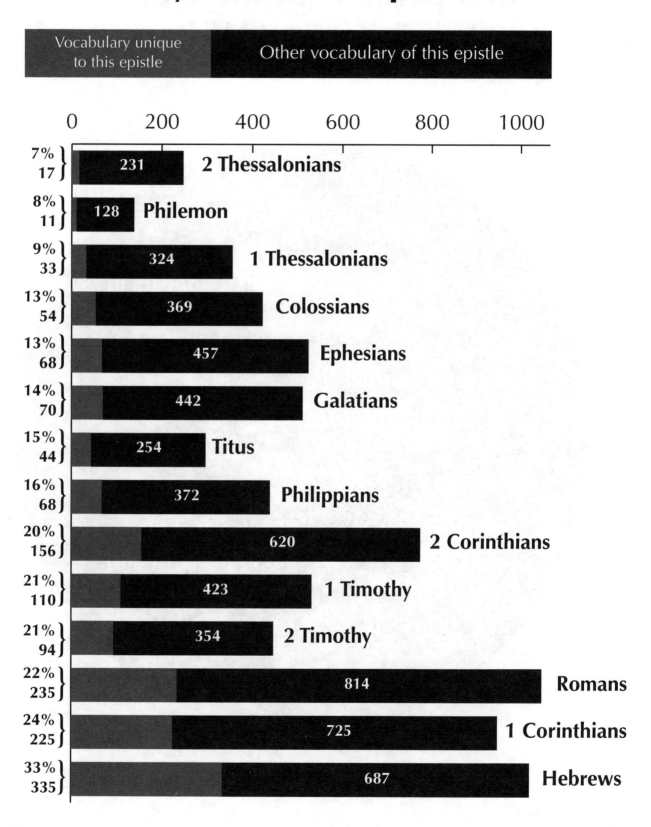

Vocabulary unique to this epistle	Other vocabulary of this epistle

0   200   400   600   800   1000

7% / 17 — **2 Thessalonians** — 231

8% / 11 — **Philemon** — 128

9% / 33 — **1 Thessalonians** — 324

13% / 54 — **Colossians** — 369

13% / 68 — **Ephesians** — 457

14% / 70 — **Galatians** — 442

15% / 44 — **Titus** — 254

16% / 68 — **Philippians** — 372

20% / 156 — **2 Corinthians** — 620

21% / 110 — **1 Timothy** — 423

21% / 94 — **2 Timothy** — 354

22% / 235 — **Romans** — 814

24% / 225 — **1 Corinthians** — 725

33% / 335 — **Hebrews** — 687

Chart 11-9

Greek Vocabulary of Paul
Compared with the Other New Testament Writers

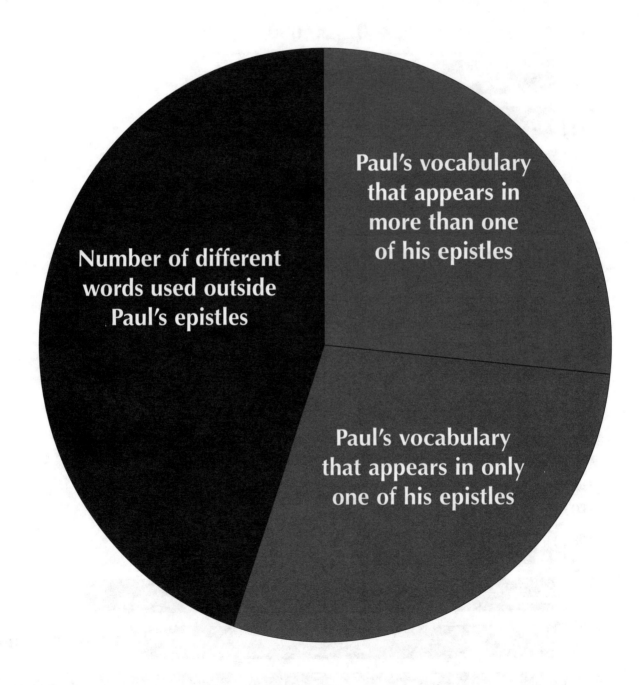

Paul's vocabulary that appears in more than one of his epistles

Number of different words used outside Paul's epistles

Paul's vocabulary that appears in only one of his epistles

Chart 11-10

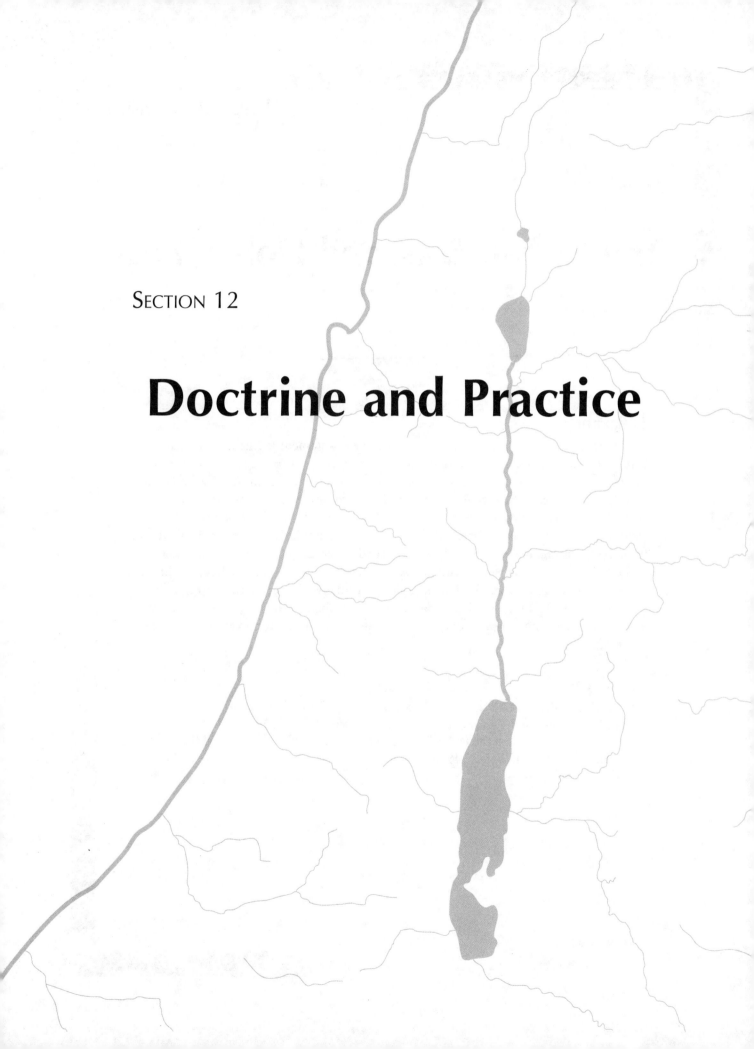

SECTION 12

Doctrine and Practice

The Father, Son, and Holy Ghost

Explanation

On several occasions and in many ways, the New Testament teaches clearly that the Father, the Son, and the Holy Ghost are three distinct beings who function with absolute unity of purpose as the Godhead. Chart 12-1 identifies key passages in the New Testament that describe in detail the divine greatness and the infinite atonement of Jesus Christ. This chart should be read in conjunction with chart 8-16, a listing of the divine names and titles of Jesus. Chart 12-2 collects references that focus on the attributes and activities of God the Father, especially noting his concerns, gifts, love, and relationships. Chart 12-3 gives attention to the Holy Ghost, perhaps the least understood member of the Godhead. His roles in the process of revelation, church leadership, spirituality, daily life, and eternal salvation are gathered and classified. These charts show how the members of the Godhead work closely together in their common cause of bringing to pass the immortality and eternal life of all the human family.

References

Bruce R. McConkie, *The Mortal Messiah* (Salt Lake City: Deseret Book, 1979).
James E. Talmage, *Jesus the Christ* (Salt Lake City: Deseret Book, 1984).
Stephen E. Robinson, "God the Father," *EM,* 2:548–50.
David H. Yarn Jr., "God," *EM,* 2:546–47.

Key Passages
on the Divine Greatness and Atonement of Christ

Christ is the head of all creation	Col 1:15–20
Prophets of old knew of Christ	1Pt 1:10–12
The greatness of the incarnate Son of God	Heb 1:1–4
The Son is greater than the angels	Heb 1:5–14
Christ's greatness and condescension	Heb 2:5–18
Witnesses of the Son	1Jn 5:6–12
Christ atones for our sins	1Cor 6:9–11
The fall and the atonement: caused by one but apply to all	Rom 5:12–21
The mystery of the spiritual life	1Tm 3:15–16
Songs of praise to the Lamb	Rev 5:9–13
The marriage supper of the Lamb	Rev 19:5–10
The rider on the white horse	Rev 19:11–16
The coming of the Alpha and Omega	Rev 22:12–17

Chart 12-1

Attributes and Activities
of God the Father

TITLES OF THE FATHER

"Husbandman of the true vine" (Jn 15:1)
"Father of mercies" (2Cor 1:3)
"Father of glory" (Eph 1:17)
"Father of Spirits" (Heb 12:9)
"Father of Lights" (Jms 1:17)

CHARACTERISTICS AND CONCERNS OF THE FATHER

The Father sees in secret (Mt 6:4, 6, 18)
The Father is merciful (Lk 6:36)
The Father has life in himself (Jn 5:26)
The Father is greater than all (Jn 10:29)
God is the Father (1Cor 8:6)
The Father has foreknowledge (1Pt 1:2)
The Father has eternal life (1Jn 1:2)
The Father wills that none be lost (Jn 6:39)
There is no variableness nor shadow of turning in the Father (Jms 1:17)
God the Father is above all, and through all, and in all (Eph 4:6)
God is love (1Jn 4:16)

ACTIONS AND GIFTS FROM THE FATHER

The Father takes care of his creations (Mt 6:26; 10:29)
Every plant which the Father hath not planted shall be rooted up (Mt 15:13)
Revelation comes from Father in Heaven (Mt 16:17)
The Bread of Life comes from the Father (Jn 6:32)
Good works come from the Father (Jn 10:32)
The Father controls the seasons (Acts 1:7)
The Father sends peace (Rom 1:7; 1Cor 1:3)
The Father raises the dead (Jn 5:21)

THE FATHER AND PRAYER

Pray to the Father in heaven (Mt 6:9; Lk 11:2)
The Father will answer prayers (Mt 18:19)
Pray to the Father in the name of Christ (Jn 16:23)
Give thanks for all things unto God the Father (Eph 5:20; Col 3:17)
Christ prays to the Father (Jn 14:16)
Christ prayed to the Father for mankind (Jn 16:25)
Christ prayed to the Father in Gethsemane (Mt 26:39, 42; Mk 14:36; Lk 22:42; Jn 17)

Chart 12-2 (1)

THE FATHER AND THE SECOND COMING

At the second coming, the Son of Man shall come in the glory of his Father (Mt 16:27; Mk 8:38)

Only the Father knows when the second coming will be (Mt 24:36; Mk 13:32)

THE KINGDOM OF THE FATHER

In the Father's house are many mansions, or stations (Jn 14:2)

He that doeth the will of the Father enters heaven (Mt 7:21)

The righteous shine like the sun in the kingdom of the Father (Mt 13:43)

The elders in heaven have the Father's name written on their foreheads (Rev 14:1)

LITTLE CHILDREN AND THE FATHER

The Father watches over little children (Mt 18:14)

Little children belong in the kingdom of the Father (Mt 18:10)

THE FATHER OPPOSED TO WICKEDNESS

If any man love the world, the love of the Father is not in him (1Jn 2:15)

The antichrist denieth the Father and the Son (1Jn 2:22)

THE FATHER AND THE HOLY SPIRIT

The Comforter was sent by the Father (Jn 14:26; 15:26)

Mankind must worship the Father in spirit and in truth (Jn 4:23)

The Spirit of the Father gives revelation (Mt 10:20)

THE GODHEAD

The Father, Son, and Holy Ghost are one (1Jn 5:7)

Mankind has access to the Father through Christ and the Spirit (Eph 2:18)

People should be baptized in the name of the Father, Son, and Holy Ghost (Mt 28:19)

COMMANDMENTS FOR MANKIND REGARDING THE FATHER

Glorify the Father which is in heaven (Mt 5:45)

Mankind must learn of the Father (Jn 6:45)

Continue in the Son and the Father (1Jn 2:24)

Honor the Son as the Father (Jn 5:23)

Be perfect, even as Father in heaven (Mt 5:48)

Chart 12-2 (2)

THE FATHER'S DOINGS TOWARDS MANKIND

Father in heaven rewards mankind (Mt 6:1)

The Father gives good things to those who ask (Mt 7:11; Lk 11:13)

The Father gives hope to mankind (2Th 2:16)

The Father directs the ways of mankind (1Th 3:11)

The Father forgives those who sin ignorantly (Lk 23:34)

The Father forgives those who forgive others (Mt 6:14–15; 18:35; Mk 11:25–26)

The Father sends revelation to the humble (Mt 11:25; Lk 10:21)

The Saints are sanctified by God the Father (Jude 1)

It is the Father's good pleasure to give the Saints the kingdom (Lk 12:32)

MANKIND'S RELATIONSHIP WITH THE FATHER

Humans are the children of our Father (Mt 5:45; 23:9)

The Father himself loveth mankind (Jn 16:27)

The Father knows what the Saints need before they ask (Mt 6:8, 32; Lk 12:30)

The Father wants mankind to worship him (Jn 4:23)

The Father is glorified by the Saints' good works (Jn 15:8)

The fellowship of the Saints is with the Father (1Jn 1:3)

No man hath seen the Father, save he which is of God (Jn 6:46)

MANKIND'S RELATIONSHIP WITH THE FATHER AND THE SON

The Father sent the Son to be the Savior of the world (1Jn 4:14)

Christ is the advocate of the Saints with the Father (1Jn 2:1)

No man cometh to the Father but by Christ (Jn 14:6)

The Father gives the Saints to Christ (Jn 6:37, 44)

The Father honors those who serve Christ (Jn 12:26)

None can come to Christ except they do the will of the Father (Jn 6:65; Mt 12:50)

Christ has made the Saints kings and priests unto his Father (Rev 1:6)

He who loveth Christ is beloved of the Father (Jn 14:21)

Those who hate Christ hate the Father (Jn 15:23)

Christ brings men before the Father (Mt 10:32; Rev 3:5)

No man sees the Father without the Son (Mt 11:27 JST; Lk 10:22 JST)

To acknowledge or deny the Son is to acknowledge or deny the Father (1Jn 2:23)

Chart 12-2 (3)

THE RELATIONSHIP BETWEEN CHRIST AND THE FATHER

Christ is the Only Begotten Son of the Father (Jn 1:14; 5:18)
The Father is greater than the Son (Jn 14:28)
The Father loves the Son (Jn 3:35; 5:20; 10:17)
Christ loves the Father (Jn 14:31)
Christ and the Father are one (Jn 8:19; 10:30, 38; 14:7, 10–11, 20)
The Father and Son know each other (Jn 10:15)
The Father is glorified in the Son (Jn 14:13)
Christ is in the bosom of the Father (Jn 1:18)

THE FATHER'S ACTIONS TOWARD CHRIST DURING HIS MINISTRY

Christ received glory and honor from the Father (Jn 8:54; 2Pt 1:17)
The Father watched over the Son during his ministry (Mt 26:53; Jn 8:29)
The Father bears witness of the Son (Jn 5:37; 8:18)
The Father taught the Son (Jn 8:28)
Christ received power from his Father (Rev 2:27)
The Father sanctified Christ (Jn 10:36)
The Father commanded the Son (Jn 12:49)
The Father hath sent Christ (Jn 5:36, 43; 6:57; 8:16)

CHRIST'S ACTIONS TOWARD THE FATHER DURING HIS MINISTRY

Christ lives by the Father (Jn 6:57)
Christ obeys the Father (Jn 5:17, 19, 30, 36; 14:31; Lk 2:49)
Christ speaks the words of the Father (Jn 12:50; 15:15)
Christ honored his Father (Jn 8:49)

THE RELATIONSHIP BETWEEN CHRIST AND THE FATHER AFTER CHRIST'S MINISTRY

The Father raised Christ from the dead (Rom 6:4)
Christ is set down with the Father in his throne (Rev 3:21)
Christ departed out of this world unto the Father (Jn 13:1; 14:12; 20:17; Lk 23:46)
Christ has all that the Father has (Mt 11:27; Jn 13:3; 16:15; Lk 10:22; Col 1:19)
The Father has appointed a kingdom for Christ (Lk 22:29)
Christ shall deliver the kingdom to the Father (1Cor 15:24)
The Father has sealed the Son (Jn 6:27)
The Father commits judgment to the Son (Jn 5:22)

The Holy Ghost

THE HOLY GHOST AND THE GODHEAD

The Holy Ghost comes from God (Jn 16:3; 1Th 4:8)
The Holy Ghost enables us to bear the presence of God (Mt 1:18, 20; Lk 1:35)
The Father, Son, and Holy Ghost bear witness of each other (1Jn 5:6–7)
Access to the Father is obtained through Christ and the Holy Ghost (Eph 2:18, 22)

THE HOLY GHOST AND JESUS CHRIST

Jesus Christ had the company of the Holy Ghost during his ministry (Mt 3:16; Lk 4:14)
The Holy Ghost invites us to come unto Christ (Heb 3:7)
We are given the Holy Ghost through Jesus Christ (2Cor 5:5)
Christ's atonement was accomplished through the Holy Ghost (Heb 9:14)
Christ was resurrected through the Holy Ghost (1Pt 3:18)
Jesus' departure allowed for the Comforter to come and abide with the people (Jn 16:7)
Those who believe in Christ receive the Holy Ghost (Jn 7:39)
The gift of the Holy Ghost comes because of Christ (Acts 1:5)
The Holy Ghost witnesses of Christ (Acts 20:23; 1Cor 12:3–4; 1Jn 4:2)

THE HOLY GHOST AND REVELATION

Prophecy comes from the Holy Ghost (Lk 2:25–27; Acts 2:17–18)
The prophets speak through the power of the Holy Ghost (Mk 12:36; Acts 1:16)
Visions are received through the Holy Ghost (Acts 7:55)
The Holy Ghost helps men to speak the words of God (Jn 3:34)
The sword of the Spirit is the word of God (Eph 6:17–18)
The scriptures were written through the Holy Ghost (Rev 1:10; 14:13; 22:17)

THE HOLY GHOST AND CHURCH LEADERSHIP

Leaders of the church are appointed by authority and by the Holy Ghost (Acts 20:28)
Leaders of the church must have the company of the Holy Ghost (Lk 1:15; Acts 6:3)
We sustain our leaders for the sake of the Holy Ghost (Rom 15:30)
The doctrine of the church is received through the Holy Ghost (Acts 1:2; 15:28)

THE HOLY GHOST AND MISSIONARIES

Missionaries must be sent forth by the Holy Ghost (Acts 13:2, 4)
Missionaries prove themselves to be from God by having the Holy Ghost (2Cor 6:6)
Missionaries testify of Christ through the power of the Holy Ghost (Acts 1:8)
The Holy Ghost protects missionaries [and others who are faithful] (Acts 8:39)

REQUIREMENTS TO RECEIVE THE GIFT OF THE HOLY GHOST

The Holy Ghost must be received from one who has the authority to bestow it (Acts 8:15–19)
Obedience is necessary in order to have the Holy Ghost (Acts 5:32)
Faith is required in order to have the company of the Holy Ghost (Gal 3:14)
The gift of the Holy Ghost is received by the laying on of hands by those with authority (Acts 19:6)

Chart 12-3 (1)

Gifts and Powers of the Holy Ghost

The Holy Ghost gives the gifts of the Spirit (1Cor 12:7–13; Heb 2:4; Acts 2:4)
The Holy Ghost brings us peace and hope (Acts 13:52; Rom 15:13)
Miracles are worked through the power of the Holy Ghost (Mt 12:28; Rev 11:11)

Baptism and the Holy Ghost

Baptism should be performed in the name of the Father, Son, and Holy Ghost (Mt 28:19)
Baptism is required to receive the gift of the Holy Ghost (Acts 2:38)
Jesus baptizes with the Holy Ghost (Jn 1:32–33)
The baptism of the Spirit is required to enter the kingdom of God (Jn 3:5–8; Acts 19:2)
The Holy Ghost baptizes the Saints with fire (Acts 11:15–16)

The Holy Ghost and Daily Life

The Holy Ghost changes our character (Gal 5:22–23)
The Holy Ghost will prompt us to do things (Acts 8:29; 11:12)
The Holy Ghost helps us with our weaknesses, especially in communicating with God (Rom 8:26-27)
The Holy Ghost witnesses of truth (Rom 9:1)
The Holy Ghost helps us to show proper judgment (Mt 12:18)

The Holy Ghost in Contrast with Worldliness

The wicked resist the Holy Ghost (Acts 5:39; 7:51; Heb 6:4)
Speaking against the Holy Ghost is unforgivable (Mt 12:31–32; Lk 12:10)
Walk not after the flesh, but after the Spirit (Rom 8:1–5)
The flesh and the Spirit are in opposition (Gal 4:29; 5:16–18)
The things of the Spirit are more important than the things of the flesh (Rom 14:17)
The gift of the Holy Ghost far surpasses all other earthly gifts (Lk 11:13)
Spiritual things must be learned through the Holy Ghost (1Cor 2:10–14)

The Holy Ghost and the Saints

The Holy Ghost teaches men (Jn 14:26; Heb 9:8; 1Pet 1:11–12)
The Saints are converted through the Holy Ghost (1Th 1:5–6)
The Father sends the Holy Ghost to comfort men (Jn 14:16–17; Acts 9:31)
The Holy Ghost strengthens the Saints (Eph 3:16)
The Holy Ghost fills the Saints with the love of God (Rom 5:5)
The Saints are united through the Holy Ghost (Eph 4:3–4; Phil 2:1; Col 1:8)
The Holy Ghost dwells in men (1Cor 3:16; 6:19)
We each need a personal relationship with the Holy Ghost (2Cor 13:14)
The Holy Ghost is available to all (Acts 10:44–47; 15:8)

The Holy Ghost and Salvation

We are made perfect through the Holy Ghost (Gal 3:2–5; Titus 3:5)
We know that we are saved because we feel the Holy Ghost (2Cor 1:22; 1Jn 4:13)
The Holy Ghost tells us that our spirits are children of God (Rom 8:9–16)
Humans are cleansed and sanctified by the Holy Ghost (Rom 15:16; 1Cor 6:11; 2Th 2:13)
The Holy Ghost liberates us and changes us to a state of glory (2Cor 3:17–18)
The faithful are sealed for exaltation by the Holy Ghost (Eph 1:13)
The Saints are the firstfruits of the Spirit (Rom 8:23)

Chart 12-3 (2)

Basic Theologies

Explanation

The teachings propagated among Christians in the first generation after Christ derived largely from Peter, John, and Paul. Through examination of the surviving writings of these three apostles, much of the nature of early Christian theology can be ascertained. Most prominent were teachings about Christ, testimonies of his divine sonship, and declarations of his atoning mission. Other teachings can be categorized as basic doctrines and as practices of the early Christian community. The three charts that follow highlight various teachings about Christ as well as Christian doctrines and Christian practices as articulated in the writings of Peter (chart 12-4), John (chart 12-5), and Paul (chart 12-6). Taken together these charts show that these three major spokesmen addressed similar subjects in similar ways. For example, John is often thought of as the apostle of love. However, Peter and Paul also spoke about this important subject, often using the same vocabulary or phraseology. How does one explain the commonalities? Most obviously, these apostles derived their teachings from Jesus Christ as their common source.

References

John F. Hall, "Peter," *EM*, 3:1077–79.

Raymond Brown, trans., *The Gospel According to John* (Garden City, N.Y.: Doubleday, 1966–70).

Richard Lloyd Anderson, *Understanding Paul* (Salt Lake City: Deseret Book, 1983).

"Paul's Teachings," *WRC*, 102–5.

Peter's Basic Theology

TEACHINGS ABOUT CHRIST

Belief in Christ essential	Acts 2:38; 1Pt 3:21
Premortal Christ	1Pt 1:20
Christ as Creator	2Pt 3:5
Atonement of Christ	1Pt 1:3; 2:21–24; 3:18
Resurrected Christ	Acts 2:29–36; 5:29–32; 1Pt 1:3
Christ's second coming	2Pt 3:10

CHRISTIAN DOCTRINES

Apostasy	2Pt 2:1–3
Latter-day restoration	Acts 3:21; 2Pt 3:3

CHRISTIAN PRACTICES

Faith, key to redemption	1Pt 1:7; 2Pt 1:5
Baptism	Acts 2:38; 1Pt 3:21
Personal revelation	1Pt 3:18
Love, charity	1Pt 1:22; 4:8; 2Pt 1:7

Chart 12-4

John's Basic Theology

TEACHINGS ABOUT CHRIST

Belief in Christ Essential	Jn 6; 1Jn 3:23; 4:1; 5:10–13
Premortal Christ	Jn 1; 6:62; 8:58; 16:28; 17:25
Christ as Creator	Jn 1:3, 10
Christ, Only Begotten	Jn 1:14, 18; 3:16
Atonement of Christ	Jn 6:51; 10:15; 11:25; 1Jn 1:7; 2:2; 3:5; 4:10
Resurrected Christ	Jn 20:14–20; 21

CHRISTIAN DOCTRINES

Apostasy	1Jn 2, 4
Fulfillment of Mosaic Law	Jn 1:17
Godhead	Jn 5:19; 8:18; 10:30, 38; 17:3, 21; 1Jn 5:7

CHRISTIAN PRACTICES

Baptism	Jn 3:1–5
Personal revelation	Jn 6:63; 14:17; 15:26; 1Jn 3:24; 4:6; 5:6
Love, charity	Jn 5:42; 12:25; 13:34–35; 15:10, 13, 19; 17:26; 1Jn 2:5; 3:1, 23; 4:7–8, 16–18, 21; 2Jn 1:5

Chart 12-5

Paul's Basic Theology

TEACHINGS ABOUT CHRIST

Belief in Christ essential	Rom 1:16; 3:26; Gal 3:22; Eph 1:13, 19; Phlp 1:29
Christ as Creator	Eph 3:9; Col 1:16; 3:10; Heb 1:2; 11:3
Atonement of Christ	Rom 3:25; 2Cor 5:18; Eph 2:16; Heb 5:9; 9:28
Resurrected Christ	Rom 6:9; 1Cor 15:5–8; 2Tm 2:8
Christ's second coming	1Cor 15:23; 1Th 4:16; 2Th 1:7; 2:8

CHRISTIAN DOCTRINES

Apostasy	1Cor 11:18; Gal 1:6; 2Th 2:1–12
Latter-day restoration	Rom 11:25; Eph 1:10; 2Tm 3:1
Baptism for the dead	1Cor 15:29
Fulfillment of Mosaic law	Rom 3:21; 6:14; 7:4; 10:4; Gal 2:21; 3:2, 13, 24; 5:18; Heb 8:13
Godhead	2 Cor 4:4; Eph 3:14; Col 1:15; Heb 1:2
Kingdoms of glory	1Cor 15:40; 2Cor 2:12
Revelation in church	1Cor 12:3; 14:6; 2Cor 12:1; Gal 1:12; Eph 1:17
Apostolic foundation	Eph 2:20; 4:11

CHRISTIAN PRACTICES

Faith, key to redemption	Rom 3:25–28; 1Cor 12:9; 13:13; 15:14; 16:13; Gal 2:20; 3:26; Eph 2:8; Heb 6:12
Baptism	Rom 6:4; Col 2:12; Titus 3:5
Personal revelation	Rom 1:4; 8:1–27; 1Cor 2:4, 10–12; 6:11; 12:1–13; 3:6; Gal 3:2, 14; 5:5, 25; Eph 2:18; 5:18; Phlp 2:1; 1Th 5:19
Love, charity	Rom 13:8–10; 1Cor 8:1; 13:1–13; 2Cor 6:6; Gal 5:6, 13–14, 22; Eph 3:17, 19; Col 2:2; 1Th 3:12

Chart 12-6

Levitical and Melchizedek Priesthoods
As Compared in Hebrews 7

Explanation

Hebrew 7 speaks of two orders of priests and priesthood: the Aaronic or Levitical Priesthood, and the Melchizedek Priesthood. The lower priesthood serves many useful functions, but it serves below the higher priesthood. Chart 12-5 details the points of comparison between these two priesthoods as articulated in the epistle to the Hebrews. With Jesus, the old was made new, the temporal became eternal, and the lower law was fulfilled with the higher law.

References

John W. Welch, "The Melchizedek Material in Alma 13:13–19," in *By Study and Also By Faith*, ed. John M. Lundquist and Stephen D. Ricks (Salt Lake City: Deseret Book, 1990), 2:238–72.

Jae R. Balif, "Melchizedek Priesthood: Powers and Offices in the Melchizedek Priesthood," *EM*, 2:882–85.

Verdon W. Ballantyne, "Levitical Priesthood," *EM*, 2:828–29.

Levitical and Melchizedek Priesthoods
As Compared in Hebrews 7

LEVITICAL	MELCHIZEDEK
Begins and ends	"Without beginning of days nor end of life" (7:3)
Mortal	"Immortal, made like unto the Son of God" (3)
Revocable	"Abideth a priest continually" (3)
Hereditary	"Without father, without mother" (3)
Limited to the tribe of Levi	Open to those outside the tribe of Levi (14)
Commanded according to the law	Blessed according to righteousness (1–2)
Takes tithing from their brethren	Receives tithing with a blessing (6)
In Abraham	Over Abraham (4, 6, 10)
Receives blessings through Abraham	Gave blessings to Abraham (6)
Not the final priesthood	Another priest beyond the Levitical (11, 15)
Governs the lower law	Governs the higher law (11–12)
After the law of carnal commandments	After the power of endless life (16)
Cannot make perfect	Brings in a better hope (19)
Made priests without an oath	Made priests with an oath (20–21, 28)
Law administered without an oath	Law administered with oaths (21, JST)
Temporal	Eternal, "for ever" (21, 28)
Old testament	Surety of a better testament (22)
Many priests needed because they die	Based on Jesus who will not die (23)
Changeable	Unchangeable (24)
Limited reconciliation of God and man	Able to intercede to the uttermost (25)
Highest Priest in this order is fallible	Highest Priest in this order is holy, undefiled (26)
Offers sacrifices to heaven for his own sins	Highest Priest higher than the heavens (27)
Daily sacrifices required	One sacrifice for all time (27)
With infirmity	"Consecrated for evermore" (28)

Chart 12-7

Offices of the Priesthood

Explanation

An important doctrinal tenet of the restored Church of Jesus Christ concerns the organization of the priesthood which it shares with its counterpart in the meridian of time. Chart 12-8 demonstrates this correlation. It lists priesthood offices or church functionaries, giving modern names and New Testament counterparts, which are noted under their Greek names along with brief translations. A scriptural reference where the Greek term occurs in the New Testament is also provided. Each of these offices and functions was crucial in the establishment and nurturing of Christian congregations, communities, and churches from the earliest decades of the New Testament era, as they are in similar although not identical ways today.

Reference

Richard G. Ellsworth and Melvin J. Luthy, "Priesthood," *EM,* 3:1133–38.

Offices of the Priesthood

OFFICE	GREEK	REFERENCE
Deacon	διάκονος (*diakonos*) attendant, deacon, minister, servant	1Tm 3:8–13
Teacher	διδάσκαλος (*didaskalos*) instructor, doctor, master, teacher	1Cor 12:28–29
Priest	ἱερεύς (*hiereus*) priest, holy one	Heb 10:11
Bishop	ἐπίσκοπος (*episkopos*) superintendent, overseer, bishop	1Tm 3:1–2
Pastor	ποιμήν (*poimēn*) shepherd, pastor	Eph 4:11
Elder	πρεσβύτερος (*presbuteros*) old one, senior, elder	1Tm 5:17; Titus 1:5
Patriarch	πατριάρχης (*patriarchēs*) progenitor, patriarch	Acts 2:29; Heb 7:4
Evangelist	εὐαγγελιστής (*euangelistēs*) preacher, evangelist, declarer	2Tm 4:5; Eph 4:11
Seventy	ἑβδομήκοντα (*hebdomēkonta*) seventy	Lk 10:1, 17
Apostle	ἀπόστολος (*apostolos*) he that is sent, delegate, ambassador, messenger	Mt 10:2; Acts 2:42
Twelve	δώδεκα (*dōdeka*) twelve	Mt 10:2
High Priest	ἀρχιερεύς (*archiereus*) high priest, chief of priests	Heb 2:17
Prophet	προφήτης (*prophētēs*) foreteller, proclaimer	Eph 4:11

Chart 12-8

Duties of a Bishop

Explanation

The early Christian bishop was originally a leader of a local congregation. In the letters of 1 Timothy and Titus, the duties and characteristics required of a bishop are spelled out. Taken together, these epistles prescribe twenty-four qualities of the bishop. These attributes are as appropriate for bishops and leaders of the church today as they were in the first generation of Christians.

Reference

John A. Widstoe, ed., *Discourses of Brigham Young* (Salt Lake City: Deseret Book, 1977), 143–46.

Duties of a Bishop

	1Tm	Titus
blameless	3:2	1:6–7
husband of one wife	3:2	1:6
faithful children	3:4	1:6
not self-willed		1:7
not soon angry		1:7
not given to wine	3:3	1:7
no striker/not a brawler	3:2–3	1:7
not given to filthy lucre	3:3	1:7
a lover of hospitality	3:2	1:8
a lover of good men		1:8
sober	3:2	1:8
just		1:8
holy		1:8
temperate		1:8
holding fast the faithful word		1:9
exhorts, convinces gainsayers		1:9
apt to teach	3:2	
vigilant	3:2	
of good behavior	3:2	
patient	3:3	
not covetous	3:3	
one that rules well his own house	3:4	
not a novice	3:6	
of good reputation in the community	3:7	

Chart 12-9

Gifts of the Spirit

Explanation

The main purpose of priesthood in the Church of Jesus Christ is to lead the faithful in such a way that they can feel and receive the gifts of the Spirit, the greatest of which is the gift of eternal life. The gifts of the spirit are rich and manifold. Chart 12-10 combines into a single profile the array of spiritual gifts that are mentioned in four scriptural lists: in 1 Corinthians 12, Moroni 10, Doctrine and Covenants 46, and the seventh Article of Faith. No two of these lists are the same, just as no two individuals are the same. To one is given one gift; to others are given other gifts.

Through priesthood ordinances, people prepare themselves to receive the gifts of the Spirit by repentance, baptism, and then righteously keeping one's covenants with God. Chart 12-11 lists the many instances in the New Testament that mention the ordinance of baptism. This substantial collection shows the importance of baptism in early Christianity. As administered by John the Baptist and the apostles of Jesus, baptism was performed by immersion as a conscious token of one's faith and repentance. Baptism opens the way for a person to receive the confirmation of the gift of the Holy Ghost and the blessings of his companionship.

References

H. George Bickerstaff, "Gifts of the Spirit," *EM*, 2:544–46.
James E. Talmage, *The Articles of Faith* (Salt Lake City: Deseret Book, 1983), 197–213.

Gifts of the Spirit

GIFT	1 Corinthians 12	Moroni 10	D&C 46	Article of Faith 7
To know that Jesus Christ is the Son of God			v. 13	
To have a testimony of the atonement			13	
To believe on the words of those who know			14	
To know the differences of administration			15	
To know the diversities of operations			16	
To have wisdom	v. 8		17	
To have knowledge	8		18	
To teach the word of wisdom		v. 9		
To teach the word of knowledge		10		
To have faith	9	11		
To have faith to be healed			19	
To heal	9	11	20	✓
To work miracles	10	12	21	
To prophesy	10	13	22	✓
To discern spirits	10	14	23	
To behold angels		14		
To speak in tongues	10	15	24	✓
To interpret tongues	10	16	25	✓
To interpret languages		16		
To receive revelation				✓
To behold visions				✓

Chart 12-10

Instances of Baptism

John performed baptisms in the river Jordan.
Mt 3:6; Mk 1:4–5; Lk 3:3; Jn 1:28

Pharisees and Sadducees come to the baptism of John.
Mt 3:7

John the Baptist criticizes hypocrites who are present at his baptisms.
Lk 3:7

Then came also publicans to be baptized, and said unto him, "Master, what shall we do?"
Lk 3:12

"I indeed baptize you with water unto repentance: but he that cometh after me is mightier than I, whose shoes I am not worthy to bear: he shall baptize you with the Holy Ghost, and with fire."
Mt 3:11; Mk 1:8; Lk 3:16; Jn 1:26–27

And they asked him, and said unto him, "Why baptizest thou then, if thou be not that Christ, nor Elias, neither that prophet?"
Jn 1:25

John prophesies that his baptism prepares the way for the Messiah.
Jn 1:31; Acts 13:24

Jesus is baptized by John to fulfill all righteousness.
Mt 3:13–16; Mk 1:9–10; Lk 3:21

John bears record of Jesus as the Messiah who will baptize with the Holy Ghost.
Jn 1:33

Humble publicans accept the baptism of John, while Pharisees and Scribes reject it.
Lk 7:29–30

"But I have a baptism to be baptized with; and how am I straitened till it be accomplished!"
Lk 12:50

Jesus asks the sons of Zebedee whether they can bear to be baptized with his baptism.
Mt 20:22–23; Mk 10:38–39

Jesus asks the chief priests, "The baptism of John, whence was it? from heaven or of men?"
Mt 21:25; Mk 11:30; Lk 20:4

The apostles are instructed to baptize in the name of the Father, Son, and Holy Ghost.
Mt 28:19

"He that believeth and is baptized shall be saved; but he that believeth not shall be damned."
Mk 16:16

"Verily, verily, I say unto thee, Except a man be born again, he cannot see the kingdom of God."
Jn 3:3–5, 7

Jesus, his disciples, and John all baptize.
Jn 3:22–23

People complain to John because of Jesus' success in baptisms.
Jn 3:26; 4:1–2

"For John truly baptized with water; but ye shall be baptized with the Holy Ghost not many days hence."
Acts 1:5

"Beginning from the baptism of John, unto that same day that he was taken up from us, must one be ordained to be a witness with us of his resurrection."
Acts 1:22

"Repent, and be baptized every one of you in the name of Jesus Christ for the remission of sins, and ye shall receive the gift of the Holy Ghost."
Acts 2:38

Chart 12-11 (1)

Peter baptizes three thousand souls.
Acts 2:41

Philip baptizes in Samaria.
Acts 8:12–13

For as yet the Holy Ghost was fallen upon none of them: only they were baptized in the name of the Lord Jesus.
Acts 8:16

Philip baptizes a eunuch.
Acts 8:36, 38

Paul was healed and baptized.
Acts 9:18

Peter commands that Gentiles should be baptized as well as Jews.
Acts 10:47–48

"Then remembered I the word of the Lord, how that he said, John indeed baptized with water; but ye shall be baptized with the Holy Ghost."
Acts 11:16

Lydia of Thyatira and her household were baptized.
Acts 16:15

The keeper of the prison in Philippi and his household were baptized.
Acts 16:33

Crispus, the chief ruler of the synagogue, believed on the Lord with all his house; and many of the Corinthians hearing believed, and were baptized.
Acts 18:8

Apollos was instructed in the way of the Lord; and being fervent in the spirit, he spake and taught diligently the things of the Lord, knowing only the baptism of John.
Acts 18:25

People in Ephesus had been baptized only with the baptism of John. Paul baptized them in the name of Jesus.
Acts 19:3–5

"And now why tarriest thou? arise, and be baptized, and wash away thy sins, calling on the name of the Lord."
Acts 22:16

Baptism is a symbol of the death and resurrection of Christ.
Rom 6:3–4; Col 2:12; 1Pt 3:21

Saints are to be baptized in the name of Christ, not in the name of the missionary who performed the baptism.
1Cor 1:13–17

"Moreover, brethren, I would not that ye should be ignorant, how that all our fathers were under the cloud, and all passed through the sea; And were all baptized unto Moses in the cloud and in the sea."
1Cor 10:1–2

"For by one Spirit are we all baptized into one body, whether we be Jews or Gentiles, whether we be bond or free; and have been all made to drink into one Spirit."
1Cor 12:13

"Else what shall they do which are baptized for the dead, if the dead rise not at all? why are they then baptized for the dead?"
1Cor 15:29

"For as many of you as have been baptized into Christ have put on Christ."
Gal 3:27

"One Lord, one faith, one baptism."
Eph 4:5

Baptism is a saving ordinance.
Titus 3:5

Paul declares the doctrine of baptisms.
Heb 6:2

Chart 12-11 (2)

Chart 12-12

Church Policies and Practices

Explanation

Scattered throughout the epistles of the New Testament are indications of how the earliest Christians worshiped and lived. Prayer and singing were important parts of their worship. They administered the sacrament of the Lord's supper. They made donations to the poor and to the church headquarters. They insisted on morality and chastity. They strengthened marriages and families. Chart 12-12 identifies these key elements present among the policies and practices of the early Christian church. These elements will always be found among the fundamental covenants and teachings of the Church of Jesus Christ.

References

Howard W. Hunter, "Organization of the Church of Christ," *Improvement Era,* December 1965, 1145–47.

Charles W. Penrose, "What is 'the Church'?" *Millennial Star* 70 (16 January 1908): 40–43.

Church Policies and Practices

ON PRAYER
    Pray for everyone   1Tm 2:1–8
    Pray and sing   Jms 5:13

ON WORSHIP
    Women in the assembly   1Tm 2:9–15
    Head coverings of men and women   1Cor 11:2–16

ON THE SACRAMENT
    The last supper   1Cor 11:23–26
    Do not partake of the sacrament unworthily   1Cor 11:27–34

ON MAKING DONATIONS
    Be generous   2Cor 8:1–9
    Blessings come from giving   2Cor 9:6–15
    Combine godliness and material contentment   1Tm 6:3–10

ON MORALITY
    Incest and other immorality in Corinth   1Cor 5:1–13
    Avoid fornication; glorify God in your body   1Cor 6:12–20

ON MARRIAGE
    Marriage is good   1Cor 7:1–11
    Marriage of a believer to an unbeliever   1Cor 7:12–16
    Wives and husbands   Eph 5:22–33
    Advice to wives: adorn your relationship with righteousness   1Pt 3:1–6
    Advice to husbands: inherit life with your wife   1Pt 3:7

ON DOMESTIC RELATIONS
    Morals and duties in household relationships   Col 3:18–4:1
    Children and parents   Eph 6:1–4
    Caring for widows   1Tm 5:3–16
    Instructions to various age groups   Titus 2:1–10

Chart 12-12

Chart 12-13

Main Doctrinal Chapters
in the New Testament

Explanation

Certain chapters in the New Testament are especially famous. These doctrinal highlights express key concepts in unforgettably eloquent or powerful terms. To the list in chart 12-13 could be added many other topics and chapters, but those listed are certainly among the top favorites concerning the first principles and ordinances of the gospel (namely faith, repentance of the prodigal son, baptism, and the gift of the Holy Ghost), Christian living (charity, love of the good Samaritan, family relations, missionary work, priesthood, and unity), and the salvation history of the world (atonement, apostasy, second coming, and resurrection).

Reference

BYU Studies Staff, "*We Rejoice in Christ: A Bibliography of LDS Writings on Jesus Christ and the New Testament*" (Provo, Utah: BYU Studies, 1995).

Main Doctrinal Chapters
in the New Testament

Apostasy	2Th 2
Atonement	Heb 10
Baptism	Jn 3; Rom 6
Charity	1Cor 13
Faith	Heb 11
Family relations	Eph 5–6
Gift of the Holy Ghost/Spirit	1Cor 12; Eph 4
Love of God and neighbors	Lk 10
Missionary work	Mt 10
Priesthood	Heb 7
Repentance	Lk 15
Resurrection	1Cor 15
Second Coming	1Th 4–5; Mt 24
Unity	Jn 17

Chart 12-13

Christian Virtues and Unchristian Vices

Explanation

One may glean from the writings of the New Testament references to dozens of virtues and vices. Chart 12-14, on the one hand, offers a simple listing of the numerous virtues expected of a true Christian. The list is long, and without the blessings of the Spirit of God no person can acquire all these many traits of righteousness. But with the help of God, lives can be transformed and these attributes of divine nature can be enjoyed by the Saints. Consulting and reviewing this list will help the meek and humble followers of Christ to grow in goodness and godliness.

Chart 12-15, on the other hand, tabulates the many vices that Christians are warned and counseled to shun. Lists of virtues and vices are often found in scripture (as in the Ten Commandments), as well as in the moralistic writings of the Hellenistic age. In the New Testament, one famous list of eight divine virtues is found in 2 Peter 1:5–7, and a trenchant list of ten wicked vices is given in 1 Corinthians 6:9–10. Charts 12-14 and 12-15 combine to produce a comprehensive profile of what it means to be a true Christian in terms of human ethics and moral behavior.

References

John T. Fitzgerald, "Virtue/Vice Lists," *ABD*, 6:857–59.
"Exemplary Life," *WRC*, 15–16.

Christian Virtues

Abhorrence of evil
Abounding in good works
Abstinence from the appearance of evil
Approval of excellent things
Bearing all things
Bearing one another's burdens
Belief in Christ
Blamelessness
Blessing those who persecute you
Boldness
Brotherly love
Charity, compassion
Chastity, virtue
Cheerfulness in giving
Circumspection
Cleanliness
Being completely filled
Confidence, trust
Constructive communication
Contentment, peace, no worry
Courtesy
Diligence
Ease in entreatment
Edification
Endurance
Entertaining strangers
Equality
Esteem, regard
Example-setting
Faithfulness
Fear, respect of God
Fervency in spirit
Fidelity, trustworthiness
Following that which is good
Foolishness to the world
Forbearance
Forgiveness
Gentleness
Glory in tribulation
Godliness, piety
Goodness, uprightness, kindness
Goodwill
Graveness, solemnity, seriousness
Harmlessness
Hearing
Holiness

Honesty
Honorability
Hope
Hospitality
Humility
Incorruption, soundness
Instance in prayer
Joy
Justice, fairness
Kindness
Knowledge
Like-mindedness, being agreeable
Longsuffering
Love
Lowliness
Making others rich
Meekness
Mercy
Might, power
Minding own business
Moderation
Modesty
Obedience
Orderliness
Patience
Peacefulness
Perfection, completion, wholeness
Perseverance
Piety
Pity, tenderheartedness
Praising
Prayerfulness without ceasing
Preferring others, deference
Proving all things, examining
Purity, sincerity, cleanliness
Quiet, peace
Reception
Recompensing no evil
Reconciliation to God
Rejoicing
Being renewed
Beyond rebuke or reproach
Repentance
Resisting the devil
Righteousness
Ruling well
Same mindedness

Separation, being set apart
Service
Shamefacedness, no pretension, respect
Silence, quiet
Simplicity, purity, innocence
Sincerity, being unsullied
Singleness of heart, frankness, dedication
Sobriety, self-control, prudence, thoughtfulness
Sorrow, grieving, sympathy
Sound mind, self-discipline
Speaking kindly and uprightly
Spirituality
Standing fast, firmness
Strength in faith
Strength in graciousness
Strength in the Lord
Striving together for good
Subjection, obedience, orderliness
Submission to righteous authority
Supplication
Support of the weak
Teaching what is good
Being temperate, in full control of oneself
Tenderheartedness
Thankfulness
Touching no unclean thing
Transformation, transfiguration
Trust in God
Truthfulness, dependability, honesty
Understanding, insight
Unity in the faith
Being unmovable
Vigilance, watchfulness
Virtue, moral excellence
Watchfulness, alertness
Weeping with those who weep
Well doing, benevolence
Wisdom, experience, helpfulness
Working with own hands
Worshipfulness
Worthiness, deserve, propriety
Zealousness, striving

Chart 12-14

Unchristian Vices

Abusing oneself with mankind, sodomy
Adultery
Anger
Being ashamed of one's testimony
Babbling
Bitterness
Blasphemy
Boasting
Brawling
Being a busybody, meddling
Childishness, immaturity
Clamoring, shouting
Conceit
Concupiscence, lust, envy
Conformity to the world
Contention, discord
Covetousness
Craftiness, trickery
Deceit
Defrauding, taking advantage
Despising, disdaining, contempt
Dishonesty, shamefulness
Disputing, arguing
Double-tonguedness, insincerity
Doubt
Drunkardness
Easy provocation, irritability
Being effeminate, transexuality
Envy, jealousy
Evil doing or speaking
Extortion, robbery, plundering
Being faint, slacking
False accusing, slander
Filthiness, indecency
Foolish questions
Foolish or silly talk
Fornication, prostitution
Genealogical boasting
Greed
Grudging, complaining
Guile, cunning
High-mindedness, pride, haughtiness
Hypocrisy
Idleness
Idolatry
Inordinate affection, passion

Jesting, coarse jokes
Judging, condemning
Leaving nature, homosexuality
Loving money, avarice
Lust, toward men or women
Lying
Malice
Murmuring, grumbling
Being a novice
Offending
Partiality, playing favorites
Provoking, irritating
Being puffed up, conceit
Purloining, embezzling
Rendering evil for evil
Respecter of persons, unfairness
Reviling, abusing
Self-seeking
Self-will, stubbornness, arrogance
Shaken in mind, wavering
Sin
Slander
Slothfulness, laziness
Spot, blemish
Strife, ambition, quarreling
Striking, fighting
Superfluity of naughtiness, wickedness
Swearing, issuing oaths
Tattling, gossip
Terror, intimidation
Theft, stealing
Being troubled or disturbed
Uncleanness, impurity
Ungodliness, impiety
Unrighteousness, injustice
Unseemly behavior, disgrace, indecency
Being unwise, foolishness, ignorance
Vainglory, empty conceit
Vanity, emptiness, frustration
Vaunting, boasting, bragging
Wavering, indecision
Weakness
Whoremongering, fornication
Being given to wine
Wrath, anger, rage

Chart 12-15

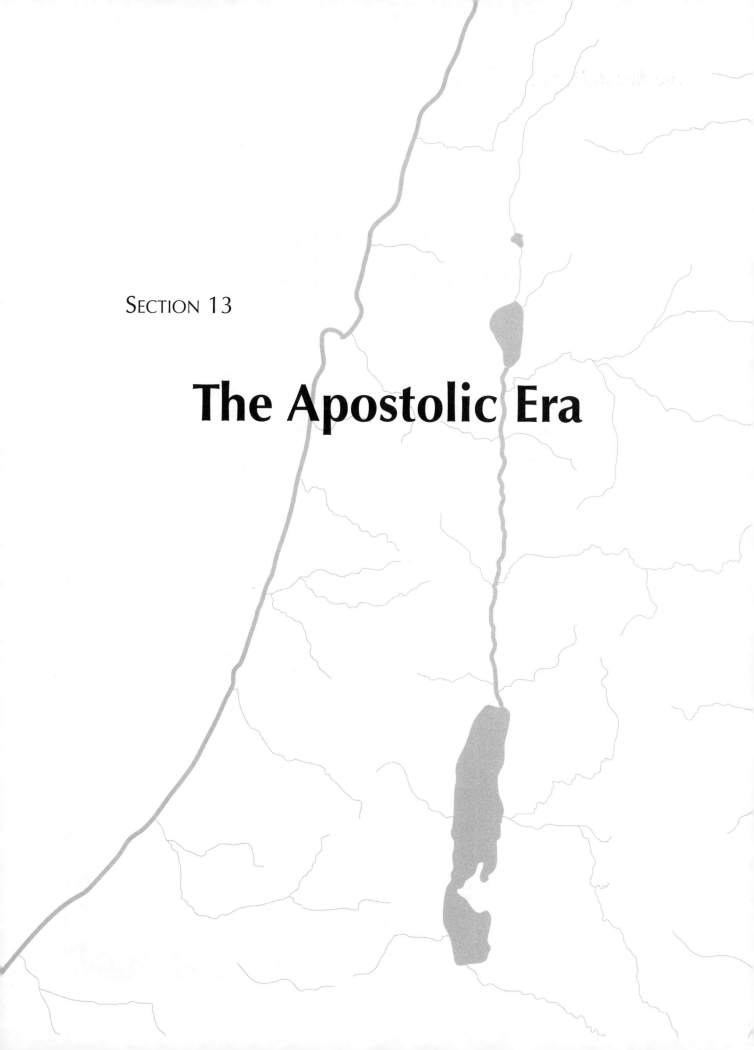

SECTION 13

The Apostolic Era

Chronology
of the New Testament Era

Explanation

The timeline of the apostolic era on chart 13-1 encompasses events from the time of Christ until the departure of the last of the apostles, John the Beloved. About half of the events noted are of certain date. Most relate to Roman governance and are documented in Roman historical records, official transcripts, or monuments. Some of the notations (in italics) are of conjectural date, based on careful reconstruction of the activities of leading individuals and the most likely chronological sequencing of events. The remaining items listed very likely occurred as dated, since they fit into a sequence of related happenings, or are confirmed by strong, though not certain, evidence. These dates are listed in accordance with the dating system of the time, that of the Roman year, with the modern date equivalent also provided. Events listed are either of particular importance to early Christian history or of empire-wide importance.

References

M. Cary and H. H. Scullard, *A History of Rome* (New York: St. Martin's, 1975).
F. E. Peters, *The Harvest of Hellenism* (New York: Simon & Schuster, 1970).

Chronology
of the New Testament Era

Chart 13-1 (1)

ROMAN YEAR	MODERN DATE	EVENT	
746–748	*7–5 B.C.*	*Birth of Christ*	**Certain Dates**
747	**6 B.C.**	**Quinctilius Governor of Syria**	Likely Dates
748	*5 B.C.*	*Slaughter of Innocents*	*Conjectural Dates*
749	**4 B.C.**	**Death of King Herod** **Herod Antipas becomes Tetrarch of Galilee** **Archelaus becomes Ethnarch of Judea**	
758	**A.D. 6**	**Quirinius Governor of Syria** **Archelaus is removed as Judean ethnarch** **Coponius first prefect of Judea**	
766	**14**	**Death of Augustus, accession of Tiberius**	
778	**26**	**Pilate prefect of Judea**	
780	**28**	**John the Baptist begins ministry in fourteenth year of Tiberius's reign**	
782	30	Christ begins his ministry	
783	31	John the Baptist is beheaded by Herod Antipas	
785	33	Crucifixion Peter and John testify and perform miracles in Jerusalem	
786	34	Caiaphas is removed as High Priest	
786–787	34–35	Paul witnesses Stephen's stoning	
787	35	Paul is converted on road to Damascus	
789	**37**	**Death of Tiberius, accession of Gaius Caligula, Marullus replaces Pilate as prefect of Judea**	
791	**39**	**Herod Agrippa becomes tetrarch of Galilee**	

793	**41**	**Gaius is assassinated, Claudius is proclaimed emperor** **Claudius appoints Herod Agrippa king of Judea**
795	43	James is executed in Herod Agrippa's persecution of Christians in Judea Paul's Antioch mission
797–799	45–47	Paul's first missionary journey
801	49	Council of Jerusalem; Peter moves to Antioch James, "the Brother of the Lord" leads church in Jerusalem *Andrew begins mission to Black Sea region* *Thomas begins mission to the East* *Philip begins mission to Asia Minor* Claudius's expulsion of Jews from Rome
801–804	49–52	Paul's second missionary journey
803–804	**51–52**	**Gallio governor at Corinth** Paul at Corinth
804	**52**	**Felix appointed procurator of Judea**
804–805	52–53	Paul labors at Antioch
805–810	53–58	Paul's third missionary journey
806	**54**	**Death of Claudius, accession of Nero**
807	*55*	*Peter at Corinth*
806–808	54–56	Paul at Ephesus
808	56	Peter arrives at Rome
809–810	57–58	Paul in Macedonia and Greece
811–812	59–60	Paul arrested by Jews at Jerusalem, held in custody at governor's palace in Caesarea **Festus replaces Felix as procurator of Judea**
813	60	Paul's voyage to Rome
813–814	61–62	Paul lives in his own house at Rome awaiting hearing before Nero
814	**62**	**James, "the Brother of the Lord," is executed at Jerusalem by the high priest Ananus.**

Chart 13-1 (2)

815	*63*	*Paul's ministry in Italy*
816–818	*64–66*	*Paul's possible missionary journey through Spain and the other western provinces*
816	**64**	**The Great Fire at Rome** **Nero's prosecution of Christians** Death of Peter
818	**66**	**Revolt of Jewish Zealots against Rome, Jewish persecution of Christians at Jerusalem, departure of Christians from Jerusalem**
818–819	66–67	Paul writes Pastoral Epistles from Rome
819	67	John arrives at Ephesus
820	*68*	*Paul's death*
820	**68**	**Nero is overthrown**
821	**69**	**Year of the Four Emperors; ends with Vespasian as sole emperor**
822	**70**	**Titus destroys Jerusalem**
831	**79**	**Death of Vespasian, accession of Titus; Eruption of Vesuvius**
832	**80**	**Colosseum constructed**
833	**81**	**Death of Titus, accession of Domitian**
846–847	*94–95*	*John resides on Patmos; Revelation is received*
847	**95**	**Domitian executes Christians at Rome**
848	**96**	**Death of Domitian, accession of Nerva** John returns to Ephesus
850	**98**	**Nerva's death, accession of Trajan**
852–862	*100–110*	*John writes the Epistles and the Gospel of John at Ephesus*
862–864	**110–112**	**Pliny is governor of Bithynia-Pontus, Trajan-Pliny correspondence about conduct of judicial proceedings involving Christians**
865	*113*	*Departure of John, removal of apostolic keys*

Chart 13-1 (3)

Chronological Order of Books

Explanation

Chart 13-2 lists the books of the New Testament in the likely chronological order of their composition. The probable place of composition is also listed. In some cases, these dates and places are conjectural, but in a few cases the dates are quite certain. An awareness of the time and place of composition helps readers today to appreciate the situations and the audiences addressed in these compositions.

Although in recent years some scholars have argued against accepting traditional authorship, we remain unconvinced. Sufficient evidence has not been produced to prove that the books of the New Testament were not written by the traditionally claimed authors. Indeed, early Christian sources corroborate that, during the generations immediately following their composition, the apostolic and evangelistic authority of these books was unchallenged. Only later, in a changed Christian church, did various clerics and scholastics raise questions of legitimacy as the New Testament canon evolved. (See chart 18-6).

References

Raymond E. Brown, *An Introduction to the New Testament* (New York: Doubleday, 1997).
Henry C. Thiessen, *Introduction to the New Testament* (Grand Rapids: Eerdmans, 1955).
L. M. McDonald, *The Formation of the Christian Biblical Canon* (Peabody, Mass.: Hendrickson, 1995).

Chronological Order of Books

BOOK	AUTHOR	DATE OF COMPOSITION	PLACE OF COMPOSITION
1 Thessalonians	Paul	51	Corinth
2 Thessalonians	Paul	51	Corinth
1 Corinthians	Paul	54	Ephesus
2 Corinthians	Paul	57	Macedonia (Philippi?)
Galatians	Paul	57	Macedonia (Philippi?)
Romans	Paul	57	Corinth
Hebrews	Paul	60	Caesarea
Colossians	Paul	61	Rome
Ephesians	Paul	61	Rome
Philippians	Paul	62	Rome
1 Peter	Peter	63	Rome
2 Peter	Peter	64	Rome
James	James, brother of the Lord	early 60s	Jerusalem
Matthew	Matthew	60s	Antioch
Mark	Mark	60s	Rome
Philemon	Paul	66–67	Rome
1 Timothy	Paul	66–67	Rome
Titus	Paul	66–67	Rome
2 Timothy	Paul	66–67	Rome
Luke	Luke	70s	Rome?
Acts	Luke	70s	Rome?
Jude	Jude	80s	?
1 John	John	80s	Ephesus
2 John	John	80s	Ephesus
3 John	John	80s	Ephesus
Revelation	John	96–98	Patmos, Ephesus
John	John	98–110	Ephesus

 Chart 13-2

Chart 13-3

Significant Parallels
between Luke and Josephus

Explanation

A number of events noted in the New Testament are also mentioned in other of the few sources from antiquity that have survived to our own time. As an example, Luke's Gospel and Acts, and the *Jewish War* (*Bellum Judaicum,* abbreviated *B.J.*) and *Jewish Antiquities* (*Antiquitates Judaicae,* abbreviated *Ant.*) of Josephus share references to many of the same events. Although both authors wrote in Rome, and despite the works being more or less contemporary (Luke probably wrote in the A.D. 70s; Josephus's *Jewish War* began to be published in 75 and *Jewish Antiquities* in 93), it is unlikely that either was familiar with the other, as a source. Of greatest importance to students of the New Testament is that the two historians corroborate the accounts of one another on several occasions.

Reference

Steve Mason, *Josephus and the New Testament* (Peabody, Mass.: Hendrickson, 1992).

Significant Parallels
between Luke and Josephus

	LUKE	JOSEPHUS
Census under Quirinius	Lk 2:1–3	*B.J.* 2.117–18; *Ant.* 18.1–5
Lysanius, tetrarch of Abilene	Lk 3:1	*B.J.* 2.215 *Ant.* 19.275
Pilate's attack on Galileans/Samaritans	Lk 13:1	*Ant.* 18.85–87
Siege and destruction of Jerusalem including slaughter of the children	Lk 19:43–44	*B.J.* 6
Mention of false prophets:		
Theudas	Acts 5:36	*Ant.* 20.97
Judas the Galilean	Acts 5:37	*Ant.* 20.102
The Egyptian prophet	Acts 21:38	*B.J.* 2.261–63; *Ant.* 20.171
Famine during the reign of Claudius	Acts 11:28–29	*Ant.* 3.320; 20.51–53, 101
King Agrippa killed by God/the gods	Acts 12:20	*Ant.* 19.343–52
Sicarii in the desert	Acts 21:38	*B.J.* 2.264

Chart 13-3

Chart 13-4

Four Lists of the Original Twelve Apostles

Explanation

The Twelve Apostles are listed not only in the three synoptic gospels, but also in Acts. While the lists vary in order, they include the same individuals. The only discrepancy is that Mark and Matthew identify Jude as Thaddeus. Scholars suggest this was done to avoid confusion with the infamous Judas Iscariot. Elder James Talmage (*Jesus the Christ,* 224–25) agrees that Jude and Thaddeus are one and the same. The listings appear in three groupings, always with the same four apostles in each group. The first group always includes the inner circle of Peter, James, and John, with Peter listed first, no doubt as an indication of his presidency within the quorum. It is unclear why the order of names within their groupings is different from one list to another.

References

James E. Talmage, *Jesus the Christ* (Salt Lake City: Deseret Book, 1972), 217–29.
John P. Meier, "The Circle of the Twelve," *Journal of Biblical Literature* 116 (winter 1997): 646.
"Church Organization," *WRC,* 10–13.

Four Lists of the Original Twelve Apostles

MARK	MATTHEW	LUKE	ACTS
3:16–19	10:2–4	6:14–16	1:13

FIRST GROUP OF FOUR

Simon Peter	Simon Peter	Simon Peter	Peter
James son of Zebedee	Andrew his brother	Andrew his brother	James
John brother of James	James son of Zebedee	James	John
Andrew	John his brother	John	Andrew

SECOND GROUP OF FOUR

Philip	Philip	Philip	Philip
Bartholomew	Bartholomew	Bartholomew	Thomas
Matthew	Thomas	Matthew	Bartholomew
Thomas	Matthew the Publican	Thomas	Matthew

THIRD GROUP OF FOUR

James son of Alphaeus	James son of Alphaeus	James son of Alphaeus	James son of Alphaeus
Thaddeus	Thaddeus	Simon the Zealot	Simon the Zealot
Simon the Cananean	Simon the Cananean	Jude brother of James	Jude brother of James
Judas Iscariot	Judas Iscariot	Judas Iscariot	

Chart 13-4

Meanings of Proper Names

Explanation

Many names of Hebrew and Greek derivation have special or natural meanings. Some of the most prominent names that occur in the New Testament are given along with their meanings in chart 13-5. Although these meanings are not deeply significant (a person today whose last name is Brown or North or the like is not thought of as a color or a cardinal direction), occasionally the texts of the New Testament make word plays or symbolic uses of a person's name.

Meanings of Proper Names

ANDREW	Stout and strong man
AUGUSTUS	Increased, augmented or royal, majestic
BARABBAS	Son of a father (bar-abba)
BAR-JONA	Son of Jonah or of a dove
BARTHOLOMEW	Son of Tholmai
CAIAPHAS	Searcher, or he that seeks with diligence
ELISABETH	God is the oath of her; or the fullness of God
GABRIEL	Man of God, or strength of God
HEROD	Hero, or like a hero
JAMES	Supplanter
JESUS	The Lord will save, the Lord of salvation
JOHN	Lord of grace, or whom the Lord graciously gave
JOSEPH	He shall add
LUKE	Light of the sun, white
MARK	Indolent, lazy
MARTHA	Lady, mistress
MARY (MIRIAM)	One who is exalted of the Lord
MATTHEW	Gift of the Lord
ONESIMUS	Profitable
PETER	Rock, or rock-like
PHILEMON	Loving, friendship
PHILIP	Lover of horses
SIMON	Hearing with acceptance
STEPHEN	Crown
TABITHA	Gazelle
THOMAS	Twin
TIMOTHY	Honored of God
TITUS	Honorable

Chart 13-5

Chart 13-6

Speeches of Peter in Acts

Explanation

Seven major speeches of the apostle Peter are recorded in a total of 97 verses in the book of Acts (compare chart 15-6). Peter spoke to a wide variety of audiences, from believing Christians on the day of Pentecost in Acts 2 to the leading apostles and elders of the church at the Jerusalem conference in Acts 15, and from the leading priests and elders of the Jews in Acts 4 and 5 to the general Jewish populace in Acts 3 and 11. His life-changing words to Cornelius are found in Acts 10. Peter's main themes were accepting Christ, obeying God, and the universal cleansing power of God's salvation.

References

Pheme Perkins, *Peter: Apostle for the Whole Church* (Columbia: University of South Carolina Press, 1993).

John Meyendorff, *The Primacy of Peter: Historical and Ecclesialogical Studies* (Crestwood, N.Y.: St. Vladimir's Seminary, 1992).

Speeches of Peter in Acts

AUDIENCES	THEMES	REFERENCE
Crowd at Pentecost	God has raised up Christ	Acts 2:14–40
Jews in the temple of Jerusalem	Prepare to receive Jesus at his return	Acts 3:12–26
Leaders of the Jews	Accept Jesus as the foundation of salvation	Acts 4:8–12
High Priest and Sanhedrin	Obey God, not man	Acts 5:29–32
Cornelius, a Gentile	God welcomes all people	Acts 10:34–43
Circumcised Jews in Jerusalem	God can cleanse all people	Acts 11:5–17
Apostles and Elders	God can cleanse all people	Acts 15:7–29

Chart 13-6

Chart 13-7

Peter's Three Affirmations
John 21:15–17

Explanation

Although Peter "denied" Jesus three times during the night of his arrest (see chart 10-13), Peter affirmed his love for Jesus three times on the shores of Galilee when the resurrected Lord appeared there to his apostles. John, the beloved disciple and evangelist of love, sensitively recorded the intimate three-fold exchange between Jesus and his chief disciple Peter, as if to reinstate Peter following his three-fold "denial." Repeatedly Jesus asked, "Do you love me?" Three times Peter answered, "You know I love you." Three times Jesus charged Peter, "Feed my sheep." Some people have tried to find subtle distinctions between the different Greek words for "love," "know," "feed/tend," and "lambs/sheep," but there appears to be little difference between the meanings of these words in these three particular verbal exchanges.

References

Sidney B. Sperry, "The Meaning of Peter's Confession," *Improvement Era*, July 1949, 430–31, 471–72; August 1949, 496–98, 537.

Samuel L. Holmes, "The Beginnings of a Conversion," *Instructor,* October 1969, 366–67.

Spencer W. Kimball, "Peter, My Brother," *Speeches of the Year* (Provo, Utah: BYU Press, 1971).

Peter's Three Affirmations
John 21:15–17

		"A third time, Do you love (*phileis*) me?"	INTERCHANGEABLE TERMS
"Do you love (*agapas*) me more than these?"	"Do you love (*agapas*) me?"		–Love deeply or love as a good friend
"You know (*oidas*) that I love (*philō*) you"	"You know (*oidas*) that I love (*philō*) you"	"You know (*ginōskeis*) that I love (*philō*) you"	–Know –Love as a good friend
"Feed (*boske*) my lambs (*arnia*)"	"Tend (*poimaine*) my sheep (*probata*)"	"Feed (*boske*) my sheep (*probata*)"	–Feed or tend –Lambs or Sheep

Chart 13-7

Recurring Names

Explanation

In the Judeo-Christian world of the first century, surnames were seldom used except by Romans. In keeping with the customs of the time, reference to individuals in the New Testament is usually made using only their given name or occasionally some other identifying factor such as filiation (who their father was, e.g., James the son of Zebedee) or provenance (place of origin, e.g., Mary of Magdala or Mary Magdalene). Such imprecise references produce a great deal of confusion about the identity of several individuals.

The following three charts differentiate, as much as possible, between the Marys mentioned in the New Testament, as well as the Jameses and the Johns. Among these people are some of the most important figures in early Christianity.

References

Raymond F. Collins, et al., "Mary," *ABD*, 4:579–82.
Camille Fronk, "Mary, Mother of Jesus," *EM*, 2:863–64.
C. Wilfred Griggs, "John the Beloved," *EM*, 2:757–58.
Loui Novak, "John the Baptist," *EM*, 2:755–57.
R. Douglas Phillips, "James the Apostle," *EM*, 2:716–17.

The Marys

Name	Identification	Description
Mary	mother of Jesus	Bore and raised Jesus (Mt 1–2; Lk 2) Was with Jesus at the wedding at Cana (Jn 2) Accompanied Jesus during his ministry (Mt 12:46; Mk 3:31; Lk 8:19) Witnessed Jesus' crucifixion (Jn 19) Was with the apostles after the ascension (Acts 1:14)
Mary Magdalene	a dear friend of Jesus	Healed by Jesus (Lk 8:2) Provided financially for Jesus and the Twelve Accompanied Jesus to Jerusalem Witnessed Jesus' death, burial, and was the first to witness the resurrection (Mt 27:56–28:8; Mk 15:40, 47; 16:1, 9; Lk 24:10; Jn 19:25; 20:14–18)
Mary of Bethany	sister of Martha and Lazarus	Listened to Jesus while Martha tended to household duties (Lk 10:39, 42) Sent for Jesus after the death of Lazarus, witnessed the raising of Lazarus, and testified of Jesus (Jn 11:1–45) Anointed Jesus (Jn 12:3–8)
Mary	mother of James	Followed Jesus during his and Joseph's Galilean ministry and possibly provided him financial support (Mk 15:40, 47; 16:1) Witnessed Jesus' crucifixion, burial, and resurrection (Mt 27:56)
Mary	a follower of Jesus	Possibly a relative of Jesus Married to a man named Cleopas (Jn 19:25)
Mary	mother of John Mark	Gave her home in Jerusalem, as a well-to-do widow, a regular place for the saints to gather and pray (Acts 12:12)
Mary	a Roman Christian	Received greetings from Paul because she had served well in Rome (Rom 16:6)

Chart 13-8

The Johns

NAME	IDENTIFICATION	DESCRIPTION
John	the Baptist	A relative of Jesus and forerunner of his ministry, declared by the Savior to be the greatest prophet born of woman (Lk 7:28).
John	the Beloved, the Apostle, the Evangelist, the Revelator	These names refer to the same individual—John, son of Zebedee and brother of James. With Andrew, the first called by the Savior as a disciple (Jn 1:37–40), John became known as the beloved disciple. Later ordained an apostle, John was found with Peter and his own brother James in the inner circle of three privileged to accompany the Savior on sacred occasions including the raising of Jairus's daughter, the transfiguration, and in Gethsemane. On the cross Christ entrusted his mother, Mary, to the care of John, and it was John who joined Peter in exercising leadership in Jerusalem after the ascension of the Lord. Later John is known to have gone to preside over the large Christian community at Ephesus. John received the book of Revelation in approximately A.D. 96 while on Patmos off the coast of Ephesus and was thereafter known as John the Revelator. Later from his residence at Ephesus John wrote his epistles and the Gospel *(evangelion)* from which derived his title, John the Evangelist. After the death of Peter, John exercised authority as the presiding officer of the church until, as revealed to the Prophet Joseph Smith (D&C 7), he was transfigured. With Peter and James, John restored the keys of the Melchizedek Priesthood to Joseph Smith.
John Mark		Generally known as Mark, he was author of the Gospel that bears his name. Relative of Barnabas who accompanied Paul to Rome (Col 4:10) and Peter to Babylon (1 Pt 5:13), Peter was probably the source for Mark's Gospel. After Peter's death, Mark is traditionally held to have founded the Christian community at Alexandria in Egypt.

Chart 13-9

The Jameses

NAME	IDENTIFICATION	DESCRIPTION
James	son of Zebedee	With his brother John, and Peter, James belonged to the inner circle of three apostles who were with Christ on the most sacred occasions, such as the raising of Jairus's daughter, the transfiguration, and in Gethsemane. To distinguish him from the other James among the original Twelve Apostles, he is known as "James the Greater." The first of the apostles to be martyred, James was killed by Herod Agrippa in A.D. 44 (Acts 12:2). With Peter and John, James restored the Melchizedek Priesthood to the Prophet Joseph Smith.
James	son of Alphaeus	Sometimes called "James the Less" to distinguish him from his fellow apostle James, son of Zebedee, little is known of this James beyond his inclusion among the Twelve.
James	the brother of the Lord	Son of Mary and Joseph, James was identified by early Christians as "James, the brother of the Lord." Paul mentions him along with Peter and John as one of the three pillars of the early church (Gal 1:19). Jude, author of the epistle of the same name, describes himself as brother of this well-known James. James seems to have been assigned supervision of the church at Jerusalem after the departure of Peter and John. In early Christian tradition he was variously believed to have been an apostle, although he is sometimes called the bishop of Jerusalem. He is the writer of the Epistle of James. His personal goodness earned him the appellation of "James the Just," whose death in A.D. 62 at the hands of the Jewish High Priest Ananus, as Josephus (*Ant.* 20.9.1) reports, was widely believed to have heralded the disasters which befell Jerusalem in the Jewish revolt that immediately followed.

Chart 13-10

Miracles in Acts

Explanation

Following in the footsteps of the Master, the apostles of Jesus performed many miracles as they took the gospel out into the world. These wonders included healing the lame, casting out evil spirits, escaping from captivity, restoring sight to the blind, raising the dead, and stopping the discharge of blood. The fact that these miracles were so similar to those performed by Jesus Christ demonstrated to the world that these disciples came endowed with his divine powers. The reactions of people were also similar: the Chief Priests continued to doubt, while others attributed these miracles to God, believed, and were baptized in the name of Jesus.

Miracles in Acts

PLACE	WHAT HAPPENED	RESULT	REFERENCE
Jerusalem	Apostles spoke in tongues	Many people were amazed while others mocked	2:1–13
Jerusalem: temple gate	Peter and John healed a man lame from birth	Many in the temple were amazed and ran to Peter and John	3:1–11
Jerusalem: in the streets	The sick passed under Peter's shadow and were healed; he cast out spirits	Apostles were thrown in prison	5:15–18
Jerusalem: in prison	Angel opened prison door freeing the apostles who returned to the temple	The Chief Priests doubted	5:19–24
Samaria	Philip cast out spirits and healed those with palsies	There was great joy in the city, and many were baptized	8:5–13
Damascus: Judas' House	Ananias restored Saul's sight	Saul baptized and people marvelled at his conversion	9:17–21
Lydda	Peter healed Aeneas, who had been sick with palsy	All turned to the Lord in Lydda	9:32–35
Joppa	Peter restored life to Dorcas	It became known throughout Joppa, and many believed	9:36–42
Judea: in prison	Peter was delivered by an angel	Disciples were astonished when Peter arrived	12:6–16
Paphos	Paul caused Elymas, the sorcerer, to be blind	The official believed	13:8–12
Lystra	Paul told a cripple from birth to stand, and he walked	People believed that gods had come in the likeness of men	14:6–11
Philippi	Paul cast a possessing spirit out of a soothsayer	Paul and Silas were beaten and cast into prison	16:16–23
Philippi: in prison	Prison doors were opened by an earthquake	Keeper of the prison believed and was baptized	16:26–33
Ephesus	An evil spirit caused a man to leap on Jewish exorcists	Fear fell on all who believed, and they burned magical books	19:13–17
Troas	Paul raised Eutychus from the dead	All were comforted	20:9–12
Melita	Paul was bitten by viper and lived, and he cured the father of Publius of a blood flux	They said Paul was a god and people came to be healed	28:7–9

Chart 13-11

Chart 13-12

The Sermon on the Mount and the Epistle of James

Explanation

Rarely noticed by general readers, yet quite evident on closer inspection, are the parallels between the phraseology of the Sermon on the Mount in Matthew 5–7 and the vocabulary of the Epistle of James. Over twenty conspicuous similarities can be identified. Various explanations may account for this similarity. Above all, this consistency shows that James and his broad, early Christian audience knew and revered the words of their Lord and Master, especially the directives found in the Sermon on the Mount.

Reference

Patrick Hartin, *James and the Q Sayings of Jesus,* Journal for the Study of the New Testament Supplement Series, vol. 47 (Sheffield: Sheffield Academic Press, 1991), 144–72.

The Sermon on the Mount and the Epistle of James

MATTHEW		JAMES	
Blessed are the …	5:3–11; 11:5	*Blessed* is the man …	1:12; 1:2; 2:5
Blessed are they that *mourn*, for they shall be comforted.	5:4	Be afflicted, and *mourn*, and weep …	4:9
Blessed are the merciful for they shall obtain *mercy*.	5:7	For he shall have judgment without mercy that hath shewed no *mercy*.	2:13
Blessed are the *pure in heart: for they shall see God.*	5:8	Draw nigh unto God, and *he will draw nigh unto you. Purify* your hands … and *hearts*	4:8
Blessed are the *peacemakers*: for they shall be called the children of God.	5:9	And the fruit of righteousness is sown in peace of them that *make peace*.	3:18
Blessed are ye, when men shall … *persecute* you … for my sake,… for *so persecuted* they the *prophets* which were before you.	5:11–12	Take … the *prophets*, who have spoken in the name of the Lord, for an example of *suffering affliction*, and of patience.	5:10
Whosoever shall *break* one *of these least commandments* … he shall be called least in the kingdom of heaven.	5:19	For whosoever shall keep the whole *law*, and yet *offend in one point*, he is guilty of all.	2:10
Thou shalt not *kill*, thou shalt not commit *adultery*.	5:21–30	Do not commit *adultery* … Do not *kill*.	2:11
Whosoever is *angry* with his brother … shall be in danger of the judgment.	5:22	The *wrath* of man worketh not the righteousness of God.	1:20
Whosoever looketh on a women to *lust* after her hath committed adultery …	5:28	But every man is tempted when he is drawn away of his own *lust*, and enticed.	1:14–15

Chart 13-12 (1)

Swear not at all; *neither by heaven ... nor by the earth.*	5:34–37	*Swear not, neither by heaven, neither by the earth.*	5:12
Be *ye* therefore *perfect ...*	5:48	*That ye* may be *perfect ...*	1:4
And *lead us not* into *temptation*, but deliver us from evil.	6:13	Let no man say when he is *tempted*, I am tempted of God ... *neither tempteth* he any man.	1:13
Lay not *up* for yourselves *treasures* upon earth, where *moth (sēs)* and *rust (brōsis)* doth *corrupt (aphanizei).*	6:19–21	Your *riches* are *corrupted (sesēpen),* and your garments are *motheaten (sētobrōta).* Your gold and silver ... the *rust (ios)* of them shall be a witness against you ... ye have *heaped treasure together.*	5:2–3
He will *hold to the one,* and *despise* the other. Ye cannot serve *God* and *mammon.*	6:24	Whosoever therefore will *be a friend* of the world is the *enemy* of *God.*	4:4
Judge not that ye be not judged.	7:1–2	He that ... *judgeth* his brother, ... judgeth the law.	2:13; 4:11; 5:6
Ask, and it shall be given ...	7:7–11	If any of you lack wisdom, let him *ask* of God ...	1:5–6
Ask, and it shall be given you ... For every one that asketh receiveth	7:7–8	Yet ye have not, because ye *ask* not.	4:2–3
If ye then, being evil, know how to give *good gifts (domata agatha) ... Father* which is in heaven give(s) good things ...	7:11	Every *good gift (dosis agathē)...* cometh down from the *Father* ...	1:17
Do men gather *grapes (staphulas)* of thorns or *figs (suka)* of thistles?	7:16	Can the *fig* tree ... bear olive berries? Either a *vine (ampelos),* a *fig (suka)?*	3:11–12
Whosoever *heareth (akouei)* these *sayings (logous)* of mine and *doeth (poiei)* them.	7:24	But be ye *doers (poiētai)* of the *word (logou),* and not *hearers (akroatai)* only.	1:22

Chart 13-12 (2)

Overviews of the Epistles

The following charts give an overview of each of the epistles in the New Testament. These twenty-one letters, among the most important ever written in the history of the world, were sent by Peter, James, John, Paul, and Jude to some of the earliest Christians.

Each chart divides the letter into thematic blocks with subheadings that outline the main contents of each block. By reading through the outline of each letter, readers can get a quick overview of each text. Used as a guide, each chart should help modern readers find their way through these letters, many of which are fairly complicated and sometimes obscure. A main purpose of these charts is to bring the messages of these letters to life by making the dominant purpose and underlying structure of each letter clear.

Most of these letters follow the pattern typically found in ancient letters. First, they begin with an introduction of greetings, salutations, or well-wishes. The New Testament letters, however, are unusually personal and religious. Next, they take time to reinforce the bonds of friendship, familiarity, loyalty, and personal concern. The body of each letter then deals with various topics: some are doctrinal; some are practical; others are filled with information or encouragement. Finally, they each conclude with farewell statements and extended greetings in accordance with standard epistolary practice.

Beyond formal similarities, however, it is important to note that each letter is addressed to a particular audience. Some congregations, such as in Corinth, were struggling with dissension; others, such as the community in Philippi, were thriving; some, like the church in Thessalonica, were new, while others, as at Rome, were well established. Thus, different levels of instruction are found in each of these letters.

In addition, Paul knew some of his audiences better than others, and thus his degree of familiarity and friendship is much higher when he wrote to the Saints in Ephesus, for example, than when he expounded more abstract teachings to the Galatians. Likewise, Paul's close working relationship with his convert Timothy explains the tone of paternal guidance found in his letters to Timothy, in contrast, for example, to the sterner tone of Jude's letter of warning.

Under the name of each letter is a subtitle profiling and highlighting its dominant point or purpose. Hopefully, these subtitles and outlines will orient readers and students to the key characteristics of each letter. The charts are grouped approximately in chronological order.

The two short letters on chart 14-1 were written close in time to each other. In 1 Thessalonians, Paul instructed his new converts, trying to move them forward beyond baptism toward other lofty goals; but his optimism fades in 2 Thessalonians, where he must admonish them to stay the course as this fledgling branch of the church struggles with failed expectations.

Chart 14-2 outlines the strong counsel Paul gave to the troubled congregation in Corinth. Paul had lived with these people for eighteen months, and he was concerned about reports of their disputes and misunderstandings. The letter is not a systematic treatise but rather a bill of particulars taking up one issue after another in an effort to keep these members on the right path.

Paul's second epistle to the Corinthians is probably a composite text but one theme of apostleship unites all of its parts. As chart 14-3 indicates, the work of an apostle is illustrated by the work of Paul, is defined through the duties of the apostles, is embedded in Paul's self defense against criticisms, and is conveyed with apostolic exhortations.

Chart 14-4 shows the single focus of the letter to the Galatians: This entire letter constitutes an orchestrated argument against Jewish-Christians who claimed that followers of Jesus should still follow the Law of Moses, at least in some respects. Paul marshals a series of six arguments of several different kinds but all leading to the same conclusion. Paul's style here is abrupt and forceful. After all, not far from Galatia he had suffered severely at the hands of Jewish leaders.

The epistle to the Romans is covered in chart 14-5. Paul wrote this letter to introduce himself to the Christians in the imperial city, many of whom he had not yet met. Perhaps to preempt or correct misunderstandings, in this letter he gives a basic manifesto of his belief in the atonement of Jesus Christ, demonstrating that all people have need of the Savior, testifying that Jesus Christ is that Savior, assuring that God will keep his covenants, and encouraging people to likewise keep their covenantal commitments.

Among Paul's closest friends were his followers in Philippi, whom he loved deeply. Here he had made his first converts on European soil. Here he had been loved and supported. Here he had been miraculously delivered from prison. Here he has nothing but praise and love to share with his yoke-fellows, as the top of chart 14-6 indicates.

Colossians is the most philosophical of Paul's letters, perhaps because the region around this small town was deeply involved with science and philosophy. The scroll on the bottom of chart 14-6 details various elements of Paul's proclamation of the Christian worldview, including such topics as cosmology, the creation of the world, true wisdom, powers and principalities, and offering a new order of moral or social duties, all of which were topics of lively philosophical interest in the Hellenistic world.

Nowhere did Paul feel a deeper sense of companionship and community than at Ephesus, where he lived for three years. Chart 14-7 summarizes this eloquent letter to the Ephesians which gives Paul's blueprint for constructing an eternal household of God, which included being brought under the patronage of God, building on the foundation of apostles and prophets, cultivating community and unity in Christ, applying the principles of Christian living within the circle of eternal family relationships, and defending against evil with the whole armor of God. Also on this chart, Paul's personal request to Philemon nicely exemplifies the spirit in which Paul, as a priesthood leader, made a difficult request of a church member.

Paul's closest companion was Timothy, an early convert and full time missionary. Charts 14-8 and 14-9 give two sorts of handbooks. In 1 Timothy, Paul gives specific instructions to Timothy as he serves as a bishop amidst faithful fellow Saints; in 2 Timothy, Paul speaks to Timothy, the Christian soldier and missionary who works to proclaim the gospel under difficult circumstances. These two books, along with the shorter but similar instructions to church leaders found in Titus are the earliest Christian handbooks of instructions for priesthood leaders

Little is known about the time and place where the epistle to the Hebrews might have been written. Entertaining the possibility that it was written or coauthored by Paul during his prolonged house arrest in Caesarea helps to see it as a doctrinal treatise, addressed to people in Judea, establishing the importance of faith in Jesus Christ as the priest of the new covenant. Paul had tried to take gentile converts into the Temple of Jerusalem, believing that the atonement of Jesus had opened the blessings of the covenant to all people. As chart 14-10 clarifies, each part of this letter serves to explain and bolster the Christian claims that stood behind the uproar in Jerusalem that led to Paul being taken into custody.

Chart 14-11 presents the guidelines for living the gospel of Jesus Christ as set forth in the epistle of James. Although its emphasis on "faith without works is dead" is often thought by some theologians to distinguish this general epistle from the teachings of Paul, these outlines show that all the New Testament apostles were concerned with righteous living according to the commandments of God.

The two letters of the chief apostle Peter are treated in charts 14-12 and 14-13. As the leader of the church, Peter focuses his attention on themes that relate to prophets, priesthood, holiness, divine nature, the atonement, loving one another, feeding the sheep, perfecting the Saints, redeeming the dead, and enduring trials that refine faith. His personal testimony, gained on the Mount of Transfiguration, shines brightly in 2 Peter 1:16–18.

Along with Paul's words on charity in 1 Corinthians 13 and Peter's exhortation to love one another, the apostle John adds his powerful witness that God is love, the Christian's watchword. Charts 14-13 and 14-14 sketch the main subheadings of the three epistles of John, concluding with Jude's voice of warning against the impending apostasy.

1 Thessalonians
Instructions to Recent Converts

1:1	Greetings
1:2–10	Congratulations on their recent baptism
2:1–12	Paul reviews how he taught them
2:13–16	The faith and patience of the Thessalonian converts
2:17–20	Paul's desire to come back to visit the Saints in Thessalonica
3:1–5	Timothy sent to preside in Thessalonica
3:6–13	Paul thanks God for good reports about the Thessalonians
4:1–12	Work next on chastity, honesty, holiness, obedience, and charity
4:13–18	The resurrection of the righteous living and the dead
5:1–11	Watch for the coming of the Lord
5:12–22	Further instructions for being a member of Christ's church
5:23–28	Closing prayer and farewell

2 Thessalonians
Staying the Course in a Struggling Branch

1:1–2	Greetings
1:3–12	Justice will come at the last judgment
2:1–12	The apostasy will come before the day of the Lord
2:13–15	Encouragement to endure
2:16–3:5	Pray for us; we have confidence in you
3:6–15	Follow our example and withdraw from those who do otherwise
3:16–18	Prayer and farewell wishes

Chart 14-1

1 Corinthians

Strong Counsel to a Troubled Congregation

1:1–3	Greetings
1:4–9	Thankfulness for a foundational testimony of Jesus Christ
1:10–16	Against factions in the church over who baptized them
1:17–25	God's wisdom is greater than the world's
1:26–31	God chooses the foolish to confound the wise
2:1–5	Paul preaches not with wisdom, but the Spirit
2:6–16	Revelation through God's Spirit
3:1–23	Against factions in the church, for we are all Christ's
4:1–13	The apostles have stewardship over God's sacred teachings
4:14–21	Accept Timothy as an authorized teacher
5:1–13	How to punish incest and other immorality
6:1–8	Do not sue each other in the pagan law courts
6:9–11	Christ atones for our sins
6:12–20	Flee fornication; some things are not permitted
7:1–11	Recognize that marriage is good
7:12–16	Allow marriage of a believer to an unbeliever
7:17–24	Give God's commandments priority over one's status
7:25–40	Advice on when to marry
8:1–6	There is none other God but one; avoid idol worship
8:7–13	Be an example; do not give others an excuse to sin
9:1–14	Give temporal support of the apostles
9:15–27	Paul explains his approach to missionary labors
10:1–13	A warning against desiring evil; lessons from Israel's history
10:14–22	Do not partake of the table of devils
10:23–11:1	If you know it is wrong, do not do it

Chart 14-2 (1)

1 Corinthians

11:2–16	Women should pray with head coverings
11:17–22	Avoid abuses in observing the Lord's supper
11:23–26	Correct details about the last supper
11:27–34	Do not partake of the Sacrament unworthily
12:1–11	Recognize the variety and unity of spiritual gifts
12:12–30	The body with its members is analogous to the church
12:31–13:13	Love is the most important spiritual gift
14:1–25	Prophecy is greater than speaking in tongues
14:26–40	Regulate spiritual gifts and show orderly restraint
15:1–19	Do not deny the physical resurrection of Christ
15:20–28	Adam and death; Christ and life
15:29	Baptism for the dead as evidence of resurrection
15:30–34	Daily life as a reflection of belief in the resurrection
15:35–53	The manner of the resurrection, various glories
15:54–58	A concluding hymn of triumph
16:1–4	Instructions on gathering financial contributions
16:5–9	Paul's plans for travel to Corinth
16:10–12	On Timothy and Apollos coming to Corinth
16:13–24	Final request and greetings

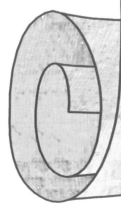

Chart 14-2 (2)

2 Corinthians

The Work of an Apostle

1:1–2	Greetings
1:3–11	Paul gives thanks after affliction
1:12–2:4	Paul changed his plans to visit Corinth not due to fickleness
2:5–11	Forgive and comfort the offender
2:12–13	In Alexandreia Troas and Macedonia
2:14–17	Apostles make manifest sweet fragrance of knowing Christ
3:1–18	Ministers of the new covenant
4:1–6	Apostles spread awareness of the Light of Christ
4:7–5:10	Apostles bring life in Christ
5:11–6:2	Apostles have ministry of reconciling the world to God
6:3–10	Apostles suffer afflictions, yet always rejoice
6:11–7:4	Separate yourself from uncleanliness
7:5–7	Paul is joined by Titus in Macedonia
7:8–16	Godly sorrow brings repentance
8:1–9	Be generous
8:10–15	Guidance on giving
8:16–9:5	Paul's commendation of his delegates to the Corinthians
9:6–15	Blessings come from giving
10:1–11	Paul's reply to accusations of weakness and overbearing
10:12–18	Paul's aversion to ambition or self-commendation
11:1–15	Paul sounds his own praises and rebukes false apostles
11:16–33	Paul's sufferings as an apostle
12:1–10	Paul's visions and revelations
12:11–21	Paul's concern for the Corinthian church
13:1–10	Paul's fears and anxieties
13:11–14	Recommendations, greetings, final good wishes

Chart 14-3

Galatians

A Defense that Christ Has Fulfilled the Law of Moses

1:1–5	Greetings
1:6–10	There is no gospel other than that of Christ
1:11–24	God called and trained Paul to be an authoritative apostle
2:1–10	The apostles accepted Paul at Jerusalem
2:11–14	Paul rebuked Peter at Antioch over the Jewish dilemma
2:15–21	Jews, like Gentiles, are saved by faith in Christ
3:1–14	The proof of justification by faith in Christ, while a curse was brought by the law
3:15–18	The law did not cancel the promise given to Abraham
3:19–22	The law was given looking toward Christ
3:23–26	The law was a schoolmaster
3:27–29	We are one in Christ
4:1–11	We are God's sons and heirs, and no more servants
4:12–20	Therefore we should remain zealous in righteousness
4:21–31	Hagar and Sarah form a compelling allegory of Jews and Gentiles
5:1–15	Christian liberty is in faith and charity
5:16–26	Fruits of spirit and works of flesh
6:1–10	On kindness, humility, perseverance, and bearing one another's burdens
6:11–18	Final warning and blessing

Chart 14-4

Romans

A Manifesto on Receiving the Atonement of Jesus Christ

1:1–7	Greetings
1:8–15	Paul's prayer and desire to visit Rome
1:16–17	The power of the gospel
1:18–32	We all need a Savior, for wickedness alienates man from God
2:1–11	God, not man, will judge everyone for their deeds
2:12–16	Doers of the law, not hearers only, are justified
2:17–29	Avoid hypocrisy; be circumcised of heart
3:1–20	All, both Jew and Gentile, are guilty—none is righteous
3:21–31	We have a Savior in Jesus Christ, not in the law
4:1–17	Abraham was justified by faith, not by the law
4:18–25	Abraham's faith, a model of Christian faith
5:1–5	We are justified by faith
5:6–11	Christ died for the ungodly and sinners
5:12–21	The fall and the atonement: caused by one, applicable to all
6:1–11	Baptism, dead to sin, alive in Christ
6:12–14	Let holiness, not sin, have dominion over you
6:15–19	The Christian becomes servant of righteousness
6:20–23	The fruits of sin and of holiness
7:1–6	Analogy of marriage: Christians are loosed from dead law
7:7–13	The relationship between law and sin
7:14–25	The inward struggle
8:1–13	Live by the spirit, not the flesh
8:14–17	We are children of God
8:18–27	Glory is the destiny of sons of God
8:28–30	Calling and foreordination

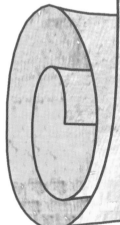

Chart 14-5 (1)

Romans

8:31–39	A concluding hymn to God's love
9:1–13	God has kept his promise and covenant with Israel
9:14–24	God is not unjust; he will keep his promises
9:25–33	Old Testament prophecies concerning Israel
10:1–13	Israel failed to see that God is the source of salvation
10:14–21	Israel's unbelief
11:1–10	The remnant of Israel
11:11–15	The Jews to be restored in the future
11:16–24	Gentiles should not boast; the Jews are still chosen
11:25–32	The future conversion and restoration of the Jews
11:33–36	A concluding hymn to God's wisdom
12:1–2	We must do our part, being a living sacrifice to God
12:3–13	Have charity and humility in exercising gifts
12:14–21	Show charity to everyone, including enemies
13:1–7	Be subject to civil authority
13:8–10	Love fulfills the law
13:11–14	Prepare for the second coming by living righteously
14:1–12	Judge not
14:13–23	Do not be a stumbling block to another
15:1–6	Please your neighbors, not yourself
15:7–13	An appeal for unity between Jews and Gentiles
15:14–21	Paul preaches the gospel of Christ
15:22–33	Paul's desires to visit Rome and Spain
16:1–16	Greetings and good wishes
16:17–20	A warning and first postscript
16:21–24	Last greetings and second postscript
16:25–27	Glorifying God

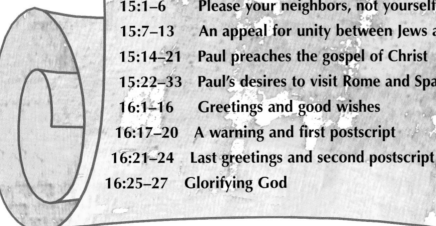

Chart 14-5 (2)

Philippians

A Message of Love and Encouragement

1:1–2	Greetings
1:3–11	Thankfulness for their righteousness and prayer that collaboration may continue
1:12–26	Paul's own choice of life through death in Christ
1:27–30	Exhortation to stand fast in the faith through adversity
2:1–11	Attain unity by following Christ's example of ultimate meekness
2:12–18	Work for salvation and shine as a light in the world
2:19–30	News about the missions of Timothy and Epaphroditus
3:1–3	Warnings against evil practices
3:4–14	Righteousness comes through faith in Christ
3:15–4:1	Let all who are perfected walk together beloved in the Lord
4:2–9	Last advice, rejoicing, and guidance
4:10–20	Praise and blessing for help received from the Philippians
4:21–23	Salutations and final wishes

Colossians

A Proclamation of the Christian Worldview

1:1–2	Greetings
1:3–14	Thankfulness for redemption and prayer for good works
1:15–20	Christ is the head of all creation
1:21–29	Be not alienated in the faith
2:1–5	Be not beguiled away from God's wisdom
2:6–8	Walk in Christ; beware the philosophy and tradition of men
2:9–15	We are made complete in Christ
2:16–23	Avoid false worship of angels and false asceticism
3:1–4	Set your affection on heavenly things
3:5–17	Rules of Christian behavior and righteousness
3:18–4:1	Morals and duties in household relationships
4:2–6	Pray for the apostles; speak always with grace
4:7–9	Recommendation of Tychicus and Onesimus
4:10–18	Greetings and final wishes

Chart 14-6

Ephesians
Building an Eternal Household of God

1:1–2	Greetings
1:3–14	Know that God has reserved an eternal inheritance for you
1:15–23	Know Christ through personal revelation
2:1–10	Accept the gift of salvation and new life in Christ
2:11–22	Become a member of God's church
3:1–13	The mystery of salvation is now revealed
3:14–21	Paul's prayer that all know the love of Christ
4:1–16	A call to unity in the body and spirit of Christ
4:17–5:21	Walk in the new life of Christ as children of Light
5:22–33	Model your marriage on eternal patterns
6:1–4	Obedience of children and kindness of parents
6:5–9	Obedience of slaves and goodness of masters
6:10–20	Be strong in the war against evil
6:21–24	Personal news and final salutation

Philemon
A Personal Request

1:1–3	Greetings
1:4–7	Thanksgiving and prayer
1:8–21	Paul beseeches Philemon to accept Onesimus back as a brother, not as a slave
1:22–25	A personal request and good wishes

Chart 14-7

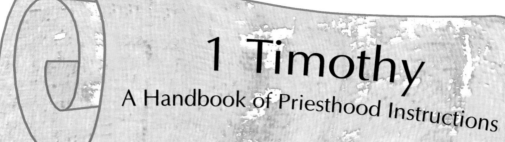

1 Timothy

A Handbook of Priesthood Instructions

1:1–2	Greetings
1:3–7	Beware of false teachers
1:8–11	The church is here to help sinners
1:12–17	Paul is proof that all may be forgiven
1:18–20	Timothy was called of God by prophecy
2:1–8	Pray for everyone; God wants all to be saved and know the truth
2:9–15	Rules for women in the church
3:1–7	Qualifications to be a bishop or local leader
3:8–13	Qualifications to be a deacon
3:14–16	The church and the mystery of the spiritual life
4:1–5	Prediction of wickedness
4:6–16	Being a good minister of Jesus Christ
5:1–2	How to treat members, old and young
5:3–16	Instructions for caring for widows
5:17–25	Instructions concerning elders
6:1–2	Instructions to slaves
6:3–10	Combine godliness and material contentment
6:11–16	The good fight of faith
6:17–21	Be rich in good works

Chart 14-8

2 Timothy
Advice to a Soldier of Christ

1:1–2	Greetings
1:3–5	Prayer for reunion, 'til we meet again
1:6–14	Be not ashamed of the gospel and of spiritual gifts
1:15–18	News about Onesiphorus in Rome and trouble in Asia
2:1–13	A good soldier of Jesus Christ must face hardships
2:14–26	Study to be an approved workman against false teachings
3:1–9	The evil character of people in the last days
3:10–17	Follow the scriptures
4:1–8	Preach, reprove, watch, and finish the race
4:9–18	Men forsake, but the Lord delivers
4:19–22	Final greetings

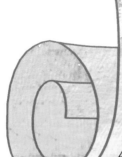

Titus
A Handbook of Priesthood Instructions

1:1–4	Greetings
1:5–9	Instructions to bishops and church leaders
1:10–16	Oppose false teachers and deceivers
2:1–2	Instructions to the elders
2:3–5	Instructions to women, as teachers of young women
2:6–8	Instructions to young men
2:9–10	Instructions to slaves
2:11–15	The grace and redemption of Christ is the basis of the Christian moral life
3:1–7	Teach the members to do good and be merciful, for God has been merciful
3:8–11	Instructions concerning discipline
3:12–15	Practical recommendations, farewells, and good wishes

Chart 14-9

Hebrews

A Doctrinal Treatise on Faith in Christ as Priest of the New Covenant

1:1–4	The greatness of the incarnate Son of God
1:5–14	The Son is greater than the angels
2:1–4	The import of Christ's teachings
2:5–18	Christ's greatness and condescension
3:1–6	Christ greater than Moses
3:7–4:11	Let us labor to enter into God's rest
4:12–13	God's power and knowledge
4:14–5:10	Jesus the compassionate High Priest
5:11–6:8	Maturing in the gospel
6:9–20	Words of hope and encouragement
7:1–10	Melchizedek greater than Abraham
7:11–14	The Melchizedek Priesthood greater than the Levitical
7:15–19	Melchizedek Priesthood binds with an eternal oath
7:20–26	Christ's Priesthood operates beyond death
7:27–28	The perfection of Christ as the heavenly High Priest
8:1–5	Christ officiates in the divine temple
8:6–13	Christ is the mediator of a better covenant
9:1–10	Herod's Temple and the inadequacy of blood sacrifice
9:11–14	The efficacy of Christ's sacrifice
9:15–28	Christ seals the new testament with his blood
10:1–10	Christ's sacrifice superior to the sacrifices of the old law
10:11–18	Christ's sacrifice brings remission of sins
10:19–25	The Christian opportunity
10:26–31	The seriousness of personal apostasy
10:32–39	Motives for perseverance
11:1–40	Examples of people who worked by faith
12:1–4	The example of Jesus Christ
12:5–17	God's fatherly instruction chastens in love
12:18–29	The old covenants transcended by the new
13:1–16	Service is well pleasing to God
13:17–19	Obey church leaders and pray for them
13:20–25	News, good wishes, and greetings

Chart 14-10

James

Guidelines for Living the Gospel

1:1	Greetings
1:2–4	Tests build faith through patience
1:5–8	God freely gives wisdom to those who ask in faith
1:9–11	May all converted Saints rejoice
1:12–18	Resisting sin brings the crown of life
1:19–27	Pure religion is doing the word that saves
2:1–9	Love the poor
2:10–11	Keep the whole law
2:12–13	Show mercy
2:14–26	Faith without works is dead
3:1–12	Talk is cheap and dangerous
3:13–16	Avoid contention
3:17–18	Be truly wise
4:1–5	Worldliness is the enemy of God
4:6–10	Submit to God
4:11–12	Judge not
4:13–17	Do good in God and boast not of yourself
5:1–6	Warning to the corrupt rich
5:7–11	Be patient
5:12	Be honest
5:13	Pray and sing
5:14–18	When sick, call the elders for a healing anointing
5:19–20	Blessings come from converting a sinner

Chart 14-11

1 Peter

Guidance from the Leader of the Church

1:1–2	Greetings
1:3–6a	God has reserved an eternal inheritance for you
1:6b–9	Trials refine faith
1:10–12	Prophets of old knew of Christ
1:13–16	Be holy
1:17–21	Revere God who bought you back with Christ's blood
1:22–23	Love one another
1:24–25	The word of God endures forever
2:1–3	Grow as a child
2:4–10	Become the people of God
2:11–17	Deal honestly with all people and rulers
2:18–25	Advice to servants: follow the example of Christ's suffering
3:1–6	Advice to wives: adorn your relationship with righteousness
3:7	Advice to husbands: inherit life with your wife
3:8–12	Love one another
3:13–18	Be not afraid to testify of Christ
3:19–22	Christ preached to the spirits in the spirit prison
4:1–11	Cease from sin and have fervent charity
4:12–19	Suffer as a Christian
5:1–4	Advice to the elders: feed the sheep of God
5:5–10	Church members are to follow the elders in humility
5:11–14	Final greetings

Chart 14-12

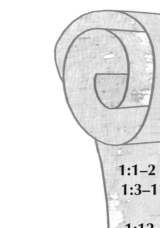

2 Peter
A Farewell Testimony

1:1–2	Greetings
1:3–11	The promise and election to partake of the divine nature
1:12–15	Remember, remember these things always
1:16–21	Witnesses of Christ's glory come from revelation and scripture
2:1–22	Avoid false prophets and the path of apostasy
3:1–10	Conditions at the time of the Lord's second coming
3:11–18	Prepare for Christ's promised coming

1 John
God is Love

1:1–4	Greetings
1:5–7	Walk in God's light
1:8–10	All have committed sins
2:1–2	Christ atones for our sins
2:3–11	Keep the commandments
2:12–14	Greetings
2:15–17	Love not the world
2:18–27	Avoid the antichrist; heed truth through the anointing
2:28–3:10	Children of God will become like God
3:11–18	Love one another in deed
3:19–24	Confidence before God comes from a clear conscience
4:1–21	God loved us, so we should love one another
5:1–5	Overcome the world by faith and obedience
5:6–12	Witnesses of the Son of God
5:13–21	Be born unto eternal life

Chart 14-13

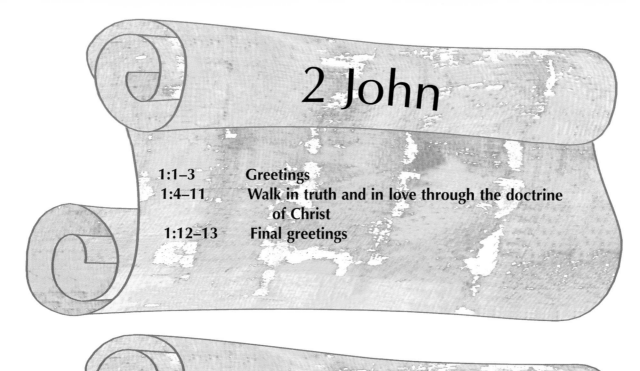

2 John

1:1–3	Greetings
1:4–11	Walk in truth and in love through the doctrine of Christ
1:12–13	Final greetings

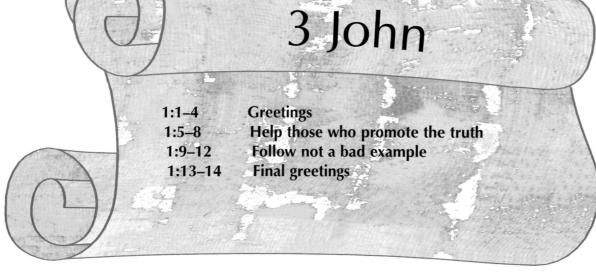

3 John

1:1–4	Greetings
1:5–8	Help those who promote the truth
1:9–12	Follow not a bad example
1:13–14	Final greetings

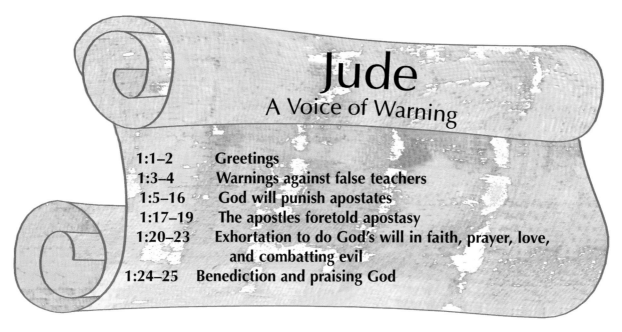

Jude
A Voice of Warning

1:1–2	Greetings
1:3–4	Warnings against false teachers
1:5–16	God will punish apostates
1:17–19	The apostles foretold apostasy
1:20–23	Exhortation to do God's will in faith, prayer, love, and combatting evil
1:24–25	Benediction and praising God

Chart 14-14

SECTION 15

Paul

Paul, a Citizen of Three Worlds

Explanation

Paul's multicultural background provided him with training and experience that uniquely prepared him to be called of God as the apostle to the gentiles. From a prominent and no doubt wealthy family of Tarsus, the major metropolitan center of southeastern Anatolia, Paul received the advantages not only of education, both Jewish and Hellenistic, but also the privilege of prized Roman citizenship.

Although a Jew of the Diaspora and the son of a Pharisee, Paul's economically advantageous background afforded him the opportunity to undertake advanced studies in Judaism under the premier rabbi of the age, Gamaliel, in Jerusalem. Paul was thoroughly familiar with the Old Testament, the Jewish law, and Jewish customs.

Paul's writings also reveal his superb training in Greek, the language of his home city, and also in Greek rhetoric and philosophy. He probably learned these subjects in Greek schools as he was growing up. Tarsus was noted for its educational institutions.

In the eastern Mediterranean less than one percent of the population enjoyed the privileges of Roman citizenship. Thus, the important place of Paul's family in Tarsus is confirmed by their possession of the rare status of *Civis Romanus*.

By birth and religious training Paul was a Jew; by his birth in Tarsus and educational training Paul was a Greek; and by his birth in a high-ranking provincial family of citizen status, Paul was a Roman. This gave him the rare and powerful ability to move in and out of political and social circles throughout the world of his day.

References

Richard Wallace and Wynne Williams, *The Three Worlds of Paul of Tarsus* (London: Routledge, 1998).

J. Phillip Schaelling, "Paul," *EM*, 3:1068–70.

Paul, a Citizen of Three Worlds

JEW

Diaspora Jew, born and raised in Tarsus

Tribe of Benjamin

Trained as a youth by local Pharasaic rabbis

Trained later in Jerusalem at the rabbinical school of Gamaliel

Learned Hebrew as a Pharisee

Worked for the inner circle of the Sanhedrin

ROMAN

Born a Roman citizen; did not have to purchase his citizenship

Paulus is a Roman name

Possibly spoke Latin to the citizens in Corinth and elsewhere

Used Roman imagery in his metaphors (citizenship, family relations, etc.)

GREEK

Read the Old Testament in the Greek Septuagint

Spoke Greek

Classical education in Greek rhetoric, Greek philosophy

Most of the Pauline Epistles follow Greek rhetorical argumentation and
figurative patterns

Versed in Greek philosophical discourse (preached in Athens)

Chart 15-1

The Life of Paul

Explanation

The book of Acts provides an excellent outline of many parts of Paul's ministry. Although exact dating can be ventured for only some of the events in Paul's life, a fairly reliable sequence of events and even the approximate dating of those events is found in chart 15-2. As far as possible, the time and place of Paul's composition of individual epistles are included. Dating is given in the Roman system used at the time, with modern equivalents. Also offered are scriptural references for the activities noted in the scriptures. Aspects of Paul's ministry after his arrival at Rome are conjectural, based on early Christian tradition.

Chart 15-3 details the missionary experiences of Paul, showing the various locations where he preached the gospel of Jesus Christ and the results thereof.

Paul was an impressive missionary. Although he may be best known through his exposition of doctrine and powerful testimony that still live in the words of his epistles, his actions speak even louder than his words. Paul displayed his faithfulness and dedication throughout his missionary labors. Chart 15-3 summarizes the information reported in the book of Acts about Paul's experiences as a missionary. Details about where he went, what events are known to have occurred there, what lengths of time were involved, and what outcomes they produced are listed along with the scriptural references.

References

Sidney B. Sparry, *Paul's Life and Letters* (1955; reprint, Salt Lake City: Bookcraft, 1995).
Richard Lloyd Anderson, *Understanding Paul* (Salt Lake City: Deseret Book, 1983).
Henry C. Thiessen, *Introduction to the New Testament* (Grand Rapids: Eerdmans, 1955).

Paul's Life and Ministry

Roman Year	Modern Date	Event	Scriptural Reference
753–56	1–3	Paul's birth at Tarsus	
771–81	19–29	Approximate period of Paul's tutelage at Jerusalem under Gamaliel	Acts 22:3
781–85	29–33	Paul departs from Jerusalem, probably for Tarsus	
786–87	34–35	Paul witnesses stoning of Stephen and persecutes the Christian community in Judea	Acts 7:54–60, 8:1–4
787	35	Paul is converted on road to Damascus;	Acts 9:1–19
		Paul preaches of Christ at Damascus	Acts 9:20–25
788	36	Paul's visit to Jerusalem to learn of Christ from Peter and other brethren	Acts 9:26–29, Gal 1:18
789–94	37–42	Paul's ministry in Tarsus, Syria, and other places	Acts 9:30, Gal 1:18–20
795	43	Paul's mission at Antioch	Acts 11:25–26
796	44	Paul's second visit to Jerusalem	Acts 11:30, Gal 2:1–10
797–99	45–47	Paul's first missionary journey	Acts 13–14
800–801	48–49	Paul's continued labors in Antioch	Acts 14:26–15:2, 25–34
801	49	Council of Jerusalem	Acts 15:2–34
801–4	49–52	Paul's second missionary journey	Acts 15:35, 16–17
803–4	51–52	Paul at Corinth	Acts 17
		1 Thessalonians written from Corinth	
		2 Thessalonians written from Corinth	
804	52	Paul's fourth visit to Jerusalem	Acts 18:27–28
804–5	52–53	Paul labors in Antioch	Acts 18:23
805	53	Paul begins his third missionary journey	Acts 18:23–24
806–8	54–56	Paul at Ephesus	Acts 19
		1 Corinthians written from Ephesus	
809	57	Paul in Macedonia (Philippi)	Acts 20:1–2
		2 Corinthians written from Macedonia	
		Galatians written from Macedonia	
		Paul returns to Corinth	Acts 20:2–3
		Romans written from Corinth	
810	58	Paul's farewell journey through Macedonia and Asia as he returns to Jerusalem	Acts 20:4–38
811–12	59–60	Paul's fifth visit to Jerusalem and arrest; in custody at the governor's palace at Caesarea	Acts 21–26
813	60	Paul's voyage to Rome	Acts 27
		Hebrews written from Caesarea	
813–14	61–62	Paul lives in his own house two years at Rome awaiting his hearing before the emperor, Nero	Acts 28
813	61	*Colossians* written from Rome	
		Ephesians written from Rome	
814	62	*Philippians* written from Rome	
815	63	Ministry in Rome and Italy	
816–18	64–66	Possible missionary journey through the western provinces (Spain, Gaul, Raetia, Noricum)	
818–19	66–67	Pastoral Epistles written from Rome	
820	68	Possible date of death	

Paul's Missionary Experiences

LOCATION	REFERENCE	DURATION	OUTCOME
Antioch	Acts 13:4		Called to be a missionary along with Barnabas
Seleucia	13:4		
Cyprus	13:4		
Salamis	13:5		Preaches in synagogues
Paphos	13:6–12		Curses Elymas, the false sorcerer; Sergius Paulus converted
Perga in Pamphylia	13:13		
Antioch in Pisidia	13:14–51	At least a week	Success among Gentiles, expelled by Jews. Shakes the dust off of his feet
Iconium	13:51–14:6	Long	Disciples filled with joy and the Holy Ghost. Great multitudes of Greeks and Jews believe. Unbelievers attempt to stone them. They flee
Lystra in Lycaonia	14:6–20		Heals a lame man. People call Paul and Baranbas Mercury and Jupiter. Paul stoned. Disciples surround him and he raises up
Derbe in Lycaonia	14:20–21		Teaches many
Lystra	14:21–23		Confirms disciples, teaches faith, ordains elders
Iconium	14:21–23		Confirms disciples, teaches faith, ordains elders
Antioch	14:21–23		Confirms disciples, teaches faith, ordains elders
Pisidia	14:24	Passed through	
Pamphylia	14:24	Passed through	
Perga	14:25		Preaches the word
Attalia	14:25		
Antioch	14:26	Long	End of first missionary journey
Phenice	15:3	Brief	Reports conversion of Gentiles to the brethren
Samaria	15:3	Brief	Reports conversion of Gentiles to the brethren
Jerusalem	15:4–29	Brief	Jerusalem conference
Antioch	15:30–40		Teaches and preaches. Splits with Barnabas and takes Silas as a companion
Syria	15:41		Confirms the churches
Cilicia	15:41		Confirms the churches
Derbe	16:1		Churches established in the faith and increase in numbers daily
Lystra	16:1		Churches established in the faith and increase in numbers daily
Phrygia	16:6		
the region of Galatia	16:6		Forbidden of the Holy Ghost to preach in Asia
Mysia	16:7		Attempts to go to Bithnyia, forbidden by the Holy Ghost
Troas	16:8–11		Has vision of Macedonian asking for help
"Samothracia in Macedonia"	16:11	1 day	

Chart 15-3 (1)

Neapolis	16:11		
Philippi	16:12–40	Certain days	Baptizes Lydia and her household. Beaten and thrown into prison. Keeper of the prison and his household baptized
Amphipolis	17:1		
Appollonia	17:1		
Thessalonica	17:1–9	3 weeks	Some Jews and a 'great multitude' of Greeks converted. The Jews stir up the rulers of the people; Paul released by the rulers, but sent away by night by the Christians
Berea	17:10–14		People prepared and many believe. The Jews of Thessalonica stir up the people, and the brethren send Paul away
Athens	17:15–18:1		Unknown God speech
Corinth	18:1–18	"18 months to 2 years"	Shakes the blood of the Jews from his garments and would henceforth go to the Gentiles. Crispus (ruler of the synagogue) and many Corinthians baptized
Cenchrea	18:18		
Syria	18:18		
Ephesus	18:19–20	Brief	People ask him to stay, but he leaves to be in Jerusalem for a feast
Caesarea	18:22	Brief	
Antioch	18:22–23	Some time	
Galatia	18:23		
Phrygia	18:23		
Upper coasts	19:1	Passed through	
Ephesus	19:1–41	3 years	Many converted
Macedonia	20:1		
Greece	20:2	3 months	
Philippi	20:6		
Troas	20:6–12	7 days	Paul raises a young man from the dead
Assos	20:13–14		
Mitylene	20:14		
Chios	20:15	1 day	
Samos	20:15		
Trogyllium	20:15	1 day	
Miletus	20:15–38	Some time	
Coos	21:1	1 day	
Rhodes	21:1		
Patara	21:1		
Tyre	21:3–6	7 days	
Ptolemais	21:7	1 day	
Caesarea	21:8–14	Many days	
Jerusalem	21:15		Imprisoned

Chart 15-3 (2)

Paul's Rights as a Roman Citizen

Explanation

Chart 15-4 enumerates several of the powerful rights enjoyed by a Roman citizen such as Paul. These rights significantly enhanced his social, financial, political and legal stature, making it possible for him to command respect and influence. Compare chart 4-6, relating similar rights to parallel spiritual blessings extended to the early members of the kingdom of God.

References

A. N. Sherwin-White, *Roman Society and Roman Law in the New Testament* (Oxford: Oxford University Press, 1963).

A. N. Sherwin-White, *The Roman Citizenship* (Oxford: Clarendon, 1939).

Paul's Rights as a Roman Citizen

SOCIAL

Right to use triple Roman name
Right to wear the toga
Right to marry a Roman citizen
Right to pass citizenship to children

FINANCIAL

Exemption from *tributum* (taxes to Rome)

POLITICAL

Right to vote if in Rome
Right to audience before Roman governors and officials in the provinces
Right to be appointed to government office
Right to stand for election to town council *(decuria)* of towns in Italy and the provinces

LEGAL

Right to make contracts under Roman law, guaranteeing standing within Roman legal system
Exemption from death or punishment without due process of trial and appeal process
Right to trial before Roman magistrate
Right of appeal for judgment to the emperor *(appellatio ad Caesarem)*
Exemption from physical abuse in interrogation
Exemption from authority of non-Roman local officials
Protection from accusation by noncitizens
Deaths of Roman citizens investigated by government

   Chart 15-4

Chart 15-5

Evidences of
Paul's Wealthy Background

Explanation

How rich was Paul? Although Acts 18:3 styles him as a "tentmaker," many factors strongly indicate that Paul was no ordinary craftsman. Indeed, he may have come from a very wealthy and privileged background. This makes the conversion of Paul all the more impressive. He not only renounced his Jewish background and a promising future among the leading men of Jerusalem, but he also left or dedicated everything he possessed to establish a kingdom greater than the Roman Empire. Although little is known for certain about Paul's childhood and upbringing, Paul's rare citizenship, his extensive education, cool savvy, unflinching boldness, aristocratic behavior, and unparalleled success all point in the same direction: It would appear that Paul came from no low- or middle-class background. He was prepared in no ordinary way. He was sent on no ordinary mission.

Reference

Robert J. Matthews, "Saul of Tarsus: Chosen for a Special Need," *Ensign*, September 1987, 60–63.

Evidences of
Paul's Wealthy Background

His father was a Roman citizen, a very rare privilege at this time.

His father was a businessman, making tents, awnings, sails, and other canvas or leather items.

His homeland was Tarsus, capital of the province of Cilicia and "no mean city" (Acts 21:39).

Tarsus was famous for its schools of philosophy and literature.

Besides being schooled in Tarsus, Paul was sent to be educated in Jerusalem.

He was tutored by Gamaliel, the best Jewish teacher money could buy.

The Sanhedrin knew Paul as a young man and entrusted him to arrest Christians.

Peter and the fishermen apostles found Paul hard to understand and to work with.

He could afford to travel extensively with companions throughout his life.

He had access to books and written materials.

Paul knew and could quote scriptures both in Hebrew and Greek.

He had the means to hire a scribe and to write copious, erudite letters.

His vocabulary and language were high class.

Paul could comfortably discuss and use the prevailing philosophies of the day.

He was humiliated when he had to work with his hands at his family's craft.

He knew how to handle and transmit money and organize and direct churches.

He stayed 18 months at Corinth, capital of Achaia, and 3 years at Ephesus, capital of Asia.

He welcomed opportunities to speak with rulers, such as Sergius Paulus in Paphos.

He converted wealthy people, such as Erastus in Corinth.

Paul knew his way around successfully in Jewish, Greek, and Roman courts.

He boldly entered the temple of Jerusalem with one of his gentile converts.

Paul was kept in special custody by Felix and Festus for a couple of years in Caesarea.

Felix detained Paul, hoping to extract a bribe from him (Acts 24:26).

When Paul arrived at Rome, he could afford to purchase a large house.

He hoped to spread the gospel to all the known world by converting the emperor himself.

Chart 15-5

Chart 15-6

Paul before Judges and Officials

Explanation

In addition to its accounts of Paul's missionary efforts, the book of Acts intriguingly chronicles Paul's appearance before many officials and judges. Often he welcomed the opportunity to explain his actions and, more frequently than not, answer charges brought by angry local Jewish leaders whose congregants Paul had converted to Christianity. On occasion the presiding official was Roman, but usually these judges were city magistrates who would have shared a Greek background with their fellow townsmen, or they were local citizens from a town of Asia Minor with a hellenized population. The typical outcome of such hearings and inquests was dismissal of the charges or a tacit agreement that Paul move on in order to assure local order. Chart 15-6 presents detailed information about each judicial appearance of Paul as recounted in Acts. Paul's repeated victories in court show that he was well trained in the law and reassured early Christians that their cause was just and defensible.

References

D. W. J. Gill and Conrad Gempf, *The Book of Acts in its First Century Setting: Greco-Roman Setting* (Grand Rapids: Eerdmans, 1994).

Brian Rapske, *The Book of Acts in its First Century Setting: Paul in Roman Custody* (Grand Rapids: Eerdmans, 1994).

John W. Mauck, *Paul on Trial: The Book of Acts as a Defense of Christianity* (Nashville: Thomas Nelson, 2001), 85–86, featuring charts on legal charges against Paul, arguments and possible exhibits in defense of Paul, countercharges against accusers of Christians, speeches and trials in Acts.

Paul before Judges and Officials

PLACE	REFERENCE	CAUSE OF ACTION	OFFICIAL OR COURT	HOLDING OR OUTCOME	CONSEQUENCE
Jerusalem	Acts 9:1–2	Paul volunteers to arrest Christians in Damascus	The High Priest	Paul given letters of introduction	Paul blinded and converted
Paphos (on Cyprus)	Acts 13:6–12	Paul and Barnabas summoned concerning Bar-jesus, a sorcerer	Sergius Paulus, the Roman proconsul	Paul blinds Bar-jesus; he is led away by the hand	The proconsul believes
Antioch (in Pisidia)	Acts 13:14–51	Jews stir up persecution	The prominent men and women of the city	They expel Paul and Barnabas from their district	They pursue Paul to Lystra
Iconium (in Lycaonia)	Acts 14:1–5	People are divided over the miracles Paul performed	Gentiles and local Jewish leaders rush against Paul	They want to humiliate and stone Paul and Barnabas	Paul and Barnabas get word of it and leave for Lystra
Lystra (in Lycaonia)	Acts 14:12–19	Paul and Barnabas received as Mercury and Jupiter	Jews from Antioch and Iconium persuade the townspeople	They stone Paul; drag him out of the city as if dead	Paul revives
Philippi (Roman capital of Macedonia)	Acts 16:16–40	Paul and Silas interfere with a soothsayer's business; trouble the city; teach unlawful customs	They take Paul and Silas to the rulers in the forum	Magistrates tear their clothes and beat them without a conviction	Held overnight in prison; do not flee when earthquake hits; released and asked to leave town

Chart 15-6 (1)

PLACE	REFERENCE	CAUSE OF ACTION	OFFICIAL OR COURT	HOLDING OR OUTCOME	CONSEQUENCE
Thessalonica (town west of Philippi)	Acts 17:5–9	Zealous Jews arouse the rabble; put the city in an uproar; Paul escapes	Jason arraigned before the city fathers for violating decrees of Caesar and saying Jesus is king	They settle the case	They take a security offering and release Paul's friends
Athens	Acts 17:17–33	Paul disputes in the synagogue and the city center	Philosophers take him to the Areopagus, the high court	They recess to hear more about the matter later	Paul leaves town voluntarily
Corinth (Roman capital of Achaia)	Acts 18:1–18	The ruler of the synagogue converts to Christianity; Jews accuse Paul of apostasy	Publicly taken before Gallio, proconsul of Achaia	Gallio declines to take jurisdiction	The new ruler of the synagogue is beaten publicly
Ephesus (Roman capital of Asia)	Acts 19:13–19	Jewish exorcists use the name of Jesus; the spirit recognizes Paul	Jews and Greeks become afraid and confess their activities	Many magic books are burned in public	The word of God prevails
Ephesus	Acts 19:24–41	Paul's preaching threatens the silversmiths' business	Ephesus city clerk and a large assembly in the theater	Chief city administrative assistant sees no cause of action	Administrator dismisses the assembly
Jerusalem	Acts 21:27–34	Asian Jews accuse Paul of desecrating the people, the law, and the temple	Israelite men seize him and attempt to kill him	The Roman captain, Claudius Lysias, intervenes	Paul is chained and taken into custody

Chart 15-6 (2)

PLACE	REFERENCE	CAUSE OF ACTION	OFFICIAL OR COURT	HOLDING OR OUTCOME	CONSEQUENCE
Jerusalem	Acts 21:37–22:29	Roman captain allows Paul to speak to the crowd, who accuse him further	Military tribunal examines Paul by scourging him in the Antonia Fortress	Paul invokes his Roman citizenship	Any Roman charges against Paul are dropped
Jerusalem	Acts 22:30–23:10	Paul taken before the Jews to answer their charges; High Priest commands Paul be hit	Sanhedrin and Chief Priests	The court becomes divided over theological differences	Roman captain takes Paul back to the Fortress
Caesarea	Acts 23:25–35	Paul's preliminary hearing based on Claudius Lysias's transmittal letter	Felix, governor of Judea	Takes jurisdiction but postpones trial until accusers can appear	Paul placed in Herod's Praetorium
Caesarea	Acts 24:1–26	Tertullus and Ananias charge Paul of disruption, sedition, and profaning temple	Felix hears Paul's denial of the charges	Case suspended awaiting Claudius Lysias's testimony	For two years, Felix holds Paul in house arrest hoping for a bribe. Paul is able to teach
Caesarea	Acts 25:6–12	Jews from Jerusalem accuse Paul of offending Jewish law, the temple, and Caesar	Festus, governor of Judea	Paul refuses to be tried in Jerusalem	Paul's appeal to Caesar in Rome is accepted
Caesarea	Acts 25:22–26:32	Festus is unsure what charges he should report when he sends Paul to Rome	King Agrippa, son of Herod Agrippa I, volunteers to hear the case	They find Paul innocent of all charges	Agrippa decides that Paul's appeal must stand

Chart 15-6 (3)

Places of Paul

Explanation

Paul's journeys took him throughout the Mediterranean world. He introduced Christianity to many areas and was responsible for conversions in other areas. The branches of the church, large and small, contained many people with whom Paul was personally acquainted. Certainly he manifested concern that all run the good race to follow the example of Christ. To better understand Paul's labors, a knowledge of Mediterranean geography is necessary, especially of the Roman provinces in Greece and in Asia Minor. The following maps offer the reader the necessary geographic orientation and depict Paul's most likely route on his three missionary journeys and his voyage to Rome.

Reference

F. W. Farrar, *The Life and Works of St. Paul* (London: Dutton, 1879).

Places of Paul

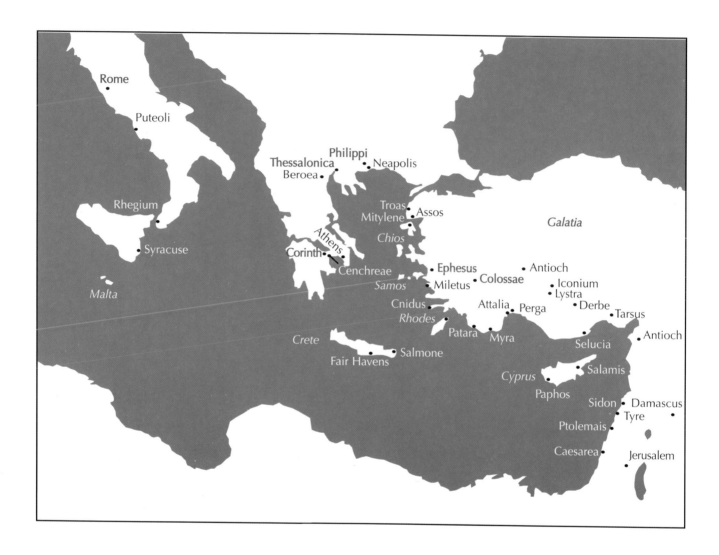

Mentioned in the Acts or the Epistles
Titles of Epistles sent by Paul

Chart 15-7

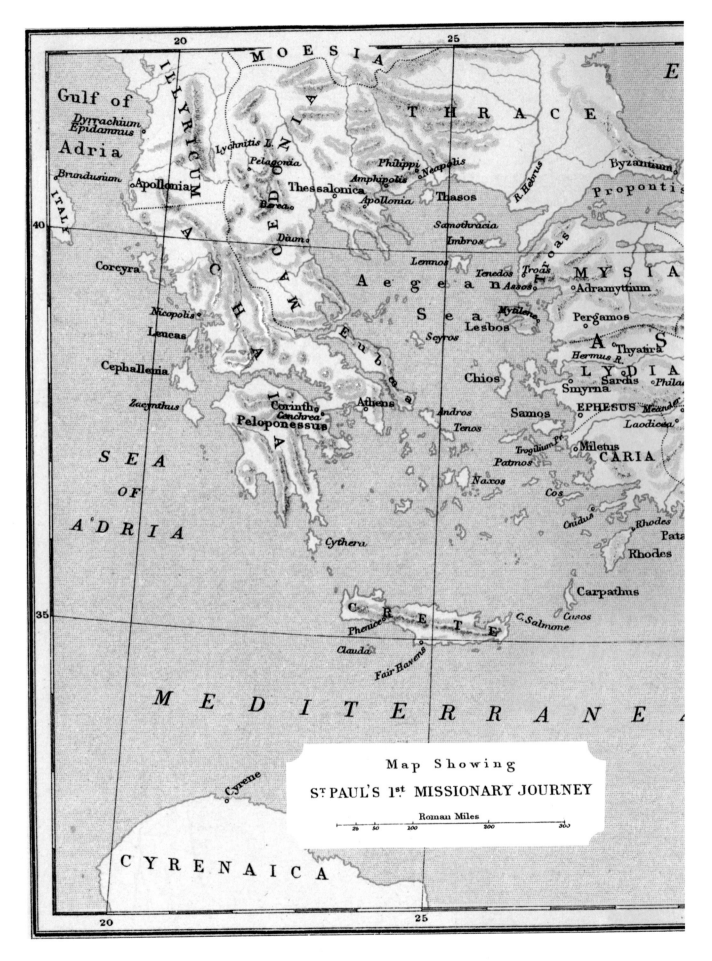

MOESIA

Gulf of

Dyrrachium
Epidamnus
Adria

ILLYRICUM

THRACE

Lychnitis L.

Pelagonia

M
A
C
E
D
O
N
I
A

Philippi
Amphipolis *Neapolis*
Thessalonica
Apollonia Thasos

Byzantium

R. Hebrus

Propontis

E

Brundusium

ITALY

Apollonia

Berea

Dium

Corcyra

Nicopolis
Leucas

Cephallenia

Zacynthus

A
C
H
A
I
A

Samothracia
Imbros

Lemnos

Aegean

Tenedos Troas
Assos

Sea

Scyros

Mytilene
Lesbos

MYSIA

Adramyttium

Pergamos

A

S

Thyatira

Chios

Hermus R.

LYDIA

Smyrna Sardis *Philad*

Eubœa

Corinth.
Cenchrea
Peloponessus

Athens

Andros
Tenos

Samos

EPHESUS *Mæand*

Laodicea

SEA

OF

A'DRIA

Cythera

Patmos

Trogilium Pr.
Miletus
CARIA

Naxos

Cos

Cnidus

Rhodes

Rhodes

Pata

Carpathus

MEDITERRANE

C
R
E
T
E

Phenice

Claudia

Fair-Havens

C. Salmone

Casos

Cyrene

CYRENAICA

Map Showing

St PAUL'S 1st MISSIONARY JOURNEY

Roman Miles

25 50   100   200   300

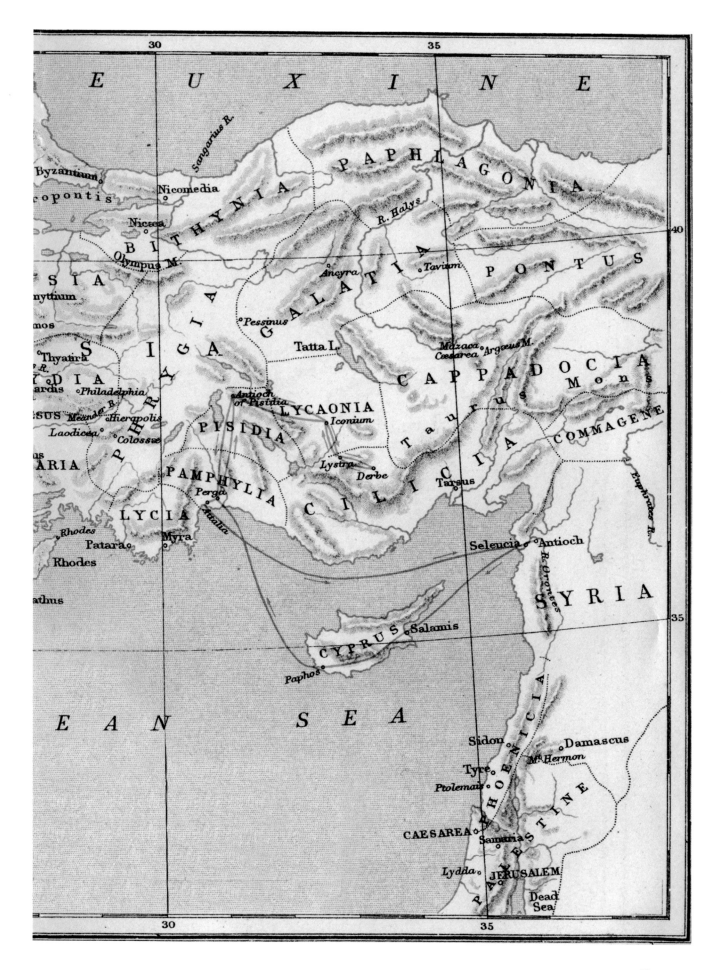

E U X I N E

Byzantium
copontis
Nicomedia
Nicaea
Olympus M.
BITHYNIA
PAPHLAGONIA
R. Halys
GALATIA
Ancyra
Tavium
PONTUS
Pessinus
Tatta L.
Mazaca
Caesarea
Argæus M.
CAPPADOCIA
Taurus Mons
COMMAGENE
Antioch
of Pisidia
LYCAONIA
Iconium
PISIDIA
Lystra
Derbe
Tarsus
CILICIA
PAMPHYLIA
Perga
Attalia
LYCIA
Myra
Rhodes
Patara
Rhodes
athus
Seleucia
Antioch
SYRIA
R. Orontes
Euphrates R.

Thyatira
R.
DIA
ardis
Philadelphia
SUS
Meander R.
Hierapolis
Laodicea
Colossæ
rus
ARIA

P H R Y G I A
MYSIA

E A N   S E A

CYPRUS
Salamis
Paphos

Sidon
Damascus
Tyre
M. Hermon
Ptolemais
PHOENICIA
CAESAREA
Samaria
PALESTINE
Lydda
JERUSALEM
Dead
Sea

Chart 15-8

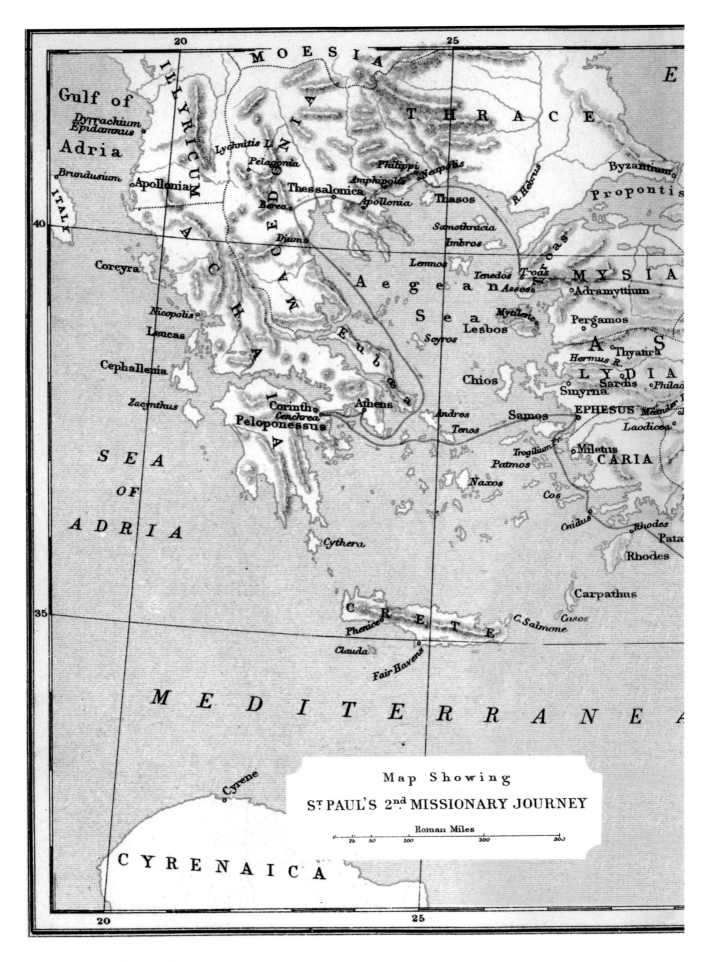

Map Showing

St PAUL'S 2nd MISSIONARY JOURNEY

Roman Miles

25 50   100   200   300

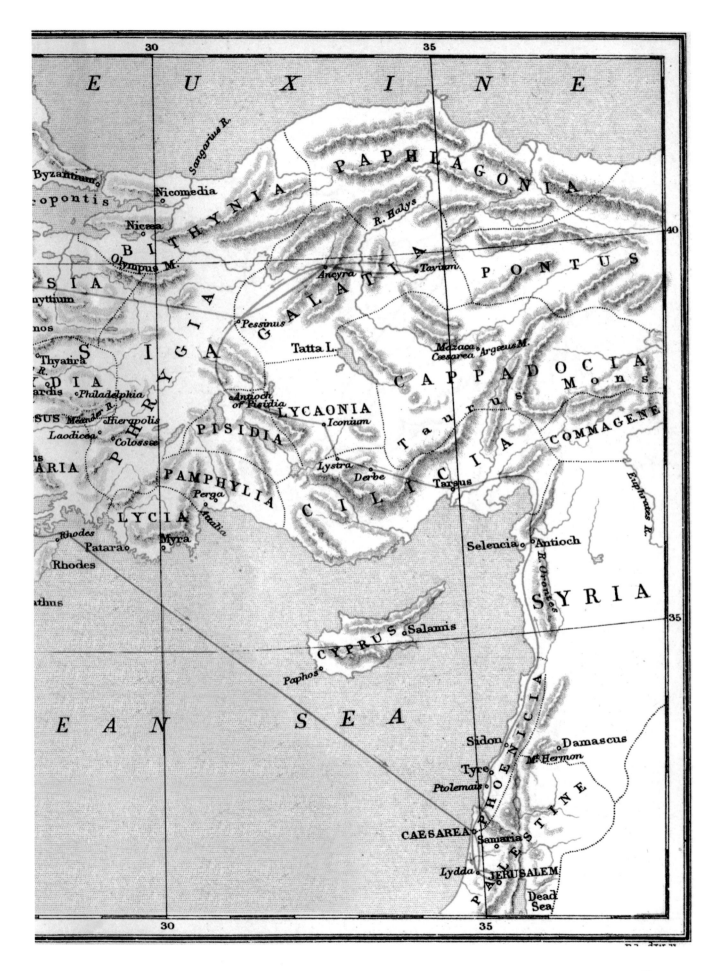

The map contains the following labels (geographic place names):

E U X I N E E

Byzantium
Nicomedia
BITHYNIA
Nicaea
PAPHLAGONIA
GALATIA
R. Halys
Olympus M.
ropontis
PONTUS
Ancyra
Tavium
Pessinus
MYSIA
PHRYGIA
Tatta L.
CAPPADOCIA
Mazaca
Caesarea Argæus M.
Taurus Mons
Thyatira
Sardis
Philadelphia
Antioch of Pisidia
LYCAONIA
COMMAGENE
Mæander R.
Iconium
Hierapolis
Laodicea
Colossæ
PISIDIA
Lystra
Derbe
CILICIA
Tarsus
CARIA
PAMPHYLIA
Perga
Attalia
LYCIA
Euphrates R.
Rhodes
Myra
Patara
Selencia
Antioch
Rhodes
SYRIA
R. Orontes
athus

E A N   S E A

CYPRUS
Salamis
Paphos

Sidon
Damascus
Tyre
Mt Hermon
Ptolemais
PHOENICIA
CAESAREA
Samaria
PALESTINE
Lydda
JERUSALEM
Dead Sea

Chart 15-9

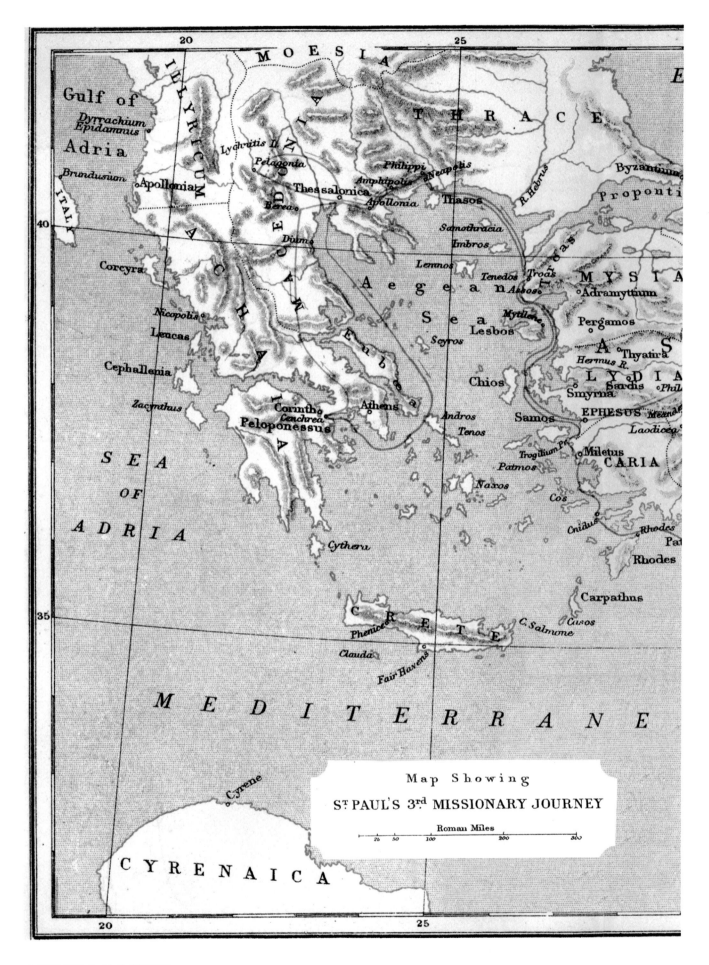

MOESIA

ILLYRICUM

Gulf of

Dyrrachium Epidamnus

Adria

THRACE

Brundusium

Apollonia

Lychnitis L.

Pelagonia

MACEDONIA

Philippi

Amphipolis *Neapolis*

Thessalonica

Apollonia *Thasos*

Byzantium

Propontis

ITALY

Berea

Samothracia

Imbros

40

Dium

Corcyra

ACHAIA

Lemnos

Aegean

Tenedos *Troas*

MYSIA

Assos

Adramyttium

Nicopolis

Leucas

Sea

Scyros

Mytilene

Lesbos

Pergamos

A S

Thyatira

Hermus R.

LYDIA

Cephallenia

Chios

Sardis *Phil*

Zacynthus

Euboea

Samos

Smyrna

EPHESUS *Mezral*

Corinth

Peloponessus

Cenchrea

Athens

Andros

Tenos

Trogilium Pr.

Patmos

Miletus

CARIA

Laodicea

SEA

Naxos

Cos

OF

Cnidus

Rhodes

Pat

ADRIA

Rhodes

Cythera

Carpathus

35

CRETE

Cusos

Phenice

C. Salmone

Clauda

Fair Havens

MEDITERRANE

Cyrene

Map Showing

St PAUL'S 3rd MISSIONARY JOURNEY

Roman Miles

25   50   100   200   300

CYRENAICA

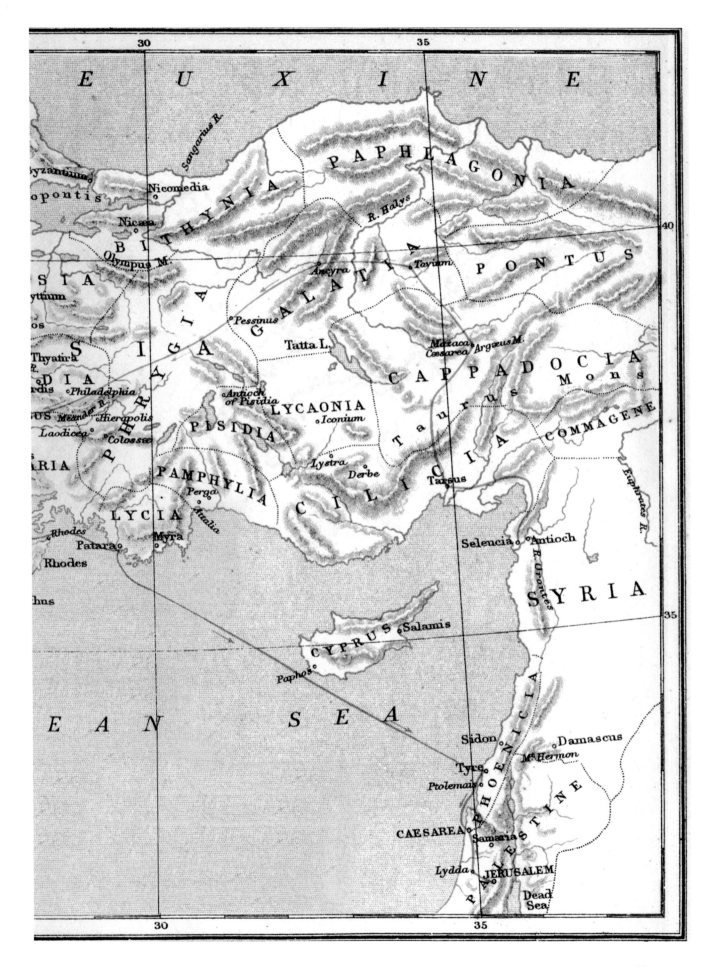

E U X I N E

Sangarius R.

Byzantium
opontis
Nicomedia
Nicæa
Olympus M.
B I T H Y N I A

P A P H L A G O N I A

R. Halys

Tavium

P O N T U S

40

S I A
yttium
os

M Y S I A

P H R Y G I A

Pessinus

G A L A T I A

Ancyra

Mazaca Cæsarea Argæus M.

C A P P A D O C I A

Mons

Thyatira
Meza R.
dis *Philadelphia*
Mænd R. Hierapolis
Laodicea Colossæ

Tatta L.

L Y C A O N I A

Iconium

T a u r u s

Mons

C O M M A G E N E

D I A

A R I A

P I S I D I A

Antioch of Pisidia

Lystra

C I L I C I A

Derbe

Tarsus

Euphrates R.

P A M P H Y L I A

Perga
Attalia

L Y C I A

Rhodes
Patara
Rhodes

Myra

Seleucia Antioch

S Y R I A

35

chus

E A N   S E A

C Y P R U S
Salamis

R. Orontes

Paphos

Sidon
Damascus
M. Hermon
Tyre
Ptolemais

P H Œ N I C I A

CAESAREA
Samaria
P A L E S T I N E

Lydda JERUSALEM

Dead
Sea

30

35

Chart 15-10

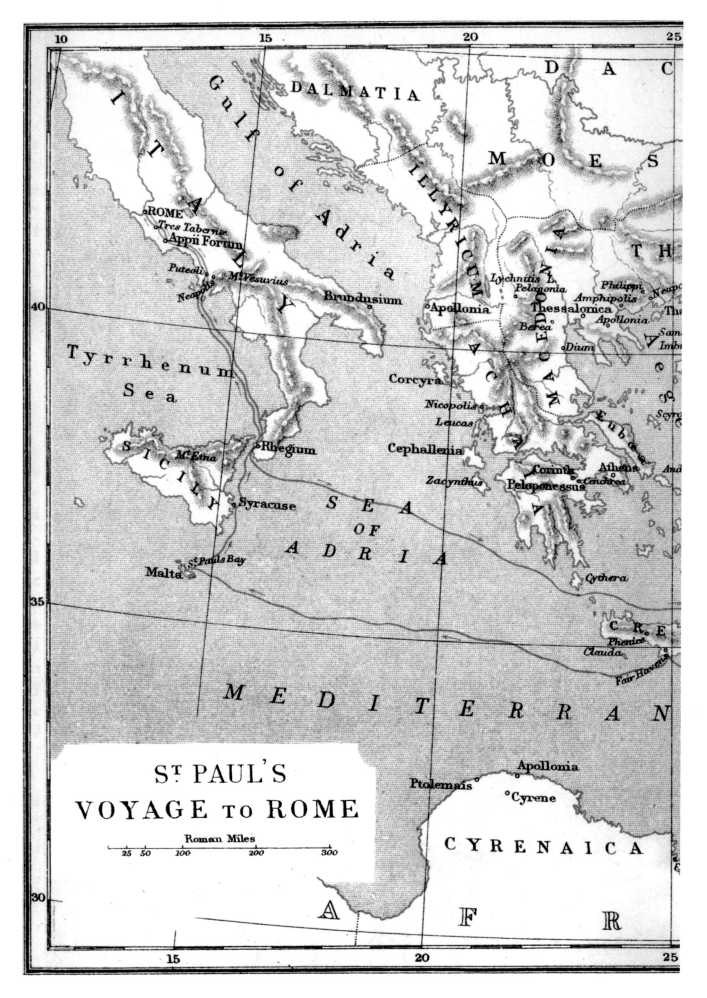

ST. PAUL'S
VOYAGE TO ROME

Roman Miles

25 50   100   200   300

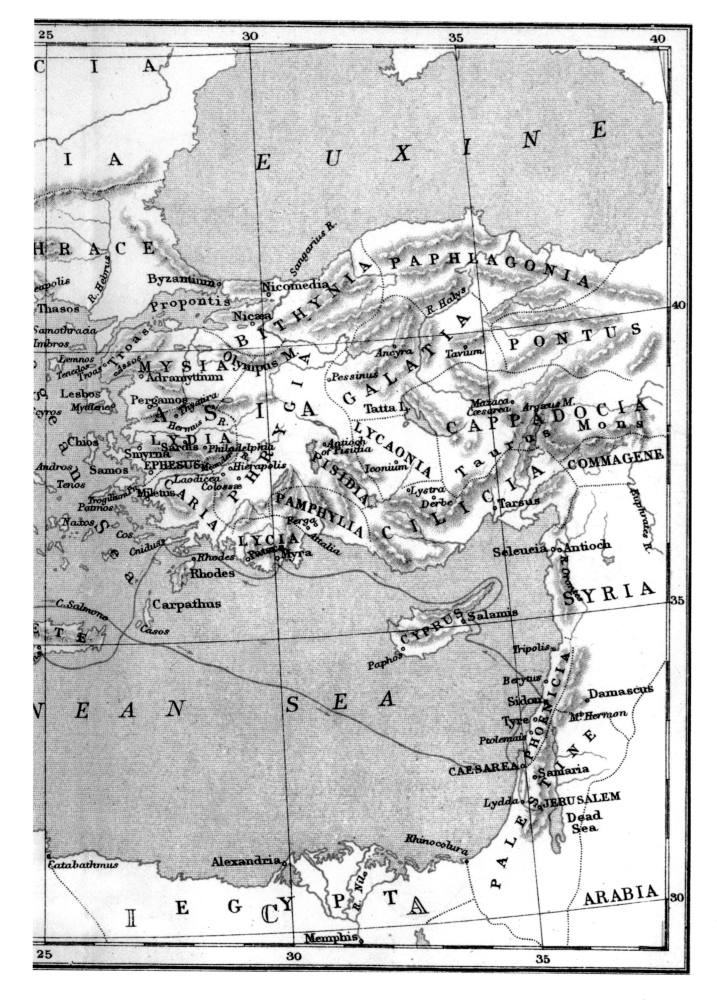

Chart 15-11

Chart 15-12

Some of Paul's Many Metaphors

Explanation

The letters of Paul are difficult to understand, for many reasons. Besides his convoluted sentence structures and huge vocabulary (see chart 11-10), Paul loved to use metaphors. This is fine for people who know the surrounding culture from which Paul drew those metaphors. But for modern readers, many of these images require clarification. Chart 15-12 displays and explains Paul's main metaphors, drawn from the worlds of city, country, and family life; law, slavery, and freedom; manufacturing, marketing, and travel; warfare, sports, and entertainment. By understanding the Greek cultural worlds of Corinth, Ephesus, Thessalonica, and the other cities where Paul worked, modern readers can better appreciate the vivid and beautiful images invoked and evoked by his writings.

Reference

Extracted from David J. Williams, *Paul's Metaphors: Their Context and Character* (Peabody, Mass.: Hendrickson, 1999).

Some of Paul's Many Metaphors

METAPHOR		WHAT IT REPRESENTS	REFERENCE

From Country Life

Cattle kicking against the goad	~	Paul's own conversion experience, denying an education in the gospel	Acts 26:14
The flock	~	The church	Acts 20:17–35
Shepherds	~	Elders of the church	Acts 20:17–35
The olive tree	~	Israel, both Jew and Gentile	Rom 11:16–24
A wild olive tree	~	From whence Gentiles came	Rom 11:24
Grafting	~	Gentiles, against their nature, brought into the realm of God and the Jews	Rom 11:24

Sheep on lintel from an early church in Constantinople.

From Family Life

The marriage contract	~	Christ and the church	Eph 5:27
Betrothal	~	A pledge to Christ	2Cor 11:2
One husband	~	Jesus Christ	2Cor 11:2
Bridegroom	~	Jesus Christ	2Cor 11:3
Friend of the bride	~	Paul, presenting the Christians to Christ pure and righteous	Rev 19:7
The father/parent	~	Paul the parent of his converts	1Cor 4:15; 2Cor 12:14; Phlmn 10
Children	~	Paul's new converts	1Cor 4:15; 2Cor 12:14; Phlmn 10
The human body	~	Church	1Cor 12
Head	~	Christ	Eph 4:15–16; Col 2:19
Veil, woman being veiled	~	Jews not seeing beyond the Old Testament to understand Christ to be the fulfillment of it	2Cor 3:12–18; 4:3–6

Chart 15-12 (1)

METAPHOR	WHAT IT REPRESENTS	REFERENCE

From the Legal Sphere

METAPHOR		WHAT IT REPRESENTS	REFERENCE
Advocate (legal adviser)	~	The Lord, the one who pleads our cause	2Tm 4:17
Justification	~	God forgives sinners by the grace of Jesus Christ	Rom 4:25; 5:18
Judge	~	God and Jesus Christ	Rom 14:10; 2Cor 5:10
Those whom [the judge] summoned [to] the judgment seat	~	All people will be judged of Jesus Christ God's executor in giving judgment	Rom 14:10; 2Cor 5:10
A last will and testament	~	God's promises which cannot be annulled or amended	Gal 3:15
Citizenship, civic pride	~	Loyalty Christians should have to Christ (not only to Rome); be as citizens of heaven	Phlp 1:27; 3:20
Fellow citizens	~	Gentiles as fellow saints	Eph 2:12, 19
An ambassador	~	Paul in his ministry	2Cor 5:20; Eph 6:20

Courtroom in Priene near Ephesus.

From Slavery and Freedom

METAPHOR		WHAT IT REPRESENTS	REFERENCE
Stewards, agents	~	Church leaders	1Cor 4:1; Titus 1:7
Slavery	~	Human condition, humans innately in service to sin	Rom 6:6, 16, 17, 20
Branding, "the marks of Jesus"	~	Paul bearing the stigmata of Jesus, demonstrating his devotion	Gal 6:17
Redemption of a slave	~	Christ's blood bought the Christians freedom	Eph 1:7
Purchase of slaves by a new master: "You were bought at a price"	~	Believers being purchased (converted) from one master (sin) to another (God) at the price of Christ's crucifixion	1Cor 6:20; 7:23
A ransom	~	Jesus Christ's atonement	1Tm 2:6

Chart 15-12 (2)

METAPHOR		WHAT IT REPRESENTS	REFERENCE
From the World of Manufacturing and Marketing			
A workman/mason	~	Timothy "cutting" the word of truth to the required dimensions	2Tm 2:15
Wage	~	What God will "pay" the teacher according to his works	Rom 4:4; 1Cor 3:8, 14; 9:17–18
Fellow worker/partner	~	Titus in his co-ministry with Paul to the Corinthian church	2Cor 8:23
A potter	~	God	Rom 9:21
Peddlers (of God's word)	~	Insincere teachers who water down the gospel, what Paul professes he and his colleagues are not	2Cor 2:17
A guarantee	~	God's promise that we belong to Christ	2Cor 1:21–22
Entered into an account	~	The believer is credited to Christ	2Cor 1:21–22
A seal ("it is he who has sealed us")	~	God's sign of ownership	2Cor 1:21–22
An installment	~	God has put his Spirit in our hearts	2Cor 1:22
Debtors	~	Those who are saved by grace who still owe it to God to live their lives righteously	Rom 8:12
Immeasurable riches	~	Spiritual reward for being a follower of Christ	Eph 1:7, 18; 2:7; 3:8, 16
Deposit	~	Paul's life, dedicated to Christ and entrusted to God	2Tm 1:12

Jars from ancient Israel.

Chart 15-12 (3)

METAPHOR		WHAT IT REPRESENTS	REFERENCE
From the World of Travel			
Paul's letter of recommendation	~	Corinthians (Paul's converts in Corinth could vouch for him as their teacher)	2Cor 3:1–3
Coming out to meet an official visitor	~	Coming up to meet Christ at his coming	2Cor 7:6–7; 1Th 4:17
Helmsmanship	~	Leadership in the church as a gift of the Spirit	1Cor 12:28
To furl or reef a sail	~	Paul assuring the Ephesian elders that he holds back none of the counsels of God	Acts 20:20
Trim his sails	~	Peter separating himself from the Jewish Christians	Gal 2:12
Departure	~	Death	2Tm 4:6
Haven for ships	~	Access to God and God's grace through Christ	Rom 5:2; Eph 2:18; 3:12
Tossed to and fro by the waves (whirled) about by every wind	~	The theological fad-following Ephesians	Eph 4:14
Shipwreck (of their faith)	~	Certain Ephesians rejecting their faith in Christ; Paul considered them no longer Christian	2Cor 11:25
Drowning in a "sea" of destruction	~	Spiritual danger of loving money more than Jesus Christ	1Tm 6:9
Walking	~	Christian life	Rom 5:7; 6:4; 8:4; 13:13; 14:15; 1Cor 3:3; 2Cor 4:2; 5:7; 10:2–3; Gal 5:16; Eph 2:1–2; 4:1, 17; 5:2, 8, 15; Col 1:10; 3:5–7; 4:5; 1Th 2:12; 4:12; 2Th 3:6,11
Walk the straight line	~	Follow the "road" Christ has set for us	Gal 2:14
The road blocked	~	Satan hindering Paul in his travels (specifically in his return to the Macedonian capital)	1Th 2:18
Clear the way	~	Hope that God instills to encourage progress toward Christ	1Th 3:11; 2Th 3:5

Oarsman on a Greek sailing vessel.

Chart 15-12 (4)

Metaphor		What It Represents	Reference
From Warfare and Soldiering			
Front liner	~	Paul as the leader of the Nazarenes	Acts 24:5
In proper battle array	~	Worshiping in a decent and orderly manner	1Cor 14:40
Ranks	~	Lines of believers, the first line being Christ in his singular glory	1Cor 15:23, 52
Keep in step (with the Spirit)	~	Enjoining Christian "soldiers" to set a pace towards likeness to Christ	Gal 5:25
Battles	~	Trials Paul faced when he returned to Macedonia	2Cor 7:5
At war	~	Skirmishes between the flesh and the Spirit	Rom 7:23
Enemy	~	Flesh	Rom 8:5–9
A prisoner of war	~	He who does not accept the Savior and submits to the flesh	Rom 7:7–25
Weapons of warfare	~	God's power	2Cor 10:3–6
Strongholds	~	Arguments against the Gospel	2Cor 10:4
Prisoner (of Christ)	~	Paul	Eph 3:1; 4:1; 2Tm 1:8; Phlmn 1, 9
Armor of light	~	Jesus Christ	Rom 13:11–13
Fiery Darts	~	Burning personal attacks	Eph 6:16
The full armor	~	God's protection	Eph 6:10–18
Belt	~	Protection	Eph 6:14
Breastplate	~	Virtue of righteousness	Eph 6:14
Sandals	~	Preparedness or readiness of the gospel of peace	Eph 6:15
Shield	~	Faith, trust in God	Eph 6:16
Helmet	~	Assurance of salvation	Eph 6:17
Sword	~	Word of God	Eph 6: 17
Fellow soldiers	~	Epaphroditus and Archippus	Phlp 2:25; Phlmn 2
A good soldier (of Jesus Christ)	~	Timothy	2Tm 2:3

Armor on gladiators from Ephesus.

Chart 15-12 (5)

Race course in Aphrodesias.

METAPHOR		WHAT IT REPRESENTS	REFERENCE
From Public Shows and Sporting Events			
Lead in triumph	~	Christ as the triumphator (the head of a victory procession), leading the apostles in his train behind him	2Cor 2:14
Chariot or foot race	~	Life in the church, the believer pressing forward, never back, with the goal to know Christ by enduring to the end	Phlp 3:13–14
Charioteer's prize	~	To be like Christ	Phlp 3:14
A spectacle	~	The apostles	1Cor 4:9
Fighting wild beasts	~	Costliness of Christian service	1Cor 15:32

Stadion at Delphi.

Chart 15-12 (6)

METAPHOR		WHAT IT REPRESENTS	REFERENCE

From Village or City Life

METAPHOR		WHAT IT REPRESENTS	REFERENCE
Nighttime darkness in narrow streets	~	Children of the world in this age	1Cor 4:5; 1Th 5:5
Light	~	Children of God	1Cor 4:5; 1Th 5:5
A thief in the night	~	Jesus' return	1Th 5:4
A doorway	~	God opening the gospel to the Gentiles	Acts 14:27
An entrance	~	Opening of Macedonia to the gospel	1Th 1:9; 2:1
Scum	~	Apostles in the sight of the world	1Cor 4:13
Offscouring, filth	~	Apostles in the sight of the world	1Cor 4:13
Refuse, dung, garbage	~	Things of the world	Phlp 3:8
Do not quench the fire of the Spirit	~	Gifts of the Spirit	1Th 5:19
The foundation platform of a building	~	Jesus Christ	1Cor 3:10–15
Builders and their materials	~	Teachers and teaching	1Cor 3:10–15
Buildings	~	Those who are taught	1Cor 3:10–15
Fine structures	~	Likeness to Christ	1Cor 3:10–15
Fire sweeping through wooden buildings	~	Second coming of Christ	1Cor 3:10–15
Expert builder	~	Paul	1Cor 3:10
Foundations laid	~	Having Christ dwell in the hearts of the believers	Eph 3:17
Built on the foundation	~	Apostles and prophets, Jesus Christ being the cornerstone	Eph 2:20–21
Cornerstone	~	Jesus Christ	Eph 2:20
The (builder's) mark	~	"The Lord knows those who are his"; God's seal	1Cor 9:2; 2Tm 2:19
Fitting together in the construction of the temple	~	Integration of the Jews and Gentiles	Eph 2:21; 4:16
Tents, tabernacles	~	Our spiritually nomadic state on earth	2Cor 5:1–5
House	~	Solidarity from God, in heaven	2Cor 5:1–5
Utensils, vessels	~	Members in God's household	2Tm 2:20

Chart 15-13

Speeches of Paul in Acts

Explanation

As with Peter (see chart 13-6), the book of Acts contains seven speeches of the apostle Paul. In 122 verses, Paul addresses Jews in Antioch, Jerusalem, and Rome; ruling Greeks in Athens; King Agrippa in Caesarea; and converts of the John the Baptist and the elders of the church in Ephesus. Paul spoke to Jews and Gentiles passionately and articulately. His major themes covered Jesus as the promised Savior and man's kinship to God assured by Christ's resurrection; receiving the Holy Ghost and laboring to remain true Christians; and conversion, calling, obedience, and testimony.

Reference

Gary L. Hatch, "Paul among the Rhetoricians: A Model for Proclaiming Christ," in *The Apostle Paul: His Life and His Testimony, Sidney B. Sperry Symposium,* ed. Paul Y. Hoskisson (Salt Lake City: Deseret Book, 1994), 65–79.

Speeches of Paul in Acts

AUDIENCE	THEMES	REFERENCE
Synagogue at Antioch in Pisidia	Jesus, the promised Davidic Savior	Acts 13:16–47
Athenians on Mars' Hill	Man's kinship to God assured by Jesus' resurrection	Acts 17:22–31
Followers of John the Baptist in Ephesus	Receive the Holy Ghost	Acts 19:2–4
Farewell speech to the elders of the church from Ephesus	Labor to remain true Christians	Acts 20:18–35
The angry mob at the temple in Jerusalem	Visions of conversion and calling	Acts 22:3–21
Defense before Agrippa	Obedience to the heavenly vision	Acts 26:2–29
Jews in Rome	Testimony delivered and turned to the Gentiles	Acts 28:17–28

Chart 15-13

Chart 15-14

Statements about Women
by Peter and Paul

Explanation

Many readers of the New Testament come away with the impression that Paul was a misogynist who did not value and esteem women. This false reaction is due in part to the King James English, which generally renders the Greek in a manner that is less flattering toward women than may be necessary. Other nuances in meaning are possible and bear reflection, even if it remains uncertain what Paul originally intended. When Paul's statements about women are read all together, especially in conjunction with similar statements by Peter, a more positive New Testament posture toward women emerges. As chart 15-14 shows, women are encouraged and welcomed as united companions working in building the kingdom of God; women are charged to train their sisters in virtue and righteousness; dress styles are to be modest and in good taste; and women are to learn in serenity and peace of soul. In reality, both men and women are given similar instructions: to be wise, reverent, orderly, and obedient.

References

Andrew Perriman, *Speaking of Women: Interpreting Paul* (Leicester: Apollos, 1998).
Joseph Fielding Smith, "Your Question," *Improvement Era*, April 1960, 224–25.

Statements about Women
by Peter and Paul

SERVICE IN THE KINGDOM

Phlp 4:2–3	Be of one mind in the Lord, and labor in the gospel
Rom 16:1–4	Minister (*diakonon;* KJV, serve) as companions (*synergous;* KJV, helpers) in building the church, preaching the gospel, even risking their own lives
Titus 2:4–5	Older women should teach younger women to be wise [KJV, sober], loving wives and mothers, and to be virtuous, holy, well organized at home (*oikourgous;* KJV, keepers at home), good, obediently supportive to their husbands, and that the word of God should not be profaned [KJV, blasphemed]
1Tm 2:12	The wife [KJV, a woman] should not teach or domineer over (*authentein;* KJV, usurp authority over) her husband [KJV, the man]

PERSONAL DECORUM

1Pt 3:3	Do not worry about outward adorning, hair styles, jewelry, or worldly apparel
1Tm 2:9	Avoid costly hair styles and apparel
1Tm 2:9	Dress modestly, in good taste (*sophrosunēs;* KJV, sobriety), in a manner that brings honorable self-respect (*aidous;* KJV, shamefacedness)

BEHAVIOR IN CHURCH

1Tm 2:11–12	Let women learn in serenity (*hēsuchia;* KJV, silence), with deference (*hypotagēi,* KJV, all subjection), in peace of soul (*hēsuchia;* KJV, silence)
1Cor 11:5	Women should dress modestly when they pray or prophesy (wearing a veil was a symbol of virtue and respectability in the world of the New Testament)
1Cor 14:29–33	Both men and women must speak in an orderly manner
1Cor 14:34–35	Women should be reverent (*sigatōsan;* KJV, keep silent) and not chatter (*lalein;* KJV, speak) but be supportive [KJV, under obedience] in church and discuss questions they may have at home with their husband

WIDOWHOOD

1Tm 5:3–10	Give honor to widows over sixty years of age who have served faithfully
1Tm 5:11	Younger widows are encouraged to remarry

Chart 15-14

Chart 15-15

Teachings of Peter and Paul
about Marriage

Explanation

Marriage was an important part of New Testament Christianity. Both Peter and Paul encouraged marriage. Paul forsook marriage (or perhaps remarriage) while he served as a missionary, and he encouraged all single men and women to remain absolutely chaste like himself (1Cor 7:8–9), but he strongly rejected the false doctrine that "it is good for a man not to touch a woman" (1Cor 7:1). He gave advice to married couples regarding sexual relations within marriage; and he discouraged divorce, even among mixed marriages of different faiths (1Cor 7:2–5, 10–17). Both Peter and Paul admonished husbands and wives to have total love and respect for each other, for the one is not without the other in the Lord. In unity, they shall be joint-heirs together of the gift of eternal life.

Reference

Monte S. Nyman, "The Stumbling Blocks of First Corinthians," in *The New Testament and the Latter-day Saints, Sidney B. Sperry Symposium* (Orem, Utah: Randall Book, 1987), 249–62.

Teachings of Peter and Paul about Marriage

1Pt 3:1–2	A wife's obedience to her unchristian husband may influence the husband by her chaste conduct coupled with respect (*phobō;* KJV, fear)
1Pt 3:5–7	Righteous women of old trusted in God and were in subjection to their husbands who gave honor to their wives, treating her as a tender instrument [KJV, weaker vessel], and also recognizing that they will be heirs together of the gift (*charitos;* KJV, grace) of life
1Pt 3:7	A husband should live according to revealed truth (*gnōsin;* KJV, knowledge), giving honor to the wife
1Cor 7:2	"Let every man have his own wife, and let every woman have her own husband"
1Cor 7:3–4	"Let the husband render unto the wife what is owed to her (*opheilēn;* KJV, due benevolence), and likewise also the wife unto the husband. The wife hath not authority (*exousia;* KJV, power) of her own body, but the husband, and likewise also the husband hath not authority [KJV, power] of his own body, but the wife"
1Cor. 7:15	"For the unbelieving husband is sanctified by the wife, and the unbelieving wife is sanctified by the husband"
1Cor 11:7	He is in the glory of God; and she is the glory of the man
1Cor 11:11	"Neither is the man without the woman, neither the woman without the man, in the Lord"
Eph 5:25, 33	The husband has pure love toward (*agapatō;* KJV, loves) his wife, as Christ has pure love for the Church; he loves his wife even as his own life
Eph 5:22–24	The wife stands behind (*hypotassetai;* KJV, submits to) her husband in all things when the husband stands behind Christ [as in a battle formation]; she shows love, reverence, and respect to her husband
Col 3:18	Wives stand behind (*hypotassesthe;* KJV, submit themselves to) their own husbands as it is fit in the Lord
1Tm 2:15	She shall be preserved during childbirth, if they [plural] continue together in faith, charity and holiness with good judgment and self-control (*sōphrosunēs;* KJV, sobriety)

Chart 15-15

The Articles of Faith in the Letters of Paul

Explanation

In the thirteenth Article of Faith, Joseph Smith declared, "Indeed we may say we follow the admonition of Paul." The writings of Paul were deeply meaningful and fully embraced by the Prophet Joseph Smith. As chart 15-16 shows, the essence of each of the Articles of Faith can be found, often verbatim, in the writings of Paul. Following the table listing the New Testament references, two pages compare the parallel words and thoughts between the letters of Paul and the Articles of Faith. Paul admonished the people in Ephesus to be united in "one Lord, one faith, one baptism, one God and Father of all" (Eph 4:5–6). The congruence between the teachings of Joseph Smith and Paul shows them to be of one mind and one will as apostles of Jesus Christ.

Reference

John W. Welch, "Co-Authors of the Articles of Faith?" *Instructor* 114 (November 1969): 422–26.

The Articles of Faith in the Letters of Paul

Articles of Faith	References in the New Testament Letters
1	2 Corinthians 13:14
2	Galatians 6:7; 1 Corinthians 15:22
3	Colossians 1:20; Hebrews 5:9
4	Hebrews 6:1–2
5	1 Timothy 4:14
6	Ephesians 4:11
7	1 Corinthians 12:8–12
8	2 Timothy 3:16; 2 Corinthians 13:1
9	1 Corinthians 2:10–11
10	Hebrews 12:22; 1 Thessalonians 2:19; 3:13
11	Romans 2:14–16
12	Romans 13:1–7
13	1 Corinthians 13:7; Philippians 4:8

Chart 15-16 (1)

The Letters of Paul and the Articles of Faith

"The grace of the Lord *Jesus Christ*, and the love of *God*, and the communion of the *Holy Ghost*, be with you all" (2Cor 13:14).	**1**	We believe in *God*, the Eternal Father, and in His Son, *Jesus Christ*, and in the *Holy Ghost*.
"Whatsoever a *man* soweth, that shall he also reap" (Gal 6:7). "For as in *Adam* all die, even so in Christ shall all be made alive" (1Cor 15:22).	**2**	We believe that men will be punished for their own sins, and not for *Adam's* transgression.
"And having made peace through the blood of his cross, by him to *reconcile all* things unto himself" (Col 1:20). "And being made perfect, he became the author of eternal *salvation* unto *all* them that *obey* him" (Heb 5:9).	**3**	We believe that through the Atonement of Christ, *all* mankind may be *saved*, by *obedience* to the laws and ordinances of the Gospel.
"The foundation of *repentance* from dead works, and of *faith* toward God, Of the doctrine of *baptisms*, and of *laying on of hands*" (Heb 6:1–2).	**4**	We believe that the first principles and ordinances of the Gospel are: first, *Faith* in the Lord Jesus Christ; second, *Repentance*; third, *Baptism* by immersion for the remission of sins; fourth, *Laying on of hands* for the gift of the Holy Ghost.
"Neglect not the gift that is in thee, which was given thee *by prophecy*, with the *laying on of the hands of the presbytery*" (1Tm 4:14).	**5**	We believe that a man must be called of God, *by prophecy*, and by the *laying on of hands by those who are in authority*, to preach the Gospel and administer in the ordinances thereof.
"And he gave some, *apostles;* and some, *prophets;* and some, *evangelists; and some, pastors* and *teachers*" (Eph 4:11).	**6**	We believe in the same organization that existed in the Primitive Church, namely, *apostles, prophets, pastors, teachers, evangelists,* and so forth.
"For to one is given by the Spirit ... the gifts of *healing ... prophecy ... discerning of spirits ... divers kinds of tongues ... the interpretation of tongues*" (1Cor 12:8–10).	**7**	We believe in the *gift of tongues*, *prophecy, revelation,* visions, *healing, interpretation of tongues,* and so forth.

Chart 15-16 (2)

"All scripture is given by inspiration of God" (2Tm 3:16). "In the mouth of two or three witnesses shall every *word* be established" (2Cor 13:1).	**8** We believe the Bible to be the word *of God* as far as it is translated correctly; we also believe the Book of Mormon to be the *word of God*.
"But *God hath revealed them unto us* by his Spirit: for the Spirit searcheth all things" (1Cor 2:10–11).	**9** We believe all that *God has revealed*, all that He does now reveal, and we believe that He will yet reveal many great and important things pertaining to the Kingdom of God.
"But ye are come unto mount *Sion … the heavenly Jerusalem*" (Heb 12:22). "Are not even ye in the *presence of our Lord Jesus Christ* at his coming?" (1Th 2:19). "He may stablish your hearts unblameable in holiness before God, even our Father, at the coming of our *Lord Jesus Christ with all his saints*" (1Th 3:13).	**10** We believe in the literal gathering of Israel and in the restoration of the Ten Tribes; that Zion *(the New Jerusalem)* will be built upon the American continent; that *Christ will reign personally upon the earth;* and, that the earth will be renewed and receive its paradisiacal glory.
"These … are a law unto themselves: Which shew the work of the law written in their hearts, their *conscience* also bearing witness" (Rom 2:14–16).	**11** We claim the privilege of worshiping Almighty God according to the dictates of our own *conscience*, and allow all men the same privilege, let them worship how, where, or what they may.
"Let every soul be subject unto the higher powers: the *powers that be* are ordained of God" (Rom 13:1–7).	**12** We believe in being subject to *kings, presidents, rulers, and magistrates,* in obeying, honoring, and sustaining the law.
"Beareth all things, believeth all things, hopeth all things, endureth all things" (1Cor 13:7). "Whatsoever things are *pure … lovely … of good report … if there be any praise,* think on these things" (Phlp 4:8).	**13** We believe in being honest, true, chaste, benevolent, virtuous, and in doing good to all men; indeed, we may say that we follow the admonition of Paul; *we believe all things, we hope all things, we* have endured many things, and *hope* to be able to *endure all things.* If there is anything *virtuous, lovely,* or *of good report* or *praiseworthy*, we seek after these things.

Chart 15-16 (3)

Chart 15-17

Comparing Conversions
Paul and Alma

Explanation

The conversions of Saul of Tarsus on the road to Damascus and of Alma the Younger in the land of Zarahemla are similar in certain fundamental respects, as one would expect since the source of their spiritual reversals was one and the same. Interestingly, in each case we have three accounts of their conversions: Paul's conversion is reported in Acts 9, 22, and 26. Alma's conversion is given in Mosiah 27, Alma 36, and 38. No two of these accounts are exactly the same. The columns on the far right and left sides of chart 15-17 show the verses of these six accounts in which each element either appears or is absent. Down the middle are found the elements shared by both Paul and Alma, and off center are words or experiences unique to either Paul or Alma. In sum, the personalized differences significantly offset and highlight the individual experiences in the two conversions.

Reference

Rex E. Lee, "Paul and Alma and Harold B. Lee: What Prophets and Common Sense Can Teach Us about Learning from Our Mistakes," *Brigham Young University Devotional and Fireside Speeches,* (Provo, Utah: BYU Press, 1993/94), 13–17.

Comparing Conversions
Paul and Alma

Conversion of Paul					Conversion of Alma		
Acts 9:	Acts 22:	Acts 26:	Three accounts		Mos 27:	Alma 36:	Alma 38:
1–2			Seeking to destroy church		8–11	6	
				Corrupting the people	8–10	14	
1–2	5	9–12	Arresting and persecuting saints				
3–8	6–11	13–19	A heavenly vision of Jesus Christ	A heavenly vision of an angel	11–18	5–9	7
3	6	13	Light shining from heaven				
				Whole earth did tremble	11, 18	7	7
				Thunderous voice	11–18	7	7
4	7	14	Fell to the earth		12, 18		
4	7	14	"Why persecutest thou me?"	"Why persecutest thou the church?"	13		
5	8	15	"Who art thou, Lord?"				
6	10		"What wilt thou have me to do?"				
				Warning of self-destruction		9, 11	
6	10	16	Told to arise		13	8	
				Commanded to repent	16		
7			Some hear, but do not see			11	
				Some hear and see, but do not understand	12, 18		
	9	13	Some see, but do not hear	Some hear and see, but Alma does not		11	
9	11		Struck blind	Struck dumb	19		
				Overcome with weakness	19	10	
9	11		Without food or drink for three days	Immobile for three days	23	10	8
				Soul racked with torment	29	12–18	8
				Prayers of fasting and righteous	21–23		
10–18	12–16		God sends Ananias to heal	Brought before a multitude	21		
18	16		Ananias invites to baptism	Reborn of the Spirit	24–30	18–19	6, 8
				Declaration of repentant joy		20–22	
15–16	14–15	16–19	Called to the ministry				
13–26	18–21		Mistrust among the disciples	Redeemed through Jesus Christ		18–19	6, 8
20–30			Proving discipleship				
				Testimony of repentant convert	30–31	22–30	4–6
		20	Taught the gospel		32–37	24–26	
		31	Maintained testimony in the face of persecution		32	27	

Chart 15-17

Chiasmus in the New Testament

Explanation

Chiasmus and several varieties of inverted parallel structures are found in many places in the New Testament. In reading Bible commentaries, students will often encounter figures displaying chiastic patterns. The following charts offer a few samples of such literary arrangements. Chart 15-18 lays out the elegant configuration of the Hymn to Charity *(Agape)* found in 1 Corinthians 13; Paul may have imported or modified this poetical unit from some other source. Chart 15-19 helps a reader to follow the logic of the Epistle to the Galatians, focusing especially on the central chiasm in Galatians 4:1–7. Chart 15-20 gives an overview of the letter of Paul to Philemon. The argument of the Epistle to the Hebrews also has a central pivot point, drawing attention to Jesus Christ as the new High Priest. These and many other examples show that Paul and other writers of the New Testament were skilled writers, conversant with the literary styles of their day.

References

John W. Welch and Daniel B. McKinley, *Chiasmus Bibliography* (Provo, Utah: Research Press, 1999), 116–45.

Nils W. Lund, *Chiasmus in the New Testament* (Chapel Hill: University of North Carolina Press, 1942).

John W. Welch, "Chiasmus in the New Testament," in *Chiasmus in Antiquity,* ed. John W. Welch (Hildesheim, Germany: Gerstenberg, 1981), 211–49.

On chiasmus in 1 Corinthians, see Lund, 176; Welch, 215–16; in Galatians, see Welch, 214; in Philemon see, Thomas Boys, *Tactica Sacra* (London: Hamilton, 1824), 65–67; Lund, 219; Welch, 225–26; in Hebrews, see Welch, 220.

Chiastic Hymn to Charity
1 Cor 12:31–14:1

A Seek after the *greatest* gifts, and indeed here is the *greatest* way:
  B If I speak in *tongues* with men, yea even with angels
    But have not love
      I am but raucous bronze and rattling cymbals.
  If I have the gift of *prophecy* and know *mysteries* all and all knowledge
    But have not love
      I am nothing.
  If I give away all I have or lay down my body to get glory
    But have not love
      I have gotten absolutely nothing.
    C *Love* is *patient* toward others
    Mercifully kind is *love*.
      D Not greedy
      Not a show-off
      Not conceited
      Not shameless
      Not with ulterior design, selfishness or cliquishness
      Not irritable
      Does not rationalize wickedness
      Has no joy when things are not right
      But rejoices in truth.
    C' *Love* is *patient* under all circumstances
    Always believing
    Always hoping
    Love endures to the end.
  B' Love will never lose its importance
    But *prophecy* will come to an end
    Speaking in *tongues* will cease
    And some day knowing *mysteries* will be nothing special.
    For now we just know little bits
    And we prophesy of little glimpses
      But when Christ comes all will be perfectly whole
      And all our partial experiences will be no more.
        When I was a child
        I spoke as a child
        I had the intellect of a child
        I figured like a child
        When I became a man
        I had no more use for childish things.
    For now we just see faint images of our real selves
      But then we shall see face to face
    Now we just know little bits
      But then I shall know and be known completely.
  What lasts are faith, hope, love, these three,
A' But the *greatest* of these is love.

Chart 15-18

Chiasmus in Galatians

A Prologue (1:1–12)

    B Autobiographical section (1:13–2:10)

        C Justification by faith (2:11–3:4)

            D Arguments from scripture (3:5–29)

                E Central chiasm (4:1–10)

      a The *heir* remains a *child* and *servant* (4:1)

         b Until the time appointed of the *father* (4:2)

            c When that time came, *God* sent forth his *Son* (4:4)

                d Made under the *law* (4:4)

                d′ To redeem those under the *law* (4:5)

            c′ Because ye are sons, *God* sent forth the Spirit of his *Son* (4:6)

         b′ That ye cry Abba, *Father* (4:6)

      a′ That ye are no more a *servant* but a *son* and *heir* (4:7)

            D′ Arguments from scripture (4:11–31)

        C′ Justification by faith (5:1–10)

    B′ Moral section (5:11–11)

A′ Epilogue (6:12–18)

Chart 15-19

Chiasmus in Philemon

A Epistolary (1–3)

  B Paul's prayers for Philemon (4)

    C Philemon's love, faith, and hospitality (5–7)

      D Paul could use his authority (8)

        E But prefers to make supplication (9–10)

          F Onesimus a convert of Paul's (10)

            G Paul has made Onesimus profitable (11)

              H Receive Onesimus as Paul's own bowels (12)

                I Paul retained Onesimus as Paul's minister in the bonds of the Gospel (13)

                  J Without Philemon's willing consent Paul will not require Philemon to take Onesimus back (14)

                  J' Perhaps the reason Onesimus left was so that Philemon could take Onesimus back forever (15)

                I' Not as a servant but as a brother in the Lord (16)

              H' Receive Onesimus as Paul's own self (17)

            G' Paul will repay any wrong Onesimus has done (18–19)

          F' Philemon indebted as a convert to Paul (19)

        E' Paul makes supplication to Philemon (20)

      D' Although he could ask for obedience (21)

    C' Paul requests hospitality of Philemon (22)

  B' Philemon's prayers for Paul (22)

A' Epistolary (23–25)

Chart 15-20

Chiasmus in Hebrews

A Jesus is forever (1:8), so great a salvation we cannot neglect (2:3), who is a Son higher than the angels, whose house is more glorious than that of Moses (1:1–3:7).

    B The word preached unto the House of Israel did not profit them because they hardened their hearts and had no faith upon their day of temptation (3:7–4:13).

        C Christ's priesthood is higher than that of Aaron or of the Levitical priests (4:14–7:28).

            D We have a High Priest who officiates in the sanctuary built by God (8:1–2).

        C' Christ's covenant is the eternal testament higher than the atonement administered in the temple by the Levites (8:3–10:35).

    B' The word preached to some did profit them by faith unto becoming heirs of righteousness who obtained a good report by pleasing God. (10:36–11:40).

A' Jesus is forever (13:8), so great a witness we cannot neglect (12:1), becoming sons (12:7–9), in Christ's house which is the heavenly Jerusalem (12:22–28).

Chart 15-21

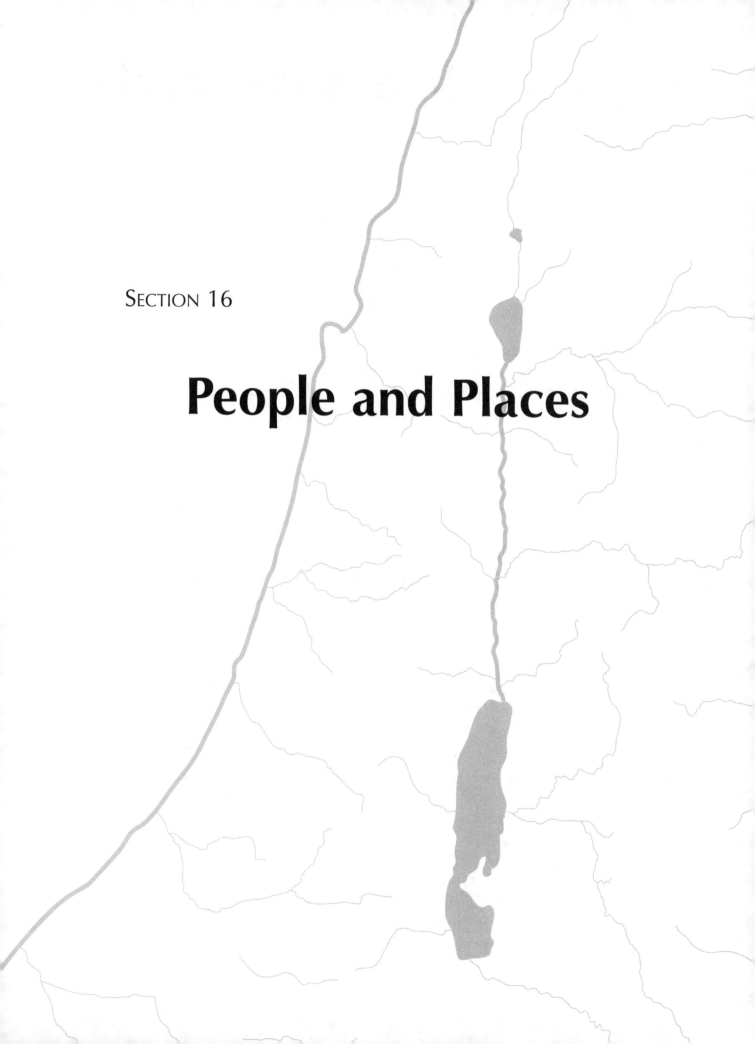

People and Places

People in Acts and the Epistles

Achaicus	A Corinthian who visited Paul in Philippi	1Cor 16:17
Aeneas	A man whom Peter healed of palsy	Acts 9:33–34
Agabus	A prophet from Judea who prophesied of dearth throughout the world and the captivity of Paul	Acts 11:28; 21:10
Agrippa	The king of Judea; he was almost persuaded by Paul to be Christian	Acts 25:22–24, 26; 26:32
Alexander	A coppersmith who did Paul much evil; Paul delivered him unto Satan to learn not to blaspheme	1Tm 1:20; 2Tm 4:14
Alexander	A Jewish leader in Jerusalem who questioned Peter; kindred of Annas	Acts 4:6
Alexander	A Jew who was in the riot in Ephesus	Acts 19:33
Ananias	A certain disciple; he healed Saul and baptized him	Acts 9:10, 12–13, 17; 22:12
Ananias	A High Priest who interrogated Paul in Jerusalem	Acts 23:2; 24:1
Ananias	The husband of Sapphira; he lied to Paul about the price of land and lost his life	Acts 5:5
Andrew	One of the Twelve Apostles	Acts 1:13
angel of God	Instructed Cornelius to send for Peter	Acts 10:3, 7, 30
angel of God	Told Paul that he would be brought before Caesar	Acts 27:24
angel of the Lord	Freed Peter from prison	Acts 12:7–11
angel of the Lord	Smote Herod for his pride	Acts 12:23
Annas	The High Priest who questioned Peter in Jerusalem	Acts 4:6
Apollos	A converted Jew from Alexandria who received instruction in the church from Aquila and Priscilla; a leader of the church; he baptized many	Acts 18:24; 19:1; 1Cor 1:12; 3:4–6; 16:12; Titus 3:13
Apphia	Paul addressed him as a beloved disciple	Phlmn 1:2
Aquila	A Jew born in Pontus, married to Priscilla; his house was the center of church activity in Corinth	Acts 18:2, 18, 26; 1Cor 16:19
Archippus	Called a fellowsoldier by Paul	Col 4:17; Phlmn 1:2
Aretas	The king of a North Arabian kingdom including Damascus	2Cor 11:32
Aristarchus	A Thessalonian; fellow laborer and fellowprisoner with Paul	Acts 19:29; 20:4; 27:2; Phlmn 1:24; Col 4:10
Augustus (Caesar)	The emperor of Rome appealed to by Paul	Acts 25:21, 25
Bar–jesus (Elymas)	A Jew; a false prophet and a sorcerer whom Paul cursed with blindness for his evil works	Acts 13:6–11
Barnabas (Joseph/Joses)	A Levite of Cyprus; he sold his possessions and gave the proceeds to the apostles; assisted in missionary work; not one of the Twelve, but was called an apostle	Acts 4:36–37; 11:22; 13–15; 1Cor 9:6; Gal 2:1, 13;
Bartholomew	One of the Twelve Apostles	Acts 1:13

Chart 16-1 (1)

Bernice	The daughter of Herod Agrippa; believed Paul to be innocent after hearing him	Acts 25:13, 23; 26:30–31
Blastus	Agrippa's chamberlain; helped Tyre and Sidon establish peace with king	Acts 12:20
Caesar	The title of the Roman emperor; Paul sought to be tried in his imperial court	Acts 17:7; 25:8–12, 21; 26:32; 27:24; 28:19; Phlp 4:22
Caiaphas	High Priest in Jerusalem who questioned Peter; kindred of Annas	Acts 4:6
Candace	The queen of the Ethiopians; sent the eunuch to Jerusalem	Acts 8:27
Captain of the Temple	Held Peter and apostles for preaching about resurrection	Acts 4:1; 5:24, 26
Carpus	A Christian at Troas; Paul left a cloak with him	2Tm 4:13
Centurion	Paul told him of his Roman citizenship and he told his chief captain	Acts 22:25–26
Centurion	Brought Paul's nephew to the chief captain to report a plot against Paul	Acts 23:17
Centurion	Commanded to guard Paul and ensure his liberty	Acts 24:23
Cephas	The name given to Peter by Christ	1Cor 1:12; 3:22; 9:5; 15:5; Gal 2:9
Chief captain (Claudius Lysias)	Stopped the beating of Paul and took him prisoner; sent him to the governor Felix	Acts 21:31–23:30
Chief priests	The ruling body among Jews who tried to subvert Christian teachings	Acts 5:24; 9:14
Claudia	Paul sent greetings to her in a letter to Timothy	2Tm 4:21
Claudius Caesar	Agabus's prophecy of dearth was under his reign; he commanded all Jews to depart from Rome	Acts 11:28; 18:2
Claudius Lysias	The name of the chief captain (see Centurion above)	Acts 23:26
Clement	A fellow laborer with Paul in the mission	Phlp 4:3
Cornelius	A centurion; Peter received a vision to visit him; he was baptized by Peter	Acts 10
Council (Sanhedrin)	The governing body of Jews	Acts 5:21, 27; 6:12
Crescens	A missionary who left Paul and the ministry and went to Galatia	2Tm 4:10
Crispus	The chief ruler of the synagogue; he believed and was baptized by Paul	Acts 18:8; 1Cor 1:14
Damaris	A woman who believed Paul on Mars' hill in Athens	Acts 17:34
Damsel	A soothsayer; Paul cast a spirit out of her	Acts 16:16
Demas	A fellow laborer in the gospel; he forsook Paul, and departed into Thessalonica	Col 4:14; 2Tm 4:10; Phlmn 1:24
Demetrius	A silversmith who feared for his trade and lead revolt against Paul in Ephesus	Acts 19:24, 38
Demetrius	A Christian commended by John	3Jn 1:12
Dionysius	An Areopagite who believed Paul on Mars' hill	Acts 17:34
Diotrephes	A Christian who wanted to have the preeminence among the church and rejected John and the missionaries	3Jn 1:9

Chart 16-1 (2)

Drusilla	The wife of Felix; a Jew	Acts 24:24
Elymas (Bar-jesus)	See Bar-jesus	Acts 13:8
Epaphras	A fellowservant and faithful minister of Christ	Col 1:7; 4:12; Phlmn 1:23
Epaphroditus	Paul's companion in labor; he became sick unto death	Phlp 2:25; 4:18
Erastus	A Christian who went to Macedonia; companion of Timotheus; he later abode at Corinth	Acts 19:22; 2Tm 4:20
Erastus	A Corinthian city official	Rom 16:23
Eubulus	A Christian who greeted Timothy through Paul's letter	2Tm 4:21
Eunice	Timothy's mother	2Tm 1:5
Eunuch	Served Candace, the queen of Ethiopia; he was converted by Phillip	Acts 8
Euodius	A Christian at Philippi whom Paul beseeched to be of the same mind in the Lord with Syntyche	Phlp 4:2
Eutychus	A youth who fell from loft during Paul's speech and was raised from the dead	Acts 20:9
Felix	The procurator of Judea at the time of Paul's arrest; he heard Paul's defense of himself	Acts 23–24
Festus (Porcius Festus)	The successor of Felix as procurator of Judea; he tried to try Paul in Jerusalem, but Paul appealed to Caesar	Acts 25–26
Fortunatus	A Corinthian who visited Paul in Philippi and assisted Paul and the Saints in Corinth	1Cor 16:17
Four daughters	Of Philip the evangelist; prophesied	Acts 21:9
Four men	Christians of Gentile birth who purified themselves with Paul and entered the temple, starting a riot among the Jews	Acts 21:23–32
Gaius	A man from Corinth who was baptized by Paul	1Cor 1:14
Gaius	A Christian from Macedonia; Paul's companion in travels	Acts 19:29
Gaius	A Christian from Derbe who accompanied Paul to Asia	Acts 20:4
Gaius	The addressee of 3 John; possibly a wealthy layman in Ephesus	3Jn 1:1
Gallio	The Roman proconsul of Achaia who refused to hear the Jews' case against Paul	Acts 18:12–17
Gamaliel	A respected pharisee; Paul was one of his pupils	Acts 5:34–40; 22:3
Hermas	Paul saluted him in his letter to the Romans	Rom 16:14
Hermes	Paul saluted him in his letter to the Romans	Rom 16:14
Hermogenes	An apostate Christian in Asia; turned away from Paul	2Tm 1:15
Herod (Agrippa I)	The king of Judea who began the persecution of the church; he put James to death but Peter escaped him; he was killed by the Lord for his pride	Acts 12:1–23
Herod Antipas	"Herod the tetrarch"	Acts 13:1
Herodion	A kinsman of Paul	Rom 16:11
High Priest	Appointed by Romans; responsible for judicial, ecclesiastical affairs; persecuted the church	Acts 5; 7:1; 9:1
Hymenaeus	Erred in doctrine of resurrection and misdirected some members	1Tm 1:20; 2Tm 2:17

Chart 16-1 (3)

Jambres	Withstood Moses; given as example of a type of apostates in the last days	2Tm 3:8
James	An apostle; the brother of John; killed by Herod with a sword	Acts 12:2; 1Cor 15:7; Jude 1:1
James	The brother of the Lord; held an important position in the church; likely the writer of the Epistle of James	Gal 1:19; 2:9–12; Jms
James	The son of Alphaeus; one of the Twelve	Acts 1:13
Jannes	Withstood Moses; given as example of type of apostates in last days	2Tm 3:8
Jason	A kinsman of Paul in Thessalonica	Acts 17:5–9
Jesus	The Christ; appears to Paul	Acts 9; 22:8; 26:15
Jesus (Justus)	A Roman Christian; fellowworker with Paul	Col 4:11
John	An apostle; he ministered the gospel with Peter	Acts 3:1; 4; 13; 8:14
Joseph (Barsabas)	Surnamed Justus; he was nominated by the apostles with Matthias to replace Judas Iscariot	Acts 1:23
Joses Barnabas	A Christian who sold his land and brought the money to the apostles	Acts 4:37
Judas Barsabas	A Christian prophet who went to Antioch with Paul and Barnabas	Acts 15:22
Judas of Galilee	The leader of a failed revolt against Roman rule	Acts 5:37
Judas	Surnamed Barsabas; the apostles sent him with Paul and Barnabas	Acts 15:27
Judas/Jude	The brother of James; one of the Twelve; the author of the Epistle of Jude	Acts 1:13; Jude 1:1
Judas	A Christian who housed Saul while he was blind	Acts 9:11
Julia	A Christian in Rome whom Paul greeted in his letter to the Romans	Rom 16:15
Julius	A centurion of Augustus's band; he allowed Paul to visit friends	Acts 27:1–3
Junia	A kinswoman and fellowprisoner of Paul	Rom 16:7
Justus	A Corinthian Christian; Paul entered his house joined to a synagogue	Acts 18:7
Lame man	A Jew who was healed by Peter and John in the temple	Acts 3:2
Linus	A Christian who greeted Timothy through Paul's letter	2Tm 4:21
Lois	Timothy's grandmother	2Tm 1:5
Lucas	A Christian who greeted Philemon through Paul's letter	Phlm 1:24
Lucius of Cyrene	A teacher of the gospel	Acts 13:1
Lucius	A Christian who saluted Roman Saints through Paul's epistle	Rom 16:21
Luke	The author of Acts; a companion of Paul; imprisoned with him in Rome	Col 4:14; 2Tm 4:11
Lydia	A Christian from Thyatira; housed Paul and Silas when they were released from prision	Acts 16:14, 40
Lysias	The chief captain who took Paul out of the hands of the Jews	Acts 24:7, 22
Macedonian	A man who appeared to Paul in a vision and asked for help	Acts 16:9
Manaen	A Christian teacher in Antioch	Acts 13:1
Marcus	A Christian who greeted Philemon through Paul's letter	Phlm 1:24

Chart 16-1 (4)

Marcus	A nephew (sister's son) of Barnabas; fellowworker with Paul	Col 4:10
Mary	The mother of Jesus; in upper room with disciples	Acts 1:14
Mary	A Christian in Rome who bestowed much labor on the apostles	Rom 16:6
Mary	The mother of John Mark	Acts 12:12
Matthew	One of the Twelve Apostles	Acts 1:13
Matthias	One of the Twelve, took Judas Iscariot's place	Acts 1:23–26
Mnason	A Christian from Cyprus; an old disciple; he lodged Paul's company	Acts 21:16
Mother of Paul	A Christian in Rome whom Paul saluted in his letter to the Romans	Rom 16:13
Mother of Rufus	A Christian in Rome whom Paul saluted in his letter to the Romans	Rom 16:13
Narcissus	A leader of the church in Rome	Rom 16:11
Nereus	A Christian in Rome whom Paul saluted in his letter to the Romans	Rom 16:15
Nereus's sister	A Christian in Rome whom Paul saluted in his letter to the Romans	Rom 16:15
Nicanor	One of seven chosen to minister over temporal affairs in Jerusalem	Acts 6:5
Nicolas	One of seven chosen to minister over temporal affairs in Jerusalem; a proselyte of Antioch	Acts 6:5
Nymphas	The church in Laodicea was in his house	Col 4:15
Olympas	A Christian in Rome whom Paul saluted in his letter to the Romans	Rom 16:15
Onesimus	A Christian in Colosse; converted slave whom Paul sent back to his owner; faithful and beloved of Paul	Col 4:9; Phlmn 1:10–19
Onesiphorus	A Christian in Ephesus who refreshed Paul; Paul sent greetings to him	2Tm 1:16; 4:19
Parmenas	One of seven chosen to minister over temporal affairs	Acts 6:5
Patrobas	A Christian in Rome whom Paul saluted in his letter to the Romans	Rom 16:14
Paul (Saul)	From Tarsus; a Pharisee active in the persecution of the saints; he saw Christ in a vision and converted, then spent the rest of his life preaching the gospel; he went on three missionary journeys; fourteen of his epistles to members are in the New Testament	Acts 8–28; Gal 1; 2Cor 11
Paul's nephew	A Christian who told the chief captain of a plot to kill Paul	Acts 23:16
Persis	A Christian who labored much in the Lord; beloved of Paul	Rom 16:12
Peter	A disciple of Christ who held the keys of kingdom of God on earth and was the chief apostle in his day; he called the church together after the death of Christ; through his ministry the gospel was first opened to Gentiles	Acts 1–5, 8–12, 15; 1Pt; 2Pt
Phebe	A Christian dwelling at Cenchrea who succored Paul and other Saints	Rom 16:1
Philemon	A Christian converted by Paul; owned the slave Onesimus whom Paul sent back	Phlmn
Philetus	A false prophet who erred in doctrine of resurrection and misdirected some members of the church	2Tm 2:17
Philip	One of seven chosen to minister over temporal affairs in Jerusalem; evangelist; converted Ethiopian eunuch	Acts 1:13; 6:5; 8, 21

Chart 16-1 (5)

Philologus	A Christian in Rome whom Paul saluted in his letter to the Romans	Rom 16:15
Phlegon	A Christian in Rome whom Paul saluted in his letter to the Romans	Rom 16:14
Phygellus	A missionary who turned away from Paul and went to Asia	2Tm 1:15
Priscilla (Prisca)	A helper in Christ Jesus; married to Aquila; her house was the center of church activity in Corinth	Acts 18:2–3, 18, 26; Rom 16:3; 1Cor 16:19; 2Tm 4:19
Prison keeper	Was converted when prison walls fell	Acts 16:27–36
Prochorus	One of seven chosen to minister over temporal affairs	Acts 6:5
Publius	The chief man of the island of Melita; housed Paul and the disciples; his father was healed by Paul	Acts 28:7–8
Pudens	A Christian who greets Timothy through Paul's letter	2Tm 4:21
Quartus	A Christian in Rome whom Paul salutes in his letter to the Romans	Rom 16:23
Rhoda	A Christian who recognized that Peter was at the door and did not open it, but ran in for gladness	Acts 12:13–14
Rufus	A Christian in Rome whom Paul saluted in his letter to the Romans; chosen in the Lord	Rom 16:13
Rufus's mother	A Christian in Rome whom Paul saluted in his letter to the Romans	Rom 16:13
Sadducees	A group of Jews who opposed the work of the apostles because they preached the resurrection	Acts 4:1; 5:17; 23:7–8
Samaritans	Missionaries preached the gospel in many of their villages	Acts 8:25
Sapphira	The wife of Ananias; she lied and held back the price of a possession and fell dead at Peter's feet	Acts 5:10
Sceva	A Jew whose sons tried to cast out evil spirits in name of Jesus	Acts 19:14
Scribes	A group of Jews who questioned the disciples' authority	Acts 4:5; 6:12
Secundus	A Thessalonian who accompanied Paul into Asia	Acts 20:4
Senate of the children of Israel	Older men allowed to join in the Sanhedrin's decisions	Acts 5:21
Sergius Paulus	The proconsul in Cyprus; a prudent man; he wanted to hear the gospel from Paul and Barnabas	Acts 13:7
Silas (Silvanus)	One of the chief men among the Christians; he accompanied Paul on journeys	Acts 15–18; 1Th 1:1; 2Th 1:1; 1Pt 5:12
Simeon (Niger)	A prophet and teacher from Antioch; a prophecy he made was quoted by James	Acts 13:1; 15:14
Simon Zelotes	One of the Twelve Apostles	Acts 1:1
Simon (Magus)	A sorcerer who was baptized and offered to buy the gift of giving the Holy Ghost	Acts 8:9–24
Simon	A tanner at Joppa; he lodged Peter many days	Acts 9:43; 10:6, 17, 32
Sopater	A Christian of Berea who accompanied Paul into Asia	Acts 20:4
Sosipater	A kinsman of Paul who saluted the Roman Saints through Paul's letter	Rom 16:21
Sosthenes	The chief ruler of the synagogue in Corinth; he was beaten by some Greeks for defending Paul	Acts 18:17

Chart 16-1 (6)

Sosthenes	A coworker of Paul's	1Cor 1:1
Stachys	A Christian in Rome; beloved of Paul	Rom 16:9
Stephanas	He and his household were baptized by Paul and devoted themselves to the ministry of the Saints	1Cor 1:16; 16:15, 17
Stephen	One of seven chosen to minister over temporal affairs in Jerusalem; performed miracles; stoned to death	Acts 6:5–15; 7
Syntyche	A Christian at Philippi whom Paul asked to be of the same mind in the Lord with Euodius	Phlp 4:2
Tabitha (Dorcas)	Peter raised her from the dead in Joppa	Acts 9:36–40
Tertius	A Christian who scribed the Epistle of Paul to the Romans	Rom 16:22
Tertullus	An orator who accused Paul before the governor	Acts 24:1–2
Theophilus	The recipient of the Acts of the Apostles	Acts 1:1
Theudas	A false Jewish Messiah; given as an example of a failed revolt	Acts 5:36
Thomas	One of the Twelve Apostles	Acts 1:13
Timon	One of seven chosen to minister over temporal affairs in Jerusalem	Acts 6:5
Timothy (Timotheus)	One of Paul's most trusted and capable assistants	Acts 16:1–3; 1Tm; 2Tm; 2Cor 1:1; Rom 16:21
Titus	Converted by Paul; with Paul on third missionary journey; bearer of letter to Corinthians	1Cor; 2Cor 12:18; Titus 1:4
Town clerk	Appeased the townspeople against Paul and dismissed the assembly in Ephesus	Acts 19:35
Trophimus	A missionary who accompanied Paul into Asia; Paul left him sick at Miletum	Acts 20:4; 2Tm 4:20
Tryphena	A Christian who labored in the Lord	Rom 16:12
Tryphosa	A Christian who labored in the Lord	Rom 16:12
Two soldiers	Peter slept between them in prison	Acts 12:6
Tychicus	A missionary who accompanied Paul to Asia	Acts 20:4; Col 4:7; 2Tm 4:12
Tyrannus	An Ephesian schoolmaster; Paul disputed daily in his school	Acts 19:9
Urbane	A Christian in Rome whom Paul saluted in his letter to the Romans; a helper in Christ	Rom 16:9
Zenas	A Christian lawyer; Paul asked that Zenas be brought to him	Titus 3:13

Chart 16-1 (7)

Places in Acts and the Epistles

Aceldama	The burial ground bought with Judas's betrayal money; the name means "field of blood"	Acts 1:19
Achaia	A Roman province forming the southern part of Greece	Acts 18:12; 27; 19:21; Rom 15:26; 16:5; 1Th 1:7, 8
Adramyttium	A seaport of Mysia in Asia Minor, where Paul took a ship to Rome	Acts 27:2
Adria/Adriatic Sea	The sea between Greece and Italy; Paul was caught in a storm on it	Acts 27:27
Alexandria	The Greek capital of Egypt; center of Jewish activity	Acts 18:24; 27:6; 28:11
Amphipolis	A city in Macedonia through which Paul and Silas passed	Acts 17:1
Antioch	In Syria; the chief meeting point of East and West; center of gentile Christianity; Barnabas preached here	Acts 6:5; 11:19–30; 15:26–35
Antioch	In Pisidia; a Phrygian city in the Roman province of Galatia; Paul and Barnabas were persecuted here	Acts 13:14; 14:19–21; 2Tm 3:11
Antipatris	A city in northern Palestine where soldiers brought Paul by night	Acts 23:31
Apollonia	A city in Macedonia through which Paul and Silas passed	Acts 17:1
Appii forum	A place south of Rome where brethren came to meet Paul and his company	Acts 28:15
Arabia	The northern part of the Arabian peninsula; Paul went here	Gal 1:17
Asia	A Roman province in western Turkey; missionary work was done there by Paul and missionaries	Acts 6:9; 16:6; 19:22–31; 20:4; 1Cor 16:19; 2Tm 1:15
Assos	A seaport of Mysia in Asia Minor where Paul's group sailed to meet him	Acts 20:13
Athens	A city in Greece; Paul preached there on Mars' hill with partial success	Acts 17:15–18:1; 1Th 3:1
Attalia	A seaport near Perga where Paul and Barnabas preached the word	Acts 14:25
Azotus/Ashdod	A Philistine city where Philip was found	Acts 8:40
Babylon	The capital of the Babylonian Empire, located on the Euphrates River, compared metaphorically with Rome	1Pt 5:13
Beautiful	A gate of the temple in Jerusalem where Peter healed	Acts 3:2, 10
Berea	A city in Macedonia to which Paul and Silas fled by night	Acts 17:10
Bithynia	A Roman province in Asia Minor where Paul and Silas wanted to go, but the Spirit forbade; Peter wrote to strangers there	Acts 16:7; 1Pt 1:1
Caesarea	A seaport town in Judea where the Roman procurators resided; Paul visited it many times	Acts 9:30; 18:22; 21:8, 16; 23:23; 25:1–13;
Cappadocia	A Roman province in Asia Minor; Peter wrote to strangers there	Acts 2:9; 1Pt 1:1
Cenchrea	The harbor city for Corinth; Phoebe lived there and Aquila shaved his head there	Acts 18:18; Rom 16:1
Chios	An island near Greece where Paul's group went	Acts 20:15
Cilicia	A Roman province in Asia Minor where Paul was from; large settlements of Jews lived there; Paul visited it many times	Acts 15:23, 41; 22:3; 23:34; Gal 1:21
Clauda	An island close to Crete that Paul's ship encountered	Acts 27:16

Chart 16-2 (1)

Cnidus	A port town in southwestern Asia Minor that Paul and his company sailed near	Acts 27:7
Colosse	A town of Phrygia; Paul greeted the Saints from there	Col 1:2
Coos	An island near Cnidus where Paul's group landed	Acts 21:1
Corinth	The capital of the Roman province of Achaia; Apollos was at Corinth; Paul visited there during his second missionary journey	Acts 18:1; 19:1; 2Cor 1:1; 2Tm 4:20
Crete	An island off the coast of Greece; Paul and his company sailed near Crete; Paul left Titus there to ordain elders	Acts 2:11; 27; Titus 1:5
Cyprus	A large island in the Mediterranean off the coast of Syria; birthplace of Barnabas; Paul and Barnabas visited there	Acts 4:37; 15:39; 21:3–16; 27:4
Cyrene	A town of Libya; large settlement of Jews there; Christian converts from there were active in missionary work in Antioch	Acts 2:10; Acts 6:9; 11:20
Dalmatia	A Roman province west of Macedonia, on the eastern coast of the Adriatic Sea; Titus left Paul to go there	2Tm 4:10
Damascus	A city in Syria; Paul had gone there to bind Christians; Jesus appeared to Paul on the way	Acts 9:2–27; 22:10–11; 26:12–20; 22:26; 2Cor 11:32
Derbe	A southern Galatian town to which Paul and Barnabas fled; Gaius and Timotheus were from there	Acts 14:6, 20; 16:1; 20:4
Egypt	A kingdom in northeast Africa; Egyptians were present on Pentecost	Acts 2:10
Ephesus	The capitol of Roman province of Asia; center for Christian church in Asia Minor; visited by Paul on his second missionary journey, stayed two years on third (4:12) missionary journey, he left because of the silversmiths in town	Acts 18–19; 1Cor 15:32; 2Tm 1:18;
Ethiopia	A country in northeast Africa; an Ethiopian eunuch came to worship in Jerusalem	Acts 8:27
Galatia	A Roman province in Asia Minor; Paul visited there on his second and third missionary journeys	Acts 16:6; 18:23; 2Tm 4:10; 1Cor 16:1; 1Pt 1:1; Gal 1:2
Galilee	A district north of Samaria whence the gospel began; Jesus was seen by Galileans; the Saints there had rest	Acts 1:8; 9:31; 10:37; 13:31
Gaza	A royal Philistine city; Philip journeyed there	Acts 8:26
Greece	The peninsula south of the Balkans; Paul preached the word there	Acts 20:2
Hierapolis	A city in the Roman province of Phrygia, in Asia Minor; Epaphrus had zeal for the people there	Col 4:13
Iconium	A city in Asia Minor; Paul and Barnabas visited there	Acts 14; 16; 2Tm 3:11
Illyricum	A Roman Adriatic province where Paul preached	Rom 15:19
Italy	The homeland of most Roman citizens; Aquila was from there; Paul preached there	Acts 18:2; 27:1, 6; Heb 13:24
Jerusalem	The Holy City for Jews and Christians in central Palestine where the apostles and elders of the church were based; much of the activity of the early church, including Pentecost, took place there	Acts 1:8; 9:26–28; 15:1; 21–22; Gal 1:17–2:1
Joppa	A town on the coast of Palestine having the only majority Jewish population on the coast of Palestine	Acts 9:36–42; 10:5, 8–32; 11:13
Judea	A Roman province in the southern part of western Palestine; there, the people heard that the Gentiles received word of God, apostles witnessed of Christ, and the gospel was published	Acts 1:8; 2:9; 9:31; 10:37; 11:1; 15:1; Gal 1:22; 2Cor 1:16

Chart 16-2 (2)

Laodicea	The chief city of Phrygia in the Roman province of Asia; Paul was concerned about the Saints there	Col 2:1; 4:13–16
Lasea	A city on Crete near which Paul and his company sailed	Acts 27:8
Lycaonia	A Roman province in Asia Minor to which Paul and Barnabas fled	Acts 14:6, 11
Lycia	A Roman province in southeast Asia Minor where Paul and Barnabas got on a ship to sail to Rome	Acts 27:5
Lydda	A city in Judea near Joppa; Paul visited the Saints there	Acts 9:32–38
Lystra	A city in Lycaonia to which Paul and Barnabas fled	Acts 14:6–8; 16:1–2; 2Tm 3:11
Macedonia	A Roman province north of Greece; the first part of Europe where Paul preached the gospel; it was an abode for saints; Philippi was its chief city	Acts 16:9–10; 19:21–29; 20:1–3; Rom 15:26; 1Th 1:7–8; Phlp 4:15
Medes	A country north of Persia; people from Medes were present on the day of Pentecost	Acts 2:9
Melita	An island in the Mediterranean where Paul and his company were shipwrecked	Acts 28:1
Miletum/Miletus	A city in the Roman province of Caria, in southwest Asia Minor; Paul's group came there, where he sent for the elders in Ephesus	Acts 20:15, 17
Mitylene	The major city of the island of Lesbos, off Asia Minor; Paul's group came there	Acts 20:14
Mt. Olivet	A hill to the east of Jerusalem where angels appeared to apostles to declare the resurrection	Acts 1:12
Myra	A city of Lycia, from which Paul's group sailed to Rome	Acts 27:5
Mysia	A Roman province in northeast Asia Minor to which Paul and Silas came	Acts 16:7–8
Nazareth	A city in Galilee where Jesus was from	Acts 22:8
Neapolis	A Macedonian seaport to which Paul and Silas came	Acts 16:11
Nicopolis	A city in Thrace where Paul wintered	Titus 3:12
Pamphylia	A province of Asia Minor where John Mark had departed from the brethren; Paul and Barnabas passed throughout the province	Acts 13:13; 14:24; 15:38; 27:5
Paphos	The capital of Cyprus where missionaries encountered Bar-jesus	Acts 13:6, 13
Patara	A city in Lycia in Asia Minor to which Paul's group came	Acts 21:1
Perga	The capital of Pamphylia where Paul and Barnabas preached the word	Acts 13:13–14; 14:25
Phenice/Phenicia	The coastal region of northern Palestine; Paul and other missionaries passed through there	Acts 11:19; 15:3; 21:2; 27:12
Philippi	A city in Macedonia to which Paul and Silas came; Paul wrote to the Saints there	Acts 16:12; 20:4; 1Th 4:2; Phlp 1:1
Phrygia	A Roman province in central Asia Minor; Paul and Silas went throughout the province	Acts 16:6; 18:23
Pisidia	A Roman province in southern Asia Minor; Paul and Barnabas went throughout the province	Acts 13:14; 14:24
Pontus	A Roman province in northern Asia Minor where Aquila was born; Peter wrote to strangers there	Acts 2:9; 18:2; 1Pt 1:1
Ptolemais	A seaport between Carmel and Tyre; Paul's group came there	Acts 21:7

Chart 16-2 (3)

Puteoli	A seaport in western Italy, south of Rome; Paul and his company came there	Acts 28:13
Rhegium	A port of southern Italy; Paul and his company came there	Acts 28:13
Rhodes	An island in the Mediterranean off Asia Minor to which Paul's group came	Acts 21:1
Rome	The capital of the ancient world; Paul and his company came there; where Paul bore witness of Jesus; Claudius commanded all of the Jews to depart from Rome	Acts 18:2; 19:21; 23:11; 28:14–16; 2Tm 1:17
Salamis	A city on Cyprus where missionaries preached the word	Acts 13:5
Salmone	A promontory on Crete against which Paul and his company sailed	Acts 27:7
Samaria	The central district of Palestine west of the Jordan; Paul, Barnabas, Philip, and other apostles preached the word there, and communities of Saints were set up	Acts 1:8; 8:1, 5, 9, 26; 9:31; 15:3
Samos	An island in the Aegean Sea to which Paul's group came	Acts 20:15
Samothracia	An island in the Aegean Sea to which Paul and Silas came	Acts 16:11
Saron	The area between Joppa and Caesarea; the Saints there turned to the Lord after seeing Aeneas	Acts 9:35
Seleucia	A city in Syria from which the missionaries departed	Acts 13:4
Sidon	A Phoenician city north of Tyre where Paul's ship landed; people from Sidon entreated Herod for favor	Acts 12:20; 27:3
Solomon's Porch	The cloister on the east side of Herod's Temple where the apostles wrought many signs and wonders	Acts 3:11; 5:12
Spain	The land at the western extremity of the Mediterranean sea that Paul visited	Rom 15:24–28
Straight	A street in Damascus where Ananias found Saul	Acts 9:11
Syracuse	A city on Sicily where Paul and his company landed	Acts 28:12
Syria	A Roman province north of Israel where Paul and Silas preached; Paul sailed there with Priscilla and Aquila	Acts 15:23, 41; 18:18; 21:3; Gal 1:21
Tarsus	The capital of the Roman province of Cilicia; Paul's home	Acts 9:11, 30; 11:25; 21:39; 22:3
Three taverns	Located in the Appii forum near Rome, where the brethren came to meet Paul and his company	Acts 28:15
Thessalonica	The capital of Macedonia; Paul and Silas preached there	Acts 17:11–13; 27:2; 2Tm 4:10
Thyatira	A city in the Roman province of Lydia in Asia Minor; home of Lydia	Acts 16:14
Troas	A Roman colony on the seacoast of Phrygia in Asia Minor; Paul and Silas came there while people waited for him	Acts 16:8, 11; 20:6; 2Cor 2:12; 2Tm 4:13
Trogyllium	A coastal town in Ionia in Asia Minor where Paul's group tarried	Acts 20:15
Tyre	A coastal town in Syria where Paul's group landed; the people of Tyre entreated Herod's favor	Acts 12:20; 21:3–7

Chart 16-2 (4)

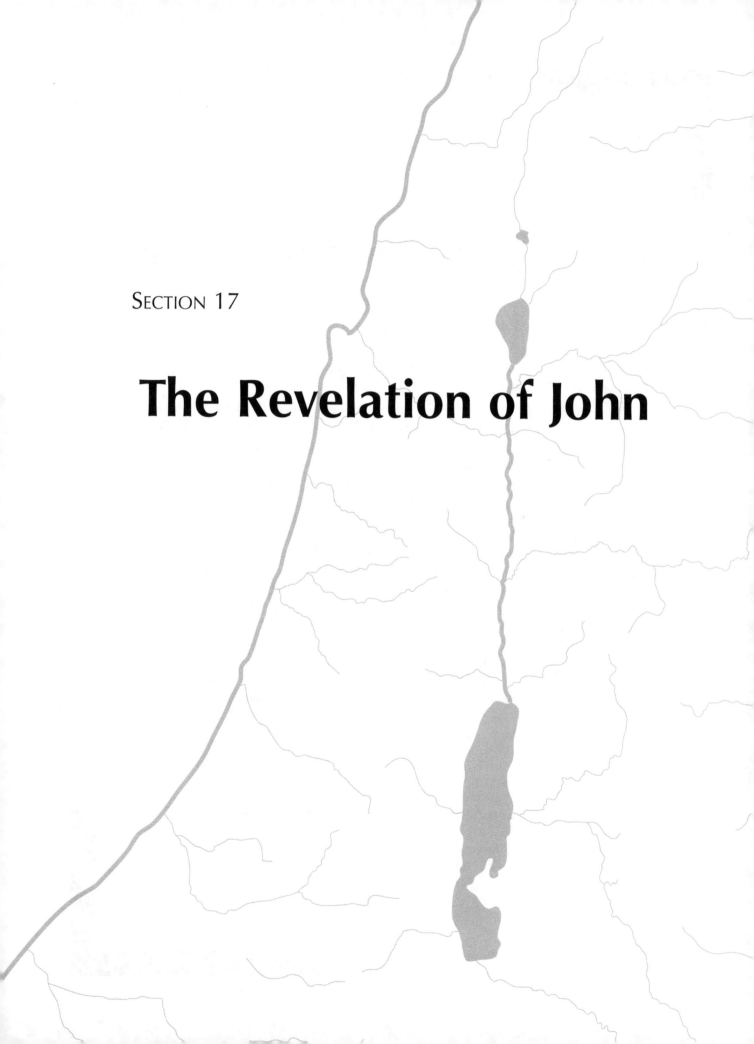

SECTION 17

The Revelation of John

Seven and the Revelation of John

Explanation

The number seven repeatedly occurs in the text of the book of Revelation. To readers living in the first century, an age when the symbolism of numbers was common, the number seven was thought to represent fulfillment or completion. For example, seven days in the week was a complete cycle; the seven wonders of the world embraced the entire scope of human experience; the seven sages were the wisest of all men. In the book of Revelation, it is not improbable that one of the meanings of the repetitive use of the number seven was to assure listeners of the complete and ultimate fulfillment of those prophecies revealed to John. Chart 17-1 lists fourteen occurrences of the number seven in Revelation.

One example of the use of the number seven in the Revelation given to John is the seven churches the text is addressed to. These seven cities in the Roman province of Asia, in modern-day western Turkey, were the most important of western Anatolia. All were near Ephesus, the largest Christian center of Asia, if not of the entire Mediterranean region. From Ephesus, John presided over the church after the death of Peter.

Each branch of the church is criticized for a particular weakness and admonished in various ways. These seven messages at the beginning of the book of Revelation follow a pattern, as chart 17-2 demonstrates. They encourage the early saints to increase in holiness and give promises anticipating the temple themes of the New Jerusalem that appear at the end of the revelation.

Additional information is provided in chart 6-2, "Major Cities of Asia Minor."

References

Colin J. Hemer, *The Letters to the Seven Churches of Asia* (Grand Rapids: Eerdmans, 2001).
W. M. Ramsay, *The Letters to the Seven Churches*, ed. Mark W. Wilson (Peabody, Mass.: Hendrickson, 1994).
Keith Burton, "Numbers," *Eerdmans Dictionary of the Bible*, ed. David Noel Freedman (Grand Rapids: Eerdmans, 2000).

The Number Seven in the Revelation of John

Seven churches in Asia	Rev 1:4, 11
Seven golden candlesticks	1:12–13
Seven stars	1:16
Seven lamps of fire, the seven Spirits of God	4:5
A book with seven seals	5:1, 5
The lamb with seven horns and seven eyes	5:6
Seven angels with seven trumpets	8:2, 6
Seven thunders	10:3–4
Seven thousand men killed by an earthquake	11:13
A dragon with seven heads and seven crowns	12:3
A beast from the sea with seven heads	13:1
Seven angels bringing seven plagues	15:1, 6, 8; 16:1; 21:9
Seven angels and seven golden vials	15:7; 17:1
A woman sitting on a seven-headed beast	17:3, 7
Seven kings	17:10–11

Chart 17-1

The Seven Churches

	DIVINE COMMISSION	RECOGNITION	CRITICISM	ADMONITION
EPHESUS *(Rev 2:1–7)*	Unto the angel of the church of Ephesus write;	I know thy works …	Nevertheless I have somewhat against thee, because thou hast left thy first love.	Remember therefore from whence thou art fallen, and repent, and do the first works …
SMYRNA *(Rev 2:8–11)*	And unto the angel of the church in Smyrna write;	I know thy works …	and I know the blasphemy of them which say they are Jews, and are not …	be thou faithful unto death …
PERGAMOS *(Rev 2:12–17)*	And to the angel of the church in Pergamos write;	I know thy works …	But I have a few things against thee …	Repent …
THYATIRA *(Rev 2:18–29)*	And unto the angel of the church in Thyatira write;	I know thy works …	Notwithstanding I have a few things against thee …	But that which ye have already hold fast till I come.
SARDIS *(Rev 3:1–6)*	And unto the angel of the church in Sardis write;	I know thy works …	Notwithstanding I have a few things against thee …	But that which ye have already hold fast till I come.
PHILADELPHIA *(Rev 3:7–13)*	And to the angel of the church in Philadelphia write;	I know thy works …	Behold, I will make them of the synagogue of Satan, which say they are Jews, and are not …	hold that fast which thou hast, that no man take thy crown.
LAODICEA *(Rev 3:14–21)*	And unto the angel of the church of the Laodiceans write;	I know thy works …	Because thou sayest, I am rich, and increased with goods, and have need of nothing …	Be zealous therefore, and repent …

Chart 17-2 (1)

	DESCRIPTIVE STATEMENT ABOUT JESUS CHRIST	CALL TO HEAR	SACRED PROMISES
EPHESUS (Rev 2:1–7)	These things saith he that holdeth the seven stars in his right hand, who walketh in the midst of the seven golden candlesticks;	He that hath an ear, let him hear what the Spirit saith unto the churches;	To him that overcometh will I give to **eat of the tree of life,** which is in the midst of the paradise of God.
SMYRNA (Rev 2:8–11)	These things saith the first and the last, which was dead, and is alive;	He that hath an ear, let him hear what the Spirit saith unto the churches;	He that overcometh shall **not be hurt of the second death.**
PERGAMOS (Rev 2:12–17)	These things saith he which hath the sharp sword with two edges;	He that hath an ear, let him hear what the Spirit saith unto the churches;	To him that overcometh will I give to eat of the hidden manna, and will give him **a white stone,** and in the stone **a new name** written, which no man knoweth saving he that receiveth it.
THYATIRA (Rev 2:18–29)	These things saith the Son of God, who hath his eyes like unto a flame of fire, and his feet are like fine brass;	He that hath an ear, let him hear what the Spirit saith unto the churches.	And he that overcometh, and keepeth my works unto the end, to him will I give **power over the nations:** And he shall rule them … even as I received of my Father. And I will give him the morning star.
SARDIS (Rev 3:1–6)	These things saith he that hath the seven Spirits of God, and the seven stars;	He that hath an ear, let him hear what the Spirit saith unto the churches.	He that overcometh, the same shall be **clothed in white raiment;** and I will not blot out his name out of the **book of life,** but I will confess his name before my Father, and before his angels.
PHILADELPHIA (Rev 3:7–13)	These things saith he that is holy, he that is true, he that hath the key of David, he that openeth, and no man shutteth; the creation of God; and shutteth and no man openeth;	He that hath an ear, let him hear what the Spirit saith unto the churches.	Him that overcometh will I make **a pillar in the temple of my God,** and he shall go no more out: and I will write upon him the name of my God, and the name of the city of my God, which is new Jerusalem … and I will write upon him my **new name.**
LAODICEA (Rev 3:14–21)	These things saith the Amen, the faithful and true witness, the beginning of the creation of God;	He that hath an ear, let him hear what the Spirit saith unto the churches.	To him that overcometh will I grant to **sit with me in my throne,** even as I also overcame, and am set down with my Father in his throne.

Chart 17-2 (2)

Key Themes Common to Genesis 2–3 and Revelation 2–3

Explanation

The Garden of Eden was a holy, sacred place. In many ways, it was a prototype of the temple built in Jerusalem, where mankind could again seek to stand in the presence of God, as had Adam and Eve. Chart 17-3 identifies seven temple elements in the primal account of Genesis 2–3. For example, the tree of life is present, clothing is given by God, and names are given. Prominent in the book of Revelation is the New Jerusalem, which houses the heavenly temple in which the Lord and his Saints shall dwell (Rev 21). As John begins his book of Revelation, he addresses seven cities of the province of Asia. The church in each of these seven cities is promised a blessing. As shown on the right hand column of chart 17-3, each of these seven blessings relate to the promise of the temple for these congregations of Saints.

References

Based on Richard D. Draper and Donald W. Parry, "Seven Promises to Those Who Overcome: Aspects of Genesis 2–3 in the Seven Letters," in *The Temple in Time and Eternity,* ed. Donald W. Parry and Stephen D. Ricks (Provo, Utah: FARMS, 1999), 121–41.

Gerald N. Lund, "John, Revelations of," *EM,* 2:753–55.

Key Themes Common to Genesis 2–3 and Revelation 2–3

	PRIMAL TEMPLE (EDEN)	TEMPLE OF HEAVEN
1. Tree of Life	Adam and Eve are forbidden to eat the fruit of the tree of life (Gen 2:17).	The elect will partake of the fruit of the tree of life (Rev 2:7).
2. Death	Death enters the world because of the transgression of Adam and Eve (2:17; 3:3).	The elect will not be hurt by the second death (2:11).
3. Bread/Manna	Adam and Eve eat bread by sweat (3:19).	The elect will eat the hidden manna (2:17).
4. Dominion	Adam and Eve replenish and subdue the earth and have dominion over the animal kingdom (1:28).	The elect will have power over the nations (2:26).
5. Sacred Clothing	God made coats of skins, clothing Adam and Eve (3:21).	The elect will be clothed in white raiment (3:5).
6. Expulsion/Return	The Lord "sent [Adam and Eve] forth from the garden" and "drove out" the man and the woman (3:23–24).	The elect will reenter and symbolically become pillars in the temple, possessing eternal temple access (3:12).
7. Receiving Names	God "called their name Adam [humankind] in the day when they were created" (5:2).	The elect of God will receive the name of God and Christ as a new name (3:12).

Chart 17-3

Chart 17-4

Earthly and Heavenly Temples

Explanation

Temple themes are prominent throughout the book of Revelation. Echoes from the Old Testament are conspicuously present in the revelation of John. Chart 17-4 lists these elements, together with their corresponding references, where applicable, from the Hebrew scriptures. It is difficult to understand the book of Revelation without a clear picture of the Jewish Temple. By the time this revelation was given to John, the temple in Jerusalem had been destroyed. Its eternal renewal and perpetual blessings were the hope and joy of the Revelator.

References

Hugh Nibley, *Temple and Cosmos* (Provo, Utah: FARMS, 1992).
Donald W. Parry, ed., *Temples of the Ancient World* (Provo, Utah: FARMS, 1994).

Earthly and Heavenly Temples

Ex 29:39	Slain Lamb of God	Rev 5:6
Ex 26:25–33	Holy of Holies	Rev 4:1–10
1Kgs 7:50	Holy place	Heb 9:11–12, 24
Ex 30:10	Altar of sacrifice	Rev 6:9
Ex 27:1–2; 39:39	Four horns of the altar	Rev 9:13
Ex 30:1–6; 39:38	Altar of incense	Rev 8:3–5
Ex 30:34–36	Incense	Rev 5:8; 8:3–4
Num 7:13–37; 1Kgs 7:50	Incense bowls	Rev 5:8
Ex 25	Ark of the Covenant	Rev 11:19
Heb 4:14	High Priest	Heb 9:6–7
Ps 110:4; Heb 7:17	Priestly officiants	Rev 8:2–5
Ex 19:13, 16, 19	Trumpet	Rev 8:2, 6
Ex 29, 39	Sacral vestments	Rev 4:4; 6:11; 15:6
1Kgs 7:50	Golden censer	Rev 8:3–5
Ex 26:35	Seven-branched lampstand	Rev 1:12
passim	Worshipers	Rev 5:11; 7:9; 19:6
passim	Rites	Rev 4:8–11; 8:2–5; 15:1–8
1 Chr 23:3–6	24 priests or elders	Rev 4:4, 10; 5:8; D&C 77:5
Ex 25:18, 22; 1Kgs 6:23–28	Cherubim	
	Four living creatures	Rev 4:6–8; D&C 77:2–3
Ex 25:22; Lev 16:2	Mercy seat or throne	Ps 11:4; Rev 7:9; 16:17
Heb 9:1–2	"Worldly sanctuary"	
	"temple in heaven"	Rev 7:15; 14:17; 15:5; 16:17
	"True tabernacle"	Heb 8:2

Chart 17-4

Joseph Smith's Explanations
of the Revelation of John

Explanation

In March 1832, in Hiram, Ohio, at the John Johnson home, Joseph Smith was at work on the Joseph Smith Translation of the Bible. In connection with his prophetic calling to understand and elucidate the meanings behind many passages in the Bible, several questions were asked and answers were given about the images and characters who figure in the book of Revelation, chapters 4–11. This information, found in Doctrine and Covenants 77 and 88, is presented conveniently in chart 17-5.

References

Joseph Fielding Smith, ed., *Teachings of the Prophet Joseph Smith* (Salt Lake City: Deseret Book, 1977), 287–94.

"Book of Revelation," *WRC*, 93–94.

Joseph Smith's Explanations
of the Revelation of John

REV	IMAGE	SIGNIFICATION	D&C
4:6	The sea of glass	Immortal sanctified earth	77:1
4:6	Four beasts full of eyes	Figurative expressions of happiness	77:2
4:7	The individual beasts	Exemplars of classes of beings	77:3
4:6	The eyes and the wings	Knowledge and power	77:4
4:4	The 24 elders	Faithful early elders now in paradise	77:5
5:1	The sealed book	God's revealed will for this earth	77:6
5:1	The seven seals	Seven periods of a thousand years	77:7
7:1	The four angels	Angels with the everlasting gospel	77:8
7:2	The other angel	Elias gathering all things together	77:9
7:1	The events of the sixth seal	Events of this 6th thousand years	77:10
7:3	The sealed 144,000	Ordained high priests in all nations	77:11
8:1	The sounding of trumpets	The beginning of the end	77:12
8–9	The sounding of the seven trumpets	Calling forth the dead by groups	88:98–110
9	The events of this chapter	After the opening of the 7th seal	77:13
10:10	The little book that was eaten	Mission of John, Elias, to restore all	77:14
11:3	The two witnesses slain	Two prophets to the Jews	77:15

Chart 17-5

The beginning of the Apostle Paul's epistle to the Colossians, from the fifth- or sixth-century Freer Codex. Courtesy of the Freer Gallery of Art, Smithsonian Institution, Washington, D.C.

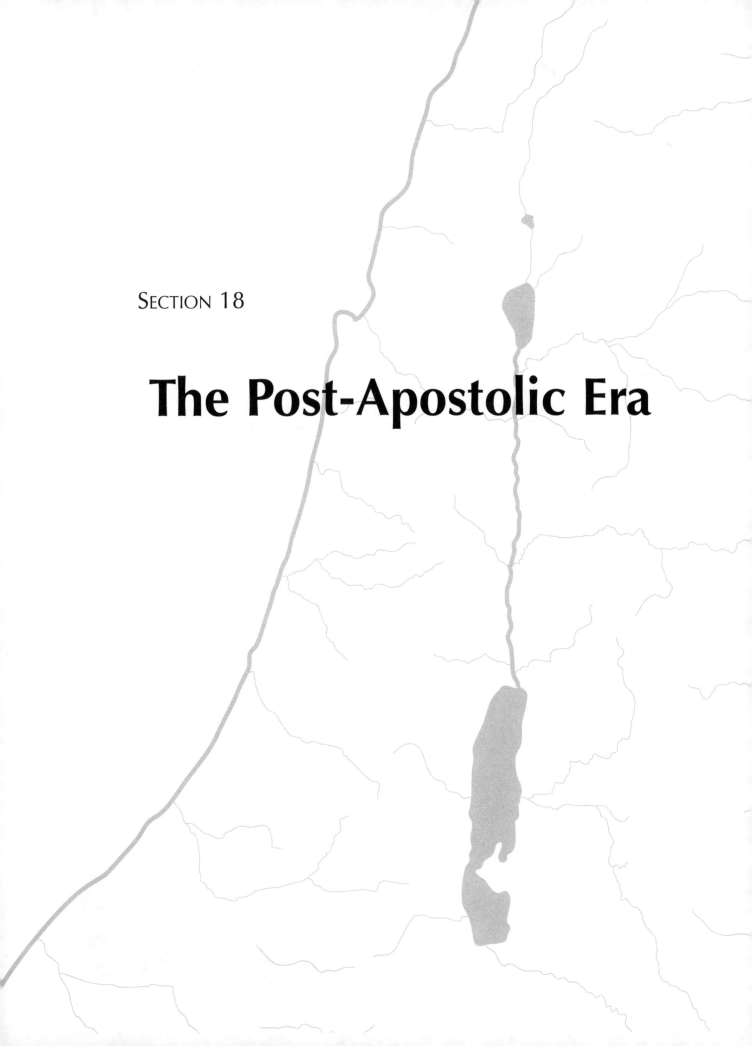

SECTION 18

The Post-Apostolic Era

Chart 18-1

The Apostolic Fathers

Explanation

After the death of the original apostles, other leaders continued to write and teach their followers. Coming from the late first and second centuries A.D., some of the exhortations and doctrinal expositions of these early Christian leaders have survived to the modern era. Because chronologically they follow the apostles, and more importantly because some had been chosen and ordained bishops by men who were apostles, these authors are collectively identified by the term "apostolic fathers."

As chart 18-1 shows, their writings reveal their struggle to maintain doctrinal purity in a rapidly growing church, for which the poor communication opportunities of the time were made more difficult by Jewish and sometimes Greek or Roman opposition to Christianity. The teachings of the apostolic fathers are varied and span a considerable time, but in general they can be categorized as (1) exhortations to Christians to continue righteous behavior, (2) explanations of Christianity to non-Christians, and (3) condemnation of doctrinal corruption and growing apostasy. Several of these writings were actually once included in early versions of the New Testament, but later they were removed by Constantine's bishops.

Reference

J. B. Lightfoot, *The Apostolic Fathers,* ed. M. W. Holmes (Grand Rapids: Baker, 1989).

The Apostolic Fathers

APOSTOLIC FATHER	PROBABLE DATE	INTERESTING CONTENT
Papias	A.D. 60–130	Strong apocalyptic and millennial influence
Barnabas	A.D. 70–135	Testimony of Christ as the Creator, exhortation to the Saints to work the will of God
1 Clement	A.D. 95 or 96	Focuses on peace and concord among the Saints; influenced by popular Greek and Roman philosophies
Ignatius	A.D. c. 110	Exhortation to martyrdom
Polycarp, Letter to the Philippians	early II	Anti-docetist; seeks to prove that Christ came physically rather than in appearance only
Didache	early II	Manual for Christian behavior
Quadratus	A.D. 124–25	Earliest known Christian Apology, addressed to the emperor Hadrian
Hermas (possibly by multiple authors)	A.D. c. 140	A series of five visions showing allegorically the struggle of repentance
2 Clement (probably had a different author than 1 Clement)	A.D. 140–60	Sermon on self-control, repentance, and judgment
Martyrdom of Polycarp	A.D. 155–56	The first martyrdom narrative from the early church
Letter to Diognetus (author unknown)	A.D. c. 200	Early Christian Apology answering pagans' questions about the nature of Christianity

Chart 18-1

Chart 18-2

Timeline of Persecutions

Explanation

As chart 18-2 shows, persecution of Christians was sporadic and varied. The earliest attacks on Christianity, from the time of its inception, came from the Jews who were angry or concerned that some of their number had embraced the new religion. They and other enemies of individual Christians sometimes brought actions against Christians in the courts of Roman magistrates, who were left with the daunting task of determining guilt or innocence. During the first and second centuries, Roman law and the general religious tolerance of Rome actually served to protect Christians from their attackers.

By the end of the second century, a heretical group of Christians in Asia Minor, known as Montanists, had formulated a doctrine that heavenly salvation would be assured, regardless of the worthiness of an individual's life, if that life were given in testimony or "martyrdom" of the Christian message. Montanist practice spread, and the third and fourth centuries witnessed in some quarters aggressive effort by Christians to effect their own death at the hands of either enemies or the Roman government.

Nevertheless, Christian numbers continued to grow so that by the time of Diocletian (A.D. 285) and Constantine (A.D. 315), the Christians comprised a force to be reckoned with. Christians became an important political factor in the dynastic struggles of Roman emperors, and under some rulers in that era they became the objects of actual government persecution for about thirty years.

References

Details and quotes extracted from W. H. C. Frend, *Martyrdom and Persecution in the Early Church* (Oxford: Blackwell, 1965).

For an extensive synopsis of events, see W. H. C. Frend, *The Rise of Christianity* (Philadelphia: Fortress, 1984), 912–85.

Robert C. Patch, "Martyrs," *EM,* 2:862–63.

Timeline of Persecutions

64	Fire in Rome—Peter, perhaps Paul, and 977 others were reportedly executed during Nero's reign
70	Jewish War—Christians fled to Pella instead of helping the Jews
70	Suspicion of Jews increased—this fear extended to Christians, who were seen as a Jewish sect
90	The Christian church had been completely severed from Judaism—"Most of the Christian persecutions of this time appear to be the direct result of Jewish hostility"
112	The Emperor Trajan ordered that Christians not be sought out
115	Second Jewish Revolt (Dispersion of Jews) (Christians showed their support of Rome)
117	The Jewish Revolt crushed under Trajan and Hadrian
124 or 125	The emperor Hadrian reinforced Trajan's ruling that Christians not be sought out. Under Hadrian, a distinction was made between Christians and Jews. Those who prosecuted Christians unsuccessfully received the penalty they sought for the Christians. (Hadrianic Rescript)
132	Third Jewish Revolt (Christians showed their support of Rome)
135	Jewish revolt crushed; Hadrian put a statue of a pig on the Bethlehem gate of Jerusalem. End of Judea, creation of Palestine
135	Mob violence against Christians forbidden through 165; Hadrian's rescript was later reaffirmed by M. Aurelius
152–65	Denunciations of Christians by private citizens for personal motives
160	Clash begins within the Church between pro-voluntary martyrdom and anti-voluntary martyrdom groups
164–68	Scattered martyrdoms in Asia
165	Great plague in Asia (believed to be due to Christian atheism), M. Aurelius sent new policies to Asia, making it easier to denounce Christians
165–80	Procedures laid down by Trajan and Hadrian whittled away and Christians began to be sought out (mostly in the provinces); rise in numbers of voluntary martyrs
165	Martyrdom of Polycarp by Greeks and Jews
170–80	Christian apologist Tatian promotes contempt of pagan society, already prevalent in Christian apocalyptic thought
172	Montanus began a pro-martyrdom sect of Christianity
177	48 martyrs in Lugdunum (Lyons), most voluntary

Chart 18-2 (1)

180	Period of peace for the Christians
180–92	Commodus's mistress, Marcia, was friendly toward the Christians and helped them
180–92	Reign of Commodus, peace for the Christians
190–240	Growth of Christianity and theological divisions between the East and West
c. 190	Irenaeus wrote *Adversus Haereses,* in which he claimed that the Roman "secular rule was also divine in character"
198–99	War between Rome and Parthia; Jewish Rebellion
200	"Outbreak of apocalyptic exultation" among Christians in Asia and Syria
202	"Severus' Edict prohibits conversion to Judaism or Christianity in response to the Jewish Rebellion of 198–199"
202–3	Outbreak of pro-martyrdom sentiment in Northern Africa
203	Perpetua and five others martyred in Carthage; "Apart from the years 202–203, and the situation which had developed between the Christians and pagans in Carthage, the reigns of Septimus Severus and his son Caracalla (211–217) were tolerant."
212	The *Constitutio Antoniniana* gave citizenship to nearly all of the freemen in the Roman Empire, making them responsible for worshiping the Roman gods.
217–18	Reign of Macrinus, no persecution
218–22	Reign of Heliogabalus, no persecution
222	Callistus, Bishop of Rome, and his presbyters were killed by a Roman mob
222–35	Reign of Alexander Severus, no persecution; "golden age of the pre-Constantinian Church"
235	Despite the ceaseless attacks by Jews, Christianity became one of the main religions of the Roman Empire
235	Maximin began his reign by executing Christian members of Alexander Severus's court and ordering the deaths of Christian leaders to restrict the growth of Christianity
235–37	Reign of Maximin, persecution against leaders, but extended to others through mob violence
c. 236	Earthquakes in Cappadocia were seen as a divine sign against Christians, causing local persecutions

Chart 18-2 (2)

248	Pogrom against Christians in Alexandria
249–51	Reign of Decius
249	Higher members of Christian clergy were arrested
250	Edict of Decius required sacrifice from all Christians in the Empire, martyrdoms over the whole empire numbered in the hundreds
251	Decius died; "within a year … the Christian message was being proclaimed openly once more"
252	Plagues in the Empire for the next 15 years caused lapsed Christians to return and numbers of Christians to boom
257	First Edict of Valerian orders bishops and priests to worship Roman gods
258	Second Edict of Valerian put to death bishops and priests who disobeyed the first edict and confiscated Christian property; approximately 300 martyrs
260–68	Reign of Gallienus, no persecution, confiscated property was returned and Christianity was granted cemeteries and places of worship
260–303	No persecution, Christianity spread throughout the Roman Empire
275	Aurelian ordered proscriptions of Christians, but they were never carried out
303	Diocletian's First Edict, beginning the Great Persecution, destroyed churches and scriptures and imprisoned church leaders. Urged by Galerius, the Second and Third Edicts expanded the first one
304	Diocletian's Fourth Edict ordered general sacrifice and the death of noncompliant Christians
305	Galerius gained control of the Roman Empire and enforced anti-Christian edicts
306–10	Persecutions continued, although many of the martyrdoms were provoked by volunteer martyrs
311	Galerius became fatally ill and rescinded all edicts against Christians; oracles spoke out against this, instigating a three-month long "savage outburst" of martyrdoms
312	Battle of Milvian Bridge, Constantine gained control of the Roman Empire. No further persecutions
13 June, 313	Constantine issued an edict granting religious freedom to everyone

Chart 18-2 (3)

Earliest Important
Greek Papyri

Explanation

All the books of the New Testament were originally written in Greek. Other sources, written and oral, certainly stood behind these final literary products, but in the end the good news of the ministry of Jesus Christ and his apostles was disseminated to the world in the common language of the day throughout the Roman Empire, namely Greek. Over 100 fragments of individual gospels or letters have been found by archaeologists or archivists that date before A.D. 325. Chart 18-3 lists the most famous of these early texts, which were written on papyrus. Some contain only a few words or verses, but a few are quite extensive and extremely precious.

References

Harry Y. Bramble, "Canon: New Testament," *ABD,* 1:852–61.

Bruce M. Metzger, *The Text of the New Testament* (New York: Oxford University Press, 1992).

Earliest Important Greek Papyri

Papyrus Number	Date	Present Location	Contents
𝔓52	early II	Manchester, John Rylands Library	Jn 18:31–33, 37–38
𝔓46	late II	Ann Arbor, University of Michigan; Dublin, Chester Beatty Library	Large Parts of Rom, 1Cor; 2Cor; Gal; Eph; Phlp; Col; 1Th; Heb
𝔓87	II or III	Cologny, Universität zu Köln, Institut für Altertumskunde	Phlmn 1:13–15, 24–25
𝔓104	II	Oxford, Ashmolean Museum	Mt 21:34–37, 43, 45
𝔓4	II or III	Paris, Bibliothèque Nationale	Parts of Lk 1–6
𝔓64 [67]	late II	Oxford, Magdalen College Library [Barcelona, Fundación San Lucas Evangelista]	Parts of Mt 26 [Parts of Mt 3; 5]
𝔓66	late II	Cologny, Universität zu Köln, Institut für Altertumskunde; Cologny-Geneva, Bibliotheca Bodmeriana	Much of Jn 1:1–7:52; 8:12–21:17
𝔓98	II	Cairo, Institut Français d'Archaeologie Orientale	Rev 1:13–20; 2:1
𝔓77	late II	Oxford, Ashmolean Museum	Mt 23:30–39
𝔓90	late II	Oxford, Ashmolean Museum	Jn 18:36–19:7
𝔓103	late II	Oxford, Ashmolean Museum	Mt 13:55–57; 14:3–5
𝔓32	late II	Manchester, John Rylands Library	Titus 1:11–15; 2:3–8
𝔓75	II or III	Cologny-Geneva, Bibliotheca Bodmeriana	Large parts of Lk 3–7; 9–18; 22–24; and Jn 1:1–15:10

Earliest Important Greek Parchments

Explanation

Chart 18-4 lists the main early texts that were written on parchment. When Christianity became the state religion, more money was available to produce copies of these books on the more expensive vellum. Parchments 1 (Sinaticus) and 3 (Vaticanus) are especially significant, as they contain virtually all of the New Testament (and other early Christian books). The textual evidence for the New Testament is earlier and more extensive than for most works from antiquity.

Reference

Bruce M. Metzger, *The Canon of the New Testament: Its Origin, Development, and Significance* (Oxford: Oxford University Press, 1987).

Earliest Important Greek Parchments

Number	Date	Present Location	Contents
189	II/III	Berlin, Staatliche Museen	Acts 5:3–21
212	III	New Haven, Yale University Library	Mt 27:56–57; Mk 15:40–42; Lk 23:49–51, 54; Jn 19:38
162	III/IV	New York, Metropolitan Museum of Art	Jn 2:11–22
171	III/IV	Florence, Biblioteca Medicea Laurenziana	Mt 10:17–23, 25–32; Lk 22:44–50, 52–56, 61, 63–64
220	III/IV	Oslo, Norway; London, The Schøyen Collection	Rom 4:23–5:3, 8–13
232	III/IV	Oxford, Ashmolean Museum	2 Jn 1:1–9
1	IV	London, British Museum	All New Testament
3	IV	Rome, Vatican Library	All NT except (1Tm, 2Tm, Titus, Phlmn, Rev)
58	IV	Vienna, Österreiches National Bibliothek	Mt 18:18–19, 22–23, 25–26, 28–29
169	IV	Princeton, Theological Seminary	Rev 3:19–4:3
185	IV	Vienna, Österreiches National Bibliothek	1Cor 2:5–6, 9, 13; 3:2–3
188	IV	Berlin, Staatliche Museen	Mk 11:11–17
206	IV	Dayton, United Theological Seminary	1Pt 5:5–13
207	IV	Florence, Biblioteca Medicea Laurenziana	Rev 9:2–15
221	IV	Vienna, Österreiches National Bibliothek	Rom 5:16–17, 19; 5:21–6:3
228	IV	Vienna, Österreiches National Bibliothek	Heb 12:19–21, 23–25
230	IV	Florence, Biblioteca Medicea Laurenziana	Eph 6:11–12
231	IV	Oxford, Bodleian Library	Mt 26:75–27:1, 3–4
242	IV	Cairo, Museum of Antiquities or Egyptian Museum	Mt 8:25–9:2; 13:32–38, 40–46
258	IV	London?	Jn 10:25–26, 40

Chart 18-4

Chart 18-5

The Canonization
of the Books of the New Testament

Explanation

At first, the books of the New Testament were individually composed and circulated. Only later were they collected and combined together. It is unknown when or where this process of collection began. Gradually, a great controversy arose as to which books should be included in the New Testament and which omitted. The standard for inclusion became the authority of the author and the authenticity of the authorship. The issue came to a head in the fourth century when prominent churchmen, entire churches, or general councils of Christians held differing opinions about what books should continue to comprise the New Testament. Chart 18-5 lists gospel writings known to have been included by various people as accepted books. Many books received widespread approval; others were accepted only in certain areas. Those meeting the criteria of particular councils or churchmen came to constitute the "canon" or "rod of scriptural integrity." The books that survived the critics of the fourth century in a canonized state are today's New Testament.

References

Lee M. McDonald, *The Formation of the Christian Biblical Canon* (Peabody, Mass.: Hendrickson, 1995).

Harry Y. Bramble, "Canon: New Testament," *ABD*, 1:852–61.

Victor L. Ludlow, "Bible," *EM*, 1:104–8.

The Canonization
of the Books of the New Testament

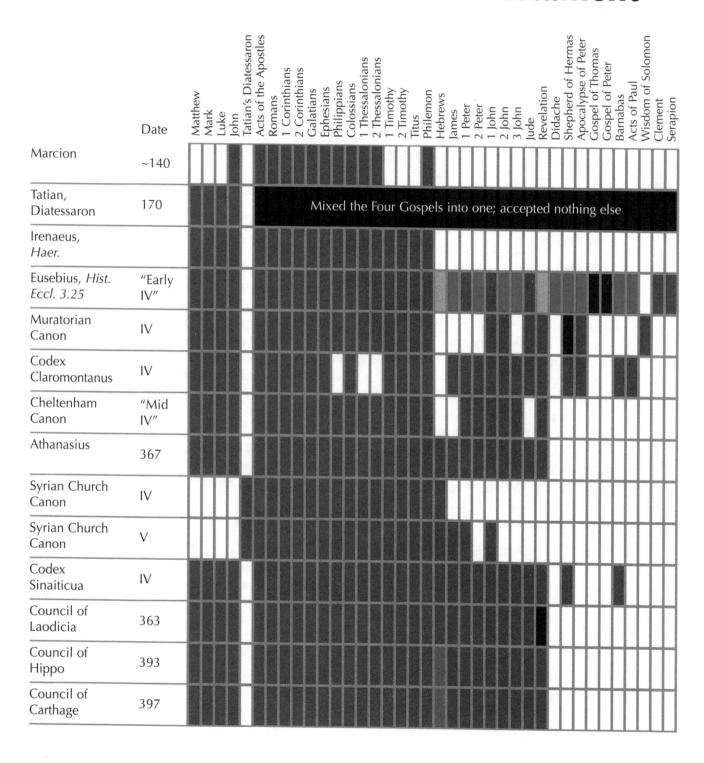

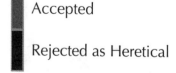

Chart 18-5

Renderings of the New Testament
Leading up to the King James Version

Explanation

The New Testament was originally written in Greek. Those original Greek texts of the individual books of the New Testament were combined into Greek codices of the entire New Testament. From these books, a myriad of manuscripts were produced over the centuries, many of which have survived. Through a long and complicated process of transmission and translation more than fifteen centuries long, the King James Version was produced.

The schematic in chart 18-6 depicts this process, including the translation or "rendering" from the original Greek into Old Latin translations, which became the basis of Jerome's Latin Vulgate translation. The latter remained the standard version of the New Testament in European countries for a millennium.

The famous classical scholar Erasmus produced a critical Greek text during the Renaissance. Martin Luther used Erasmus's Greek edition to translate the New Testament into German, and Tyndale made use of the same for his English Bible. The King James Version followed very closely three previous English renderings which were based not only on Tyndale's earlier English Bible, but also directly on the Latin Vulgate.

References

Philip W. Comfort, ed., *The Origin of the Bible* (Wheaton, Ill.: Tyndale House, 1992).

Alister McGrath, *In the Beginning: The Story of the King James Bible* (London: Hodder & Stoughton, 2001).

Renderings of the New Testament
Leading up to the King James Version

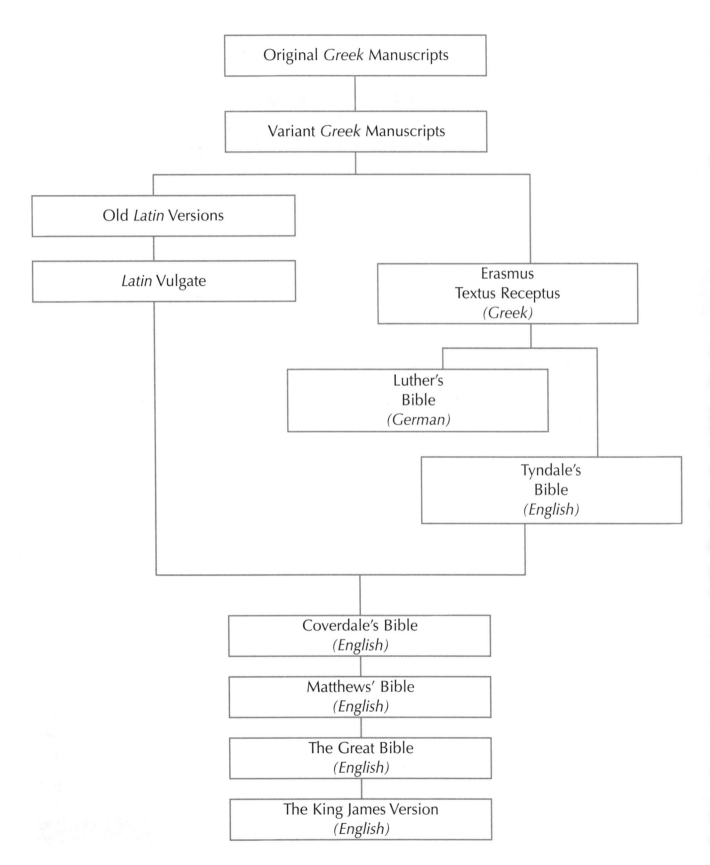

Chart 18-6

Chart 18-7

Biblical Precreedal
Statements of Belief

Explanation

Christians have always declared their faith in Jesus Christ. Nathanael, Peter, Thomas, the eunuch baptized by Philip, Paul, and John each bear testimony that Jesus is the Christ. These statements begin as early individual declarations, "I believe that Jesus Christ is the Son of God," but soon become group affirmations, "We know that the Son of God is come." Each of these testimonies is unique. They are spontaneous utterances of the Spirit; their wording is flexibly formulated. Out of these biblical, precreedal expressions would eventually grow the much more formal and elaborate creeds of Christianity. But originally, these statements were simple, pure, plain, and precious.

Biblical Precreedal Statements of Belief

NATHANAEL	Thou art the Son of God; thou art the King of Israel	Jn 1:49
PETER	Thou art the Christ, the Son of the living God	Mt 16:16
	And we believe and are sure that thou art that Christ, the Son of the living God	Jn 6:69
THOMAS	My Lord and my God	Jn 20:28
A EUNUCH	I believe that Jesus Christ is the Son of God	Acts 8:37
PAUL	God was manifest in the flesh, justified in the Spirit, seen of angels, preached unto the Gentiles,… believed on in the world, received up into glory	1Tm 3:16
	[We believe that] by him were all things created … he is the head of the body, the church … For it pleased the Father that in him should all fullness dwell; and, having made peace through the blood of his cross, by him to reconcile all things unto himself	Col 1:16–20
JOHN	We know that we are of God, and the whole world lieth in wickedness. And we know that the Son of God is come, and hath given us an understanding, that we may know him that is true, and we are in him that is true, even in his Son Jesus Christ. This is the true God, and eternal life	1Jn 5:19–20

Chart 18-7

Chart 18-8

The Post-Apostolic Creeds

Explanation

Beginning around the third century, Christians began to espouse and require of each other adherence to particular creeds demonstrating and propagating their belief in Jesus Christ. Such creeds were needed because many people were teaching a wide range of doctrines about Jesus. Some of these heretical groups, indeed, were way off the center mark. The creedal cure, however, went too far in the opposite direction, taking the liberty of the pure and simple spirit that had prevailed in the apostolic era (see chart 18-7) and prescribing extensive definitions and boundaries on the faithful. As chart 18-8 shows, this difficulty became increasingly severe. What began as fairly straightforward, biblically based declarations in the Old Roman, Apostles', and Caesarean Creeds, became more and more arcane, philosophical, and delimiting as the fourth and fifth centuries played themselves out. This process of accretion, adding phrase on phrase, from creed to creed, is traced on chart 18-8. Most problematic, ornate, and obscure, the so-called Athanasian Creed is of unknown authorship, was never adopted by a church council, and probably dates to the seventh or eighth century.

References

J. N. D. Kelly, *Early Christian Creeds* (New York: McKay, 1972).
Gary P. Gillum, "Creeds," *EM*, 1:343.
Bijan Nasser-Faili, "Early Christian Creeds and LDS Doctrine," *Journal of Latter Day Saint History* 12 (2000): 12–23.

The Post-Apostolic Creeds

THE EARLIER CREEDS COMMENCE
ON THE FOLLOWING PAGES
(2nd–5th centuries) ⟶

THE ATHANASIAN CREED

(date uncertain, c. 7th century)

Whosoever will be saved: before all things it is necessary that he hold the Catholic Faith: Which Faith except every one do keep whole and undefiled: without doubt he shall perish everlastingly.

And the Catholic Faith is this: That we worship one God in Trinity, and Trinity in Unity; Neither confounding the Persons: nor dividing the Substance [Essence].

For there is one Person of the Father: another of the Son: and another of the Holy Ghost. But the Godhead of the Father, of the Son, and of the Holy Ghost, is all one: the Glory equal, the Majesty coeternal.

Such as the Father is: such is the Son: and such is the Holy Ghost.

The Father uncreate [uncreated]:
the Son uncreate [uncreated]:
and the Holy Ghost uncreate [uncreated].

The Father incomprehensible [unlimited]:
the Son incomprehensible [unlimited]:
and the Holy Ghost incomprehensible [unlimited, or infinite].

The Father eternal: the Son eternal: and the Holy Ghost eternal.
And yet they are not three eternals, but one eternal.

As also there are not three uncreated: nor three incomprehensibles [infinites], but one uncreated: and one incomprehensible [infinite].

So likewise the Father is Almighty: the Son Almighty: and the Holy Ghost Almighty. And yet they are three Almighties: but one Almighty.

So the Father is God: the Son is God: and the Holy Ghost is God.
And yet they are not three Gods: but one God.

So likewise the Father is Lord: the Son Lord: and the Holy Ghost Lord.
And yet not three Lords: but one Lord.

For like as we are compelled by the Christian verity: to acknowledge every Person by himself to be God and Lord: So are we forbidden by the Catholic Religion: to say, There be [are] three Gods, or three Lords.

The Father is made of none: neither created, nor begotten.

The Son is of the Father alone: not made, nor created: but begotten.

The Holy Ghost is of the Father and of the Son:
neither made, nor created, nor begotten: but proceeding.

So there is one Father, not three Fathers:
one Son, not three Sons:
one Holy Ghost, not three Holy Ghosts.

And in this Trinity none is afore, or after another:
none is greater, or less than another
[there is nothing before, or after: nothing greater or less].

But the whole three Persons are coeternal, and coequal.

So that in all things, as aforesaid:
the Unity in Trinity, and the Trinity in Unity, is to be worshiped.

He therefore that will be saved, must [let him] thus think of the Trinity.

Furthermore it is necessary to everlasting salvation: that he also believe rightly [faithfully] the Incarnation of our Lord Jesus Christ.

[continued on 18-8 (3)]

Chart 18-8 (1)

OLD ROMAN AND AFRICAN FORM OF THE APOSTLES' CREED (2nd or 3rd century)	THE APOSTLES' CREED (2nd or 3rd century)	THE CAESAREAN CREED according to Eusebius, (A.D. 325)	AN OLD ITALIAN FORM OF THE APOSTLES' CREED (about A.D. 350)
I believe in God the Father Almighty.	I believe in God the Father Almighty; Maker of heaven and earth.	We believe in one God the Father Almighty, Maker of all things visible and invisible;	We believe in God the Father Almighty, Ruler and Creator of all ages and creatures.
And in Jesus Christ his only begotten Son our Lord,	And in Jesus Christ his only [begotten] Son our Lord;	And in one Lord Jesus Christ, the Word of God, God of God, Light of Light, Life of Life, the only-begotten Son, the first-born of every creature, begotten of God the Father before all ages, by whom also all things were made; who for our salvation was made flesh and made his home among men;	And in Jesus Christ, his only Son, our Lord;
who was born of the Holy Ghost and the Virgin Mary;	who was conceived by the Holy Ghost, born of the Virgin Mary;		who was born of the Holy Ghost and from the Virgin Mary;
crucified under Pontius Pilate, and buried; the third day he rose from the dead;	suffered under Pontius Pilate, was crucified, dead, and buried; he descended into hell [Hades, spirit-world]; the third day he rose from the dead;	and suffered; and rose on the third day;	who was crucified under Pontius Pilate, and buried; on the third day he rose from the dead;
he ascended into heaven, and sitteth at the right hand of the Father;	he ascended into heaven; and sitteth at the right hand of God the Father Almighty;	and ascended to the Father;	ascended into the heavens; sitteth on the right hand of God the Father;
from thence he shall come to judge the quick and the dead.	from thence he shall come to judge the quick and the dead.	and will come again in glory, to judge the quick and the dead.	from thence he shall come to judge the quick and the dead.
And in the Holy Ghost;	I believe in the Holy Ghost;	We believe also in one Holy Ghost.	And in the Holy Ghost;
the holy Church;	the holy Catholic Church; the communion of saints;		and the holy Catholic Church;
the forgiveness of sins;	the forgiveness of sins;		the remission of sins;
the resurrection of the body; [the life everlasting].	the resurrection of the body [flesh]; and the life everlasting. Amen.		the resurrection of the flesh.

Chart 18-8 (2)

THE NICEAN CREED
(As received from the Protestant Churches)
→ (A.D. 325/381)──────

I believe in one God the Father Almighty;

Maker of heaven and earth, and of all things visible and invisible.

And in one Lord Jesus Christ, the only-begotten Son of God,

begotten of the Father before all worlds [God of God], Light of Light, very God of very God, begotten, not made, being of one substance [essence] with the Father; by whom all things were made; who, for us men and for our salvation, came down from heaven,

and was incarnate by the Holy Ghost of the Virgin Mary, and was made man;

and was crucified also for us under Pontius Pilate; he suffered and was buried; and the third day he rose again, according to the Scriptures;

and ascended into heaven, and sitteth on the right hand of the Father;

and he shall come again, with glory, to judge both the quick and the dead; whose kingdom shall have no end.

And [I believe] in the Holy Ghost, the Lord and Giver of Life; who proceedeth from the Father [and the Son]; who with the Father and the Son together is worshiped and glorified; who spake by the Prophets.

And [I believe] one Holy Catholic and Apostolic Church.

I acknowledge one Baptism for the remission of sins;

and I look for the resurrection of the dead, and the life of the world to come. Amen.

THE SYMBOL OF CHALCEDON
→ (A.D. 451) ──────────

We, then, following the holy Fathers, all with one consent, teach men to confess one and the same Son, our Lord Jesus Christ, the same perfect in Godhead and also perfect in manhood; truly God and truly man, of a reasonable [rational] soul and body; consubstantial [coessential] with the Father according to the Godhead, and consubstantial with us according to the Manhood; in all things like unto us, without sin; begotten before all ages of the Father according to the Godhead, and in these latter days, for us and for our salvation,

born of the Virgin Mary, the Mother of God, according to the Manhood;

one and the same Christ, Son, Lord, Only-begotten, to be acknowledged in two natures, inconfusedly, unchangeably, indivisibly, inseparably; the distinction of natures being by no means taken away by the union, but rather the property of each nature being preserved, and concurring in one Person and one Subsistence, not parted or divided into two persons, but one and the same Son, and only begotten, God the Word, the Lord Jesus Christ; as the prophets from the beginning [have declared] concerning him, and the Lord Jesus Christ himself has taught us, and the Creed of the holy Fathers has handed down to us.

THE ATHANANASIAN CREED
[continued from 18-8 (1)]
→ (date uncertain, c. 7th century) ──────

For the right Faith is, that we believe and confess: that our Lord Jesus Christ, the Son of God, is God and Man;

God, of the Substance [Essence] of the Father: begotten before the worlds: and Man, of the Substance [Essence] of his Mother, born in the world.

Perfect God: and perfect Man, of a reasonable soul and human flesh subsisting.

Equal to the Father, as touching his Godhead: and inferior to the Father as touching his Manhood.

Who although he be [is] God and Man; yet he is not two, but one Christ.

One; not by conversion of the Godhead into flesh: but by taking [assumption] of the Manhood into God.

One altogether; not by confusion of Substance [Essence]: but by unity of Person.

For as the reasonable soul and flesh is one man: so God and Man is one Christ;

Who suffered for our salvation: descended into hell [Hades, spirit-world]: rose again the third day from the dead.

He ascended into heaven, he sitteth on the right hand of the Father God [God the Father] Almighty.

From whence [thence] he shall come to judge the quick and the dead.

At whose coming all men shall rise again with their bodies;

And shall give account for their own works.

And they that have done good shall go into life everlasting: and they that have done evil, into everlasting fire.

This is the Catholic Faith: which except a man believe faithfully [truly and firmly], he can not be saved.

Chart 18-8 (3)

Missing Scriptures

Explanation

In the New Testament itself, other writings of the apostles are mentioned that have not survived. For example, lost letters of Paul to the Saints in Laodicea, Corinth, Philippi, and Ephesus are alluded to. Another epistle of Jude is also known to have once existed.

Based on Luke's statement that "many have taken in hand to set forth in order a declaration" of the life of Jesus (Lk 1:1) and other data, scholars have toiled to reconstruct these early records of the words and deeds of Jesus. Scattered among many early Christian writings are words or phrases attributed to Jesus. If these original writings had survived in full, they would have added much to our knowledge of the history of Jesus and his apostles. The restoration of all things looks forward to the time when these lost scriptures will once again be revealed.

References

Richard Lloyd Anderson, "Missing Scriptures of New Testament Times," *Instructor,* October 1968, 419.

Keith Marston, *Missionary Pal: Reference Guide for Missionaries and Teachers* (Salt Lake City: Publishers, 1987), 165.

Stephen E. Robinson, "The Noncanonical Sayings of Jesus," *BYU Studies* 36/2 (1997): 74–92.

Robert A. Cloward, "Scripture: Forthcoming," *EM,* 1282–83.

Missing Scriptures

FROM CHRIST'S MINISTRY

OTHER GOSPELS OR RECORDS: "Many" authors compiled Jesus' history (Lk 1:1–4).

MIRACLES: These are often partially described or not even recorded (Mk 1:32–34; Jn 20:30–31).

TEACHINGS: Some of Jesus' known sayings are not in the Gospels (Acts 20:35).

DEEDS: Only a fraction of his life is reported in the Gospels (Jn 21:25).

FROM THE MINISTRY OF THE APOSTLES

EARLY LETTERS OF PAUL: None preserved from the first seventeen years of Paul's ministry (Compare 2Th 3:17).

LETTER FROM LAODICEA: "Likewise read the epistle from Laodicea" (Col 4:16).

LOST CORINTHIAN LETTER: "I wrote unto you in an epistle not to company with fornicators" (1Cor 5:9).

LOST PHILIPPIAN LETTERS: Bishop Polycarp alludes to more than one Philippian letter (Polycarp to Philippians 3:1).

ANOTHER EPISTLE OF PAUL TO THE EPHESIANS: "How that by revelation he made known unto me the mystery, as I wrote afore in a few words" (Eph 3:3–4).

FORMER EPISTLE OF JUDE: "Beloved, when I gave all diligence to write unto you" (Jude 1:3).

PAUL: No record of the close of his ministry exists.

OTHER APOSTLES: There is no connected record of their ministries.

Chart 18-9

New Testament Apocrypha

Explanation

The word *apocrypha* derives from a Greek word meaning "hidden away." It was originally used to refer to books kept hidden away since they had not been canonized. Many of these books claim to have been written by the apostles. It is not impossible that some of them derive, at least in part, from actual apostolic writings. Some apocryphal books exist today; others remain lost. Some existing books have been available since ancient times; others have been rediscovered during the past century as a result of archaeological research.

Chart 18-10 groups these apocryphal books in a wide variety of genres including gospels, apocalyptic writings (book of Revelation), treatises, letters, acts, and liturgies. The chart gives the titles of these apocryphal writings, known in whole or by fragmentary remains, or simply mentioned in other writings. These writings are useful in tracing the change and development of various ideas in the early centuries of Christianity. If studied carefully and with enlightenment of the Spirit, New Testament apocryphal writings, like the Old Testament Apocrypha, can be beneficial, although "there are many things contained therein that are not true, which are interpolations by the hands of men" (D&C 91:2).

References

Edgar Hennecke, *New Testament Apocrypha* (Philadelphia: Westminster, 1963).
Stephen J. Patterson, "Apocrypha, New Testament," *ABD*, 1:94–97.
C. Wilfred Griggs, "Apocrypha and Pseudepigrapha," *EM*, 1:55–56.

New Testament Apocrypha

1. GOSPELS AND RELATED FORMS

Narrative Gospels

The Gospel of the Ebionites

The Gospel of the Hebrews

The Gospel of the Nazoreans

The Gospel of Nicodemus (The Acts of Pilate)

The Gospel of Peter

The Infancy Gospel of Thomas

P. Egerton 2 (a fragment of an unknown narrative gospel)

P. Oxy 840 (a fragment of an unknown narrative gospel)

The Protevangelium of James

Revelation Dialogues and Discourses

The (First) Apocalypse of James

The (Second) Apocalypse of James

The Apocryphon of James (a revelation discourse cast in an epistolary framework)

The Apocryphon of John

The Book of Thomas the Contender

The Dialogue of the Savior

The Gospel of Mary

The Gospel of Philip

The Epistula Apostolorum (a revelation discourse cast in an epistolary framework)

The Gospel of the Egyptians (distinct from the Coptic Gospel of the Egyptians)

The Letter of Peter to Philip (a revelation discourse cast in an epistolary framework)

Pistis Sophia

The Questions of Mary

The Questions of Bartholomew

The Second Treatise of the Great Seth

The Sophia of Jesus Christ

The Two Books of Jeu

Bodlian Copt. MS d54 (a fragmentary dialogue between Jesus and John)

Chart 18-10 (1)

Sayings Gospels and Collections

The Gospel of Thomas

The Synoptic Sayings Source

The Teachings of Silvanus

2. TREATISES

On the Origin of the World

The (Coptic) Gospel of the Egyptians

The Gospel of Truth

The Hypostasis of the Archons

The Treatise on Resurrection (a treatise cast in epistolary form)

The Tripartite Tractate

3. LETTERS

The Abgar Legend

The Correspondence between Paul and Seneca

The Epistle of Pseudo-Titus

Paul's Letter to the Laodiceans

4. APOCALYPSES

The (Coptic) Apocalypse of Elijah

The (Arabic) Apocalypse of Peter

The (Coptic) Apocalypse of Peter

The (Greek/Ethiopic) Apocalypse of Peter

The (Coptic) Apocalypse of Paul

The (Latin) Apocalypse of Paul

The Apocalypse of Sophonias

The Apocalypse of Thomas

The Ascension of Isaiah (chap. 6–11)

The Christian Sibyllines

The Concept of Our Great Power

The Book of Elchasai

V and VI Ezra

Melchizidek

The Mysteries of St. John the Apostle and the Holy Virgin

Chart 18-10 (2)

5. ACTS

The Acts of Andrew

The Acts of Andrew and Matthias

The Acts of John

The Acts of Paul (and Thecla)

The (Coptic) Act of Peter

The (Greek) Acts of Peter

The Acts of Peter and the Twelve

The Acts of Philip

The Acts of Thomas

The Kerygmata Petrou

6. LITURGICAL MATERIALS

Homilies

The Interpretation of Knowledge

The Kerygma of Peter

The Testimony of Truth

A Valentinian Exposition

Psalms

The Odes of Solomon

Prayers

On the Anointing

On Baptism A

On Baptism B

On the Eucharist A

On the Eucharist B

A Prayer of the Apostle Paul

Chart 18-10 (3)

Final Words

Explanation

The writers of the New Testament were not timid. They were eager to bear testimony of the things that they had seen and heard and to give "a reason of the hope" that was in them (1Pt 3:15). While these writers may have commenced their gospel narratives and personal spiritual lives at different points of departure (see, for example, chart 7-2), these chosen witnesses all conclude their work at the same point of arrival. As chart 18-11 shows, Peter's bottom line is that Jesus was the Son of God. John's ultimate reality is that the Son of God has come. Paul's final assurance is that nothing can separate us from the love of God which is in Jesus Christ. Jude's lasting testimony is that Jesus is the only true and wise God.

Probably the last New Testament book to be written was the Gospel of John, not the Revelation of John (which stands out of chronological order at the end of the New Testament collection today). John 21, the final appendix to the beloved apostle's Gospel, ends with the firm attestation, "and we know that his testimony is true" (Jn 21:24) and with the sober reminder that Jesus did many other things not mentioned in the Bible—so many, in fact, that it would be impossible for all the books in the world to contain them.

Final Testimonies

PETER For we have not followed cunningly devised fables, which we made known unto you the power and coming of our Lord Jesus Christ, but were eyewitnesses of his majesty. For he received from God the Father honour and glory, when there came such a voice to him from the excellent glory, "This is my beloved Son, in whom I am well pleased." And this voice which came from heaven we heard, when we were with him in the holy mount. (2Pt 1:16–18)

JOHN And we know that the Son of God is come, and hath given us an understanding, that we may know him that is true, and we are in him that is true, even in his Son Jesus Christ. This is the true God, and eternal life. (1Jn 5:20)

PAUL For I am persuaded, that neither death, nor life, nor angels, nor principalities, nor powers, nor things present, nor things to come, nor height, nor depth, nor any other creature, shall be able to separate us from the love of God, which is in Christ Jesus our Lord. (Rom 8:38–39)

JUDE Now unto him that is able to keep you from falling, and to present you faultless before the presence of his glory with exceeding joy, to the only wise God our Saviour, be glory and majesty, dominion and power, both now and ever. Amen. (Jude 1:24–25)

Chart 18-11

The Last Words Written
in the New Testament

And there are also many **other things** which **Jesus did,** the which, if they should be written

every one,

I suppose that even **the world** itself **could not contain**

the **books** that should be **written.**

John 21:25 (see chart 13-2)

Chart 18-12

Index of Key Terms

Index of Key Terms